MEDIA CULTURES OF THE RUSSIAN 1990s

MEDIA CULTURES OF THE RUSSIAN 1990s

INVENTING THE POST-SOVIET PUBLIC SPHERE

EDITED BY

MAYA VINOKOUR

Amherst College Press

The complete manuscript of this work was subjected to a fully closed ("double anonymous") review process. For more information, visit https://acpress.amherst.edu/peerreview/.

Published in the United States of America by Amherst College Press

Manufactured in the United States of America

Library of Congress Control Number: 2024944257

DOI: https://doi.org/10.3998/mpub.14527198

ISBN 979-8-89506-009-4 (paperback)
ISBN 979-8-89506-010-0 (open access)
ISBN 979-8-89506-011-7 (hardcover)

Table of Contents

Acknowledgments

The editor and contributors would like to thank the National Endowment for the Humanities for supporting us with a Collaborative Research Grant, which helped fund the creation of this volume's companion piece: the Multimedia Sourcebook of the Russian 1990s[a].

We are also grateful to the project's Advisory Board of senior REEES scholars for their feedback on early drafts of this volume's chapters, and to NYU's Jordan Center for the Advanced Study of Russia and the University Research Challenge Fund, which helped defray costs connected to constructing the Sourcebook.

[a] https://postsoviet90s.com/

INTRODUCTION

From Perestroika and the "Wild" 1990s to "Putin's Russia": A Multimedia History

Maya Vinokour

Many features of today's global media environment—from the pervasive atmosphere of political virtuality to the proliferation of disinformation and conspiracy theory—found early and potent expression in the media landscape of the Russian 1990s. Post-Soviet Russian society emerged simultaneously with an explosion of new media, especially recently liberated broadcast, cable, and satellite television and the fledgling Internet. TV stations, radio channels, print outlets, and early social media platforms like LiveJournal enjoyed a brief and contested period of independence as pure creativity and free expression collided with profit-seeking, journalistic integrity with burgeoning political ambition, and fringe with mainstream. By the late 1990s, most recently emancipated media undertakings had succumbed to domination by Russia's political and economic elites. The causes and nature of this co-optation, which set the stage for Vladimir Putin's systematic destruction of independent outlets after 2000, are embedded in the era's media artifacts. To study the Russian 1990s, then, is to study a global media history whose legacy and material traces the Putin regime has actively sought to erase.

This volume and the accompanying online Sourcebook interpret Russian-language print, video, audio, and Web 1.0 media, along with select elements of performance and material culture, dating to the "long 1990s." This period begins in the late 1980s, when Mikhail Gorbachev introduced his signature policies of perestroika ("restructuring") and glasnost ("publicity" or "openness"), and ends with Putin's rise to the Russian presidency in 2000. We interrogate the perception that the 1990s media environment of this period was a freewheeling "Wild West", investigating vectors of influence among popular culture, commercial advertising, political journalism, and nascent social media.[1] As a joint platform, this volume and the Sourcebook present the media culture of the Russian 1990s as simultaneously rooted in (pre-)Soviet history, and deeply influential on the global present.

For most of its history, Russian society enjoyed neither freedom of speech nor freedom of association, perhaps the two most important legal guarantees of a truly free media. It is debatable whether Russia's public culture, either shortly before or after 1991, can properly be called a "public sphere"—that is, a discursive space where ordinary people can freely discuss politics and culture without fear of governmental reprisal or marginalization.[2] In the Brezhnev era, which some scholars consider a direct inheritor of late-Stalinist social and political mores, the idea that Western-style civil liberties could arise within the Soviet system would have appeared far-fetched.[3] Yet Brezhnev's eventual successor, Mikhail Gorbachev, began to chip away at seemingly immutable realities of Soviet political and social life through the policy of glasnost. Our volume and Sourcebook investigate the historically anomalous period of media freedom that followed the advent of this new "openness," charting its gradual devolution and the consequences for Russia and the world.

Together, this volume and the Sourcebook examine the relationship between Russian media subcultures and the rise of global far-right movements; uncover the impact of flooding mainstream public discourse with fraudulent, alternative, or underground material through advertising and entertainment; and consider the significance of shifting cultural canons following the introduction of market capitalism in the Russian Federation. The flexibility of digital publishing allows readers to view these scholarly contributions alongside a curated selection of the media artifacts themselves. Through this format, which encourages browsing and potentially unexpected connections, we strive to link media developments of the Russian 1990s to global phenomena like the decline of democratic governance in the developed West and the growth of right-wing nationalism across the world.

Our timeline begins in the late 1980s, when Gorbachev initiated a restructuring of Soviet society that not only failed to renew and stabilize the regime, but ultimately precipitated its collapse. The liberalizing influence of glasnost, initially conceived as a tool to promote economic development, instead enabled previously unmentionable historical episodes to enter headline news and long-forbidden films and books to be released or published. Along with a public re-examination of history, especially the era of Stalinism and the Second World War, glasnost brought intense public scrutiny of the current Soviet leadership as muckraking television and radio programs mobilized huge swathes of disenchanted citizens for political action. These seismic shifts simultaneously encouraged and depended upon the emergence of a modern news and entertainment media. Radio, print media, and especially television helped publicize, critique, and amplify many elements of perestroika. As glasnost accelerated, television and print media began exposing not only the ugliness of the Soviet past, but the flaws of the Soviet present—from the government's botched management of nationalist conflict around Nagorno-Karabakh in 1988–1991 to permanent features of the planned economy like endless queuing and consumer-goods shortages.

When the economic promise of perestroika failed to materialize, the press turned on Gorbachev and anointed a new popular favorite: Boris Yeltsin, who would go on in June 1991 to receive 57% of the vote in the first and only democratic election for President of the Russian Soviet Federative Socialist Republic. The 1917 Bolshevik Revolution may not have been televised, but the collapse of the Soviet Union certainly was. When a group of hardline Gorbachev opponents tried to take control of the government on August 19, 1991, the media mobilized to defend hard-won democratic reforms. After the putschists shut down the press, editors banded together to form *Obshchaia gazeta* ("Common Newspaper"), which exhorted citizens to resist the coup (Artifact 00009[a]). Meanwhile, a televised press conference with the coup's leaders revealed their lack of political vision and retrograde manner to an international audience.[4] By August 21, the putsch had failed. The Soviet Union itself soon followed suit, with Gorbachev resigning in a televised address on December 25 of that same year.

After 1991, market forces increasingly drove Russian media, politics, and the public sphere closer together. At first, newspapers, television stations, and radio broadcasters managed to elude both state and private influence. Soon, however, dramatic economic reforms (collectively known as "shock therapy") pushed many media outlets to bankruptcy, toward alliances with the government, or into the arms of newly minted oligarchs enriched in privatization blitzes. In the fall of 1993, tensions between Yeltsin and his parliament, "exacerbated" by the disastrous consequences of rapid marketization, erupted in a full-blown constitutional crisis. After a referendum failed to grant him expanded powers, Yeltsin disbanded parliament. In response, armed protesters occupied the offices of Moscow's mayor and the Ostankino television station, leading to a battle with police that left some 50 people dead—casualties Yeltsin-aligned television would entirely fail to report. The following morning, October 4, Yeltsin ordered the military to storm the Russian White House, the symbolic seat of the new Russian democracy. According to official figures, 187 people died in the resulting shelling, but other estimates put the total closer to 2,000.[5]

In a televised address that evening, Yeltsin called the pro-parliament demonstrators "communist revanchists" and "fascists."[6] By delegitimizing his opponents as bloodthirsty thugs bent on sowing disorder, Yeltsin primed Russians for the radical consolidation of power he would enact through a combination of constitutional changes and executive decrees. Russian media after 1993 followed a similar path: soon, ownership of most major outlets had passed to billionaires, the state, or some combination of the two.

This oligarchic restructuring of media assets proved useful in propelling Yeltsin to victory in the 1996 presidential campaign. It was already clear by 1995 that Yeltsin had lost his perestroika-era verve and was genuinely vulnerable to challenger Gennady Zyuganov and his resurgent Communist Party. Fearing the prospect of a Communist government, several Russian oligarchs formed an alliance to launch a vicious media offensive against Zyuganov. In addition to securing the presidency for Yeltsin, the

[a] https://postsoviet90s.com/artifacts/democracy-must-know-how-to-defend-itself-obshchaia-gazeta/

tactics pioneered in 1996 had two important effects. First, the success of the oligarch-backed attacks against Zyuganov demonstrated the political indispensability of cornering the information market. Second, perfecting the technique of ambushing economic and political opponents with *kompromat*-laden media "hit jobs" laid the groundwork for the online culture wars of the global 2000s.

By the end of the 1990s, television had far outstripped radio and print in terms of its reach and impact. In theory, as Ivan Zassoursky writes, "politicized and commercial capital" were at cross-purposes, since the former sought to "capture the greatest audience" whereas the latter "aimed at making profits."[7] In practice, however, these two projects often coincided. During the run-up to the 1996 elections, for example, Russian banks not only channeled hundreds of millions of dollars into the Yeltsin campaign, but also funded pro-Yeltsin advertising like the short-lived newspaper *God Forbid!* (Artifact 00275[b]), which detailed the horrors that would follow a Communist victory.[8] Some observers have even speculated that a series of lavishly produced television spots for Bank Imperial—directed by future *Night Watch* (2004/ 2006) franchise creator Timur Bekmambetov—conveyed a hidden pro-Yeltsin message in their portrayals of eccentric yet lovable rulers.[9] Yeltsin's 1996 re-election campaign exemplifies the intertwining of apocryphal and confirmed conspiracy theories so common in the Russian 1990s. In our Sourcebook, artifacts pertaining to the events of 1996 and related moments open fruitful avenues of inquiry into historical spectacle, propaganda, and popular dissent.

In the Russian 1990s, the infiltration of fringe phenomena into the mainstream was common in economic as well as in political life. One illustrative example is the saga of "entrepreneur" Sergei Mavrodi, which encapsulates a typically post-Soviet intermixing of politics, media, and mythology (Artifact 00014[c]). With the aid of state-owned television channels, which gave extensive airtime to entertaining ads for his pyramid-scheme investment company, MMM, Mavrodi defrauded tens of millions of Russians before declaring bankruptcy in 1997. By then, he had already won a seat in the State Duma (1994) and had even considered a presidential run (1996). The apparent impunity with which Mavrodi conducted his deceptions inspired thousands of imitators, who also snapped up airtime on the major television channels to peddle dubious financial products to a gullible public. Long after his original schemes failed, Mavrodi founded an international "social financial network" called the "MMM Global Republic of Bitcoin" in 2014. Iterating a familiar pattern, the "Global Republic" attempted to capitalize on popular media trends (social networks) and financial fads (alternative currencies) in order to, as the site's copy claimed, "destroy the world's unjust financial system." Although the

---

[b] https://postsoviet90s.com/artifacts/the-pro-yeltsin-propaganda-paper-god-forbid-subjects-communist-presidential-candidate-gennady-zyuganov-to-blistering-critique

[c] https://postsoviet90s.com/artifacts/tv-commercials-for-the-mmm-pyramid-scheme

"Global Republic" officially closed in 2016—two years before Mavrodi's own death—individual branches remain active in countries around the world.

MMM's metastases in the Internet age point to the continuity between the Russian 1990s and the global 2000s, 2010s, and 2020s. The expansion of the Russian-language Internet toward the end of the decade created new venues for self-expression and social connection, even as it provided new opportunities to manipulate public opinion for political and financial ends. With the popularization of social media platforms like LiveJournal—which quickly transformed from an online diary portal to a launching pad for public figures—the Internet seemed poised to become the newest bastion of free speech in Russia. Ultimately, however, many of these platforms succumbed to pro-Kremlin elements, proving the Internet no less susceptible to economic and political co-optation than older types of media.

By the end of the first decade of the new millennium, when state control of nearly all televised media was a *fait accompli*, social media began to seem like a viable alternative for expressing dissent and organizing anti-state actions. Platforms like Facebook became key mobilizational tools in 2011–13, fueling mass protests against Putin and his government among Russia's urban elites. Yet already by 2014, international media outlets were reporting the proliferation of pro-Kremlin trolls (posters of deliberately offensive or off-topic material) on LiveJournal, Facebook, Twitter, and other sites.[10] Just as they would later do during the annexation of Crimea in 2014 and the US presidential election in 2016, fake users created dummy accounts and flooded social media platforms with Kremlin-approved content. Russian-owned sites like LiveJournal relocated their servers to Russian territory, which exposed them to the draconian Internet laws instated in 2013–16 following the anti-Putin demonstrations of 2011–13.[11]

Although the affordances being restricted were new, post-Soviet media-company consolidation, political manipulation, and the proliferation of fringe or fraudulent content had created the script for this crackdown. The arrival of trolling, *kompromat*, and astroturfing onto the global political scene in 2016 in particular—all tactics honed in the Russian 1990s—shows that the story of Russian media since Gorbachev is anything but niche or local: on the contrary, it has had far-reaching, long-lasting impacts.

Just as this volume does not aim to describe the era in question exhaustively, so too is the collection of media artifacts featured in the Sourcebook neither an encyclopedia nor a museum. It does not seek to archive the long 1990s comprehensively, nor is it the first project of its kind.[12] The core group of contributors, who are also this volume's authors, have focused on their own areas of academic expertise and interest to create a curated overview of a decade characterized by political and economic instability, aesthetic experimentation, and dramatic social change. At the same time, we have tried to make the post-Soviet 1990s compelling and legible to the curious non-expert. Visitors to our page will find artifacts representing key events, people, and institutions that can help orient them in the recent social, political, and cultural history of Russia, acquainting them with elements of official and establishment discourse like newspaper op-eds or video clips of important speeches. Yet the Sourcebook also demonstrates the contingent nature of categories like "establishment" and "mainstream" through the inclusion of artifacts that radically destabilized them, like a clip of Sergey Kuryokhin's "Lenin Was a Mushroom" television hoax from 1991, or the cover of a 1997 issue of *Limonka*, then the press organ of Russia's National Bolshevik Party.

Beyond the political realm, the Sourcebook includes significant material from popular culture. Visitors interested in the history of music will find footage of iconic performances, like a 1990 Kino concert held some six weeks before frontman Viktor Tsoi died in a car accident (Artifact 00124[d]). Those wishing to explore 1990s-era entertainments will find information about popular video games, television talk shows, and cult advertisements. Our collection also documents the period's material culture through artifacts like an advertisement for a Lada car (Artifact 00107[e]); a picture of a marketization-themed, Monopoly-style board game called *Kommersant* (Artifact 00063[f]); and an image of Henkel's "Moment" hobby glue (Artifact 00106[g])—a popular huffing drug from its introduction to the Soviet market in 1979 to the end of the 1990s, when its German manufacturer removed the hallucinogenic ingredient toluene.

For those seeking scholarly coverage of issues raised in artifact annotations—and in some cases, more information on specific objects—this essay collection examines Russia's first post-Soviet decade from a variety of disciplinary angles, including history, media theory, art history, cultural studies, musicology, and gender and sexuality studies. Despite this diversity of scholarly approaches, our essays collectively surface prominent themes and paradigmatic typologies within 1990s-era media, with certain figures and events recurring in multiple essays. For instance, late-Soviet irony and *stiob*, predecessors of modern-day trolling—as exemplified in Sergei Kuryokhin's "Lenin Was a Mushroom" television hoax from 1991 (Artifact 00205[h])—appear in Chapters 3 and 4, while Eduard Limonov, a seasoned troll and professional *épateur*, is discussed in Chapters 1, 3, 4, and 6 (Artifact 00197[i]). Nina Andreeva's "I Cannot Forsake My Principles," her 1988 open letter decrying Gorbachev's glasnost (Artifact 00177[j]), which epitomizes the ever-present threat of conservative backlash to even mild attempts at reform, appears in chapters by Courtney Doucette and by Pavel Khazanov.

[d] https://postsoviet90s.com/artifacts/kino-s-last-concert-luzhniki-stadium-moscow
[e] https://postsoviet90s.com/artifacts/lada-110-series
[f] https://postsoviet90s.com/artifacts/kommersant-board-game
[g] https://postsoviet90s.com/artifacts/klei-moment
[h] https://postsoviet90s.com/artifacts/lenin-was-a-mushroom
[i] https://postsoviet90s.com/artifacts/limonov-becomes-a-post-soviet-nationalist-rock-star
[j] https://postsoviet90s.com/artifacts/i-cannot-forsake-my-principles/

Meanwhile, the youth-oriented television show *Vzgliad*, which both Fabrizio Fenghi and Pavel Khazanov consider at length, epitomizes the unkept promise of muckraking journalism-cum-entertainment in the early post-Soviet years. Although it initially took up the cause of Russian "liberalism"—for instance, by sharply critiquing the anti-Gorbachev putschists of August 1991—the show ultimately contributed to the creation of a vast, under-politicized public ripe for exploitation by neoliberal "reformers" and would-be dictators alike. The statistical analyses and opinion polls discussed in Bradley Gorski's essay (as well as my own) functioned in a similar way: rather than measuring objective social realities, they sought actively to create them in the service of, first, the immiserating economic experiments of "shock therapy" and, later, Yeltsin's 1996 re-election campaign.

The volume's authors are also interested in the fusion of Western forms and practices, from television ads for consumer goods to tabloid reportage to opinion polling, with formerly "underground" or nonconformist elements of late-Soviet culture, and, in a related phenomenon, the passage of seemingly niche or "extreme" cultural products into the political and social mainstream. As Fabrizio Fenghi shows, perestroika-era shakeups promoted an association of "violence and *chernukha*" with "sincerity and truth, and with a moral mission to reveal and amend society's darkest evils." The result was a "keen fascination with transgression and the extreme" that persisted into the 1990s, animating seemingly counterintuitive combinations like the alliance of ironic punk rocker Sergei Kuryokhin with the fascist Eurasianist Alexander Dugin. A corollary of these developments was the interpenetration of apparently nonconformist practices with state-sponsored oversight or outright collaboration, underway, as Rita Safariants shows in her investigation of Russophone rock music, since the late-Soviet era.

Another of the volume's prominent themes is the co-optation of "free" media environments by a combination of economic and political interests, as Courtney Doucette explains on the example of what she calls the "disappearing reader" of post-Soviet newspapers. By the mid-1990s, as Doucette demonstrates, readers of many regional publications were no longer contributing to them as they had habitually done in Soviet times, for instance via letters or requests for coverage. At the very moment when politics were supposedly becoming "more democratic and participatory," newspapers "abandoned" reader contributions in favor of "seemingly endless advertisements." In place of "political participation through the press," however limited or performative, the public was offered "content generated and paid for by aspiring politicians." These changes, argues Doucette, "contributed to the erosion of readers' trust in newspapers, if not democracy itself."

Most broadly, all eight of this volume's contributors attempt to reckon with the most recent incarnation of "Putin's Russia": a personalist dictatorship that, as of this writing, is continuing to lay waste to Ukraine and violently repress its own citizens. By investigating the origins of Putinist authoritarianism specifically through the lens of media, we argue for a direct link between developments in the immediate post-Soviet years—especially the rapid formation of media monopolies, the suppression of engaged publics, and the brute commodification of information and its transmission—and the Russia of the present day.

In "The Sociological Turn: Public Opinion Polling and the Dream of an Open Society," Bradley Gorski discusses the genesis of opinion polling in the final years of the Soviet project. Starting with Tatyana Zaslavskaya's bombshell "Novosibirsk Report" (1983)—a paper that sharply critiqued the Soviet planned economy and caused a sensation in both the USSR and the West—what Gorski calls the "sociological turn" in late-Soviet social science paved the way for a shift from analysis of primarily economic data to public opinion. In 1987, Zaslavskaya founded the Russian Public Opinion Research Center (VTsIOM), which began presenting its findings in the last years of the Soviet Union. VTsIOM implicitly argued that the Soviet person was receding as a type, rejecting the Soviet-Marxist legacy of materialism in favor of Hegelian idealism and promoting neoliberal values of transparency, openness, and democracy. In the post-Soviet era, public opinion formed an alliance with the market that surfaced specific cultural products as representative of objective social trends—with surprising consequences. The collection of public opinion data collided with the disintegration of post-Soviet space and the various national independence movements of the late 1980s and early 1990s, inhibiting data-gathering efforts and ultimately undermining the very ideals of public opinion polling VTsIOM originally represented.

Courtney Doucette's "The Disappearing Reader: The Disintegration of the Press–Reader Relationship in the Soviet/Post-Soviet Press, 1985–1995" considers transformations of the press during perestroika and immediately after the Soviet collapse. Through a study of the popular daily newspaper *Komsomol'skaia pravda*, Doucette shows that, between 1985 and 1995, the voice of the reader all but disappeared from the printed page. Gone were letters and articles by readers, interactive activities, and announcements of reader-centric events like surveys, telethons, and receptions. This change was no mere casualty of a more general turn away from print media and toward television, but the result of deliberate editorial decision-making. The erosion of the Soviet-era relationship between readers and newspapers undermined the democratic potential of the press—and of early post-Soviet society as a whole—by discouraging popular investment in civic life.

Fenghi's "Russian Media in the 1990s, Fully Disclosed: Gore, Tabloids, and Countercultural Nationalism" and the selection of media artifacts connected to it focus on three overlapping sets of issues. The first is the emergence of sensationalist reporting and, more generally, of tabloids (*zheltaya pressa*) in Russia during perestroika and the 1990s. Next is *chernukha* (gore or dark content, literally "black stuff") and the centrality of violence and sex in the context of glasnost and the attempts at creating truthful accounts of social and political events. The third element is the blurring of the boundaries between underground and mainstream culture that occurred during this period.

Within post-Soviet Russian media, *chernukha* and sensationalist reporting often degenerated into sheer surrealism. At the same time, the taste for the violent, sexual, absurd, and politically incorrect fed specific countercultural or transgressive forms of national identity. The surreal physicality displayed in some of the media artifacts Fenghi's essay discusses reveals and reflects the "biopolitical essence" of the post-Soviet transition, in the sense of a total control over "bare life"—following Giorgio Agamben's definition—as something inherent to the exercise of political power in contemporary Russia.

In "The Rock-and-Roll State: Popular Music, Print Media, and Soviet Bureaucracy," Rita Safariants shows the proximity of underground to mainstream culture in the years leading up to perestroika, evaluating the long-term implications of symbiosis between establishment and counterculture. By the early 1990s, government authorities had shifted their policy on rock music from control and curation to promotion and collaboration. By popularizing late-Soviet rock and inscribing its personalities into the ranks of national heroes, state-controlled public media promoted the very Western influences it had once opposed. Ultimately, Safariants argues, this approach provided a blueprint for "soft" government intervention into popular culture after 1991, facilitating the development of a modern propaganda apparatus that co-opts youth and popular movements to its own ends. In making the case that state collaboration and government support were essential contributors to the popularization of late- and post-Soviet rock music, Safariants challenges the assumption that "underground" music existed in direct opposition to the state. In so doing, Safariants links the recent authoritarian trends in Russian mass culture to a history of bilateral ideological compromise.

The next chapter, by Daniil Leiderman, considers a related problematic through the case study of self-professed "punk-*skomorokh*" B. U. Kashkin. Drawing on a nuanced understanding of "underground" paradigms that carried over from late-Soviet times, Leiderman's "B. U. Kashkin: The Underground Seeking the Public in the 1990s" argues that the artist developed his absurdist collective gift-giving performances in response to the disappearance, after 1991, of organizations that had underpinned cultural production in the USSR. In place of this centralized support network, artists now faced a volatile global art market in which the only available communities were those created by artists themselves. B. U. Kashkin's project, Leiderman shows, relocates artistic practice from the production of either artworks or concepts to the creation of social formations, socially positive activity, and performances that are closer to social work than to traditional art or even 1990s-era actionism.

Thomas Keenan's "Russia's Gay (and Not-So-Gay) Nineties: Sexual and Gender Pluralism in the First Post-Soviet Decade" examines the origins of contemporary Russian authoritarianism through the prism of the LGBTQIA+ experience. For Keenan, the status of queerness in Russian society is a useful index for more general fluctuations in the freedom of self-determination and expression. As the rigid, oppressive structures of late-Soviet life gave way to apparent openness and self-discovery, new selfhoods and self-presentations thrived. Assertions of fluidity and pluralism in post-Soviet media not only challenged earlier gender binaries and sexual mores, but also expressed the broader spirit of excitement and anxiety that suffused the evolving Russian public sphere. In the 2000s, it was precisely the privileged position of sexuality as a potentially ungovernable form of personal expression that rendered it the synecdochic target for proudly illiberal and anti-Western forces.

In "The Revolution of the New *Narod*: Perestroika, the 1991 *GKChP* Coup, and the Televised Post-Soviet Subject at *Vzgliad*/ *ViD*," Pavel Khazanov investigates the televisual sources of nationalist authoritarianism in Russia after 2000, demonstrating that the popular perestroika-era television show *Vzgliad* and its successor, *ViD*, helped shape early post-Soviet Russian audiences into a new *narod* or people. The teams crafting this updated, mediatized *narod* represented its future as emancipatory, but not necessarily liberal. Although they worked to defeat the GKChP-led coup of August 1991, for instance, they remained distant from the liberal-democratic ambitions of late-Soviet intellectual elites. Instead, the creators of *Vzgliad* and *ViD* shaped the *narod* as the stateless, apolitical subject of an essentially anarcho-libertarian system. The blurriness of this collective identity was arguably necessary to unite divergent interests against the GKChP, but became problematic in the later 1990s, when the new *narod* proved incapable of coalescing around a common vision of post-Soviet statehood. This void at the heart of Russian liberalism, in turn, set the scene for the return of authoritarianism under Putin.

My own chapter, "Memory and Media in Post-Soviet Russia: The 1990s to the Present," looks back at thirty-plus years of media history, showing that the repressions Putin's government unleashed on independent outlets following Russia's full-scale invasion of Ukraine in 2022 were decades in the making. Governmental decisions that appear contingent or spontaneous are, instead, the product of two parallel processes that unfurled after perestroika and the USSR's collapse. The first is the economic transformation of the early 1990s, which produced an oligarchy that commodified and consolidated television and print media. This process culminated in Boris Yeltsin's contentious re-election campaign of 1996, a highly mediatized affair that set the stage for subsequent political machinations. The second process is Russia's perennial drive to "remember" its difficult past, which is generally followed by a backlash that seeks to force memory back underground. Although they may appear unrelated, these two processes are tightly entwined—in particular, because both have facilitated the application of Schmittean frameworks like the "friend/ enemy" distinction to contemporary Russian politics. The collective effect of these processes is a dangerous ideological presentism that forecloses the creation of truly independent media institutions and the development of publics that would demand them.

The same structural breakdowns that dissolved social and aesthetic inhibitions—and led to skyrocketing crime rates, unimaginable corruption, and mass immiseration—also complicate the study of the Russian 1990s. In her introduction to the volume associated with the media portal Colta.ru's "Museum of the 90s[k]," Galina Orlova points to the "rapid changes, ruined infrastructures, and bureaucratic slackening" that stymied "official documentation," even as "writing disciplines" and "institutions responsible for storing documents" decayed and "failed to keep up with lived reality." Orderly archiving fell by the wayside partly for systemic reasons, but also because the very "value of what was being stored was undetermined and not obvious."[13] The artifacts, annotations, and essays comprising our Sourcebook seek to counteract this epistemic disorder, preserving and elevating the traces of a recent history that feels increasingly distant and ephemeral.

This project was created with three overlapping audiences in mind. Within East European and Eurasian Studies, we hope the Sourcebook will provide a valuable research tool. Using the platform's dynamic, searchable, and interconnected format, students of the era can gain insight into the cultural and political factors contributing to the rapid collapse of Russian journalistic independence after 1991—especially the relationship between commercial advertising and politics and the competition between new capitalist elites and state actors. We also anticipate that, as a global story, our project will be of interest to other humanities fields. The account of a briefly flourishing free media and its subsequent co-optation contributes to our collective understanding of media and memory; of the relationships among political policy, the media, post-Soviet democracy, and authoritarianism; and of changes in public representations of gender and sexuality.

Finally, we have conceived the Sourcebook as a way for Anglophone and diasporic Russophone readers, particularly those interested in current events, politics, and the history of social media, to access the crucial years following Soviet collapse. We have also worked to make these important years legible to journalists, public-facing writers, and non-academic readers focusing on post-Soviet politics and culture. By investigating the rise and fall of Russia's only public sphere to date, we hope to offer insight into the period's ongoing effects on global history, aesthetics, and politics.

Notes

1 Notable works on the media and political culture of the post-Soviet 1990s include Anna Arutunyan, *The Media in Russia* (Berkshire, UK: Open University Press, 2009); Adele Marie Baker, ed., *Consuming Russia: Popular Culture, Sex, and Society since Gorbachev* (Durham, NC: Duke University Press, 1999); Eliot Borenstein, *Overkill: Sex and Violence in Contemporary Russian Popular Culture* (Ithaca, NY: Cornell University Press, 2007); Michael S. Gorham, *After Newspeak: Language Culture and Politics in Russia from Gorbachev to Putin* (Ithaca, NY: Cornell University Press, 2014); Helena Goscilo, "Style and S(t)Imulation: Popular Magazines, or the Aestheticization of Postsoviet Russia," *Russian Culture of the 1990s, Special Issue of Studies in 20th Century Literature* 24, no. 1 (2000): 15–50; Caroline Humphrey, *The Unmaking of Soviet Life: Everyday Economies after Socialism*, Culture and Society after Socialism (Ithaca, NY: Cornell University Press, 2002); Sergei Kuznetsov, *Oshchupyvaia slona: Zametki po istorii russkogo interneta* (Moscow: Novoe literaturnoe obozrenie, 2004); Birgit Menzel, *Bürgerkrieg um*

---

[k] https://www.colta.ru/90s

Worte: Die russische Literaturkritik der Perestrojka (Köln: Böhlau, 2001); Reino Paasilinna, *Glasnost and Soviet Television* (Helsinki: Finnish Broadcasting Corporation, 1995); Natalia Roudakova, *Losing Pravda: Ethics and the Press in Post-Truth Russia* (Cambridge: Cambridge University Press, 2017); Olga Shevchenko, *Crisis and the Everyday in Postsocialist Moscow* (Bloomington: Indiana University Press, 2009); Ivan Zassoursky, *Media and Power in Post-Soviet Russia* (London: M. E. Sharpe, 2004); Vladislav Zubok, *Collapse: The Fall of the Soviet Union* (New Haven, CT: Yale University Press, 2021).

2 Although scholars and laypeople habitually apply the term to Russia, strictly speaking it is impossible for the country to have had a "public sphere" in the precise sense meant by philosopher Jürgen Habermas—simply because his *Structural Transformation of the Public Sphere: An Inquiry into a Category of Bourgeois Society* (1962) defined it exclusively in terms of Western European cultural history from the eighteenth century forward. There is, however, significant scholarly precedent for modifying Habermas's framework to analyze the Russian case. See, for example, Boris Gorshkov, "Democratizing Habermas: Peasant Public Sphere in Pre-Reform Russia," *Russian History* 31, no. 4 (Winter 2004): 373–95; Tomila Lankina, "Mapping Society and the Public Sphere in Imperial Russia," in *The Estate Origins of Democracy in Russia*, 82–121 (New York: Cambridge University Press, 2021); and Ingrid Oswald and Viktor Voronkov, "The 'Public–Private' Sphere in Soviet and Post-Soviet Society: Perception and Dynamics of 'Public' and 'Private' in Contemporary Russia," *European Societies* 6, no. 1 (March 2004): 97–117. For more colloquial or received usages of the term, see e.g. Alexander Etkind, "The Decay of the Russian Public Sphere," *Current History* 114, no. 774 (2015): 278–81, or this 2012 event announcement from the Wilson Center (https://www.wilsoncenter.org/event/angry-townspeople-the-internet-and-the-market-ideas-vectors-change-the-russian-public-sphere).

3 Evgeny Dobrenko, *Late Stalinism: The Aesthetics of Politics*, trans. Jesse M. Savage (New Haven, CT: Yale University Press, 2020), 9–10.

4 For more on the role of television in the putsch, see Gregory Freidin and Victoria Bonnell, "Televorot: The Role of Television Coverage in Russia's August 1991 Coup," *Slavic Review* 52, no. 4 (1993): 810–38.

5 Kristyna Foltynova, "The Day the Russian White House Was Shelled," *RussiaFreeEurope/RadioLiberty*, October 4, 2019, https://rb.gy/hogvs.

6 "Obrashchenie prezidenta Borisa Yel'tsina k grazhdanam strany 4-go oktiabria 1993," October 4, 1993, https://www.youtube.com/watch?v=GERxlYw5d2k.

7 Zassoursky, *Media and Power in Post-Soviet Russia*, 31.

8 Juliet Johnson, *A Fistful of Rubles: The Rise and Fall of the Russian Banking System* (Ithaca, NY: Cornell University Press, 2000), 182.

9 Vasily Avchenko, *Teoriia i praktika politicheskikh manipuliatsyi v sovremennoi Rossii*, http://psyfactor.org/polman3.htm.

10 For one of many popular accounts of this situation, see Daisy Sindelar, "The Kremlin's Troll Army," *The Atlantic*, August 12, 2014, https://www.theatlantic.com/international/archive/2014/08/the-kremlins-troll-army/375932/.

11 For a detailed articulation of the connection between the Putin administration's Internet censorship laws and the protest movement of 2011–13, see Anton Nossik, "Russia's First Blogger Reacts to Putin's Internet Crackdown," *The New Republic*, May 15, 2014, https://newrepublic.com/article/117771/putins-internet-crackdown-russias-first-blogger-reacts. For an account of the situation on the Russian Internet after February 2022, see my chapter in this volume. For more on the relationship between Putin's government and Russia's public sphere since the 2010s, see Elena Chebankova, "The State and the Public Sphere in Russia," *Demokratizatsiya* 19, no. 4 (2011): 317–41; Anastasia Denisova, "Democracy, Protest and Public Sphere in Russia after the 2011–2012 Anti-government Protests: Digital Media at Stake," *Media, Culture, and Society* 1, no. 19 (2016): 1–19; Alexander Etkind, "The Decay of the Russian Public Sphere," *Current History* 114, no. 774 (2015): 278–81; Gorham, *After Newspeak*, 166–91; Peter Pomerantsev, "Beyond Propaganda: How Authoritarian Regimes Are Learning to Engineer Human Souls in the Age of Facebook," *Foreign Policy*, June 23, 2015, http://foreignpolicy.com/2015/06/23/beyond-propaganda-legatum-transitions-forum-russia-china-venezuela-syria/; Alyssa Rosenberg, "How Censorship Works in Vladimir Putin's Russia," *The Washington Post*, February 9, 2016, www.washingtonpost.com/news/act-four/wp/2016/02/09/how-censorship-works-in-vladimir-putins-russia/?utm_term=.da6c1f7ec6a1; Maria Snegovaya, *Stifling the Public Sphere: Media and Civil Society in Russia* (National Endowment for

Democracy, October 14, 2015), http://www.ned.org/wp-content/uploads/2015/10/Stifling-the-Public-Sphere-Media-Civil-Society-Russia-Forum-NED.pdf.

12 Predecessor projects and inspirations include Colta.ru's "Museum of the 90s," a version of the eponymous (and now defunct) creation of the Yegor Gaidar fund (traces of it can be found, for now, at this archived link: https://web.archive.org/web/20190313103159/https://museum.gaidarfund.ru/), as well as Natalia Rostova's "Flourishing of Russian Mass Media" (hosted by the Yeltsin Center at http://www.yeltsinmedia.com/about/) and "Birth of the Russian Mass Media" (https://gorbymedia.com/).

13 Translation mine. Galina Orlova, "Kod dostupa: arkhiv nedavnego proshlogo," in *Muzei 90x: territoria svobody*, 107–10 (Moscow: Novoe literaturnoe obozrenie, 2016), 107.

Bibliography

Anand, N., and Richard A. Peterson. "When Market Information Constitutes Fields: Sensemaking of Markets in the Commercial Music Industry." *Organization Science* 11, no. 3 (2000): 270–84.

Arutunyan, Anna. *The Media in Russia*. Berkshire, UK: Open University Press, 2009.

Ashwin, Sarah. *Gender, State, and Society in Soviet and Post-Soviet Russia*. London; New York: Routledge, 2000.

Baer, Brian James. *Other Russias: Homosexuality and the Crisis of Post-Soviet Identity*. New York: Palgrave Macmillan, 2009.

Baker, Adele Marie, ed. *Consuming Russia: Popular Culture, Sex, and Society since Gorbachev*. Durham, NC: Duke University Press, 1999.

Borenstein, Eliot. *Overkill: Sex and Violence in Contemporary Russian Popular Culture*. Ithaca, NY: Cornell University Press, 2007.

Borogan, Irina, and Andrei Soldatov. *The Red Web: The Kremlin's War on the Internet*. New York: Public Affairs, 2017.

Bourdieu, Pierre. *The Field of Cultural Production: Essays on Art and Literature*. New York: Columbia University Press, 1993.

Caves, Richard E. *Creative Industries: Contracts between Art and Commerce*. Cambridge, MA: Harvard University Press, 2000.

Clements, Barbara Evans, Rebecca Firedman, and Dan Healey. *Russian Masculinities in History and Culture*. New York: Palgrave, 2002.

Clover, Charles. *Black Wind, White Snow: The Rise of Russia's New Nationalism*. New Haven, CT: Yale University Press, 2016.

Dobrenko, E. A. *Late Stalinism: The Aesthetics of Politics*. Translated by Jesse M. Savage. New Haven, CT: Yale University Press, 2020.

Dolinin, Ivanov, and Severiukhin Ostanin, eds. *Samizdat Leningrada: Entsiklopediia 1950e–1980e*. Moscow: Novoe literaturnoe obozrenie, 2003.

Essig, Laurie. *Queer in Russia: A Story of Sex, Self, and the Other*. Durham, NC: Duke University Press, 1999.

Etkind, Alexander. "The Decay of the Russian Public Sphere." *Current History* 114, no. 774 (2015): 278–81.

Fenghi, Fabrizio. "Making Post-Soviet Counterpublics: The Aesthetics of Limonka and the National-Bolshevik Party." *Nationalities Papers: The Journal of Nationalism and Ethnicity* 45, no. 2 (2017): 182–205.

Foltynova, Kristyna. 2019. "The Day the Russian White House Was Shelled." *RussiaFreeEurope/RadioLiberty*. October 4, 2019. https://rb.gy/hogvs.

Freidin, Gregory, and Victoria Bonnell. "Televorot: The Role of Television Coverage in Russia's August 1991 Coup." *Slavic Review* 52, no. 4 (1993): 810–38.

Gabowitsch, Mischa. "Fascism as Stiob." *Kultura*, no. 4 (December 2009).

Gatov, Vasily. "Putin, Mar'ivanna i 'Ukraintsy v Televizore.'" *Svoboda.Org*. February 2015.

Gessen, Masha. *Dead Again: The Russian Intelligentsia after Communism*. New York: Verso, 1997.

Gorham, Michael S. *After Newspeak: Language Culture and Politics in Russia from Gorbachev to Putin*. Ithaca, NY: Cornell University Press, 2014.

Gorshkov, Boris. "Democratizing Habermas: Peasant Public Sphere in Pre-Reform Russia." *Russian History* 31, no. 4 (2004): 373–95.

Goscilo, Helena. "Style and S(t)Imulation: Popular Magazines, or the Aestheticization of Postsoviet Russia." *Russian Culture of the 1990s, Special Issue of Studies in 20th Century Literature* 24, no. 1 (2000): 15–50.

Goscilo, Helena, and Vlad Strukov, eds. *Celebrity and Glamour in Contemporary Russia*. London: Routledge, 2011.
Habermas, Jürgen. *Structural Transformation of the Public Sphere: An Inquiry into a Category of Bourgeois Society*. Cambridge, MA: The MIT Press, 1989.
Healey, Dan. *Russian Homophobia from Stalin to Sochi*. London: Bloomsbury Academic, 2017.
Humphrey, Caroline. *The Unmaking of Soviet Life: Everyday Economies after Socialism*. Culture and Society after Socialism. Ithaca, NY: Cornell University Press, 2002.
Idlis, Iuliia. *Runet. Sotvorennye kumiry*. Moscow: Al'pina non-fikshn, 2010.
Johnson, Juliet. *A Fistful of Rubles: The Rise and Fall of the Russian Banking System*. Ithaca, NY: Cornell University Press, 2000.
Kalinin, Ilya. "Arkheologiia natsional'nogo znaniia." *Neprikosnovennyi zapas* 81, no. 1 (2012).
Kharkhordin, Oleg. *The Collective and the Individual in Russia: A Study of Practices*. Berkeley: University of California Press, 1999.
Komaromi, Ann. *Uncensored: Samizdat Novels and the Quest for Autonomy in Soviet Dissidence*. Evanston, IL: Northwestern University Press, 2015.
Kuznetsov, Sergei. *Oshchupyvaia slona: Zametki po istorii russkogo interneta*. Moscow: Novoe literaturnoe obozrenie, 2004.
Lankina, Tomila. "Mapping Society and the Public Sphere in Imperial Russia." In *The Estate Origins of Democracy in Russia*, 82–121. Cambridge; New York: Cambridge University Press, 2021.
Laruelle, Marlène. *Russian Eurasianism: An Ideology of Empire*. Baltimore: Johns Hopkins University Press, 2008.
Lipovetsky, Mark. "The Poetics of ITR Discourse: In the 1960s and Today." *Ab Imperio* 1 (2013).
Menzel, Birgit. *Bürgerkrieg um Worte: Die russische Literaturkritik der Perestrojka*. Köln: Böhlau, 2001.
Miller, Laura J. "The Best-Seller List as Marketing Tool and Historical Fiction." *Book History* 3 (2000): 286–304.
"Obrashchenie Prezidenta Borisa Yel'tsina k grazhdanam strany 4-go oktiabria 1993." 1993. https://www.youtube.com/watch?v=GERxlYw5d2k.
Orlova, Galina. "Kod dostupa: Arkhiv nedavnego proshlogo." In *Muzei 90x: Territoria svobody*, 107–10. Moscow: Novoe literaturnoe obozrenie, 2016.
Oswald, Ingrid, and Viktor Voronkov. "The 'Public–Private' Sphere in Soviet and Post-Soviet Society Perception and Dynamics of 'Public' and 'Private' in Contemporary Russia." *European Societies* 6, no. 1 (2004): 97–117.
Paasilinna, Reino. *Glasnost and Soviet Television*. Helsinki: Finnish Broadcasting Corporation, 1995.
Proskurin, Oleg. "Maksim Sokolov: Genesis i funktsii 'zabavnogo sloga.'" *Novoe Literaturnoe Obozrenie* 41, 2000.
Prozorov, Sergei. *The Ethics of Postcommunism: History and Social Praxis in Russia*. New York: Palgrave Macmillan, 2009.
Roudakova, Natalia. 2017. *Losing Pravda: Ethics and the Press in Post-Truth Russia*. Cambridge: Cambridge University Press.
Shevchenko, Olga. *Crisis and the Everyday in Postsocialist Moscow*. Bloomington: Indiana University Press, 2009.
Shul'man [Schulmann], Ekaterina. "Tsarstvo politicheskoi imitatsii." *Vedomosti*, August 2014.
Smith, Kathleen E. *Mythmaking in the New Russia: Politics & Memory During the Yeltsin Era*. Ithaca, NY: Cornell University Press, 2002.
Velminski, Wladimir. *Homo Sovieticus: Brain Waves, Mind Control, and Telepathic Destiny*. Cambridge, MA: The MIT Press, 2017.
Warner, Michael. *Publics and Counterpublics*. New York: Zone Books, 2005.
Yurchak, Alexei. *Everything Was Forever, Until It Was No More: The Last Soviet Generation*. Princeton, NJ: Princeton University Press, 2005.
Yurchak, Alexei. "A Parasite from Outer Space: How Sergei Kurekhin Proved That Lenin Was a Mushroom." *Slavic Review* 70, no. 2 (2011): 307–33.
Zassoursky, Ivan. *Media and Power in Post-Soviet Russia*. London: M. E. Sharpe, 2004.
Zhuk, Sergei. *Rock and Roll in the Rocket City: The West, Identity, and Ideology in Soviet Dnepropetrovsk*. Baltimore: Johns Hopkins University Press, 2010.
Zubok, Vladislav. *Collapse: The Fall of the Soviet Union*. New Haven, CT: Yale University Press, 2021.

CHAPTER 1
The Sociological Turn: Public Opinion Polling and the Dream of an Open Society

Bradley A. Gorski

POSTSOCIALISM AS EPISTEMOLOGICAL CRISIS

The Soviet Union ended when the state no longer knew its people. This might be said of any political regime that loses legitimacy in the eyes of its populace, but in the Soviet Union, the epistemological crisis was both a long-term problem and acutely felt. Already in the post-Stalinist era anxieties about ways of knowing (and controlling) the populace waxed as the most brutal forms of political violence waned.[1] The Thaw saw both a general liberalization of political and social life and, at the same time, the launch of the first public opinion institute in the Soviet Union, run out of the friendly pages of *Komsomol'skaia Pravda*. The youth-oriented newspaper constantly asked readers to write in with questions about socialist norms, observations about themselves and others, and facts about their lives.[2] Many of their responses were printed in subsequent issues of the newspaper as questions, requests for improvement, or guides to behavior and style.

Further from the public eye, state planning recognized the need for better knowledge of the Soviet consumer, and launched a surprising number of surveys meant to determine what Soviet citizens needed and what they were buying.[3] Such information gathering resulted in a flurry of publications throughout the Brezhnev era, mostly printed in small runs exclusively for internal government readerships. The Academy of Sciences also opened an "Institute of Concrete Sociological Studies" (*Institut konkretnykh sotsial'nykh issledovanii*, or IKSI) in 1966 with a young professor of philosophy named Iurii Levada as its director. The next year, Levada offered a series of lectures on sociology—the first such course in the Soviet Union—at the Journalism Department of Moscow State University. But when a copy of the lectures began to circulate the next year, it came in for harsh criticism in a special session of the Academy of Social Sciences of the Central Committee of the Communist Party. Levada's course was canceled, he was stripped of the title of Professor, and banned from teaching any courses in the future. But he was allowed to continue working at the Academy of Sciences.[4]

The split decision on Levada's fate reflected a broader ambivalence about sociology at the time. The state recognized the need to gather data for its continuing functioning but also feared ascribing too much importance to popular opinion. The Party, after all, was meant to guide the populace, and not the other way around. Furthermore, theoretical sociology, with its Western roots and connections to bourgeois thought, remained anathema in the Soviet Union.[5] For these reasons, even amid a recognized need for its work, the IKSI was shut down in 1972, and its employees were scattered throughout the state bureaucracy. Some of the most influential ended up in the vast state library system, where they had access to huge flows of more or less uncensored and unprocessed data. Meanwhile, Levada continued working with students in informal seminars held at his home, where he would develop his influential vision of the Soviet person as a special type, a "Homo sovieticus," molded by the revolutionary experiences and traumas of terror and war that characterized early Soviet life.

In official circles, sociology remained acceptable especially in economic investigations, and it was this context that ultimately changed the fate of sociology in the late- and post-Soviet era. A study with the unassuming title "On the Improvement of Socialist Industrial Relations and the Tasks of Economic Sociology" became, in the words of Boris Firsov, "without exaggeration the bravest and most radical scholarly work written by USSR sociologists."[6] Composed for a conference of agrarian economists in Novosibirsk in 1983 and marked "for internal use only," the text was deemed so dangerous that when two copies went missing, the KGB not only searched all conference locations, but even scoured the homes of conference attendees.[7] Nevertheless, it leaked to the West, where it became known as the Novosibirsk Report.[8]

Its author, Tatiana Zaslavskaia, argued that the basic assumptions of the Soviet economy were outdated, if not entirely wrong. Under Stalin, the Soviet Union had codified the fundamental harmony between productive forces (labor, technology, raw materials) and the mechanisms for their organization and interrelation (central planning). In a socialist state, there could be no contradiction between the two. The Soviet Union, it was believed, had overcome any inherent tensions among individual, group, and social interests, and the classless society had long moved beyond class antagonisms. Socialist economic relations, in other words, were assumed to be harmonious because such harmony was foundational to—indeed the raison d'être of—Soviet economic organization. But this assumed harmony, according to Zaslavskaia, was both wrong and dangerous. Labor and technology had developed enormously in the five decades since the foundations of the Soviet economy had been laid, while central planning remained much the same. Moreover, the assumption of a lack of internal contradictions blinded Soviet bureaucrats to pressing issues on the ground and led to stagnation. Under capitalism, Zaslavskaia pointed out, it is precisely class antagonisms that lead to economic development: the struggle between interested groups brings innovation which is embraced by some, resisted by others, and regulated by a decentralized market. Without markets, socialist economies lack the decentralized organization and data-gathering mechanisms that can provide constant and automatic feedback. A functioning socialist economy would need to actively compensate for this lack. But instead, the Soviet stance of assumed harmony "deprives [production] of its social content," she argued, deliberately obscuring any internal conflict and stymying dynamism. The assumption of harmony, in other words, had blindfolded the Soviet Union and was leading to economic crisis.[9]

Zaslavskaia's "Strategy for Perfecting Production Relations," as she titled the most influential section of her report, included acknowledging the possibility of a disconnect between productive forces and planning, and even between various interests involved in the economy. Once such contradictions were acknowledged, they could only be addressed by broad information gathering and even the cautious introduction of market mechanisms as part of overall economic restructuring.

Shortly after the scandal around the Novosibirsk Report—but before it had been published in the West—the Central Committee of the Communist Party admitted that, while the "Party has many modes of flexible and effective feedback, which allow it to clearly understand any changes in the mood of the masses," nevertheless, "under contemporary conditions the necessity has ripened [*sozrela neobkhodimost'*] to create a specialized system for studying the needs, opinions, and moods of the working masses."[10]

The reaction to Zaslavskaia's report, in other words, was a harbinger of larger changes in Soviet society that in the coming years would open the door for Mikhail Gorbachev's policies of perestroika and glasnost. Indeed, it is no accident that the seeds of many of Gorbachev's reforms can be found in Zaslavskaia's report. Gorbachev was enamored with Zaslavskaia, and when he became General Secretary in 1985, he immediately brought her on as one of his chief economic advisors. The Novosibirsk Report became one of the blueprints for Gorbachev's policies, which recognized the need for economic restructuring—but even more important—acknowledged that such restructuring should be informed by broad-based data collection in the form of open communication. Such data collection became part of the larger project of glasnost, Gorbachev's policy of openness. Though glasnost was a sweeping initiative that loosened censorship, lifted taboos, published previously banned literature, and even, as Courtney Doucette has argued, reformed Soviet subjectivity, it was also a data-gathering initiative, meant to inform the economic restructuring of perestroika.[11] In other words, glasnost was introduced not only as the constant companion of perestroika, but also as its driving force. Openness, and the honest feedback it would encourage, would help save the Soviet economy from collapse.

Things, to put it mildly, turned out differently. Instead of saving the Soviet Union, Gorbachev's perestroika restructured it right out of existence. But the epistemological crisis that had precipitated the Soviet Union's end outlasted it. One organization that embodied the highest aspirations of perestroika-era data collection went on to become one of the most influential organizations in *post*-Soviet Russia's self-knowledge and self-representation. That organization was the All-Union (and soon All-Russian) Center for the Study of Public Opinion, known most often by its Russian acronym VTsIOM (for *Vsesoiuznyi/Vserossiiskii tsentr izucheniia obshchestvennogo mneniia*). It was founded in 1987 by order of the Central Committee of the Communist Party with the broadest possible mandate for data-gathering and sociological analysis. Its head was Tatiana Zaslavskaia.

Statistics and statistical analysis had been important throughout the Soviet era. Production statistics were at the heart of central planning and socialist communication strategies. Both domestic and international propaganda broadcast statistics about, for instance, literacy gains immediately after the revolution and leaps in production during the first five-year plans. In the post-war era, the new discipline of cybernetics captured the bureaucratic imagination as the technical capabilities of data processing grew alongside the complexity of the Soviet economy.[12] By the mid-1970s—the middle of the era that would come to be known as the "Stagnation"—the statistical demands of the state had become so pervasive that statistics even served as the unexamined backdrop of melodrama, as in El'dar Riazanov's wildly popular *Office Romance* (*Sluzhebnyi roman*, 1977). The film's romantic entanglements and personal tragedies all unfold within an office named simply "Statistical bureau" ("*Statisticheskoe uchrezhdenie*"). Unlike in the production films of an earlier era, the work in this office plays no role in the film. By the mid-1970s, in other words, despite the enthusiasms of some cyberneticists, statistics seemed drab enough to serve as the most neutral of backdrops for melodrama.

The sociological turn of the late- and post-Soviet years, then, was new not for its use of statistical indicators to better understand society, but for a revival and a reinvention of what statistics could do. Put simply, the reinvention meant a shift from primarily economic data to sociology and public opinion. It was a way of using statistics to model not the economy, but the people, the "new narod" that was forming under the new social and political circumstances (see Pavel Khazanov's article in this volume). Despite Zaslavskaia's background in agrarian economics, the revolution that she helped launch actually represented a shift away from her area of expertise toward the more nebulous realm of broad-based subjective opinions. The organization that she helped to found would not gather production statistics directly from enterprises, nor would it collate direct consumption statistics from points of sale. Instead, it would have to create from scratch a complex apparatus for asking a broad sample of the population qualitative questions about their subjective opinions and then representing their answers quantitatively. Practically, this was an enormous and complex undertaking. Ideologically, it was a seismic shift.

This chapter is devoted to that shift. VTsIOM brought members of the late-Soviet intelligentsia together in an unexpected new way: philosophers, poets, economists, and sociologists turned to public opinion as a new way of knowing and representing the world. At stake was nothing less than a new understanding of truth. The fall of the Soviet Union was also the fall of a regime of truth. As the state admitted that its previous systems of knowledge had failed, questioning old truths, surfacing hidden truths, and producing new truths became major themes of perestroika and glasnost. The stated goals of openness and restructuring led to broader questions about epistemology, knowledge production, and rethinking investigative pathways. How had Soviet practices obscured truth rather than revealing it? And just as important, how could new systems be established that would more reliably bring truth to light? In the late- and post-Soviet years, VTsIOM represented some of the most influential answers to these questions. Its vast data-gathering apparatus, prominent media presence, and proximity to political power helped to define a new post-Soviet regime of truth.

If the Soviet regime of truth was premised on party-guided dialectical materialism, VTsIOM would offer something new. Its data-driven approach was premised on neoliberal values of transparency and technocratic governance, while its focus on respondents' subjective opinions rejected the Soviet-Marxist legacy in favor of a coyly stated but deeply held Hegelian idealism. It was modeled on Western institutions—such as Gallup in the United States and Allensbach in West Germany—which had explicitly framed themselves as bulwarks of democracy. But it was founded not amid the 1940s rise of authoritarianism, but during the neoliberal wave of the 1970s–2000s. In this context, it presented itself as a tool for governance—for gauging the acceptability of policies enacted by an executive—much more than as a responsive indicator of electoral politics. Among its most important early issues was the privatization of state industries, a staple of global neoliberalism and a process over which citizens had no control. For this reason, its polls were filled with subjective measures, for instance, asking, "How do you feel about the fact that private individuals own large factories?" (from a 1990–92 study), or developing an "Optimism Index" (beginning in 1994). Such measures distilled the subjective feelings of the populace into apparent social facts. They sought to represent what VTsIOM researchers would later call the objective Spirit of the age as sociological truth.

The approach proved powerful and enormously influential in its first decade, but it brought with it significant blind spots. By representing public opinion statistically, rather than directly and qualitatively, VTsIOM played a significant role in the disappearance of the reader from post-Soviet press, which Courtney Doucette details in Chapter 2. VTsIOM's polling also underappreciated the roles of nationality and ethnicity, even as the Soviet Union disintegrated into the various national independence movements of the late 1980s and early 1990s. By the mid-1990s, public faith in polling was replaced by a widespread belief in the manipulability of sociologically represented truth. By the early 2000s, VTsIOM had become ripe for state capture, and polling would go on to play a very different role in the rising authoritarianism of Putin's Russia.

VTSIOM: A GATHERING OF THE LATE-SOVIET INTELLIGENTSIA

The All-Union Center for the Study of Public Opinion was officially founded by decree of the Central Committee of the Communist Party on December 7, 1987. Zaslavskaia, who would serve as its founding director, envisioned a center modeled on the West German Allensbach Institute of Demoscopy (*Institut für Demoskopie Allensbach*) created forty years earlier and tasked with carrying out monthly public opinion surveys of the West German populace. But, by her own admission, she had little experience with the study of public opinion. Her area of expertise was agrarian economy and she was asked to lead the center in large part because of the moral authority and respect she had earned among both the intelligentsia and the political elite. As she remembered ten years later, she agreed to take the position "only under the non-negotiable condition that my deputy be Boris Grushin."[13]

Grushin was perhaps the only person in the country with real experience executing public opinion surveys. He had studied at Moscow State University's Philosophy Faculty alongside Levada in the late 1940s and 1950s, and the two knew and respected one another. But unlike Levada, Grushin did not immediately turn to sociology, but remained devoted to philosophy. He became one of the founding members of the Moscow Logic Circle (later known as the Moscow Methodological Circle), whose other members included Alexander Zinoviev and Merab Mamardashvili. Despite earning the respect of peers and professors alike, Grushin was not allowed to defend his thesis due to accusations of anti-Marxism, and his promising career in academic philosophy was cut short. He soon found a job in the propaganda department of *Komsomol'skaia Pravda*, where, after rising to editor, he launched the first public opinion surveys in the USSR from its pages. They were a wild success. Even Nikita Khrushchev explicitly endorsed the endeavor. But as the postwar Thaw receded into Brezhnev's stagnation the Institute of Public Opinion at *Komsomol'skaia Pravda* came under attack. By 1967, it was closed, and Grushin was once again out of work.[14]

His next effort was a short-lived Center for the Study of Public Opinion at the IKSI at the Soviet Academy of Sciences. But it too was closed down after conducting just one study.[15] Grushin spent the balance of the decade campaigning in vain for state support for public opinion polling, but his pleas met with silence and rejection. "We don't need that kind of thing here," he was told when he offered to open a public opinion section in *Pravda*, "Let them do that kind of thing at home [in the West]." He collected these and other rejections in his memoir of the era, *The Bitter Taste of Being Unwanted* (*Gor'kii vkus nevostrebovannosti*, 1987).

So it was with the enthusiasm of a lifelong dream fulfilled that Grushin agreed to work under Zaslavskaia in 1987. He quickly set about fulfilling the VTsIOM's mandate to create not only the central office in Moscow, but also "25 field offices, located in each of the capitals of the Union Republics and in a range of other cities in the country."[16] The field offices would be staffed through connections Grushin had made over the course of his career working on the borderlands between sociological research and state power. For the first time, Grushin was able to implement many of the ideas and methodologies he had pursued during the previous decades. The single study he had conducted at IKSI would be particularly influential. Remembered as the "first all-union representative survey of 2000 respondents," it would serve as VTsIOM's model for nationwide population sampling.[17]

Grushin invited his old acquaintance Levada, known by then as the Soviet Union's leading theoretical sociologist, to join VTsIOM. Many of Levada's former students soon followed. Among the most influential was Lev Gudkov, who had attended Levada's lectures on sociology in the 1960s and had worked briefly with him at the Academy of Sciences before finding himself—like all those interested in theoretical sociology—turned out of mainstream academic circles. Gudkov eventually found work in the Institute of the Book inside the State Lenin Library, where he met Boris Dubin, who would become his constant co-author until Dubin's death in 2014. Dubin was not a sociologist at all. He was a poet and a translator who had come of age in Moscow's underground art scene. He had been part of a loose grouping of artists and writers which called itself SMOG (meaning either "The Youngest Organization of Geniuses" (*Samoe molodoe obshchestvo geniev*) or "Boldness, Thought, Image, Depth" (*Smelost', mysl', obraz, glubina*)) and included Leonid Gubanov, Sasha Sokolov, Iuliia Vishnevetskaia, and Eduard Limonov.[18] It was through the literary underground, and not through sociology, that Dubin eventually found his way to the Institute of the Book where he met Gudkov. When the two combined forces—alongside colleagues Aleksei Levinson and Abram Reitblat—they realized the enormous potential of their out-of-the-way post.

Not only did they have the vast holdings of the Lenin Library at their fingertips—including access to ideologically sensitive materials unavailable to most researchers—they could also request volumes from the Library of Foreign Literature. But even more enticing was the stream of data that came into the Institute of the Book. The institute was connected to the Book Chamber, which tracked publication and print runs of all new books published in the Soviet Union. At the same time, libraries across the country sent in data on library holdings, reader requests, and deficit titles. In this way, the Institute of the Book became a central clearing house for data on what was published, in how many copies, and—most important—what people actually read. As Gudkov told me in an interview, "We knew that data could tell us something about what people were thinking."[19] But they hadn't yet developed the theoretical apparatus to process that information.

Gudkov and Dubin compiled an exhaustive bibliography of Western theories on the sociology of literature. Because of their special position within the library system, they had access to many (though far from all) of the volumes they listed. "Those were good times," Gudkov said, "despite the gloom [*mrak*]. You could sit all day and read. No one made us do anything else...Of course, we couldn't publish or present our work publicly...But we could do what we wanted. Those were good times."[20] They were especially enamored of reader-response theory and its leading theorists Wolfgang Iser and Hans-Robert Jauss. Iser argued that every literary text implies a certain kind of reader, and that careful reading of the text can then help reconstruct this "implied reader."[21] Jauss saw literature as a constant interaction between text and reader, writing and response, to which the reader brings a certain "horizon of expectations" specific to an historical moment, which, once again, could be reconstructed through concerted hermeneutic effort.[22] These theories gave Dubin and Gudkov the apparatus they needed to make reading habits into sociologically useful data. Since they knew what people were reading across the country through library data, they could analyze the population's favorite texts. Through careful literary interpretation, they could reconstruct the "implied reader" of those texts and the "horizon of expectations" they brought with them, which would in turn reveal something essential about the masses of Soviet citizens requesting these texts.

Iser and especially Jauss were banned in the Soviet Union for their connections to the Nazi Party. Though not public knowledge at the time, Jauss had been an SS officer who oversaw atrocities on the Eastern Front.[23] But both theorists' more anodyne loyalties to National Socialism were well known, and as a result reader-response theory remained anathema in Soviet literary criticism. Curiously, then, it was Dubin and Gudkov's work that introduced this influential strain of literary theory into Soviet and post-Soviet discourse, and it did so as a sociological, not a literary, methodology. As glasnost settled in, Dubin and Gudkov were able to discuss preliminary findings and even prepare them for publication. Many were collected in *The Book and Reading in the Mirror of Sociology* (1990), which—as the introduction noted—was motivated by "a united sociological idea—the relationship to reading as a social phenomenon and to literature and the structures of its dissemination as social institutions."[24] What Gudkov and Dubin discovered in the Institute of the Book was that books and reading, approached the right way, could serve as sociological material. And they would carry that innovation into their work at VTsIOM.

In fact, literature and the publishing world played an outsized role in the sociological picture of Soviet and post-Soviet Russian society that VTsIOM constructed. VTsIOM's broad-based public opinion surveys often included questions on how much people were reading, which genres they favored, and how they found their reading materials. For comparison, no such questions were consistently asked in Gallup's or Allensbach's regular studies of the American or West German populace. The Soviet Union's proud reputation as the best-read country in the world (*samaia chitaiushchaia strana v mire*) helps explain the appetite for such questions in the Russian context, but Dubin and Gudkov's background at the Institute of the Book was also an essential component. When these two researchers joined VTsIOM, they brought with them their bibliographic experience and theoretical apparatus as they continued to work on the sociology of culture—and especially of literature. Their writings within the influential publications of VTsIOM gave literature a central place in post-Soviet Russia's self-understanding and self-representation, and this alliance between literature and sociology shifted the position of the intelligentsia in post-Soviet Russia. Suddenly close reading, careful analysis of cultural texts, and literary hermeneutics—the skills the late-Soviet intelligentsia had developed in part to avoid public life through codes of Aesopian language and double meanings—could now prove central to the developing public sphere.

The motley collection of not-quite-sociologists who gathered under the umbrella of VTsIOM brought together some of the most important tendencies of the late-Soviet intelligentsia—from the economist Zaslavskaia to the underground poet Dubin, from the repressed theoretician Levada to the philosopher-turned-technocrat Grushin. Their work at VTsIOM transformed them from outcasts—each pushed to the edges of late-Soviet life—into central figures in the post-Soviet public sphere. All of the late-Soviet experiences they brought with them—their diverse backgrounds and their years of academic exile—influenced how they saw their work, and how they crafted the mirror they would hold up to post-Soviet society. They hoped to provide a clear reflection of the post-Soviet citizen amid seismic social transformations. But that clarity proved both theoretically complex and ultimately elusive. Their work would transform post-Soviet society at least as much as it measured and reflected it.

COLLECTING AND REPRESENTING PUBLIC OPINION

Logistically, the institutionalization of VTsIOM and its procedures was a major undertaking. Not least because "the majority of the staff knew almost nothing about the study of public opinion."[25] Zaslavskaia knew little. Levada, despite his deep theoretical knowledge of sociology, was equally inexperienced. Only Grushin had any practical experience and he spent his first year pulling his hair out bringing the others up to speed.[26] But there were even more fundamental problems. Almost $500,000 earmarked to buy computer technology suddenly disappeared in an international bank transfer. (The promised technology was delivered only two years later.) And most essentially, VTsIOM needed to set up twenty-five offices across the Soviet Union, and somehow connect them.

In order to measure public opinion from across the vast swathes of Soviet territory, VTsIOM's surveys would have to be standardized and disseminated to the new regional offices. In each of the twenty-five locations, workers would then go out to physically knock on doors and conduct interviews with representative members of the local populations, chosen according to Grushin's sampling method. The completed surveys would then have to make their way back to the Moscow office for processing. The material realities of the Soviet Union made these tasks much more difficult than they were in either the United States or West Germany, where VTsIOM's model organizations operated. The Soviet Union was much vaster than either country, it was technologically behind, and crucially it was more ethnically and linguistically diverse. These realities complicated the task of setting up a nationwide network in ways that can be roughly grouped under three terms: quality control, communication, and standardization.

Local offices, thousands of miles from Moscow, were staffed by the best people Grushin could find, but the lack of official education in sociology—and especially public opinion polling—throughout the Soviet Union meant that many office directors might have been well-respected but had little practical experience or comprehension of sociological methods. For the first two years, interviewers and their supervisors came to Moscow for training courses in summer and senior VTsIOM researchers often traveled from Moscow to the field offices to train regional staff, carry out quality control checks, and even conduct interviews among the local populations.[27] Still, worries about survey quality and uniformity lingered, especially in VTsIOM's first years. The Moscow office, as Zaslavskaia worried, "could do little to control how a survey was actually conducted in Dushanbe or Khabarovsk."[28]

Once the survey was conducted, the results had to make their way back to Moscow. In the late-Soviet era, fax machines still had not appeared even in the capitals, phone connections were unreliable, and the mail could take months to reach the farthest regional offices. The trains, however, still ran. VTsIOM paid train conductors to take packets of blank surveys across the country, where they would be met at the station by local employees who would take the forms to the field offices, conduct surveys, and send the results back by the same means. The system worked relatively well, though not without its problems. One tranche of results from Almaty, for instance, was lost and the Kazakh section of a nationwide survey had to be completely redone.[29]

The need for standardization and communication meant that the network of field offices was created not only on Soviet-era infrastructure, but also through Soviet-era connections (mostly those Grushin had developed) and under Soviet-era assumptions. Those with bureaucratic knowledge and connections to Moscow were chosen to lead field offices over those with other skills, such as local knowledge, embeddedness in local and indigenous populations, or fluency in local languages. These priorities were set out of expediency rather than any philosophical preference. Standardization and efficiency was key to pulling off VTsIOM's all-but-impossible task. But standardization came at certain costs. Leaders of field offices and poll workers were trained in Russian to ask questions and collect responses in Russian. When VTsIOM researchers from Moscow traveled to field offices, quality control checks were handled in Russian. To my knowledge, VTsIOM did not conduct any polls in local languages. The preference for Russian was likewise one of expediency and standardization. The vastness of Soviet space and the unprecedented sampling ambitions made VTsIOM's data-gathering complex enough without translating among several languages. But the overreliance on Soviet networks, legacies, and Russocentrism created blind spots that would haunt the center and puncture its truth claims by the middle of the first post-Soviet decade.

By the end of 1988, however, the most basic logistical hurdles had been overcome and VTsIOM launched its first survey. It was a survey on the "problem of electing leaders," requested by the Gorbachev administration in an early effort to gauge the effects of undermining the Communist Party's monopoly on power. The second survey, launched around the same time, asked about the demand for literary journals. "Literary journals," as Gudkov explained to me, "were a deeply political question. The Central Committee of the Communist Party wanted to limit the print runs of the perestroika journals [*perestroechnye zhurnaly*, meaning those legacy Soviet journals such as *Znamia* and *Novyi mir*, which had gained enormous popularity during perestroika by publishing previously banned literature] in favor of more conservative publications such as *Pravda*."[30] VTsIOM's research showed that demand—and in fact readership—far outstripped supply and recommended that Goskompechat', the Soviet body responsible for mass media, not only increase print runs, but also allow journals to raise circulation from month to month rather than only once a year. Perhaps unexpectedly, VTsIOM's second-ever survey combined literature and politics in a way that brought the market reasoning of supply and demand into late-Soviet decision-making.

The next year, in 1989, VTsIOM launched its first large-scale public opinion surveys under the title "New Year." The survey grew into an annual longitudinal study led by Levada that asked citizens how they felt about everything from travel restrictions to alcohol consumption to socially marginalized groups. As the results rolled in, VTsIOM sought ways to represent its findings to a public unused to polling. Alongside narrative publications in various periodicals, academic articles, and policy recommendations, VTsIOM commissioned a series of comics that appeared in the pages of *Izvestiia*, the official newspaper of the Soviet government.

The comics were accompanied by short narratives written by VTsIOM researchers, while the illustrations themselves show human figures who are meant to represent respondents giving certain answers to a single survey question. The figures seem to roughly correspond to these respondents' demographic characteristics and are drawn in dynamic and often humorous situations meant to both catch the reader's eye and reflect something about the results of the survey. For instance, one such drawing that appeared on the front page of *Izvestiia* under the headline "The State and Us" shows three older men on the left representing three positions that the accompanying text describes as that of those who have "become used to state support." In the middle, two younger men stand under an apple tree. One says that the state is now so weak that citizens should be ready to make sacrifices to help the state (as he picks an apple with his left hand and gives away another with his right). The other insists on the opposite, that citizens should make the state serve their interests. A final figure sits on the ground, representing those who "had trouble answering" (Figure 1).

In this illustration, the represented ages of the figures roughly correspond to the demographic characteristics of the respondents who chose those answers, as described

Общественное мнение ● Опрос и комментарий социологов

ГОСУДАРСТВО И МЫ

Многие десятилетия органы государства концентрировали в своих руках все наличные ресурсы, а населению отводилась роль очереди за дефицитом. Это не могло не породить «зависимого сознания» у многих и многих. Выявить резервы гражданской самостоятельности, оценить объем групп, готовых к независимым решениям,— такую задачу поставили перед собой социологи.

Предполагались три возможные позиции, и в ответах на вопрос об отношении к государству выделялись три группы. **Первая** — привыкшие к опеке государства. В данную группу объединились те, кто обязан государству всем (они составляют примерно одну шестую ее), кто совершенно не удовлетворен своей долей (их вдвое больше) и кто рассчитывает на прибавку (таких — около половины). В целом — с той или иной степенью удовлетворения — ощущают зависимость от государства около четверти ответивших. Среди них чаще всего можно встретить людей пожилых, недостаточно образованных и малообеспеченных (особенно — пенсионеров, колхозников, отчасти — учащихся). Они чаще прочих согласны на самое низкое вознаграждение, лишь бы труд не был тяжелым и оставлял немало свободного времени.

Вошедшие во **вторую** группу готовы для благосостояния государства идти на жертвы (около трети ответивших). Данную точку зрения чаще других разделяют люди активных возрастов (особенно тридцати- и пятидесятилетние), с высшим образованием, представители руководства, научные сотрудники, интеллигенция, в максимальной степени члены КПСС, в минимальной — беспартийные. Приверженцы этого взгляда — работники со средними (от 126 до 200 рублей) доходами, ценят прежде всего уверенность в завтрашнем дне (даже при недостаточном вознаграждении за сегодняшний).

Третья группа включает тех, кто требует свободы решений и поступков, которой должна быть подчинена деятельность государства, коллектива и т. д. Среди них много зрелой молодежи (25—29 лет), минимум — членов КПСС. Доходы этой группы выше средних, значительнее и ее культурные ресурсы (например, домашние собрания книг). Чаще всего эту позицию разделяют люди с высшим образованием, реже других — колхозники и пенсионеры. Они предпочитали бы вести собственное дело на свой страх и риск, одобряют появление в перспективе отечественных миллионеров и критически относятся к незаслуженным привилегиям. Группа составляет чуть меньше трети опрошенных.

Итак, уровень терпимости к экономическим инициативам пока еще выше, нежели степень готовности к гражданским свободам и связанной с ними ответственности.

Б. ДУБИН,
старший научный сотрудник ВЦИОМ.

FIGURE 1 Image from Artifact 00095.[a] Boris Dubin and V. Rozantsev, "Gosudarstvo i my," *Izvestiia* 49, no. 22952 (February 18, 1990): 1. The voice bubbles in the illustration read: under 4.4%, "The state gave us everything, no one has the right to demand anything else"; under 8.4%, "The state gives us so little that we do not owe it anything"; under 11.3%, "The state gives us more than a little, but we could demand more"; 33.2%, "The state is currently in such a position that we should help it, even be ready to make sacrifices"; under 32.5%, "We should become free people and make the state serve our interests"; and under 10.3%, "I have difficulty answering."

in the accompanying text. More confusing, perhaps, is the setting. Nothing in the accompanying text explains the apple tree or why the two young men would be helping each other pick and distribute its fruits. Meanwhile, the text itself seems to push interpretation in a direction not necessarily implied by the results. "For many decades," reads the teaser text in bold, "state organs have concentrated in their hands all of the available resources and the populace was left with the role of waiting in line. This could not help but instill a 'dependent consciousness' in many." This is a surprising way to open this short text, since only a small minority opinion (the 4.4% who responded that "The state gave us everything, no one has the right to demand anything else") seems to represent such a dependent consciousness.

But the apparent contradiction actually aligns with one of Levada's major projects and one which VTsIOM's findings were often used to support. Levada had been discussing the Soviet person, or Homo sovieticus, as a "specific socio-anthropological phenomenon" throughout the late-Soviet years in the private seminars he held with many of his former students. When he joined VTsIOM, a direct study of the phenomenon was among his top priorities. For Levada, the Soviet person was formed by the experiences of revolution and state terror and had taken on the central characteristics of exceptionalism (*iskliuchitel'nost'*), state paternalist orientation (*gosudarstvenno-paternalistskaia orientatsiia*), and hierarchical thinking (*ierarkhichnost'*).[31] This Soviet person was never demographically distinct. The model applied equally across genders and nationalities,

[a] https://postsoviet90s.com/artifacts/the-rise-of-public-opinion-polling

which might help account for the fact that all the figures in the illustration in Figure 1 appear to be male, even though VTsIOM disaggregated results according to sex (though not according to nationality, which was implicitly assumed by VTsIOM's methodology to play little role in most polls). The Homo sovieticus model helps explain not only certain methodological decisions, but also some of the apparent incongruities in VTsIOM's presentation of its data. For instance, the "dependent consciousness" mentioned above might not correspond to the largest group of respondents, but it does correspond to important characteristics of Homo sovieticus.

Levada argued that Homo sovieticus was on its way out. It was no longer the dominant force in society, especially among the younger generations. Those born after the Second World War had missed the revolution, were too young for Stalin's terror, and had experienced only milder forms of state violence.[32] A series of studies designed by Levada set out to show how society was changing—becoming more tolerant, for instance. In one such study, VTsIOM researchers asked citizens in late 1991 what should be done with certain people "whose behavior deviates from generally accepted norms." Answers ranged from "liquidate" to "provide help" to "leave them to their own devices," and the groups included drug addicts, murderers, hippies, prostitutes, the poor, the homeless, and homosexuals. Setting aside the enormous ethical problems in grouping these "behaviors" under one rubric, the study shows that society was relatively tolerant (more tolerant, certainly, than the Soviet state had often been): most thought these people needed help and or should be left to their own devices. However, thanks to the study's disaggregation of results by demographic characteristics of respondents, it is clear that there is no straightforward correlation between age and tolerance. The group most likely to advocate for the "liquidation" of, say, hippies or drug addicts were 20–24-year-old men, and 25–29-year-old women, respectively (Figures 2 and 3).

Nevertheless, VTsIOM's publications often made the case that younger generations were more tolerant, open, and forward-looking, while it was the older generations who held fast to conservative views. For instance, when VTsIOM published an illustration in *Izvestiia* on a similar subject ("The Strength and Weakness of Taboos", Figure 4), the visuals made an implicit argument about the tolerance of various demographic groups. This question asks which topics should be off-limits for public discussion. An older woman in a kerchief covers her mouth in apparent shame as she voices the two most popular answers, "Sex techniques" (17%) and "Sexual relations between people of the same gender" (14%). An old man with a cane voices several other potential taboos, while a relatively young apparently blind man has "difficulty answering" and the youngest and most able-bodied figure feeds a power cord to a TV camera while responding, "There are no such topics." In contrast to the illustration, the text reveals that the group most likely to have trouble answering is women over 60 years old. It says nothing about the demographics of those who see no topics worth banning, and instead lets the illustration speak for itself.

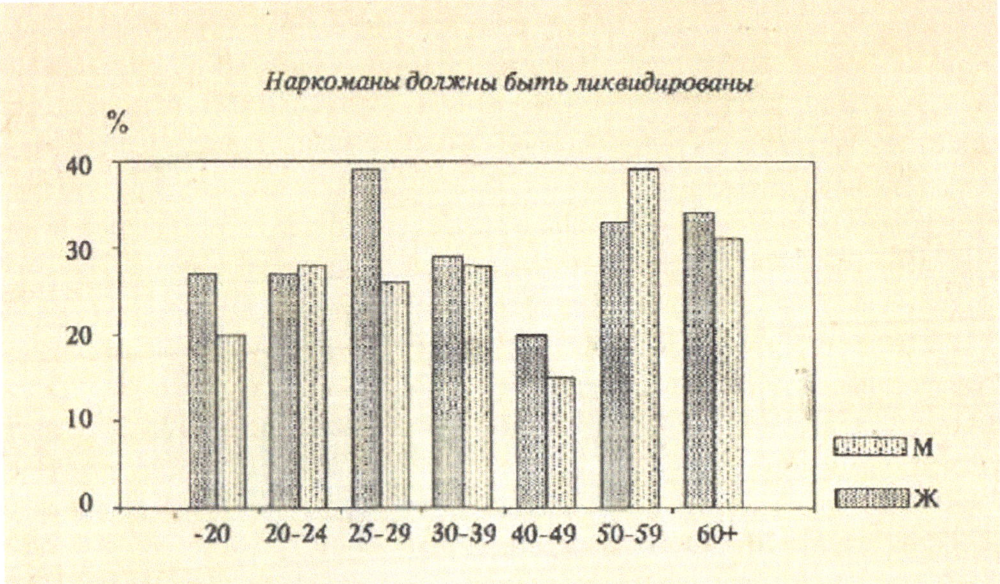

FIGURES 2 AND 3 Images from Artifact 0095.[b] Respondents who said that hippies (top) and drug addicts (bottom) should be "liquidated," broken down by age group and gender. (The lighter colored bars marked M represent men, the darker colored bars marked Ж represent women.) Iurii Levada, ed., *Prostoi sovetskii chelovek* (Moscow: VTsIOM, 1993), 287–88.

[b] https://postsoviet90s.com/artifacts/the-rise-of-public-opinion-polling

Общественное мнение ● Опрос и комментарий социолога

СИЛА И СЛАБОСТЬ ЗАПРЕТОВ

НИЧЕМ не ограниченной и никому не подотчетной власти свойственно умножать запреты. Наше общество — с различной на разных его участках скоростью — движется к демократии. Меньше стало людей, готовых слепо вручать свою судьбу лицам, которые мандата на свои полномочия не получали, реже они безропотно подчиняются безапелляционно сказанному: «Не положено». При ответе на вопрос социологов о темах, которые недопустимо обсуждать в печати и на телевидении, 26 процентов опрошенных—за полную гласность по любым вопросам, а 24 — доля заметная! — затруднились высказаться с должной определенностью. Среди воздержавшихся чаще других оказываются женщины (среди них эта доля достигает 28 процентов), респонденты старше 60 (32) и 20—25 лет (34), люди с неполным средним образованием (38), занятые в сельском хозяйстве (34) и пенсионеры (32), не выписывающие периодики (35) и не имеющие дома книг (40).

Примерно половина опрошенных сочли необходимым пока ограничить открытую полемику по наиболее напряженным моментам сегодняшнего развития общества и интимным сторонам повседневной жизни. Среди тех, кто чаще других готов отказать своим согражданам в праве на объективную информацию и независимую точку зрения, лидируют две группы. С одной стороны, самые молодые: они еще не во всем определились и потому склонны к жестким, однозначным решениям. Для них наиболее закрытыми представляются такие темы, как «политические качества нынешних руководителей», «ответственность партии за нынешнее кризисное состояние», «особенности и недостатки национальных характеров» (тема, заметим, наиболее напряженная для интеллигенции), «политические программы некоммунистических партий и групп». С другой стороны, пожилые люди, тяготеющие к известному консерватизму: особенно это касается таких тем, как «возможность замены нашего строя на капиталистический», «правильность политического курса Ленина», «возможность отделения республик», «положение дел в армии», но прежде всего — интимные стороны жизни. И та, и другая группы объединяются в том, что нужно ограничить обсуждение «полномочий КГБ» (не желающие касаться этого вопроса более других склонны вообще запрещать полемику), «личной жизни политических деятелей».

Наименее зависимы в своих оценках учащиеся и ИТР наиболее активных возрастов. Напротив, наиболее склонны полагаться на логику запретов пенсионеры и военнослужащие, достаточно часто — научная и творческая интеллигенция (этот момент стоит, пожалуй, отметить). Склонность ограничить гласность в том или другом вопросе связана с общим отношением респондентов к государству. Те, кто полагается на государственное попечительство, благодарен за любое вознаграждение, лишь бы оно было твердым, и требует постоянной «сильной руки» в стране, гораздо чаще готовы выгораживать особые зоны вне общественного внимания и критики.

Этим представителям «государственно - распределительного» комплекса противостоят те, кто взыскателен к работе и ориентирован на успех, полученный собственными усилиями, требует дальнейшей демократизации принятия общественно важных решений, настаивает на подконтрольности власти обществу.

Б. ДУБИН,
ст. научный сотрудник
ВЦИОМ.

Рис. В. РОЗАНЦЕВА, А. БЕЗИКА.

FIGURE 4 Image from Artifact 0095.[c] B. Dubin with illustrations by V. Rozantsev and A. Bezik, "Sila i slabost' zapretov," *Izvestiia* 86 (March 27, 1990): 2.

The illustrated format began as a way to introduce public opinion data to a new audience. But the intended accessibility of the format led to oversimplification and even, at times, misrepresentation. While not always true to the data, the illustrations projected the prejudices and hopes that Levada's Homo sovieticus project articulated: that an overdependence on the state, inculcated over generations, led to the paternalism and intolerance that characterized Soviet society, but that these characteristics were receding as the older generations aged. The illustrations suggest that the perestroika-era and post-Soviet subject would be more independent, more tolerant, more liberal. In other words, as they oversimplified and even misrepresented the data they were intended to elucidate, the illustrations attempted to create a post-Soviet subject that the data did not necessarily support.

When VTsIOM launched its own monthly journal in 1993, *Monitoring of Public Opinion* (*Monitoring obshchestvennogo mneniia*), it eschewed the simplification of such illustrations and instead combined theoretical complexity with radical transparency.[33] The journal would be divided into two sections. The first, comprising roughly 30% of the journal's pages, was given over to in-depth analytical articles that treated the group's findings with a level of complexity and nuance that illustrated newspaper write-ups did not allow. The articles treated both broad longitudinal trends and more

---

[c] https://postsoviet90s.com/artifacts/the-rise-of-public-opinion-polling

narrow results of a specific month's surveys. These articles not only presented findings, they also developed the center's methodology and sociological theory. The second two-thirds of every issue was filled with reams of raw data, pages upon pages of the disaggregated results of that month's surveys. The idea was to disseminate widely all of the information gathered, without the distraction of illustrations or visualizations, in the hope that transparency would lead to uptake, and the public opinion surveys would lead to a populace that better understood itself and a government that was more responsive to its needs.

The publication of raw data also suggested that VTsIOM's efforts were but one aspect of this new way of knowing the world it was projecting. Other researchers, both domestic and international, might be able to use the data in their own research. In this way, VTsIOM was adopting and amplifying the worldwide practice of public opinion polling that it saw as an essential aspect of joining the post-Cold War world. Indeed, in the first issue of *Monitoring*, VTsIOM's head researchers Levada and Gudkov invoked George Gallup as the international founder of public opinion polling and its best advocate for the practice's importance for an open society.[34] For Gallup, public opinion polling was a necessary aspect of political life, for "In the democratic community, the attitudes of the mass of people determine policy." Even more important, public opinion was a bulwark against authoritarianism. Writing in 1940, Gallup wanted public opinion polling to respond to critiques of democracy from the likes of Mussolini, Hitler, and Stalin, who suggested (in Gallup's paraphrase) that "democracy is cumbersome and slow-moving." While the will of a strong leader can act quickly and boldly, the logic went, democracy has to consider the consent of the governed. Public opinion—broad-based, statistically represented, and transparently published—would help address this problem. It would give democratic society the tools it needed to respond to its populace and ultimately to survive the threat of authoritarianism. Furthermore, public opinion had at its heart a very democratic principle: "It believes in the value of every individual's contribution to political life, and in the right of ordinary human beings to have a voice in deciding their fate. Public opinion, in this sense, is the pulse of democracy."[35]

THE OBJECTIVE SPIRIT AND THE MARKET

Looking back on their years at VTsIOM, however, Dubin and Gudkov saw something more than the pulse of democracy in their version of public opinion polling. In a 2008 volume, they wrote that they were drawn to the kind of broad-based sociological analysis practiced at the center, because they saw it as the only "reasonable foundation" from which to begin the kind of research that might approach society's "objective Spirit" (*ob"ektivnyi Dukh*).[36] On one level, the sentiment expresses something that VTsIOM's monthly journal also emphasized, that broad sociological analysis could lead to a clearer and even objective vision of society.[37] VTsIOM's monthly journal carried the slogan "From Opinions to Understanding" ("*Ot mnenii k ponimaniiu*"), suggesting that the collation of huge numbers of comparable opinions would allow a meta-level of understanding of the country as a whole that was previously inaccessible. But the use of "objective Spirit" suggests something beyond straightforward objectivity.

The phrase is patently Hegelian, as Dubin and Gudkov's capitalization of Spirit (*Dukh*) underlines. For Hegel, the objective Spirit is the driving force of history.[38] It is the human spirit as it expresses itself in the world, and in a broadly held reading of Hegel, it culminates in the ethnic nation-state.[39] What is at stake in defining the object of sociology in these Hegelian terms is nothing less than a full refutation of the Soviet-Marxist vision of history. In place of materialism—the primacy of economic and material conditions in the unfolding of history—VTsIOM sided with Hegel's idealism. Broadly defined, philosophical idealism holds that external reality can best be known through our perception, our ideas about that reality, and therefore reality is above all a mental construct. For Hegel, history should be understood from this position. It is driven not by the material world alone, but by ideas about the world in constant dialogical tension with the world itself. That dialectic creates the objective Spirit. VTsIOM, through its broad-based public opinion surveys, mirrored this dialectic. It asked about material conditions but gave primacy to respondents' subjective answers in its attempt to model post-Soviet society. In other words, it reconstructed the changing world primarily by asking for people's subjective experience of and ideas about that world. In this way, it was public opinion as idealist philosophy. Or perhaps the other way around.

Emblematic of this position was VTsIOM's relationship to literature and the bourgeoning book market. VTsIOM surveys on reading habits were often published in *Knizhnoe obozrenie*, the major trade publication of the book industry. *Knizhnoe obozrenie* had eagerly embraced market thinking even before the fall of the Soviet Union, and in the 1990s, it developed post-Soviet Russia's first bestseller lists, which became central to the newspaper's reputation and to the publishing world. As VTsIOM placed its studies alongside bestseller lists and articles like "How to Become the Russian Agatha Christie" and "The Formula for Success," it seemed to suggest that its sociology might also have market potential.[40] For instance, VTsIOM published the feature "What Are Russians Reading?" (Figure 5), which showed genre preferences disaggregated for gender, age, and education levels. The study found that action thrillers ("*ostrosiuzhetnaia slovesnost*'") had become the "gravitational pole for young men" while "the interests of young and more educated women are concentrated first and foremost on romance novels."[41]

Though such statistics do not include individual titles, the bestseller lists printed in the very same newspaper confirm the findings with names of actual bestsellers including, in this particular week, Nikolai Leonov's *Confessions of a Spy* and an unauthorized

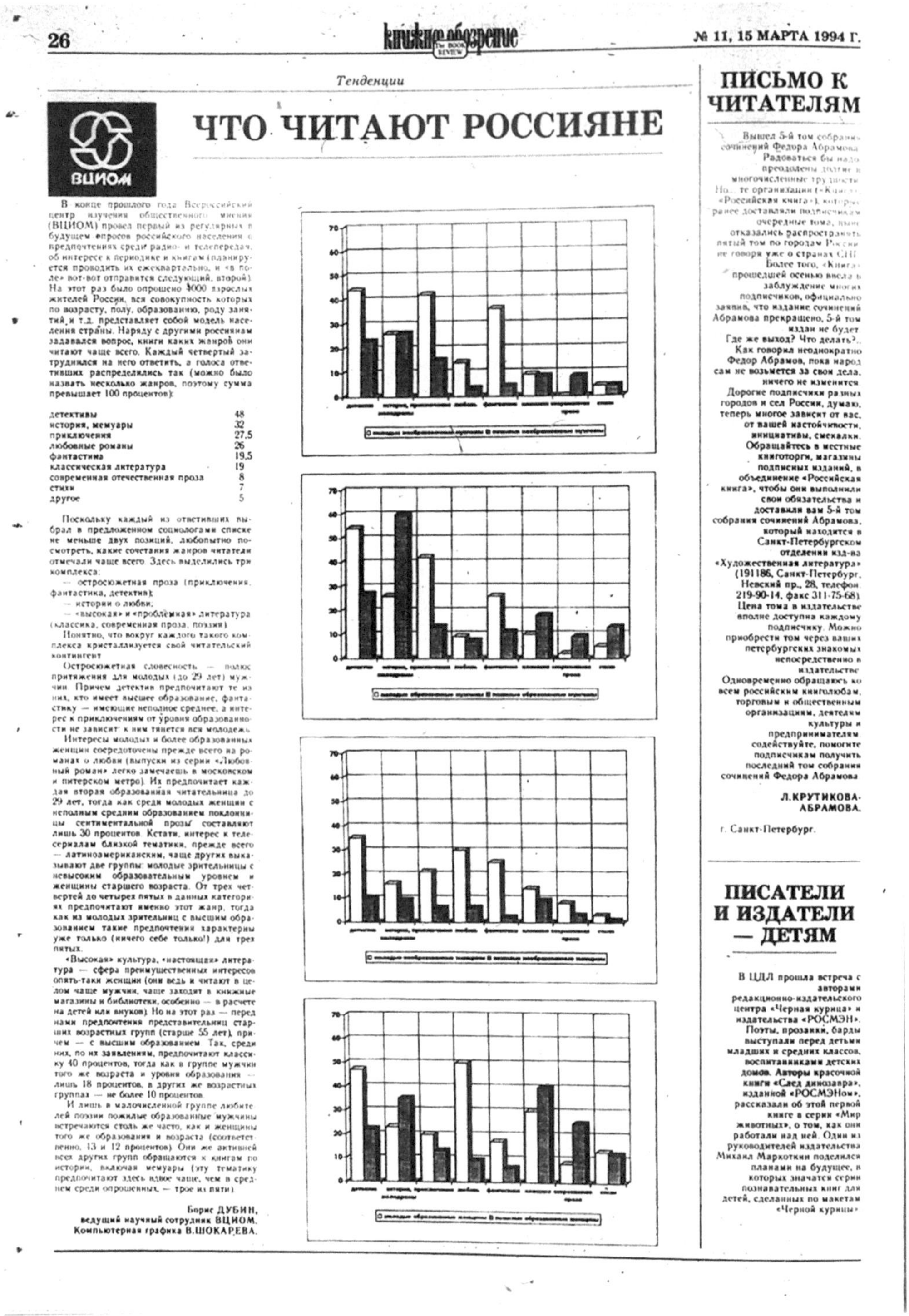

26 | Книжное обозрение | № 11, 15 МАРТА 1994 Г.

Тенденции

ЧТО ЧИТАЮТ РОССИЯНЕ

ВЦИОМ

В конце прошлого года Всероссийский центр изучения общественного мнения (ВЦИОМ) провел первый из регулярных в будущем опросов российского населения о предпочтениях среди радио- и телепередач, об интересе к периодике и книгам (планируется проводить их ежеквартально, и «в поле» вот-вот отправится следующий, второй). На этот раз было опрошено 3000 взрослых жителей России, вся совокупность которых по возрасту, полу, образованию, роду занятий и т.д. представляет собой модель населения страны. Наряду с другими россиянам задавался вопрос, книги каких жанров они читают чаще всего. Каждый четвертый затруднился на него ответить, а голоса ответивших распределились так (можно было назвать несколько жанров, поэтому сумма превышает 100 процентов):

детективы	48
история, мемуары	32
приключения	27.5
любовные романы	26
фантастима	19.5
классическая литература	19
современная отечественная проза	8
стихи	7
другое	5

Поскольку каждый из ответивших выбрал в предложенном социологами списке не меньше двух позиций, любопытно посмотреть, какие сочетания жанров читатели отмечали чаще всего. Здесь выделились три комплекса:

— остросюжетная проза (приключения, фантастика, детектив);
— истории о любви;
— «высокая» и «проблемная» литература (классика, современная проза, поэзия).

Понятно, что вокруг каждого такого комплекса кристаллизуется свой читательский контингент.

Остросюжетная словесность — полюс притяжения для молодых (до 29 лет) мужчин. Причем детектив предпочитают те из них, кто имеет высшее образование, фантастику — имеющие неполное среднее, а интерес к приключениям от уровня образованности не зависит: к ним тянется вся молодежь.

Интересы молодых и более образованных женщин сосредоточены прежде всего на романах о любви (выпуски из серии «Любовный роман» легко замечаешь в московском и питерском метро). Их предпочитает каждая вторая образованная читательница до 29 лет, тогда как среди молодых женщин с неполным средним образованием поклонницы сентиментальной прозы составляют лишь 30 процентов. Кстати, интерес к телесериалам близкой тематики, прежде всего — латиноамериканским, чаще других выказывают две группы: молодые зрительницы с невысоким образовательным уровнем и женщины старшего возраста. От трех четвертей до четырех пятых в данных категориях предпочитают именно этот жанр, тогда как из молодых зрительниц с высшим образованием такие предпочтения характерны уже только (ничего себе только!) для трех пятых.

«Высокая» культура, «настоящая» литература — сфера преимущественных интересов опять-таки женщин (они ведь и читают в целом чаще мужчин, чаще заходят в книжные магазины и библиотеки, особенно — в расчете на детей или внуков). Но на этот раз — перед нами предпочтения представительниц старших возрастных групп (старше 55 лет), причем — с высшим образованием. Так, среди них, по их заявлениям, предпочитают классику 40 процентов, тогда как в группе мужчин того же возраста и уровня образования — лишь 18 процентов, в других же возрастных группах — не более 10 процентов.

И лишь в малочисленной группе любителей поэзии пожилые образованные мужчины встречаются столь же часто, как и женщины того же образования и возраста (соответственно, 13 и 12 процентов). Они же активней всех других групп обращаются к книгам по истории, включая мемуары (эту тематику предпочитают здесь вдвое чаще, чем в среднем среди опрошенных, — трое из пяти).

Борис ДУБИН,
ведущий научный сотрудник ВЦИОМ.
Компьютерная графика В.ШОКАРЕВА.

ПИСЬМО К ЧИТАТЕЛЯМ

Вышел 5-й том собрания сочинений Федора Абрамова. Радоваться бы надо: преодолены долгие и многочисленные трудности. Но... те организации («Книга», «Российская книга»), которые ранее доставляли подписчикам очередные тома, ныне отказались распространять пятый том по городам России, не говоря уже о странах СНГ. Более того, «Книга» прошедшей осенью ввела в заблуждение многих подписчиков, официально заявив, что издание сочинений Абрамова прекращено, 5-й том издан не будет.

Где же выход? Что делать?.. Как говорил неоднократно Федор Абрамов, пока народ сам не возьмется за свои дела, ничего не изменится.

Дорогие подписчики разных городов и сел России, думаю, теперь многое зависит от вас, от вашей настойчивости, инициативы, смекалки. Обращайтесь в местные книготорги, магазины подписных изданий, в объединение «Российская книга», чтобы они выполнили свои обязательства и доставили вам 5-й том собрания сочинений Абрамова, который находится в Санкт-Петербургском отделении изд-ва «Художественная литература» (191186, Санкт-Петербург, Невский пр., 28, телефон 219-90-14, факс 311-75-68). Цена тома в издательстве вполне доступна каждому подписчику. Можно приобрести том через ваших петербургских знакомых непосредственно в издательстве.

Одновременно обращаюсь ко всем российским книголюбам, торговым и общественным организациям, деятелям культуры и предпринимателям: содействуйте, помогите подписчикам получить последний том собрания сочинений Федора Абрамова.

Л.КРУТИКОВА-АБРАМОВА.

г. Санкт-Петербург.

ПИСАТЕЛИ И ИЗДАТЕЛИ — ДЕТЯМ

В ЦДЛ прошла встреча с авторами редакционно-издательского центра «Черная курица» и издательства «РОСМЭН». Поэты, прозаики, барды выступали перед детьми младших и средних классов, воспитанниками детских домов. Авторы красочной книги «След динозавра», изданной «РОСМЭНом», рассказали об этой первой книге в серии «Мир животных», о том, как они работали над ней. Один из руководителей издательства Михаил Маркоткин поделился планами на будущее, в которых значатся серии познавательных книг для детей, сделанных по макетам «Черной курицы».

FIGURE 5 Image from Artifact 00095.[d] Boris Dubin, "Chto chitaiut rossiane?" *Knizhnoe obozrenie* (March 15, 1994): 26.

[d] https://postsoviet90s.com/artifacts/the-rise-of-public-opinion-polling

6 Книжное обозрение № 33, 16 АВГУСТА 1994 г.

МАГИЯ БЕСТСЕЛЛЕРА

что читают сегодня за рубежом и что печатают у нас

№ 33, 16 АВГУСТА 1994 г. Книжное обозрение 7

БЕСТСЕЛЛЕРЫ МОСКВЫ

на 11 августа 1994 г.

ХУДОЖЕСТВЕННАЯ ЛИТЕРАТУРА | ДРУГАЯ ЛИТЕРАТУРА

В ТВЕРДОМ ПЕРЕПЛЕТЕ

В МЯГКОЙ ОБЛОЖКЕ

«ИНТЕЛЛЕКТУАЛЬНЫЕ» БЕСТСЕЛЛЕРЫ

FIGURE 6 Image from Artifact 00017.[e] On the right page, list of "Bestsellers of Moscow"; on the left, the headline "The Magic of the Bestseller" tops an article about what is read abroad and what is published in Russia today. *Knizhnoe obozrenie* (August 16, 1994): 6–7.

sequel to Margaret Mitchell's *Gone with the Wind* called *Rhett Butler* (Figure 6).[42] The latter was part of a trend of bestsellers which had specifically followed the market data published in *Knizhnoe obozrenie* to produce ready-made bestsellers. *Rhett Butler* was one of six sequels and prequels to Mitchell's international sensation all penned by an anonymous collective of Minsk-based writers and published under the name Dzhuliia Khilpatrik. The Khilpatrik collective was only one (and perhaps the most successful) of several such groups which used the new market data to drive the creative process (Artifact 00098[f]).[43]

In this particular context, VTsIOM's sociological study distills the market, providing a higher level of abstraction. VTsIOM's researchers took this orientation one step further. Dubin and Gudkov argued that literature—including the pulp fiction bestsellers that enjoyed such popularity at the time—could be seen as an important social institution, "the basic functional significance of which we take to be the support of the cultural identity of society." In this light, each type of literature could provide insight into the

[e] https://postsoviet90s.com/artifacts/bestsellers-of-moscow

[f] https://postsoviet90s.com/artifacts/gone-with-the-wind-the-post-soviet-sequels

"structure of the normative-value systems of certain social groups."[44] In other words, as they argued at length in their co-authored book *Literature as a Social Institution* (1994), through the hermeneutic strategies championed by Iser and Jauss, what people read could be a promising approach to that ever-elusive objective Spirit.

In a series of essays, Dubin showed how this methodology might be applied to specific genres. Among essays on romance and historical fiction, Dubin wrote on the "Sociological Poetics of the Russian Action Novel [*roman-boevik*]," in which he analyzed the rising popularity of violent action thrillers by the likes of Danil Koretskii and Viktor Dotsenko and their protagonists Antikiller and Mad Dog.[45] In a subtle analysis of dozens of bestselling works, Dubin argued that action thrillers provided a symbolic test of Russian masculinity during the transitional years, as Russia moved from "an ideology of collectivism to an ideology of individualism." Nearly all the protagonists in this genre, Dubin notes, are orphans, and in the novels, they almost always act alone. The protagonist, Dubin writes, is the sole "source of 'reality' in the novel."

> [He] is at the cutting edge of time, he alone gives it its pace and rhythm of events, he directs himself and what happens. More than that, he feels himself to be on the cutting edge of world history, if not of all of civilization: "I am the edge of humanism: its sharpened end [*ia krai gumanizma; ego zaostrennoe okonchanie*]," the protagonist says of himself, justifying his destructive mission and confirming his own reality.[46]

The hero not only guides the reader through the difficulties of the new world; he creates the values of that new world through his own ability to navigate it. The new world is corrupted by selfish interests, but it is only the extraordinary individual, guided by a strict (but individual) moral code, who can set things right. The hero of the action thriller is in many ways the opposite of Homo sovieticus, whose decline VTsIOM had so long been tracking. If the Soviet person had a "dependent consciousness" characterized by "state-paternalist orientation" and "hierarchical thinking," then the hero of the action thriller is the individualist extraordinaire, fully independent and able to navigate and even transform a world almost entirely bereft of state power. The implied reader of these texts does not correspond directly to their heroes but the texts are constructed in such a way to make it clear that a reader is intended to admire the hero, his actions, and his values. The popularity of such novels, in turn, suggested a widespread aspiration toward the values which the protagonists express both explicitly and implicitly.

Though Dubin's genre analyses were inspired by research done at VTsIOM (the results of which were often published in VTsIOM's monthly journal), they appeared in literary journals such as *Novoe literaturnoe obozrenie*, *Znamia*, or *Novyi mir*.[47] These articles, and others like them, changed the relationship between literature and the social sciences. They showed that literary criticism, especially criticism that took on mass literature, might grow out of the social sciences. More specifically, the social sciences might guide critics' attention, and in turn the tools of criticism might be used to deepen sociological analysis. Though an "anthropological turn" in literary studies was discussed in subsequent decades—following a similar turn in the Anglo-American scholarship—the researchers at VTsIOM, and especially Dubin, brought the social sciences and literary studies together much earlier.[48] This synthesis, however, was different from the later anthropological turn. Based as it was on public opinion surveys, statistical data, and sociological theories, it might instead be thought of as the sociological turn in literary studies. It suggested that sociology and statistically represented public opinion, rather than aesthetics, might guide a critic's attention, and that the analysis of commercial culture—rather than of high art—might reveal society's most resonant symbolic representations.

Crucially, this kind of literary criticism connects the market to symbolic cultural representation. *Knizhnoe obozrenie*'s bestseller lists identify individual novels with broad appeal, VTsIOM's representative surveys suggest who reads what, and essays like Dubin's extract an understanding of the collective psyche by reading the bestselling books in the most popular genres. But something else happens in between: the market intervenes. As we saw with "Dzhuliia Khilpatrik," the availability of bestseller lists and sociological information on readers' preferences pushed writers and publishers to create literature based on the demands identified in the market data. The bestselling action thrillers that Dubin analyzed, then, were partly what readers demanded, but partly what the market had made profitable to produce at high volume. In this way, as VTsIOM constructed and represented an image of post-Soviet Russian society through the literature it chose to read, it empowered the market to guide those representations. In other words, if post-Soviet society's "objective Spirit" might be pursued through broad-based statistical sampling, then its reflection in mass culture was inevitably mediated by the market. Combined, these two developments might be seen as part of a broader marketization of culture, but not in the way that phrase is usually understood. Cultural products were indeed exchanged on capitalist markets in new ways. But the market was not simply a place of exchange; it became an integral part of how culture was received, how it was evaluated, and how its meanings—and their broader implications for society—were extracted.

That the market might play such a central role in the transition away from the Homo sovieticus model that had been at the center of Levada and the VTsIOM researchers' investigations from the late 1980s is perhaps no surprise. Yearly surveys had shown that even as post-Soviet Russians were exhausted by and often opposed to some of the economic reforms that ushered in the market economy, they had adopted many of the values of neoliberal capitalism. Over the course of the 1990s, even as more respondents say they could not find their way in the new society, they showed a stronger orientation toward individual success, for instance, and they began to value private property over collective responsibility.[49] But what is perhaps more surprising is that the combination of state disintegration and post-Soviet capitalism that characterized the Russian 1990s not only moved society away from Levada's Soviet person, but moved it toward the testosterone-charged hero of the action thriller. Through the market and VTsIOM's representations of post-Soviet society, in other words, it appeared that Homo sovieticus was replaced not by a liberal democratic subject, but by something closer to Savelii "Mad Dog" Govorkov.

NATIONAL INDEPENDENCE AND THE MANIPULATION OF PUBLIC OPINION

Levada argued that as Homo sovieticus receded, the Soviet Union weakened and eventually fell, opening the way for a new liberal, independent subject. But as the Union disintegrated, something else happened to Soviet citizens: they became Russians, Ukrainians, Belarusians, Kazakhs, Kyrgyz, and so on. The proliferation of citizenship categories was dwarfed by those of ethnic identification. VTsIOM had neither the linguistic resources, the demographic sophistication, nor the local staffing to measure and respond to all the rapidly shifting ethnic rifts threatening to pull societies apart across the former Soviet Union. Simultaneously, many of the logistical hurdles VTsIOM had overcome in its first two years resurfaced. Several regional offices found themselves divided from the central hub by newly drawn international borders. Some reorganized into private polling firms that cooperated with VTsIOM on occasional projects, others disappeared entirely. Customs regulations exacerbated the communication problems that had dogged VTsIOM from the start. But the problems went beyond the logistical. The question of national independence was among the most fraught during the transition years—making it one of the most important topics for VTsIOM to study. But nationalities and ethnicities had always been a blind spot, with linguistic specificity and local knowledge often sacrificed in the name of standardization and expedience. As the Soviet Union ended, the increasing violence of national independence movements made such study both more pressing and more difficult.

Gudkov recalled one vivid example in his interview with me. A routine quality control trip took him to the Dushanbe office in the fall of 1991. He was in the process of conducting interviews in an apartment block with a local colleague when a machine gun fired. It was close by. Then an artillery shell exploded even closer. The conversation was cut short, and Gudkov and his colleague rushed back to safety as the Tajikistani civil war started in earnest. Less than an hour later, Gudkov was on the last civilian flight out of the city, with unfinished survey results in his carry-on luggage.[50] Though VTsIOM and its flagship publication continued to cover national independence movements extensively, including the unfolding civil war in Tajikistan, this moment shows the difficulty of implementing VTsIOM's ideals in the post-Soviet context. Public opinion, as articulated by Gallup, was supposed to provide the "pulse of democracy." It was to give an open society a clear and transparent vision of itself, so that well-informed decisions could be made quickly that would benefit the populace. Yet when warfare literally interrupted and overtook VTsIOM's data-gathering operations, it became clear that the violence moved faster than reliable information in the post-Soviet peripheries. The open society to which post-Soviet Russia aspired did not have time to understand—much less undertake decisions to stem—the violence that accompanied its birth.

The Tajikistani civil war did not silence VTsIOM. (The center and its successor the Levada Center would continue their work through much more dire straits up to the present day.) Indeed, throughout the 1990s VTsIOM's *Monitoring of Public Opinion* devoted a huge proportion of its pages to polling on the various national independence movements across post-Soviet space, from Dushanbe to the Crimean Peninsula. Gudkov himself moved away from literary sociology for much of the early 1990s in order to concentrate on the various national independence movements that were pulling the country and its neighbors apart. Among the regions in his portfolio was Chechnya, which had declared its independence even before the Soviet Union dissolved. A civil war had been raging in the region since, with refugees streaming into Russia and unchecked violence on the ground. As Boris Yeltsin entered the last years of his first term, it was clear that the conflict in Chechnya—along with the catastrophic transition to a market economy—was among the most serious domestic issues he would face.

For Gudkov, the entanglement between the First Chechen War and Yeltsin's 1996 re-election campaign changed the place of polling in Russia forever. After Yeltsin's re-election, public opinion polling was no longer seen as a transparent metric of popular sentiment. It was seen as one more tool to be manipulated by the new breed of PR strategists who came to be known as "political technologists." Indeed, the manipulability of public opinion became a dominant theme of the second half of the 1990s, as the hopes that were invested in the possibility of an open society gave way to a society that seemed manipulable through the very mechanisms that were charged with its protection. For most, the turn came with the 1996 presidential campaign. When Yeltsin announced his intentions to run for a second term in January that year, his approval rating hovered around 6%, and for the first two months of the campaign, he polled well behind Communist Party candidate Gennady Ziuganov.[51] Yeltsin first led (at 28% to Ziuganov's 26%) in an April 4 poll conducted just days after an International Monetary Fund loan was approved (at the urging of US President Bill Clinton).[52] Soon the Yeltsin campaign hired a panel of British and American strategists and enlisted the help of media tycoons Boris Berezovsky and Vladimir Gusinsky, and for much of April and all of May, Yeltsin led in the polls, though he never captured majority support and after the first round of voting in June, he was forced into a runoff election the next month, in which he squeaked out a narrow victory (Artifact 00102[g]).[53] The election is remembered not only

[g] https://postsoviet90s.com/artifacts/a-way-out-of-the-dead-end

for the heavy hand of Western (largely American) involvement, but also for the frequency of polls that not only followed the developing narrative, but drove it.[54]

But for Gudkov, the loss of trust in public opinion polling started not in Moscow, but in Chechnya. Gudkov had been overseeing VTsIOM's polling on Chechnya since 1992, which had shown consistent and widespread support within the republic for independence from Russia (if not always for the leadership of Dzhokar Dudaev). But in late 1994, he was invited into the Russian White House and asked to explain a recent poll that showed the opposite. The poll was not VTsIOM's; it was commissioned by Russian intelligence and carried out by Nugzar Betaneli, a Georgian specialist in public opinion. "I was horrified," Gudkov told me. "Because this information was on Yeltsin's desk and essentially it said that the Chechen people would greet Russian soldiers with flowers in their hands...It was pure manipulation of information, manipulation of leadership. I was horrified and said that it was pure falsification."[55] Nevertheless, the decision to invade was undertaken and Yeltsin launched the disastrous First Chechen War. But Chechnya's place in VTsIOM's surveys—and in Yeltsin's political fate—only grew. In fact, Gudkov recalls that the end of the First Chechen War was also connected to public opinion. "In 1996, we showed that without a peace treaty in Chechnya," Gudkov told me, "Yeltsin couldn't win re-election. That was the main condition. And relying on our data, Yeltsin unwillingly agreed to peace."[56]

It is a nice story about a good poll setting right the sins of a bad poll. And Yeltsin did indeed sign a temporary ceasefire in the weeks before the election. He even flew down to Grozny and declared victory over the "rebellious Dudaev regime."[57] But the peace barely lasted through election day and the brutality of the third Battle of Grozny in August 1996 made the last-minute ceasefire look like a cynical campaign stunt. Indeed, the twin roles public opinion played in the First Chechen War represent not the good and bad side of polling, but rather two ways in which polling can be manipulated, and two ways in which the faith in polling was undermined. First, VTsIOM's success had made public opinion polling an influential and profitable enterprise, and polling agencies proliferated. Some—like Boris Grushin's commercial Vox Populi, or the Public Opinion Foundation (FOM)—grew directly out of VTsIOM's operations. Others were connected to VTsIOM's regional offices or started independently. Almost all worked for hire, often producing the results clients desired. But the second way polling was undermined was perhaps more insidious. The right polls could be used for anything—both stoking war and ending it. And as Yeltsin's declaration of victory in Grozny made clear, even transparent, rigorous, good-faith polling could be used cynically.

By the second half of the 1990s, the hopes for a transparent metric that would clearly reflect the pulse of democracy, that would hold up a reliable mirror to a newly open society, had transformed to something more equivocal. Public opinion surveys still provided essential information about society, and VTsIOM and its researchers worked tirelessly, honestly, and idealistically toward the open society that they had envisioned since the center was founded the previous decade. But after 1996, it had become clear that a truly world-class polling agency—and VTsIOM had made itself into that—was not enough to ensure an open society. Under the chaotic and violent conditions of post-Soviet capitalism, openness, transparency, and information flows were as manipulable as their opposites. After Yeltsin's cynical use of polling in the 1996 campaign, he mostly ignored the poll numbers as he stumbled through his second term in office. His successor, on the other hand, would pay close attention to polling and soon transform its role in society.

Vladimir Putin was appointed Deputy Prime Minister and then acting Prime Minister in August 1999, but it wasn't until September that he first entered the public consciousness. At a press conference, he was asked about the recent bombing of Russian forces outside of Grozny, Chechnya. His response ("We will follow the terrorists wherever they go…That means, if you'll excuse me, we'll find them in the toilet, we'll soak them in the latrine if it comes to that. That's it. The question is closed.") became emblematic of the hard line he intended to take in prosecuting the Second Chechen War, and boosted his poll numbers immediately.[58] He became a national figure, Yeltsin's handpicked successor, and on December 31, 1999, acting President. VTsIOM's polls predicted his easy victory in the March 2000 elections and rising oil prices buoyed his poll numbers for much of his first term.[59] But the polls also recorded the first disaster of his presidency with a clear dip in August 2000 when the Kursk submarine sank and Putin's bloodless response was seen as distant and even heartless.

Two years later, as VTsIOM's polls began to show popular dissatisfaction with the Second Chechen War, the organization found itself on a list of government agencies slated for privatization. The polling agency was still officially a government entity, reporting to the Ministry of Labor, but it had received no state funding since 1992 and had operated with *de facto* independence. Levada saw the upcoming changes as a government takeover, cloaked as the opposite. Through privatization, he feared, VTsIOM's independence would disappear. Over the next year, VTsIOM polls continued to surface politically unwelcome results. Perhaps most damning, Putin's party, United Russia, had earned little trust. Less than six months from the December 2003 parliamentary elections, VTsIOM showed that neither the working class (who preferred the Communists) nor intellectuals (who preferred the liberal party Yabloko) trusted United Russia to represents their interests.[60] According to Levada and other VTsIOM researchers, it was results like this that put VTsIOM in the administration's crosshairs. But the Ministry of Property, who handled the privatization, denied any political motivation. "Levada is a civil servant who reports directly to the Labor Minister," said ministry spokesman Aleksandr Parshukov. "It just so happened that [Labor Minister Aleksandr] Pochinok hasn't been interfering in his affairs."[61] In September 2003, VTsIOM was turned into a joint stock company, with a new board of directors (which included no VTsIOM researchers) and 100% of shares owned by the state.

Levada left and much of the staff followed. Unwilling to let go of the organization he and colleagues had built, Levada opened VTsIOM-A and continued to publish independent, rigorous polling data under the same logo. An inevitable lawsuit forced the new agency to drop the Soviet-era acronym and take on the name Levada Center, under which it has continued to conduct the most reliable polls in Russia ever since. Meanwhile VTsIOM continues to exist, operating since 2003 as something like the state's internal polling agency while also trading on the VTsIOM brand to garner commercial contracts for market research and other side projects.

The takeover—a combination of bureaucratic maneuvering, neoliberal capitalist procedures, and resurgent state power—was perhaps a fitting end for VTsIOM and its ideals. Brought into the world to build a new regime of truth for the post-Soviet era, it combined Western models with previously suppressed theory, all energized by the diverse legacies of the late-Soviet intelligentsia. And it created something truly groundbreaking that transformed the society it served. For its first years of existence, VTsIOM played a vital role in the energetic and open public sphere that seemed poised to fulfill the promises of glasnost and perestroika. As its researchers strove to accurately portray society, to deeply analyze trends their research surfaced, VTsIOM gave post-Soviet society perhaps its most accurate picture of itself. More important, through its publications and prominent presence in other media outlets, VTsIOM propounded the idea that such an accurate picture might be possible. But it was, from its very beginning, a project of political power. It was formed by directive of the Communist Party and its first poll was commissioned by the General Secretary. It had built its nationwide network through bureaucratic connections and, as it gained independence and theoretical sophistication, it had formed a relationship with the capitalist market. So it was perhaps no surprise that it was vulnerable to a new combination of neoliberalism and state power in the guise of what would become Putin's capitalist authoritarianism.

Perhaps just as important, from its founding, VTsIOM had often treated public opinion polling not as a tool of popular sovereignty—a method by which broad swathes of the population might influence government decision-making—but as a barometer of public sentiment in reaction to decisions already made. Its first poll asked how people felt about democratic reforms already instituted. Early surveys on privatization asked not whether to continue, but how respondents felt about the current state of affairs. This relationship to polling subordinated public opinion to state prerogatives and opened the door to state takeover. It is worth reiterating that the state did not shutter VTsIOM after taking it over. It is as active as ever, executing weekly polls ordered by the state with results broadcast on state television and published in the press. In fact, polling remains central to the state's view of itself and its communication with the populace under Putin today. Greg Yudin has recently argued that "Russia exists in a state of constant plebiscite in which the regime aims to continuously demonstrate popular support for Putin to domestic and foreign audiences."[62] Never fully a tool for popular sovereignty, polling has now transformed into the opposite: a tool for the legitimation of the state and the depoliticization of the populace. State-commissioned polls bombard the populace with Putin's popularity, making it very clear that opposition is doomed and the leader's every decision will be supported. Even independent polls (such as those by the Levada Center) show extremely high support for Putin's delusional invasion of Ukraine. But as Yudin has argued, this support reflects the populace's relationship to polling more than it does their feelings about the war. Yudin cites a recent poll which asked both "If Putin signed a peace treaty with Ukraine tomorrow would you support it?" (73% would) and "If Putin announced a renewed attack on Kyiv, would you support it?" (64% would), which suggests that respondents see polls as little more than an opportunity to agree with decisions already made, what pollsters call "acclaimation."[63]

This problem has certainly been exacerbated by the current regime. As Putin's state has become more repressive, respondents are only more likely to express agreement with all government decisions, not only because they fear reprisal, but also because they feel as though they are speaking directly to the state, with whom the only appropriate communication is supplicant flattery. Polls increasingly play a role similar to Putin's annual call-in shows, Direct Line (*Priamaia liniia*). They encourage a feeling of direct connection between the populace and political power, while providing evidence of the President's popularity and modeling the standards of correct behavior, all in a clearly stage-managed, but nevertheless convincing manner. These feedback mechanisms have become simulacra of democratic institutions with an importance that is perhaps surprising within an authoritarian regime. But Putin, like many of his modern autocratic peers, is addicted to polling. His administration commissions hundreds of polls a year from several different agencies, including the now-state-administered VTsIOM. And he pays close attention to their results, even if at times pressuring pollsters to adjust methodologies to produce better numbers.[64] Polling, even state-commissioned polling, plays such a central role in maintaining the legitimacy of the regime, in part, because of the democratic ideals invested in it in the early years of VTsIOM. The idealistic vision that a new regime of truth in the post-Soviet era might be possible, that through broad-based sampling of the public's subjective opinions, a sufficiently sophisticated sociology might be able to find (and represent) something approaching society's true interests, needs, and desires, was a powerful one, and something of that vision carries through in the perversion of public opinion that we see today.

Even if VTsIOM's early development embedded some of the weaknesses that have allowed Putin's authoritarian regime to turn polling into yet another tool of "sovereign democracy," its idealism should not be forgotten. Zaslavskaia's bravery in her 1983 "Novosibirsk Report" not only detailed a well-known secret—that Stalinist assumptions about the economy were leading to catastrophe—but also proposed a bold solution—a shift in the way the state was to understand society, economy, and the populace. Levada's deep theoretical knowledge of Western sociology and Grushin's Soviet-era polling experiences and tireless bureaucratic efforts made Zaslavskaia's solution not only feasible, but practicable and influential even before the Soviet Union fell. The complex modeling of VTsIOM researchers such as Dubin and Gudkov made public opinion polling into something more than a feedback mechanism for state projects. It became a dominant mode of self-knowledge and self-reflection for post-Soviet society. For better and for worse, the liberal, transparent, market-adjacent thinking that energized VTsIOM's early research, theoretical investigations, and statistical modeling of Soviet and post-Soviet society became the prevailing regime of truth in the post-Soviet era. But the dream of this new kind of truth proved no match for state power. Its mechanisms and use value proved at least as serviceable for a rising autocrat as they had for understanding a newly democratic populace. Polling helped bring into existence an active post-Soviet public sphere. And it also helped pave the way for its demise.

Notes

1 Oleg Kharkhordin, for instance, points to the development of *druzhiny*, comrades' courts, and other institutions of the collective as the locus of mutual surveillance during the Thaw. See his *The Collective and the Individual in Russia: A Study of Practices* (Berkeley: University of California Press, 1999), esp. pp. 279–328.

2 Boris Grushin, "Institut obshchestvennogo mneniia 'Komsomol'skoi pravdy'," in *Obshchestvennyi razlom i rozhdenie novoi sotsiologii. Dvadtsat' let monitoringa*, ed. Lev Gudkov and Boris Dubin (Moscow: Novoe izdatel'stvo, 2008), 443–62.

3 For a discussion of several such studies of late-Soviet consumption, see Serguei Oushakine, "'Against the Cult of Things': On Soviet Productivism, Storage Economy, and Commodities with No Destination," *The Russian Review* 73, no. 2 (2014): 198–236.

4 Lev Gudkov, "Sotsiologiia Iuriia Levady," introduction to Iurii Levada, *Vremia peremen: Predmet i pozitsiia issledovatelia* (Moscow: Novoe literaturnoe obozrenie, 2016), 10. For a discussion of several of the major works of IKSI, see pp. 10–14.

5 Grushin, "Istoriia izucheniia obshchestvennogo mneniia," *Monitoring obshchestvennogo mneniia* 63 (Jan–Feb 2003): 60–74.

6 Boris Firsov, *Istoriia sovetskoi sotsiologii. 1950-e–1980-e gody* (St. Petersburg: Iz-stvo Evropeiskogo universiteta, 2012), 301.

7 Firsov, *Istoriia sovetskoi sotsiologii*, 301.

8 Original publication in *The Washington Post*, August 1983. Full version: Tatyana Zaslavskaia, "The Novosibirsk Report," *Survey* 28, no. 1 (March 1984): 83–109.

9 Zaslavskaia, "The Novosibirsk Report," 93.

10 Materialy Plenuma Tsentral'nogo Komiteta KPSS, 14–15 iiunia 1983 goda (Moscow, 1983), 79. Quoted in Boris Grushin, "Na dal'nykh i blizhnykh podstupakh k sozdaniiu VTsIOMa," in *Obshchestvennyi razlom i rozhdenie novoi sotsiologii*, 18.

11 Courtney Doucette, "Glasnost in the Mailroom: The Soviet Subject in Gorbachev's Perestroika, 1985–1988," *The Soviet and Post-Soviet Review* 48 (2021): 171–88.

12 Adam E. Leeds, "Dreams in Cybernetic Fugue: Cold War Technoscience, the Intelligentsia, and the Birth of Soviet Mathematical Economics," *Historical Studies in the Natural Sciences* 46, no. 5 (2016): 633–68.

13 T. I. Zaslavskaia, "K desiatiletiiu VTsIOM," *Monitoring obshchestvennogo mneniia* 1, no. 33 (1998): 9.

14 Grushin, "Institut obshchestvennogo mneniia 'Komsomol'skoi pravdy'."

15 The project was the Taganrog Study, which sought to understand the mechanisms and effects of Soviet mass media on the populace. See Boris Doktorov, "B.A. Grushin. Chetyre desiatiletiia izucheniia rossiiskogo obshchestvennogo mneniia," *Gefter.ru*, December 2, 2015, accessed December 15, 2022, http://gefter.ru/archive/16807.

16 Grushin, "Na dal'nykh i blizhnykh podstupakh k sozdaniiu VTsIOMa."

17 Doktorov, "B.A. Grushin."

18 See "Dissidenty o dissidentstve," *Znamia* 9 (September 1997).

19 Lev Gudkov. Personal interview. Zoom. August 26, 2022.

20 Gudkov. Personal interview.

21 For more on Iser's implied reader, see Wolfgang Iser, *The Implied Reader: Patterns of Communication in Prose Fiction from Bunyan to Beckett* (Baltimore: Johns Hopkins University Press, 1974).

22 For the paradigmatic English-language publication on Jauss's "horizon of expectations," see Hans Rober Jauss and Elizabeth Benzinger, "Literary History as a Challenge to Literary Theory," *New Literary History* 2, no. 1 (Autumn 1970): 7–37.

23 Revelations of Jauss's involvement in war crimes and his falsification of his war record began to emerge in the mid-1990s. The definitive report is Jens Westemeier, *Hans Robert Jauss: Jugend, Krieg und Internierung* (Konstanz: Konstanz University Press, 2016).

24 V. D. Stel'makh and N. K. Lobachev, *Kniga i chtenie v zerkale sotsiologii* (Moscow: Knizhnaia palata, 1990), 4.

25 Tatiana Zaslavskaia, "Kak rozhdalsia VTsIOM," in *Obshchestvennyi razlom i rozhdenie novoi sotsiologii*, ed. Gudkov and Dubin (Moscow: Novoe izdatel'stvo, 2008), 13.

26 Zaslavskaia, "Kak rozhdalsia VTsIOM," 11.

27 Gudkov. Personal interview.

28 Zaslavskaia, "Kak rozhdalsia VTsIOM," 15.

29 Zaslavskaia, "Kak rozhdalsia VTsIOM," 14.

30 Gudkov. Personal interview.

31 Iurii Levada, "Fenomen 'Chelovek sovetskogo': sotsiologicheskie parametry" [1993], in his *Vremia peremen*, 502–4.

32 Iurii Levada, "Ukhodiashchaia natura?" [1992], in his *Vremia peremen*, 481–98.

33 See Artifact #00095: "The Rise of Public Opinion Polling," *Monitoring obshchestvennogo mneniia: ėkonomicheskie i sotsial'nye peremeny: al'manakh*. Vserossiiskii tsentr izucheniia obshchestvennogo mneniia. 1992–2009.

34 Iurii Levada and Lev Gudkov, "Ot mnenii k ponimaniu," *Monitoring obshchestvennogo mneniia. Sotsial'nye i politicheskie izmeneniia*, no. 1 (January 1993): 1.

35 George Gallup and Saul Forbes Rae, *The Pulse of Democracy: The Public-Opinion Poll and How It Works* (New York: Simon and Schuster, 1940), 8.

36 *Obshchestvennyi razlom i rozhdenie novoi sotsiologii*, 5–9.

37 Gudkov wrote that Levada saw sociology as a "system of positive knowledge, free from ideology, and for that reason, to a certain degree, allowing the researcher to take control of his own illusions alongside mass prejudices." Gudkov, "Sotsiologiia Iuriia Levady," in Iurii Levada, *Vremia peremen*, 6.

38 G. W. F. Hegel, *Phenomenology of Spirit*, trans. A. V. Miller (Oxford: Oxford University Press, 1977), 266–409. See also: Paul Redding, "Georg Wilhelm Friedrich Hegel", *The Stanford Encyclopedia of Philosophy*, Winter 2020 Edition, ed. Edward N. Zalta, accessed December 15, 2022, https://plato.stanford.edu/archives/win2020/entries/hegel.

39 Terry Pinkhard, "Objective Spirit: The Pulse of Self-Consciousness," in *Hegel's Philosophy of Spirit: A Critical Guide*, ed. Marina F. Bykova (Cambridge: Cambridge University Press, 2019), 147–63.

40 Oleg Leont'ev, "Kak stat' Agatoi Kristi v Rossii," *Knizhnoe obozrenie* 13 (April 1, 1997), 6.

41 "Ostrosiuzhetnaia slovesnost'—polius pritiazhenii dlia molodykh (do 29 let) muzhchin…Interesy molodykh i bolee obrazovannykh zhenshchin sosredotocheny prezhde vsego na romanakh o liubvi," Boris Dubin, "Chto chitaiut rossiane?" *Knizhnoe obozrenie* 11 (March 15, 1994), 26.

42 See Artifact #00017: "Bestsellery Moskvy," *Knizhnoe obozrenie* 11 (March 15, 1994): 2.

43 See Artifact #00098: "Gone with the Wind: The Post-Soviet Sequels." For more on the phenomenon of collective bestsellers, see Bradley A. Gorski, "Bestseller, or the Cultural Logic of Postsocialism," *Slavic Review* 79, no. 3 (Fall 2020): 613–35.

44 Boris Dubin and Lev Gudkov, *Literatura kak sotsial'nyi institut* (Moscow: Novoe literaturnoe obozrenie, 1994), 12–13.

45 Boris Dubin, "Ispytanie na sostoiatel'nost': Sotsiologicheskaia poetika russkogo romana-boevika," *Novoe literaturnoe obozrenie* 22 (1996): 252–74; quoted here from his *Ocherki o sotsiologii kul'tury. Izbrannoe* (Moscow: Novoe literaturnoe obozrenie, 2017), 386–419. A translated (and somewhat abridged) version of this text can be found as "The Action Thriller (Boevik) in Contemporary Russia," in *Reading for Entertainment in Contemporary Russia: Post-Soviet Popular Literature in Historical Perspective*, ed. Stephen Lovell and Birgit Menzel (Munich: Verlag Otto Sagner, 2005), 101–16. Quoting Dubin, among others, Eliot Borenstein develops a related argument about 1990s Russian masculinity with Dotsenko's Mad Dog in a central role. See Borenstein, *Overkill: Sex and Violence in Contemporary Russian Popular Culture* (Ithaca, NY: Cornell University Press, 2008), esp. ch. 6, "Men of Action: Heroic Melodrama and the Passion of Mad Dog," 159–94.

46 Boris Dubin, "Ispytanie na sostoiatel'nost'," 389.

47 For instance, see "Chtenie i obshchestvo v Rossii," *Novyi mir* 3 (1993): 32–35; or "Ideologiia besstrukturnosti: Intelligentsiia i konets sovetskoi epokhi," *Znamia* 11 (1994): 166–79, both by Dubin. For a full list of Dubin's work, see *Ocherki o sotsiologii kul'tury*, 845–82.

48 See Nikolai Poseliagin, "Antropologicheskii povorot v rossiiskiikh gumanitarnykh naukakh," *Novoe literaturnoe obozrenie* 113 (January 2012). A key text in this turn is Valery Podoroga, *Mimesis. Materialy po analiticheskoi antropologii* (Moscow: Kul'turnaia revoliutsiia, 2006).

49 Levada, "Homo Post-Soveticus," in his *Vremia peremen*, 550, 568–69; Boris Dubin, "Uspekh po-russki," *Monitoring obshchestvennogo mneniia* 5, no. 37 (September–October 1998).

50 Gudkov. Personal interview. In another example, Gudkov recalled a 1994 telephone conversation with Movladi Udugov, the Minister of Information of Chechnya. Gudkov had heard that VTsIOM interviewers had been surrounded by fighters. Udugov said he would love to help, but it was Russian tanks surrounding the particular building where the interviews were being conducted.

51 All the polls for this campaign are collected at Wikipedia, "Opinion Polling for the 1996 Russian Presidential Campaign," accessed December 15, 2022, https://en.wikipedia.org/wiki/Opinion_polling_for_the_1996_Russian_presidential_election.

52 "10.2 Billion Loan To Russia Approved," *The New York Times* [Reuters], March 27, 1996.

53 Berezovsky and Gusinsky were two signatories to the "Letter of the 13," an open letter signed by the most powerful rising oligarchs decrying the possible return to communism and pleading for an alliance between private capital and a corporate-friendly neoliberal state. See Artifact #00102: "Vyiti iz tupika!" *Nezavisimaia gazeta*, April 27, 1996.

54 For an overview of the 1996 election, see Michael McFaul, *Russia's 1996 Presidential Election: The End of Polarized Politics* (Stanford, CA: Hoover Institution Press, 1997); for an overview of the use of polling, see David S. Mason and Svetlana Sidorenko-Stephenson, "Public Opinion and the 1996 Elections in Russia: Nostalgic and Statist, Yet Pro-Market and ProYeltsin," *Slavic Review* 56, no. 4 (Winter 1997): 698–717.

55 Gudkov. Personal interview.

56 Gudkov. Personal interview.

57 See Teimuraz Mamaladze, "Skazano—sdelano. Boris El'tsin v Chechne pobyval," *Izvestiia* 98, no. 24705 (May 29, 1996): 1.

58 The phrase "soak them in the latrine" ("*v sortire ikh zamochim*") became one of the first so-called "Putinisms," or memorable phrases from his public appearances celebrated by his followers. It even has a Wikipedia page devoted to it. See Wikipedia, "Mochit' v sortire," accessed July 15, 2023, https://ru.wikipedia.org/wiki/%D0%9C%D0%BE%D1%87%D0%B8%D1%82%D1%8C_%D0%B2_%D1%81%D0%BE%D1%80%D1%82%D0%B8%D1%80%D0%B5.

59 Daniel Treisman used VTsIOM data to argue that Putin's popularity had everything to do with the economic circumstances (much of it global) of his first term in office. See Daniel Treisman, "Presidential Popularity in a Hybrid Regime: Russia under Yeltsin and Putin," *American Journal of Political Science* 55, no. 3 (July 2011): 590–609.

60 Aleksandr Golov and Orkhan Jemal, "Za chto razgoniaiut VTsIOM," *Novaia gazeta*, August 14, 2003, accessed July 15, 2023, https://novayagazeta.ru/articles/2003/08/14/17565-za-chto-razgonyayut-vtsiom.

61 Oksana Yablokova, "Ministry Defends VTsIOM Overhaul," *Moscow Times*, September 3, 2003, archived copy accessed July 15, 2023, https://web.archive.org/web/20110617012356/http://www.eng.yabloko.ru/Publ/2003/PAPERS/9/030903_mt.html.

62 Greg Yudin, "The War in Ukraine: Do Russians Support Putin?" *The Journal of Democracy* 33, no. 3 (July 2022): 31.

63 "Spetsial'naia voennaia operatsiia" v Ukraine: otnoshenie rossiian." 12 volna (July 16–19, 2023), https://russianfield.com/12volna.

64 See Sergei Guriev and Daniel Triesman, *Spin Dictators: The Changing Face of Tyranny in the 21st Century* (Princeton, NJ: Princeton University Press, 2022), esp. 121–28.

Works Cited

"'Spetsial'naia voennaia operatsiia' v Ukraine: otnoshenie rossiian. 12 volna (16–19 iunia 2023)." *Russian Field*. June 2023. Accessed December 15, 2023. https://russianfield.com/12volna.

"Dissidenty o dissidentstve." *Znamia* 9 (September 1997).

Wikipedia. "Mochit' v sortire." Accessed July 15, 2023. https://ru.wikipedia.org/wiki/%D0%9C%D0%BE%D1%87%D0%B8%D1%82%D1%8C_%D0%B2_%D1%81%D0%BE%D1%80%D1%82%D0%B8%D1%80%D0%B5.

Wikipedia. "Opinion Polling for the 1996 Russian Presidential Campaign." Accessed December 15, 2022. https://en.wikipedia.org/wiki/Opinion_polling_for_the_1996_Russian_presidential_election.

Borenstein, Eliot. *Overkill: Sex and Violence in Contemporary Russian Popular Culture*. Ithaca, NY: Cornell University Press, 2008.

Doktorov, Boris. "B.A. Grushin. Chetyre desiatiletiia izucheniia rossiiskogo obshchestvennogo mneniia." *Gefter.ru*. December 2, 2015. Accessed December 15, 2022. http://gefter.ru/archive/16807.

Doucette, Courtney. "Glasnost in the Mailroom: The Soviet Subject in Gorbachev's Perestroika, 1985–1988." *The Soviet and Post-Soviet Review* 48 (2021): 171–88.

Dubin, Boris. "Chtenie i obshchestvo v Rossii." *Novyi mir* 3 (1993): 32–35.

Dubin, Boris. "Chto chitaiut rossiane?" *Knizhnoe obozrenie* 11 (March 15, 1994): 26.

Dubin, Boris. "Ideologiia besstrukturnosti: Intelligentsiia i konets sovetskoi epokhi." *Znamia* 11 (1994): 166–79.

Dubin, Boris. "Ispytanie na sostoiatel'nost': Sotsiologicheskaia poetika russkogo romana-boevika." *Novoe literaturnoe obozrenie* 22 (1996): 252–74.

Dubin, Boris. "The Action Thriller (Boevik) in Contemporary Russia." In *Reading for Entertainment in Contemporary Russia: Post-Soviet Popular Literature in Historical Perspective*, edited by Stephen Lovell and Birgit Menzel, 101–16. Munich: Verlag Otto Sagner, 2005.

Dubin, Boris. "Uspekh po-russki." *Monitoring obshchestvennogo mneniia* 5, no. 37 (September–October 1998).

Dubin, Boris, and Lev Gudkov. *Literatura kak sotsial'nyi institut*. Moscow: Novoe literaturnoe obozrenie, 1994.

Firsov, Boris. *Istoriia sovetskoi sotsiologii. 1950-e–1980-e gody*. St. Petersburg: Iz-stvo Evropeiskogo universiteta, 2012.

Gallup, George, and Saul Forbes Rae. *The Pulse of Democracy: The Public-Opinion Poll and How It Works*. New York: Simon and Schuster, 1940.

Golov, Aleksandr, and Orkhan Jemal. "Za chto razgoniaiut VTsIOM." *Novaia gazeta*, August 14, 2003. Accessed July 15, 2023. https://novayagazeta.ru/articles/2003/08/14/17565-za-chto-razgonyayut-vtsiom.

Gorski, Bradley A. "Bestseller, or the Cultural Logic of Postsocialism." *Slavic Review* 79, no. 3 (Fall 2020): 613–35.

Gudkov, Lev, and Boris Dubin, eds. *Obshchestvennyi razlom i rozhdenie novoi sotsiologii. Dvadtsat' let monitoringa*. Moscow: Novoe izdatel'stvo, 2008.

Gudkov, Lev. Personal interview. Zoom. August 26, 2022.

Guriev, Sergei, and Daniel Triesman. *Spin Dictators: The Changing Face of Tyranny in the 21st Century*. Princeton, NJ: Princeton University Press, 2022.

Hegel, G. W. F. *Phenomenology of Spirit*. Translated by A. V. Miller. Oxford: Oxford University Press, 1977.

Iser, Wolfgang. *The Implied Reader: Patterns of Communication in Prose Fiction from Bunyan to Beckett.* Baltimore: Johns Hopkins University Press, 1974.

Jauss, Hans Robert, and Elizabeth Benzinger. "Literary History as a Challenge to Literary Theory." *New Literary History* 2, no. 1 (Autumn 1970): 7–37.

Kharkhordin, Oleg. *The Collective and the Individual in Russia: A Study of Practices.* Berkeley: University of California Press, 1999.

Leeds, Adam E. "Dreams in Cybernetic Fugue: Cold War Technoscience, the Intelligentsia, and the Birth of Soviet Mathematical Economics." *Historical Studies in the Natural Sciences* 46, no. 5 (2016): 633–68.

Leont'ev, Oleg. "Kak stat' Agatoi Kristi v Rossii." *Knizhnoe obozrenie* 13 (April 1, 1997): 6.

Levada, Iurii. *Vremia peremen: Predmet i pozitsiia issledovatelia.* Moscow: Novoe literaturnoe obozrenie, 2016.

Levada, Iurii, and Lev Gudkov. "Ot mnenii k ponimaniu." *Monitoring obshchestvennogo mneniia. Sotsial'nye i politicheskie izmeneniia* 1 (January 1993): 1.

Mamaladze, Teimuraz. "Skazano—sdelano. Boris El'tsin v Chechne pobyval." *Izvestiia* 98, no. 24705 (May 29, 1996): 1.

Mason, David S., and Svetlana Sidorenko-Stephenson. "Public Opinion and the 1996 Elections in Russia: Nostalgic and Statist, Yet Pro-Market and Pro-Yeltsin." *Slavic Review* 56, no. 4 (Winter 1997): 698–717.

McFaul, Michael. *Russia's 1996 Presidential Election: The End of Polarized Politics.* Stanford, CA: Hoover Institution Press, 1997.

Oushakine, Serguei. "'Against the Cult of Things': On Soviet Productivism, Storage Economy, and Commodities with No Destination." *The Russian Review* 73, no. 2 (2014): 198–236.

Pinkhard, Terry. "Objective Spirit: The Pulse of Self-Consciousness." In *Hegel's Philosophy of Spirit: A Critical Guide*, edited by Marina F. Bykova, 147–63. Cambridge: Cambridge University Press, 2019.

Podoroga, Valerii. *Mimesis. Materialy po analiticheskoi antropologii.* Moscow: Kul'turnaia revoliutsiia, 2006.

Poseliagin, Nikolai. "Antropologicheskii povorot v rossiiskiikh gumanitarnykh naukakh." *Novoe literaturnoe obozrenie* 113 (January 2012). https://magazines.gorky.media/nlo/2012/1/antropologicheskij-povorot-v-rossijskih-gumanitarnyh-naukah.html.

Redding, Paul. "Georg Wilhelm Friedrich Hegel." In *The Stanford Encyclopedia of Philosophy* (Winter 2020 Edition), edited by Edward N. Zalta. Accessed December 15, 2022. https://plato.stanford.edu/archives/win2020/entries/hegel.

Stel'makh, V. D., and N. K. Lobachev. *Kniga i chtenie v zerkale sotsiologii.* Moscow: Knizhnaia palata, 1990.

Treisman, Daniel. "Presidential Popularity in a Hybrid Regime: Russia under Yeltsin and Putin." *American Journal of Political Science* 55, no. 3 (July 2011): 590–609.

Westemeier, Jens. *Hans Robert Jauss: Jugend, Krieg und Internierung.* Konstanz: Konstanz University Press, 2016.

Yablokova, Oksana. "Ministry Defends VTsIOM Overhaul." *Moscow Times*, September 3, 2003. Archived copy accessed July 15, 2023. https://web.archive.org/web/20110617012356/http://www.eng.yabloko.ru/Publ/2003/PAPERS/9/030903_mt.html.

Yudin, Greg. "The War in Ukraine: Do Russians Support Putin?" *The Journal of Democracy* 33, no. 3 (July 2022): 31–37.

Zaslavskaia, Tatiana. "K desiatiletiiu VTsIOM." *Monitoring obshchestvennogo mneniia* 1, no. 33 (1998): 9.

Zaslavskaia, Tatyana. "The Novosibirsk Report." *Survey* 28, no. 1 (March 1984): 83–109.

CHAPTER 2

The Disappearing Reader: The Disintegration of the Press–Reader Relationship in the Soviet/Post-Soviet Press, 1985–1995

Courtney Doucette

From 1985 to 1995, the Soviet and early post-Soviet press experienced a transformation on par with the changes that the region's press underwent during the tumultuous Revolutions of 1917.[1] The start of perestroika in 1985–1986, and especially governmental promotion of glasnost, or openness, gave way to a "golden age" of the Soviet press. Media outlets published on a range of new topics, from economic problems facing the USSR and shortcomings of certain political leaders to the Stalinist terror, Stalin's shortcomings in the Second World War, and shortages after the Second World War. From 1985 to 1989, the Soviet press appeared to shake free of earlier Soviet traditions that prevented a flourishing of free speech, despite the fact that little had changed in the institutions that governed the press: each newspaper remained affiliated with a Party organization (*Pravda* with the Community Party itself, *Sovetskaia Rossiia* with the Party's Central Committee, and *Komsomol'skaia pravda* with the Komsomol, to name three examples); at least one state-appointed censor continued to occupy an office in the editorial board headquarters of every publication; and the Party maintained control of circulation rates and, relatedly, each media outlet's budget.

Fundamental changes to the institutions governing the Soviet press appeared on paper with the Press Law of 1990, which went into effect on August 1 of that year. Even though in practice censorship had largely become defunct by the time of the new law's passing, the Press Law officially removed censors from editorial offices, unhinged major print organs from the Party, and left newspapers to set their own circulation rates and balance their own budgets, while continuing to offer state subsidies that covered at least part of media outlets' expenses. Newspapers earned income by selling advertisements, and, when state subsidies dried up in 1992 in step with the evaporation of state tax revenue after Russian President Boris Yeltsin freed prices, editors turned to bartering, subletting space in their headquarters, and taking in electoral cash to keep pages in print.[2] The path to a free press reminiscent of Western media, which some might have expected to easily come from Gorbachev's reforms in conjunction with the Soviet collapse, turned out to be far more tortuous than anticipated. And, in the end, the endeavor failed. By 1995, major newspaper circulation rates fell and readers became distrustful of the press.

One of the little examined questions in the transformation of the Soviet/post-Soviet press is how the place of the reader in the newspaper changed at this time. Here I attempt to address this gap. Using the popular daily newspaper *Komsomol'skaia pravda* as a case study, I examine the reader–newspaper relationship from 1985 to 1995. These particular years reveal a striking phenomenon: the near total disappearance of the reader from the printed page. By 1995, the newspaper published staggeringly few (by comparison to 1985) readers' letters, articles by readers, interactive activities for readers to complete, and announcements about ways readers could engage the paper (such as surveys, telethons, and invitations to the newspaper's reception). It is this transformation I'm referring to in the title "The Disappearing Reader," rather than the better-known phenomenon of readers abandoning newspapers for newer media, like television or new post-Soviet publications.[3] I am interested not just in changing subscription rates, or readers' judgements of the quality of the press, but more precisely the role readers played in shaping and generating content for the newspaper, the extent to which editors made the print organ interactive with its readership, and the significance editors assigned to readers on the printed pages of the newspaper. The key source for this article is the printed newspaper itself.

My argument that the decade from 1985 to 1995 witnessed the disappearance of readers from newspapers maps onto recent scholarship on the late-Soviet and early post-Soviet press, while also expanding it. Natalia Roudakova's *Losing Pravda: Ethics and the Press in Post-Truth Russia*, the seminal work in the field since its publication in 2017, counters the more common narrative that the genie of uninhibited free speech was let out of the bottle, so to speak, during Gorbachev's reforms and most certainly with the Soviet collapse, only to be shoved back in after Putin came to power and "reintroduced" very "Soviet" limitations like censorship. In contrast, Roudakova argues that privatization of the press and the legally unstructured relationship between politicians and the press in the early- to mid-1990s eroded citizens' trust in journalists and newspapers that had actually flourished during perestroika. She introduces an ethics-based language to trace the declining trust in newspapers and increasing doubt that the printed press would deliver the truth.[4]

In addition to the erosion of trust, readers disappeared from the pages of major dailies like *Komsomol'skaia pravda*. While it might be the case that decreasing trust led to readers themselves abandoning newspapers, I argue that we are seeing something additional here: the printed page itself suggests the reader disappeared by editorial decision, too. The transformation raises a number of questions that resonate with Roudakova's study: to what extent did the erosion of the reader–newspaper relationship and the disappearance of the reader from the printed page undermine the democratic transformation of the press in the early 1990s? To what extent did late-Soviet media practices—especially, in this case, the strong emphasis on the reader–newspaper connection—inform readers' expectations about what democratic media would look like in the post-Soviet period and set off their disappointment about what eventually happened? And to what extent did the ways citizens use the press to participate in politics shape their expectations and frustrations about the intersection of politics and the press in the early post-Soviet period?

Taken alongside other phenomena spotlighted in this volume, the reader–press relationship and the public letter help illuminate the profoundly contradictory nature of the end of the Soviet period and the first post-Soviet decade. In contrast to statistical data discussed by Bradley Gorski, the proliferation of public letters in the late 1980s and throughout the 1990s suggests there was not so much a crisis in knowing the population; rather, there seems to have been a crisis of making the most of the subjective information various outlets collected about the broader population—information they collected in greater quantities than ever before. Unlike the LGBTQ population, which experienced the post-Soviet 1990s as a kind of mass coming out, as Thomas Keenan discusses, readers of some of the most mainstream periodicals seemed to have experienced a reduction in visibility. The press–reader relationship seems to offer a far rosier picture of the late-Soviet 1980s, and a far grimmer one of the post-Soviet 1990s, challenging more hopeful narratives about the possibility of "free speech" and democracy after the Soviet collapse.

To understand the reader's disappearing act, we first must have a sense of the reader's presence in the newspaper in the mid-1980s. A headline published in *Komsomol'skaia pravda* (KP) on September 16, 1986 captured the energy in the relationship between newspaper editors and readers in the early years of Gorbachev's reform. It read: "EDITORS RECEIVE ONE MILLION LETTERS SINCE THE BEGINNING OF THE YEAR" (Figure 1). The announcement came from the Light Blue Hall in KP's headquarters on Pravda Street in Moscow, where all important editorial meetings took place. The author of the article, A. Murtazaev, described the quantity as "majestic." He noted that the previous year, KP had received only 643,000 letters in a full calendar year. In 1986, by contrast, they received a million letters in eight and a half months. This meant that, on average, KP received 1,761 letters per day in 1985, whereas in 1986, they received an average of 3,922 letters per day. Murtazaev noted that the letter count included mail of all kinds: "complaints and observations, thank you notes and requests, articles and correspondence."[5]

Despite Murtazaev's enthusiasm, we should take the article's headline with a grain of salt. Throughout 1986, as the letter to the editor became a way of measuring the strength of the relationship between reader and newspaper, N. Morzhina, assistant editor of the letter department, reported on the number of letters received nearly every single month. In January, she reported a total of 72,922 letters; in March, 39,280; in April, 62,394; in May, 33,704; in June, 27,442; in July, 21,253; in August, 29,308; and for the entirety

Орган Центрального Комитета ВЛКСМ
КОМСОМОЛЬСКАЯ ПРАВДА
ПРИТЯЖЕНИЕ ДРУЖБЫ
ВЫБИРАЮ ДЕРЕВНЮ НА ЖИТЕЛЬСТВО
1000 000
ВАС ЖДУТ!

FIGURE 1 Page 1 of *Komsomol'skaia pravda* no. 211 (September 16, 1986). The red box demarcates Murtazaev's article announcing the millionth letter of the year on the front page of the paper. Also on this page, in the upper-right-hand corner (in black) is a photograph of letters sent to two KP readers who had published an article in an earlier issue of the newspaper. With the help of readers, the editorial statement suggests, the two young men found work on a collective farm. In the lower-right-hand corner is a "coupon" to cut out and fill out. It prompts the reader to state what kind of work they'd like to find. The left portion of the coupon is to be sent to the regional Komsomol office. The right portion is to go to the Letter Department at KP.

of September, 100,055. Added together, we get a total of 386,313 letters for the period included in the millionth letter article.[6] February was the only month not accounted for in Morzhina's regular reports, but it's unlikely that the daily received 613,687 letters in the shortest month of the year. The discrepancy could be explained by the kind of mail that was counted. Perhaps Morzhina's numbers did not include everything swept into Murtazaev's totals. Nonetheless, the gap between the two numbers casts doubts on the millionth letter milestone.

Yet that KP might *not* have received a million letters only underscores the significance of the millionth letter report. The proclamation was part of a much larger celebration of the letter to the editor that exploded in 1986. The phenomenon built on an already strong practice across Soviet periodicals of working with readers' letters. Since the early 1920s, Soviet law required editorial staff of newspapers to respond to every letter received from readers. Even in the midst of civil war, early Soviet newspapers like *Pravda* boasted elaborate letter departments, meaning even in a time of starvation and when it was unclear if the Revolution itself would survive, the fledgling government invested in institutions for working with readers' mail to newspapers.[7] Newspapers also encouraged readers to provide a portion of their content for print through the worker and rural correspondents' movement, in which laborers sent in articles about regional news that the newspaper then published.[8] Throughout the Soviet period, letter departments remained a key part of each periodical, charged most importantly with facilitating the newspaper's relationship with its readers.[9]

Looking at the distribution of content in an issue of KP from early 1985, just before Gorbachev's election as General Party Secretary, shows how much space was devoted to readers' voices even before the letter's prestige exploded in 1986. Issue 12 of KP published on January 15, 1985 was four pages long (see Figure 2). Three out of four pages included columns that featured readers' letters: "Who will win the prize?" (*Kto zavoiuet priz?*) and "In preparation for the elections" (*Navstrechu vyboram*) in addition to a spread of readers' letters and a telegram on page 1, "Letters, letters" (*Pis'ma, pis'ma*) on page 2, and "Who? Where? When?" (*Chto? Gde? Kogda?*) on page 4. Additionally, page 2 included an article by regional correspondent E. Chernykh on a particularly troubling letter from a reader, which he investigated in person. On page 4, KP editors also provided information for contacting the newspaper's headquarters, including the address for letters and phone numbers of the newspaper's hotline. Without using any complex software for measuring the amount of space devoted to reader content, it appears that upwards of 30% of the newspaper was covered in reader content. To be fair, this is a slightly extreme example from 1985. Some issues featured less, especially when the newspaper was covered in speech transcripts the day following a major political event. But in general not much less, which is clear from the front page of the September 16, 1986 issue. Reader-generated content dominated the printed page.

What, then, changed in 1986 as reformers rolled out perestroika? There was an even stronger attention to letters and to readers more generally, which appeared in proclamations of record-setting amounts of letters, like the millionth letter article. That we can cross-check the number of letters received in 1986 is also a sign of greater devotion to letters. N. Morzhina's column that provided the monthly overview of the post plus the number of letters received the previous month appeared eleven out of twelve months in 1986. This consistency remained unmatched either before or after that year. Indeed, there was an influx in letters, too. Newspapers across the USSR received higher quantities of mail in 1986 than any other year on record. That more readers were writing and were doing so more frequently reflected a broader trend in public letter writing that year. Even the Central Committee (CC) of the Communist Party received 954,294 letters in 1986, which was more mail than it had ever received in any other year in its history. For comparison, in 1985, the CC received only 646,549 letters.[10]

It would be misguided, however, to interpret citizens' independent ambition to write more letters as the sole cause of the influx in mail in 1986. Important political and institutional (within the newspapers themselves) forces also generated this moment, and it

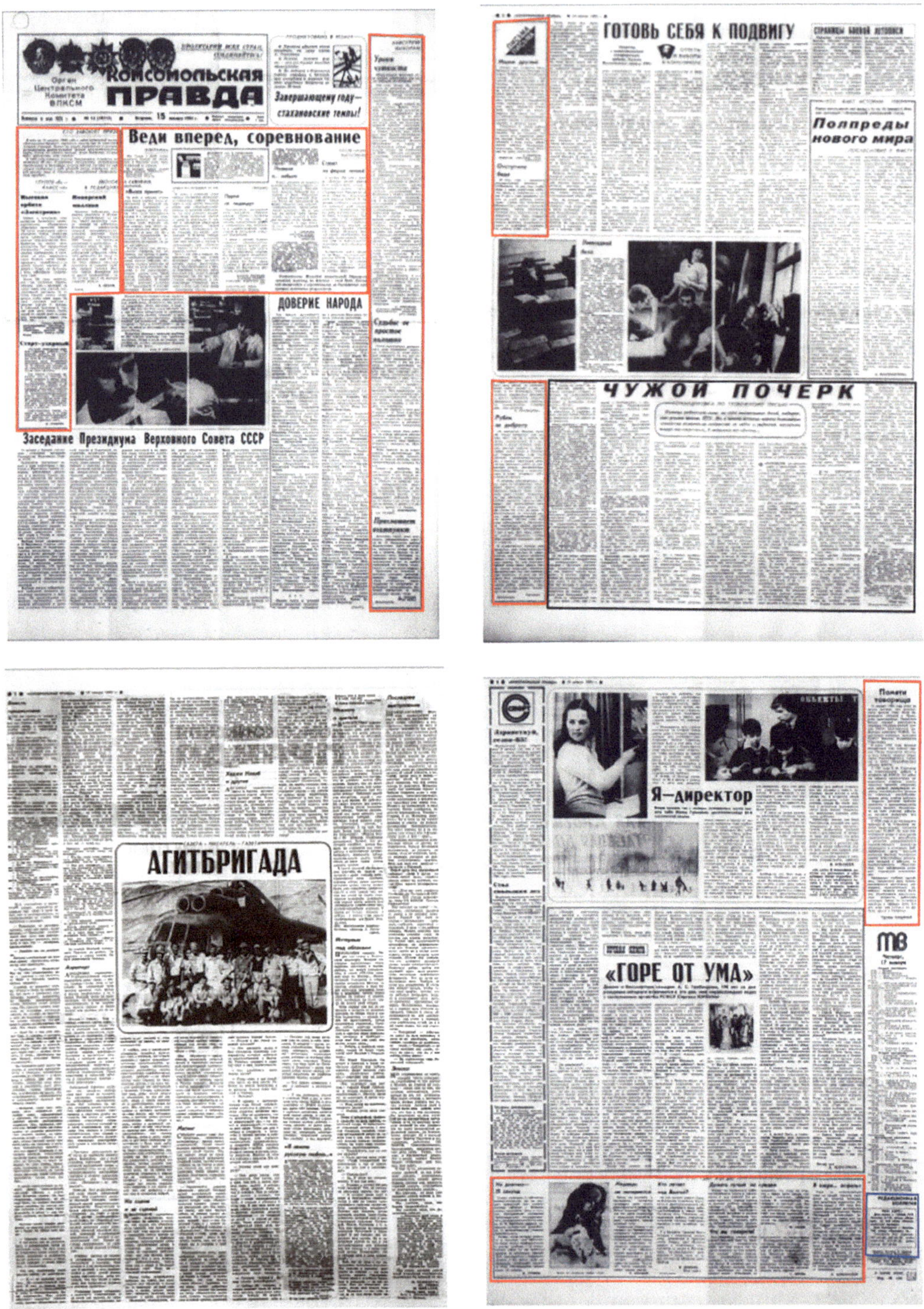

Комсомольская правда

Веди вперед, соревнование

Доверие народа

Заседание Президиума Верховного Совета СССР

Готовь себя к подвигу

Полпреды нового мира

Чужой почерк

Агитбригада

Я—директор

«Горе от ума»

FIGURE 2 Pages 1–4 of *Komsomol'skaia pravda* no. 12 (January 15, 1985). Reader-generated content and moments where the newspaper speaks directly to readers are marked off in boxes. Readers' letters and telegrams are highlighted in red. An article on a letter department journalist's investigation of a troubling letter from a reader, titled "Another Person's Handwriting" ("Chuzhoi pocherk") is demarcated in black. The address and phone numbers for writing and calling into the paper are highlighted in blue. Note the absence of advertisements from the paper.

had everything to do with the emphasis on the press–reader relationship. On March 14, 1986, immediately after the Twenty-Seventh Party Congress where Gorbachev had articulated his most detailed perspective on reform to date, the Soviet leader called a meeting at the Kremlin with high-ranking journalists and newspaper editors (Artifact 00081[a]). In his speech, he explained that much of the success of reform depended on them. It was not simply that the press could be the mouthpiece of the government, as one might expect. Rather, Gorbachev emphasized that the press was key to reform because of its relationship with readers. "We need a burst of energy," he stated:

> We need to search near and far, like bees drawing nectar and turning it to honey, for new cutting-edge phenomena, synthesizing and publicizing them. It's important that the people...see support for good work of collectives, brigades, the worker, the collective farmer, engineer, scholar. You have to convey all this in the media so that people see that *here's* how you have to work.[11]

In short, Gorbachev believed newspapers had the power to *activate* the population. At the heart of his conceptualization of press work was the relationship with the reader.

Transcripts of editorial board meetings at KP show that newspaper staff registered heightened concern for work with readers' letters in 1986 as well. On May 23, 1986, also in the Light Blue Hall at the KP headquarters on Pravda Street, the young and recently promoted Assistant Editor of KP Vladislav Fronin (today editor in chief of *Edinstvennaia Rossiia*, the newspaper of Putin's Party) delivered a speech to the Party Committee titled "The Letter in the Newspaper." As Fronin himself acknowledged, the topic was not new to editorial discussions at KP. In fact, just three years earlier in 1983, the minor newspaper worker K. N. Lavrova had reported on shortcomings in work with letters.[12] It's noteworthy, however, that the second most senior leader of the newspaper, also a man, delivered the address on letters in 1986. His gender and rank underscore the heightened significance of work with mail at the start of perestroika. In his speech, he emphasized that letters were important because they provided a sign of readers' activation (the very goal Gorbachev had underscored in his March speech to press workers) and—this is significant—a measure of the strength of the newspaper's connection to its readers.[13]

Fronin asked his colleagues to consider new ways to work with mail, beginning with asking readers to write in on postcards instead of paper stuffed in envelopes, introducing computers to the letter department (a global discussion in the mid-1980s), and even having men (albeit young men) join the predominantly female staff of letter departments. "It probably isn't right that we assign work with letters exclusively to women," he noted. "Why can't a young energetic boy become a correspondent in the letter department?"[14]

---

[a] https://postsoviet90s.com/artifacts/gorbachev-speaks-with-state-media-leaders

FIGURE 3 Image from Artifact 00083.[b] Photographs of office workers at the magazine *Govorit i pokazyvaet Moskva*, the "TV Guide" of Moscow, working with mail responding to the New Edition of the Party Program in December 1985. A special office in the letter department was set up specifically to work with these letters. Photographs like these put the spotlight on letter departments and the letter to the editor. Source: *Govorit i pokazyvaet Moskva* no. 52 (December 23–29, 1985), 19.

Fronin's call for changes echoed across letter departments in Moscow, perhaps because of across-the-board increases in the number of letters received in addition to heightened political attention to the letter. In 1986, editors of *Literaturnaia gazeta* issued a statement on its own search for new ways to process mail because of the steady influx.[15] Similarly, the same year, the Letter Department of the CC of the Communist Party discussed revisions to the ways it would work with mail, including introducing new computerized technologies and increasing the staff of the department. Newspapers further advertised the work of letter departments by noting the work they completed and even featuring photographs of work with letters, as the television guide *Govorit i pokazyvaet* did in December 1985 (Artifact 00083[c]) (see Figure 3).

Though editorial discussion focused on the letter throughout 1986, it's important to underscore that the letter itself was a stand in for the broader relationship between the newspaper and the reader. The letter was just one way of cultivating this relationship. The printed pages of KP show the variety of ways the newspaper interacted with readers: the newspaper's hotline, which on occasion was staffed by certain experts whose hours of answering the newspaper's phone were announced so readers could call in at that time; the newspaper's reception, which accepted readers who wanted to file complaints or other expressions in person instead of in writing or by phone; surveys and letter campaigns that readers could participate in by cutting out small forms published in

---

[b] https://postsoviet90s.com/artifacts/letter-department-workers-process-mail-from-citizens-writing-about-the-upcoming-26th-party-conference

[c] https://postsoviet90s.com/artifacts/letter-department-workers-process-mail-from-citizens-writing-about-the-upcoming-26th-party-conference

a corner of the newspaper; and readers' clubs that met across the USSR. Soviet newspapers like KP also published articles submitted by readers, which echoed the early Soviet worker correspondents' movement in the 1920s. The amount of space devoted to reader-generated content on the printed page underscores the centrality of the reader–newspaper relationship to the very enterprise of the newspaper. In some ways, it seems that work with readers was just as important as the "news" in the first years of perestroika.

As the relationship between readers and the press flourished, readers turned to the press for a variety of reasons, as materials published on the printed page make clear. They turned to the paper to keep abreast of the news, and wrote letters responding to reported content (*otkliki*). Readers wrote in for advice on relationships and family, and could participate in discussions about everyday activities, like playing chess or perfecting recipes. One column, "Correspondence" (*Perepiska*), sought to make friends between readers, publishing letters and then soliciting responses to them, which the newspaper then forwarded to the original published letter writers. Readers sent in articles they had penned about notable regional or sometimes national events that they hoped to get published. But readers looked to newspapers not only for social and cultural reasons.

It's important to underscore that readers wrote in to achieve political ends, too. They wrote in with problems they faced in their workplace, schools, or region, seeing the newspaper as an advocate for citizens' rights, and in many cases hoping that the letter would be sent to correct political authorities who had the authority to address the issue. Additionally, readers saw national dailies as a means for participating in political discussions and shaping the future course of the country. Even a state-controlled press provided what some saw as potential for democratic participation. The ways citizens used the newspaper for political participation flourished and evolved from 1985 to 1990, taking on distinctly Soviet forms, but nonetheless marking a central part of the reader–newspaper relationship in this period and offering readers one way of participating in politics. In other words, the reader–press relationship constituted an important part of Soviet notions of democracy, and it makes sense that it would have been part of expectations for democracy in the post-Soviet period, too.

When Gorbachev came to office in 1985, there were already well-established forms of political participation for citizens via the press: namely, letter campaigns in advance of new policies or governmental proposals under discussion. Such discussions, staged in the newspapers through published letters to the editor, took place throughout the Soviet period, including topics as varied as, for example, laws on abortion in the 1930s and policies on art in the 1950s. Newspapers also published letter clusters before and during major Party Congresses, as they did in winter 1985–1986 in anticipation of the Twenty-Seventh Party Congress in February–March 1986. This Congress was significant because in addition to passing the new five-year plan for economic production, the Congress would approve a new Party Program. In October 1985, newspapers published drafts of the Party documents and solicited feedback from readers on the materials.

Throughout December, January, and February, major national dailies, especially *Pravda*, published clusters of excerpted letters responding to the documents. Comparing the drafts of Party documents published in October 1985 and then approved in February–March 1986 suggests that citizens' responses did not necessarily shape the content of the documents much. However, the inclusion of their voices in a staged national discussion set a standard for citizen participation in national politics. It also shaped how discussions played out off the pages of the newspaper, as readers took in what was published and talked it over with friends and colleagues, and then (sometimes) wrote their own letters to the newspaper.

The scandal surrounding Nina Andreeva's well-known letter published in the national daily *Sovetskaia Rossiia* on March 13, 1988 (Figure 4) marked the peak of public letter writing in the late Soviet period and highlighted the extent to which citizens looked to the newspaper to participate in and influence the course of politics (Artifact 00177[d]).[16] Andreeva's conservative letter criticized perestroika, arguing that it had gone too far, especially when it came to now-permissible public criticism of the Stalin period. Andreeva was quite fond of Stalin, believing that he had transformed the country for the better and seen the USSR successfully through the Second World War. She framed her comments on perestroika in terms of her students. She was a chemistry lecturer at Leningrad Polytechnic Institute. It was not in her own interest, she insisted, but in the interest of young people to change the course of reform.[17] Andreeva's letter covered the *entire* third page of the newspaper—an honor rarely bestowed on any single reader submission to a newspaper. The sheer amount of space it received underscored the new potential of readers' letters in the Soviet press three years into perestroika.

The letter and the ensuing discussion of it highlights the degree to which the letter to the editor had become an established way for citizens to participate in politics. That Andreeva's letter covered an entire page was, of course, not her own doing. Layout was clearly an editorial choice. The letters excerpted in *Pravda* in 1985 provide a far better indication of the amount of space typically given to any single letter to the editor, including political letters. And yet Andreeva herself regarded her letter as a great achievement. She saw its publication not as the work of other hands, but as her own hard work and sharp ideas. Moreover, those who read her letter saw it as a new standard for the way the Soviet press could amplify citizen intervention in politics. Yuri Nesterov, whose critical response to Andreeva was excerpted in *Sovetskaia Rossiia*'s spread of responses to the chemist's publication, stated that he dreamed that his letter would cover an entire page in the newspaper, just like hers.[18] His comment underscores how Soviet newspaper readers took what was printed to heart as an indication of the possibilities of their own engagement with the press.

---

[d] https://postsoviet90s.com/artifacts/i-cannot-forsake-my-principles

СОВЕТСКАЯ РОССИЯ — 13 марта 1988 г. — № 60 (9611) — 3 стр.

Письмо в редакцию преподавателя ленинградского вуза

НЕ МОГУ ПОСТУПАТЬСЯ ПРИНЦИПАМИ

Нина АНДРЕЕВА

FIGURE 4 Image from Artifact 00177.[e] Nina Andreeva's letter in *Sovetskaia Rossiia*, published in no. 60 (March 13, 1988), covered the entire third page of the four-page newspaper. By all accounts, the amount of space devoted to this letter was unconventional, but it highlighted the potential of a letter to the editor in 1988, the newspaper's willingness to give letters pride of place, and, as the ensuing national discussion demonstrated, a citizen's ability to use the letter and the printed press to advance her own political positions.

---

[e] https://postsoviet90s.com/artifacts/i-cannot-forsake-my-principles

Long editorials like Andreeva's and Nesterov's constituted just one more way in which readers could use the press to further their political ambitions. Perhaps the most Soviet of all forms of political engagement via the press appeared in September 1990. Just as reformers launched Stanislav Shatalin's "500 Day Plan" to begin marketizing the economy (Artifact 00007[f]), editors of KP called for readers to track the progress of economic reform by keeping "kitchen diaries." On September 29, 1990, they published a sample diary by "Citizen K." on the front page of the newspaper, in which she noted items she could buy and deficit items, the cost and quality of goods she could purchase, and how long she needed to stand in line to procure goods (see Figure 5).

Newspaper editors invited readers to keep similar diaries in order to track the progress of reform—and perhaps to give them an outlet for dealing with anticipated difficulties of introducing market forces into the economy. The archive of letters received by KP suggests that readers took the invitation to heart. At least two readers dutifully kept logs in the style of Citizen K. and sent them to the newspaper, suggesting that this peculiar and very Soviet way of engaging politics gained traction as a way of engaging politics through the newspaper (Artifact 00224[g]).

The year 1990, in which Citizen K.'s diary was excerpted in KP, proved to be a year of unprecedented change for newspapers across the USSR, and not just because of movement to marketize the economy or the official removal of Article 6, which made the USSR a one-party state. In June 1990, the government finally passed the new Press Law (Artifact 00084[h]). While Party censorship had in practice been phased out before 1990, the Press Law officially removed censors from editorial headquarters. It also gave editors control over print runs, which until 1990 had been dictated centrally, like every other commodity in the planned economy. In turn, editors were now responsible for managing the publication's budget and for making ends meet. Government subsidies helped editors keep pace, but newspapers' income increasingly came from advertisements, which began to appear in the press in 1989. There is little research on how the transition of individual periodicals took place during this year, and to a large extent, it seems like it was periodical specific.[19] Even though the Press Law went into effect on August 1, 1990, KP announced its independence from the Komsomol on December 1, 1990, when it officially removed the closing line of Marx's *Communist Manifesto* ("Workers of the world unite!") from its logo on page 1 in addition to its identification as the print organ of the Central Committee of the Komsomol (see Figure 6).

One might expect that sweeping changes to the USSR as a whole and drastic reform to the press itself gave way to a tumultuous year for Soviet newspapers. But at KP, just the opposite was true. The year 1990 marked a high point. Editors and journalists were

---

[f] https://postsoviet90s.com/artifacts/500-days-program-summary

[g] https://postsoviet90s.com/artifacts/kitchen-diary-by-s-piskunov-sent-to-komsomol-skaia-pravda-october-november-1990

[h] https://postsoviet90s.com/artifacts/press-law-of-1990

АКТУАЛЬНО!

Дневник гражданки К. накануне перехода к рынку

КОМСОМО
ПРАВ

ОСНОВАНА В МАЕ 1925г.

В РСФСР до рынка, похоже, рукой подать. Первого ноября стартует программа «500 дней». Оправдает ли она надежды наших исстрадавшихся сограждан?..

1 сентября

Вчера в универсаме давали вареную колбасу, и можно было подходить и брать просто так. Если бы я знала, что это в последний раз, взяла бы три куска. Сегодня за колбасой очередь, стояла 30 мин.

2 сентября

Давно нет яиц, муки, никаких консервов, кроме морской капусты и болгарской чечевицы. Нет картошки, лука. Очередь за помидорами, стояла 45 минут.

3 сентября

Исчез хлеб.

5 сентября

Час простояла в очере[illegible] мяса так и не вынесли. По[illegible] дали карпов.

6 сентября

В магазине не было ничего, кроме хлебного кваса, горохового супа и минеральной воды. Стояла очередь, думала, за мясом, оказалось, за пряниками.

11 сентября

Появился хлеб! Илюша на радостях купил к хлебу три пачки соли.

16 сентября

Возле универсама давали картошку по 40 копеек за килограмм. Шел дождь, и я не выстояла. Какая-то женщина по старой московской привычке потребовала заменить ей мелкую на крупную, и продавщица отказалась торговать совсем. Полчаса все стояли просто так.

20 сентября

Бабушка обижается, когда мы говорим, что в магазинах ничего нет. Подозревает, что врем. Колбаса — 1 час, 560 гр. Помидоры — около часа, 3 кг.

В социологии есть такой метод: оценивать социальное событие по отношению к нему частных лиц. Т. е. изучать дневники и письма. Довольно объективная получается картина, несмотря на субъективность впечатлений. Так что благодарим гражданку К. за возможность опубликовать ее дневник и ждем. От парламента, Президента, правительства, группы Шаталина — ждем перемен. А от граждан и гражданок — писем. Ведите на кухне дневники и присылайте нам. Это будет термометр под мышкой у реформы.

(Читайте вкладку).

*Хлеб.
Бензин.
Вино.
И т. д.*

Фото И. ТУМАМБАЕВА и Г. ОБРЕЗКОВА.

FIGURE 5 Image from Artifact 00079.[i] On the front page of *Komsomol'skaia pravda* on September 29, 1990, editors printed an excerpt from the "Diary of Citizen K. on the eve of the transition to the market," which included entries from seven days that note the cost of groceries, the quality, what was available where and when, and how long she had to wait in line to purchase them. At the end of the excerpted diary, editors invited readers to keep their own kitchen diaries and send them into the newspaper in an effort to track the course of reform.

[i] https://postsoviet90s.com/artifacts/kitchen-diary-from-citizen-k

FIGURE 6 On the top is the KP logo that appeared at the top of the paper for almost all of its Soviet existence, including the last line of Marx's *Communist Manifesto* ("Workers of the world, unite!") and the newspaper's affiliation with the Komsomol. On the bottom is the KP logo as of December 1, 1990. It no longer bears the Marxist slogan or the statement of Komsomol affiliation, which had been dissolved per the Press Law of 1990.

ecstatic about the passing of the Press Law, which had been in the works since 1986, when high-ranking members of the press met with Gorbachev in the Kremlin following the Twenty-Seventh Party Congress, and which to their minds was long overdue. The same year, KP also made an unprecedented achievement: it set the Guinness World Record for print run of a daily paper (Artifact 00279[j]). That year circulation reached 21,975,000 copies per day. The newspaper's newly granted ability to set its own print run did not shape its record, as the number had been recorded in May 1990, before the Press Law officially passed.[20] The achievement is particularly noteworthy because it flew in the face of global trends. The 1980s witnessed the decline in print runs of newspapers across the globe nearly everywhere except the Soviet Union. KP not only defied the global trend, but exhibited an altogether new possibility for daily newspapers.

Just as perestroika-era newspapers hit their stride and achieved global recognition as they did so, Gorbachev's regime crumbled. The federal government of the Soviet Union became defunct on January 1, 1992. Surprisingly, this, too, had little immediate effect on the newspaper itself. On January 1, 1992, the front page of the paper quietly stated: "There is no longer a Komsomol, but there is still Komsomol Truth [*Komsomol'skaia pravda*]."[21] Institutional changes like unhinging from the Komsomol and setting print runs and budgets internally had already taken place. As far as I understand, state subsidies were still supposed to appear, coming now from the Russian government. It is unclear what kind of offices KP had in the post-Soviet republics (now independent states) outside of Russia in 1992, and if the newspaper retained them. In 1992, the newspaper continued to report news from the former Soviet sphere, especially the Caucasus and Central Asia.

Moreover, in terms of reader-generated content, KP exhibited little change in 1992. Letters were still published in abundance. Commentary from members of the letter

---

[j] https://postsoviet90s.com/artifacts/komsomolskaia-pravda-sets-world-record

department continued to appear regularly on the pages. Editors published interactive exercises for readers and reports on investigations of particularly troubling letters. Readers could still meet friends through the paper. The column "Correspondence" (*Perepiska*), the sole purpose of which was to help readers make friends, had been discontinued during perestroika but reintroduced on July 19, 1991 in response to editors' observation that so many Soviet citizens suffered from depression.[22] The only noticeable difference in terms of the presentation of reader-generated content was the phasing out of organized columns that many letters had been published in earlier, like "Letters, letters," where letter department staff had previously summarized the monthly mail and detailed the number of letters received.

The phasing out of columns of letters provides one indication of how the reader–newspaper connection was presented on the printed page, but also raises questions about how work with letters changed more broadly. On the one hand, the Press Law of 1990 maintained the same standard for work with mail: every reader's letter required, by law, an answer. Little is known, however, about other requirements and practices of working with mail. Were letter departments still required to submit weekly and monthly summaries of mail (*obzory*) to the government? To what extent did they still forward readers' letters to relevant governmental bodies for solutions? I am not currently aware of sources that would allow me to address these questions, but the answers would help provide a better sense of how the relationship between newspapers and the state changed from 1990 to 1993.

Eventually, political and especially economic changes drastically affected newspapers, including *Komsomol'skaia pravda*. According to Roudakova, 1992 witnessed the drying up of state subsidies to newspapers after Yeltsin freed prices, inflation soared, and state tax revenue petered out.[23] Inflation is starkly evident in the price of KP, which jumped from 3 kopeks in 1985, to 20 kopeks in 1991, to between 40 and 60 kopeks in 1992–1993, depending on the day, with some days priced "by agreement" at the news stand, likely to accommodate for very sudden fluctuation in the cost of printing.

As prices increased and Russian citizens experienced the devaluation of their salaries, circulation rates also dropped precipitously from the end of 1991 to the beginning of 1995. *Pravda*, for instance, went from 2,628,000 copies to 204,000; *Izvestiia* from 4,700,000 to 811,000; *Literaturnaia gazeta* from 1,200,000 to 325,000; and *Argumenty i fakty* (AiF) from 24,527,000 to 4,200,000. Subscription practices changed in step with print runs. I do not know the print run of KP in 1995, but AiF likely makes a good comparison. Like KP, AiF set the Guinness World Record in 1990 (in this case for print run of a weekly periodical), with a circulation of 33,432,100 copies. Its print run fell to 12% of that number by 1995. By 1995, most Russians subscribed to at most one newspaper and usually a regional newspaper instead of a central periodical. David Wedgewood Benn points out, however, that subscription rates and print runs imperfectly reflected readership. Polls suggested that in 1995, one in four Russians still read AiF.[24] It's also important to keep in mind that Russian periodicals continued to defy global trends.

Across the world, print runs continued to shrink. Even drastically scaled-back circulation put post-Soviet newspapers in an elite class. In 2001, for example, KP maintained a circulation of 785,000 copies, which was the ninth highest print run of a daily paper in Europe at the time.[25]

Yet even more striking than the changing print run is the change in the quality of the newspaper itself. By 1995, reader-generated content practically disappeared from the printed page. A glance at a full issue published on July 15, 1993 shows that the newspaper had significantly expanded since the 1980s: it was now a full eight pages long (Figure 7). Most issues did not include any readers' letters or reader-generated content. On July 13, 1995, there was a spread of letters, yet it appeared only on page 8. Advertisements dominated at least two pages that came closer to the start of the paper. While ads had started to appear in the paper in 1989, by 1993 they came to take up as much space as had previously been devoted to reader-generated content.

Archival material at the Russian State Archive for Socio-Political History (RGASPI), at the Central Archive for the Social and Political History of Moscow (TsAOPIM), and in the personal collection of former Letter Department director Margarita Kechkina demonstrates that readers did not stop writing letters, even if the number of letters received by print periodicals decreased by 1995. The kind of phenomenon we witness by examining content printed on the page, however, is not a function of what readers *sent* to the paper. It's a result of editorial decision and reflects editors' vision of what the news should be as well as their understanding of the place of the reader in generating content for the pages. It's also a function of institutional changes, namely in the size of letter departments. At KP, the number of employees in this department shrank from dozens during perestroika to a handful in 1995.

By comparison to American dailies (for example) at the time, there's nothing surprising about the lack of reader-generated content on the pages of Soviet newspapers in 1995. But by comparison with Soviet newspapers just a few years earlier, the change is stunning. Gone were nearly all of the ways that the newspaper had formerly engaged its audience, from interactive columns to surveys to in-person investigations in response to troubling letters. Most stunning of all, however, is the disappearance of explicit ways in which readers used the newspaper to engage in politics. This came right at a time when regional politics were supposed to be more democratic, and more participatory, yet the familiar ways of engaging politics had been abandoned. In place of this content appeared seemingly endless advertisements. And in place of political participation through the press, shaped as it was by editorial decision and governmental expectations during the Soviet period, appeared content generated and paid for by aspiring politicians. It seems likely that this swift change in the newspaper itself, and the reader's place within it, contributed to the erosion of readers' trust in newspapers, if not democracy itself.

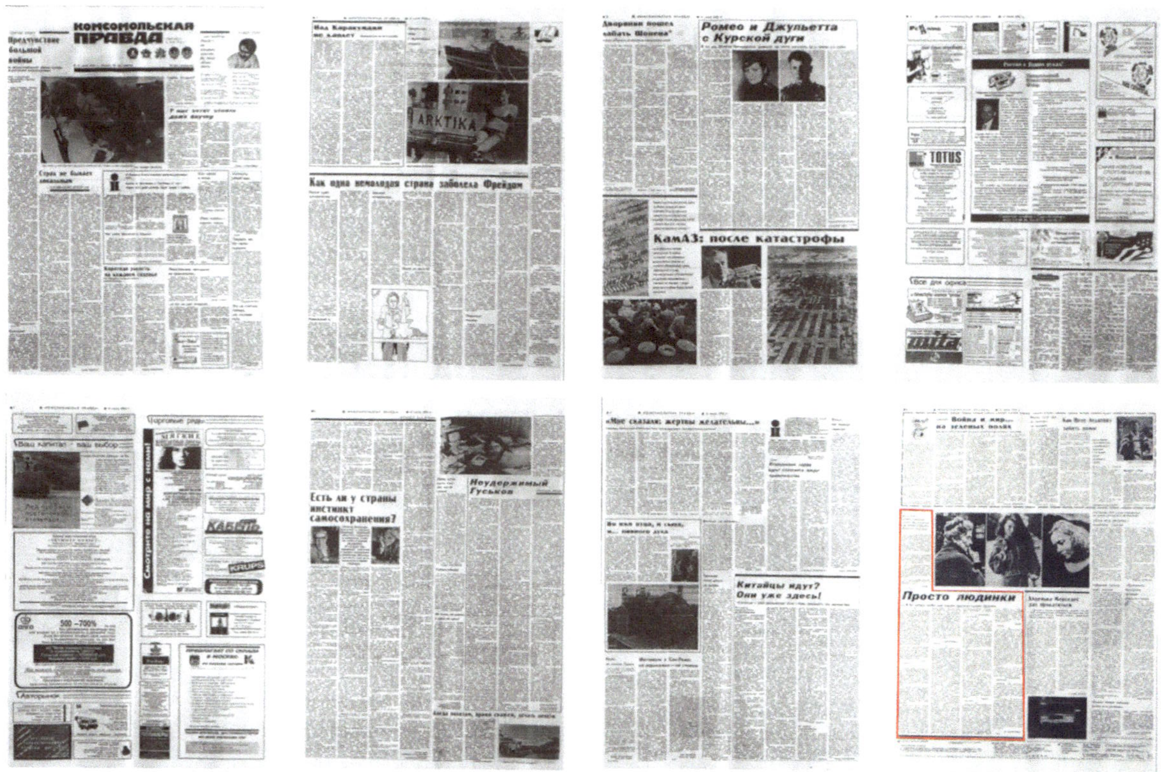

FIGURE 7 Pages 1–8 of *Komsomol'skaia pravda* No. 130 (July 15, 1993). The red box on the last page highlights the only reader-generated content—in this case, a collection of letters published under the title *Prosto liudniki*. The letters appeared only on page 8 of the paper. In contrast, there are nearly two full pages of advertisements on pages 4 and 5.

Notes

1 On the earlier press revolution, see Matthew Lenoe, *Closer to the Masses: Stalinist Culture, Social Revolutions, and Soviet Newspapers* (Cambridge, MA: Harvard University Press, 2004).

2 Natalia Roudakova, *Losing Pravda: Ethics and the Press in Post-Truth Russia* (New York: Cambridge University Press, 2017), 106.

3 On the revolution in Soviet and post-Soviet television, see Christine Evans, *Between Truth and Time: A History of Soviet Central Television* (New Haven, CT: Yale University Press, 2016); and Sabina Mihelj and Simon Huxtable, *From Media Systems to Media Cultures: Understanding Socialist Television* (Cambridge: Cambridge University Press, 2018).

4 In addition to Roudakova, see Thomas Wolfe, *Governing Soviet Journalism: The Press and the Socialist Person after Stalin* (Bloomington: Indiana University Press, 2005, as well as the later chapters of Dina Fainberg, *Cold War Correspondents: Soviet and American Reporters on the Ideological Front Lines* (Baltimore: Johns Hopkins University Press, 2021), and Simon Huxtable, *News from Moscow: Soviet Journalism and the Limits of Postwar Reform* (Oxford: Oxford University Press, 2022).

5 A. Murtazaev, "1 000 000 pisem s nachala nyneshnego goda poluchila redaktsiia," *Komsomol'skaia pravda* no. 211 (September 16, 1986), 1.

6 N. Morzhina, "Pis'ma, pis'ma," *Komsomol'skaia pravda* no. 29 (February 4, 1986), 2; no. 83 (April 8, 1986), 2; no. 105 (May 6, 1986), 2; no. 137 (June 3, 1986), 2; no. 165 (July 8, 1986), 2; no. 180 (August 6, 1986), 2; no. 202 (September 4, 1986), 2; no. 228 (October 5, 1986), 2. In the last three months of the year, KP reported receiving the following number of letters: October—78,875, November—45,871, December—45,741. See N. Morzhina, "Pis'ma, pis'ma," *Komsomol'skaia Pravda* no. 256 (November 11, 1986), 2; no. 282 (December 12, 1986), 2; no. 10 (January 13, 1987), 2.

7 Matthew Lenoe, "Letter-Writing and the State. Reader Correspondence with Newspapers as a Source for Early Soviet History," *Cahiers du Monde russe* 40, no. 1/2 (1999): 139–69.

8 Steven Coe, "Struggles for Authority in the NEP Village: The Early Rural Correspondents Movement, 1923-1927," *Europe-Asia Studies* 48, no. 7 (November 1996): 1151–71; Jeremy Hicks, "Worker Correspondents: Between Journalism and Literature," *The Russian Review* 66, no. 4 (October 2007): 568–85.

9 On letter writing in the late-Stalin period and the post-Stalin Soviet Union, see Juliana Fürst, "In Search of Soviet Salvation: Young People Write to the Stalinist Authorities," *Contemporary European History* 15, no. 3 (August 2006): 327–45; Alex Inkeles and Kent Geiger, "Critical Letters to the Soviet Press: Areas and Modes of Complaint," *American Sociological Review* 17, no. 6 (1952): 694–703; Alex Inkeles and Kent Geiger, "Critical Letters to the Soviet Press: Social Characteristics and Interrelations of Critics and the Criticized," *American Sociological Review* 18, no. 1 (1953): 12–22; Gleb Tsipursky, "'As a Citizen, I Cannot Ignore These Facts.' Whistleblowing in the Khrushchev Era," *Jahrbücher für Geschichte Osteuropas* 58, no. 1 (2010): 52–69; Stephen White, "Political Communications in the USSR: Letters to Party, State and Press," *Political Studies* XXXI (1983): 43–60.

On the role of letters in the transformation of the state and society and the limitations of that transformation during the Thaw, see Miriam Dobson, *Khrushchev's Cold Summer: Gulag Returnees, Crime, and the Fate of Reform after Stalin* (Ithaca, NY: Cornell University Press, 2009); Polly Jones, *Myth, Memory, Trauma: Rethinking the Stalinist Past in the Soviet Union, 1953–70* (New Haven, CT: Yale University Press, 2013); Denis Kozlov, *The Readers of Novyi Mir: Coming to Terms with the Stalinist Past* (Cambridge, MA: Harvard University Press, 2013).

10 Rossiiskii gosudarstvennyi arkhiv noveishei istorii (RGANI), f. 100, op. 1, d. 285, l. 2.

11 "Soveshchanie v TsK KPSS s rukovoditeliami sredstv massovoi informatsii (14 marta 1986 g.)," RGANI, f. 9, op. 5, d. 43, ll. 19–20.

12 "Protokol No 2 otkrytogo partiinogo sobraniia redaktsii gazety 'Komsomol'skaia prada' ot 22 dekabria 1983 goda," Tsentralynyi arkhiv obshepoliticheskoi istorii Moskvy [TsAOPIM], f. 1968, op. 1, d. 67, ll. 128–62.

13 "Protokol No 7 otkrytogo partiinogo sobraniia redaktsii gazety 'Komsomol'skaia pravda' ot 23 maia 1986 g.," TsAOPIM, f. 1968, op. 1, d. 73, l. 63.

14 "Protokol No 7 otkrytogo partiinogo sobraniia redaktsii gazety 'Komsomol'skaia pravda' ot 23 maia 1986 g.," TsAOPIM, f. 1968, op. 1, d. 73, l. 69.

15 "Spravka o rabote s pis'mami v redaktsii 'Literaturnoi gazety' v 1986," Rossiiskii gosudarstvennyi arkhiv literatury i iskusstv [RGALI], f. 634, op. 6, d. 75, ll. 1–11.

16 Nearly every account of perestroika makes note of the letter. See Archie Brown, *Seven Years That Changed the World* (New York: Oxford University Press, 2007), 197 n. 17, 287; R. W. Davies, *Soviet History in the Gorbachev Revolution* (Bloomington: Indiana University Press, 1989), 141–46, 152, 153, 191, 194; Ben Eklof, *Soviet Briefing: Gorbachev and the Reform Period* (Boulder, CO: Westview Press, 1989), 29–31, 36; Stephen Kotkin, *Armageddon Averted: The Soviet Collapse, 1970–2000* (New York: Oxford University Press, 2008), 73–80; Kathleen E. Smith, *Remembering Stalin's Victims. Popular Memory and the End of the USSR* (Ithaca, NY: Cornell University Press, 1996), 56–57; William Taubman, *Gorbachev: His Life and Times* (New York: Basic Books, 2016), 337–75; Thomas C. Wolfe, *Governing Soviet Journalism. The Press and the Socialist Person after Stalin* (Bloomington: Indiana University Press, 2005), 158–63; Vladislav Zubok, *Zhivago's Children: The Last Russian Intelligentsia* (Cambridge, MA: The Belknap Press of Harvard University, 2009), 342–43.

17 Nina Andreeva, "I Cannot Forsake My Principles," *Sovetskaia Rossiia* no. 60 (March 13, 1988), 3.

18 For Nesterov's excerpted letter, see *Sovetskaia Rossiia* (April 15, 1988), 3. The full text of his letter is available at the Archiv Museia politicheskoi istorii, f. 2, Inv. No. VS-7430-1, ll. 1–10. Nesterov expressed his desire for his letter to cover an entire newspaper page, just like Andreeva's, in an interview with the author conducted on October 14, 2014 in St. Petersburg.

19 Roudakova offers an account of *Leninskaia smena* in Gorky (now Nizhnyi Novgorod) in chapter 3 of *Losing Pravda*.

20 Reported at https://www.guinnessworldrecords.com/world-records/67027-highest-ever-daily-newspaper-circulation (accessed December 11, 2022).

21 *Komsomol'skaia pravda* no. 1 (January 1, 1992), 1.

22 G. Yanchuk, introduction to column *Perepiska, Komsomol'skaia pravda* no. 164 (July 19, 1991), 2.

23 Roudakova, *Losing Pravda*, 106.

24 David Wedgewood Benn, "The Russian Media in Post-Soviet Conditions," *Europe-Asia Studies* 48, no. 3 (1996): 474.

25 Adam Smith, "European Newspapers: Europe's Top Papers," *Campaign*, November 15, 2002, accessed December 11, 2022, https://www.campaignlive.co.uk/article/european-newspapers-europes-top-papers/164161.

Works Cited

Andreeva, Nina. "I Cannot Forsake My Principles," *Sovetskaia Rossiia* no. 60 (March 13, 1988), 3.

Benn, David Wedgewood. "The Russian Media in Post-Soviet Conditions." *Europe-Asia Studies* 48, no. 3 (1996): 471-479.

Brown, Archie. *Seven Years That Changed the World*. New York: Oxford University Press, 2007.

Coe, Steven. "Struggles for Authority in the NEP Village: The Early Rural Correspondents Movement, 1923–1927." *Europe-Asia Studies* 48, no. 7 (November 1996): 1151–71.

Davies, R. W. *Soviet History in the Gorbachev Revolution*. Bloomington: Indiana University Press, 1989.

Dobson, Miriam. *Khrushchev's Cold Summer: Gulag Returnees, Crime, and the Fate of Reform after Stalin*. Ithaca, NY: Cornell University Press, 2009.

Eklof, Ben. *Soviet Briefing: Gorbachev and the Reform Period*. Boulder, CO: Westview Press, 1989.

Evans, Christine. *Between Truth and Time: A History of Soviet Central Television*. New Haven, CT: Yale University Press, 2016.

Fainberg, Dina. *Cold War Correspondents: Soviet and American Reporters on the Ideological Front Lines*. Baltimore, MD: Johns Hopkins University Press, 2021.

Fürst, Juliana. "In Search of Soviet Salvation: Young People Write to the Stalinist Authorities." *Contemporary European History* 15, no. 3 (August 2006): 327–45.

Hicks, Jeremy. "Worker Correspondents: Between Journalism and Literature." *The Russian Review* 66, no. 4 (October 2007): 568–85.

Huxtable, Simon. *News from Moscow: Soviet Journalism and the Limits of Postwar Reform*. Oxford: Oxford University Press, 2022.

Inkeles, Alex and Kent Geiger. "Critical Letters to the Soviet Press: Areas and Modes of Complaint." *American Sociological Review* 17, no. 6 (1952): 694–703.

———. "Critical Letters to the Soviet Press: Social Characteristics and Interrelations of Critics and the Criticized." *American Sociological Review* 18, no. 1 (1953): 12–22.

Jones, Polly. *Myth, Memory, Trauma: Rethinking the Stalinist Past in the Soviet Union, 1953–70.* New Haven, CT: Yale University Press, 2013.

Kotkin, Stephen. *Armageddon Averted: The Soviet Collapse, 1970–2000.* New York: Oxford University Press, 2008.

Kozlov, Denis. *The Readers of Novyi Mir: Coming to Terms with the Stalinist Past.* Cambridge, MA: Harvard University Press, 2013.

Lenoe, Matthew. *Closer to the Masses: Stalinist Culture, Social Revolutions, and Soviet Newspapers.* Cambridge, MA: Harvard University Press, 2004.

———. "Letter-Writing and the State. Reader Correspondence with Newspapers as a Source for Early Soviet History." *Cahiers du Monde russe* 40, no. 1/2 (1999): 139–69.

Mihelj, Sabina and Simon Huxtable. *From Media Systems to Media Cultures: Understanding Socialist Television.* Cambridge: Cambridge University Press, 2018.

Morzhina, N. "Pis'ma, pis'ma," *Komsomol'skaia pravda* no. 29 (February 4, 1986), 2;

———. "Pis'ma, pis'ma," *Komsomol'skaia pravda* no. 83 (April 8, 1986), 2;

———. "Pis'ma, pis'ma," *Komsomol'skaia pravda* no. 105 (May 6, 1986), 2;

———. "Pis'ma, pis'ma," *Komsomol'skaia pravda* no. 137 (June 3, 1986), 2;

———. "Pis'ma, pis'ma," *Komsomol'skaia pravda* no. 165 (July 8, 1986), 2;

———. "Pis'ma, pis'ma," *Komsomol'skaia pravda* no. 180 (August 6, 1986), 2;

———. "Pis'ma, pis'ma," *Komsomol'skaia pravda* no. 202 (September 4, 1986), 2;

———. "Pis'ma, pis'ma," *Komsomol'skaia pravda* no. 228 (October 5, 1986), 2.

———. "Pis'ma, pis'ma," *Komsomol'skaia Pravda* no. 256 (November 11, 1986), 2;

———. "Pis'ma, pis'ma," *Komsomol'skaia pravda* no. 282 (December 12, 1986), 2;

———. "Pis'ma, pis'ma," *Komsomol'skaia pravda* no. 10 (January 13, 1987), 2.

Murtazaev, A."1 000 000 pisem s nachala nyneshnego goda poluchila redaktsiia," *Komsomol'skaia pravda* no. 211 (September 16, 1986), 1.

Nesterov, Yuri. Response to Nina Andreeva. Archiv Museia politicheskoi istorii, f. 2, Inv. No. VS-7430-1, ll. 1–10.

———. Excerpted letter. *Sovetskaia Rossiia* (April 15, 1988), 3.

"Protokol No 2 otkrytogo partiinogo sobraniia redaktsii gazety 'Komsomol'skaia prada' ot 22 dekabria 1983 goda," Tsentralynyi arkhiv obshepoliticheskoi istorii Moskvy [TsAOPIM], f. 1968, op. 1, d. 67, ll. 128–62.

"Protokol No 7 otkrytogo partiinogo sobraniia redaktsii gazety 'Komsomol'skaia pravda' ot 23 maia 1986 g.," TsAOPIM, f. 1968, op. 1, d. 73, l. 63.

Roudakova, Natalia. *Losing Pravda: Ethics and the Press in Post-Truth Russia.* New York: Cambridge University Press, 2017.

Smith, Adam. "European Newspapers: Europe's Top Papers," *Campaign*, November 15, 2002, accessed December 11, 2022, https://www.campaignlive.co.uk/article/european-newspapers-europes-top-papers/164161.

Smith, Kathleen E. *Remembering Stalin's Victims. Popular Memory and the End of the USSR.* Ithaca, NY: Cornell University Press, 1996.

"Soveshchanie v TsK KPSS s rukovoditeliami sredstv massovoi informatsii (14 marta 1986 g.)," RGANI, f. 9, op. 5, d. 43, ll. 19–20.

"Spravka o rabote s pis'mami v redaktsii 'Literaturnoi gazety' v 1986," Rossiiskii gosudarstvennyi arkhiv literatury i iskusstv [RGALI], f. 634, op. 6, d. 75, ll. 1–11.

Taubman, William. *Gorbachev: His Life and Times.* New York: Basic Books, 2016.

Tsipursky, Gleb. "'As a Citizen, I Cannot Ignore These Facts.' Whistleblowing in the Khrushchev Era." *Jahrbücher für Geschichte Osteuropas* 58, no. 1 (2010): 52–69.

White, Stephen. "Political Communications in the USSR: Letters to Party, State and Press." *Political Studies* XXXI (1983): 43–60.

Wolfe, Thomas. *Governing Soviet Journalism: The Press and the Socialist Person after Stalin.* Bloomington: Indiana University Press, 2005.

Yanchuk, G. *Perepiska, Komsomol'skaia pravda* no. 164 (July 19, 1991), 2.

Zubok, Vladislav. *Zhivago's Children: The Last Russian Intelligentsia.* Cambridge, MA: The Belknap Press of Harvard University, 2009.

CHAPTER 3

Russian Media in the 1990s, Fully Disclosed: Gore, Tabloids, and Countercultural Nationalism

Fabrizio Fenghi

My essay focuses on three overlapping sets of issues. The first is the emergence of sensationalist reporting and, more generally, of tabloids (*zheltaia pressa*) in Russia during perestroika and the 1990s. The second is *chernukha* (gore) and the centrality of violence and sex in the context of glasnost and the attempts at creating truthful accounts of social and political events. The third is the blurring of the boundaries between underground and mainstream culture that occurred during this period of time. Within post-Soviet Russian media, *chernukha* and sensationalist reporting often degenerated into sheer surrealism and, at the same time, this taste for the overtly violent, sexual, absurd, and politically incorrect became the source of specific countercultural or transgressive forms of national identity.[1] In addition, the surreal physicality displayed in some of the media artifacts discussed here reveals and reflects a "biopolitical essence" of the post-Soviet transition, in the sense of a total control over "bare life"—to use Giorgio Agamben's definition—as something inherent to the exercise of political power in contemporary Russia. Drawing primarily on Michel Foucault's *History of Sexuality* and Hannah Arendt's discussion of human rights, Agamben argues that biopolitics, seen as a "growing inclusion of man's natural life in the mechanisms and calculations of power," is the defining feature of modern forms of sovereign power and, as a consequence, of both totalitarianism and mass democracy.[2] This is particularly true for post-Soviet Russia, where, primarily because of the country's abrupt transition to a radical form of unregulated capitalism, the exercise of power can be described through the prism of a total control over bare life and a prolonged "state of exception." In line with this view, in one of the most authoritative economic studies of Russia's transition to capitalism, Peter Reddaway and Dmitri Glinski describe the shock therapy of the 1990s as a tool intentionally used to hinder democratic change and create systemic inequality by wiping out the savings of an emergent middle class.[3] Biopolitics, in this sense, could be seen as an element of fundamental continuity between Yeltsin's and Putin's forms of "neoliberal authoritarianism."

The idea of a state of exception is also connected to the possibility of looking at the 1990s—which are both demonized and romanticized as a time of unlimited possibilities—as a foundation myth and a source for defining a post-communist Russian identity and conception of statehood. For Agamben, the state of exception is the condition characterizing the creation of the excluded "other" as the premise for creating "the body of the people," or "the sacred life that may be killed but not sacrificed." But on the basis of Greek and Roman conceptions of sacred life—which Agamben uses as a starting point for his reflection—the state of exception also coincides with the origins of sovereign power and the political more broadly. The state of exception marks the moment in which political change and transformation (albeit potentially violent) is possible: Oedipus is both the *pharmakos*—"the impure" who is expelled from the community so that said community can atone and be purified from its sins—and "the tyrant"—the extraordinary individual who determines the fate of this same community.[4] In a similar vein, the vision of the 1990s as *bespredel* (mayhem) plays an important role in defining the post-Soviet condition and its temporality as a specific state of exception. The lawlessness and transgressions of the 1990s establish, through negation, the accepted ethical and legal norms of the latter decades in the form of a sort of apophatic identity—"what we are not, what we don't want." And, at the same time, they affirmatively (or "positively") define subsequent discursive and political styles in terms of a withdrawal from any form of ideology or teleology.[5] As far as the nascent post-Soviet media industry is more specifically concerned, during the 1990s popular culture and mass media became privileged loci for defining and presenting "Russia and 'Russianness' for domestic consumption, usually framed within the discourse of total collapse and cultural degradation." In this context, Russian media both "condensed and magnified the anxieties that gripped the nation" by providing the fundamental framework for expressing these anxieties, and by turning into the object and motivation of these same anxieties.[6]

Starting from these assumptions, I look at the artifacts in my selection through the prism of a specific construction of identity through negativity. In doing that, I follow a trajectory that moves, metaphorically, from the "positive" deconstruction of perestroika—where transparency, plurality, and the commitment to truth are themselves sources of a new identity that is largely based on overcoming the oppressive immobility and well-intended hypocrisy of the late Soviet system—to the dissipation, or quite literally decomposition, of "revolutionary negativity" into *chernukha*. In some cases, this process resulted in a surreal reclaiming of the darkest sides of post-Soviet reality as part of an imperial project—in the form of a more or less conscious reclaiming of the stereotypical vision of the Soviet Union (and, by extension, Russia) as an "Evil Empire," or a space that has fallen on the wrong side of history.[7] In this context, the essay argues, discourses surrounding identity and *chernukha* or *bespredel* in the nascent post-Soviet mediascape also reflect an underlying dialectic tension between virtual reality and manipulation on the one hand, and true belief and the authenticity of physical experience on the other.

CRIME NOVELS, INVESTIGATIVE JOURNALISM, AND SENSATIONALISM DURING PERESTROIKA

The first issue of the monthly magazine *Sovershenno sekretno* (Top Secret), the first privately owned periodical in Soviet Russia since 1917, perfectly captures the emergent journalistic style and media discourse of the 1980s, in that it combined investigative journalism—and a yearning for transparency and truth—with sensationalism and salaciousness (Artifact 00190[a]).[8] *Sovershenno sekretno* was a creation of the best-selling author Yulian Semyonov, widely known in Russia as the creator of Stierlitz, the Soviet undercover spy working in Nazi Germany from the popular Soviet TV series *Semnadtsat' mgnovenii vesni* (Seventeen Moments of Spring, 1973). The magazine was published by the International Association of Crime and Political Fiction (MADP), also founded and directed by Semyonov, and initially it was periodically sold in combination with the almanac *Detektiv i politika* (Crime Fiction and Politics).[9]

The front page of *Sovershenno sekretno*'s first issue (June 1989) displayed the graphic image of the lifeless body of Soviet actress Zoya Fyodorova, who was found dead in mysterious circumstances in her apartment in the center of Moscow on December 11, 1981, killed by a single gunshot to the back of the neck fired from a German-made Sauer pistol. The column provided a brief account of the case, promising a novella focusing on these events, "The Mystery of Prospekt Kutuzov," to be published in installments.[10] In contrast with the somewhat grabby, entertaining-cum-macabre headline, Semyonov's editorial for the same issue switched to a much more poised analysis of current events. The piece, entitled "Fully Public" (a wordplay on the magazine's name—which in Russian means, literally, "Fully Secret"), presents a curious combination of Reaganism and Leninism, or Semyonov's very specific interpretation of both, and one of the rallying cries of perestroika, "the fight against bureaucratism."[11] Semyonov, a strong supporter of Gorbachev's reforms, expressed admiration for the efficiency and wealth of "the West" and voiced some concern over the "Stalinist elements" within the Soviet nomenklatura, which he saw as a potential threat to the country's modernization process. He called for throwing into the street "the 18 million bureaucrats who are only tasked with tallying up the earnings of the most successful factory directors"; for allowing Soviet citizens to travel abroad; and for promoting tourism to counteract the country's chronic shortage of currency.[12]

Looking at some of *Sovershenno sekretno*'s early issues, one is indeed struck by the combination of serious reporting and in-depth political analysis with salacious stories and true crime. The magazine alternated articles about serial killers and unsolved murders with scholarly essays by prominent Russian economists and political scientists,

[a] https://postsoviet90s.com/artifacts/top-secret-investigative-journalism-and-true-crime-during-perestroika

literary and philosophical sections with previously unpublished pieces on, and by, such authors as Nikolay Berdiaev and Yevgeny Zamyatin, and political commentaries about Soviet dissidents, the origin of *Solidarność*, and the emergence of national movements throughout the Soviet bloc.[13] *Detektiv i politika* served as the magazine's literary counterpart by offering a mix of fictional and semi-fictional reportages, historical exposés, and spy stories by, or in the style of, John le Carré, Martin Cruz Smith, and Ian Fleming, as well as short stories and essays by more experimental writers, not necessarily of crime fiction, like Kurt Vonnegut, Stanislaw Lem, Viktor Erofeev, and Eduard Limonov.

Both the magazine and its attachment used the genres of crime and spy fiction (with some excursions into political fantasy and sci-fi) as an underlying thread that connected popular entertainment with investigative journalism, but also with advanced scholarly writing and daring literary experiments. In many respects, *Sovershenno sekretno*'s editorial line reflected and encapsulated larger cultural trends during perestroika. In part due to a lack of affordable alternatives, crime novels or *detektivy* (especially the foreign ones) were one of the main forms of popular entertainment throughout the 1980s and well into the 1990s. During perestroika, violence and *chernukha* themselves became implicitly associated with sincerity and truth, and with a moral mission to reveal and amend society's darkest evils. At the same time, the proliferation of overtly violent and sexual materials in the first Russian independent media represents a response to the "culture of shortage" affecting attitudes toward consumer goods, print culture, and entertainment more broadly. As a consequence, the acute yearning for truth, transparency, and information characterizing media discourses in this period goes hand in hand, and often overlaps, with a keen fascination with transgression and the extreme.[14] And the appearance of these new themes coincides with the emergence of new journalistic languages that, in contrast with the largely flat and hypernormalized language of the Soviet press, allowed for the use of personal, original styles and involved strong elements of irony and provocation.[15]

A perfect example of this combination of transparency, sensationalism, and political irony during the 1990s was the weekly magazine *Novyi vzgliad* (New View, Artifact 00192[b]). Initially conceived as an extension of the popular TV show *Vzgliad*, *Novyi vzgliad* was founded by a former correspondent of *Sovershenno sekretno*, Evgeny Dodolev, who was widely known for having published, in 1986, the first article on prostitution in the Soviet Union.[16] As far as salaciousness goes, *Novyi vzgliad* followed in *Sovershenno sekretno*'s footsteps and pushed things a little further, as exemplified by the general tone of some of its headlines: "Boobs Coated in Flour"; "The Cannibal-Lover"; "Serial Murders"; and "Uxoricides."[17]

Most notably, *Novyi vzgliad* became closely associated with new forms of political irony and was widely known for the fierce debates that took place on its pages—as well as for the few public trials that some of these debates caused. In accordance with

---

[b] https://postsoviet90s.com/artifacts/novyi-vzgliad-violence-political-irony-and-national-pride

its slogan—"Total Pluralism"—the magazine regularly published, side-by-side, opposite and often quite radical political views: the Stalinist, ultranationalist essentialism of Aleksandr Prokhanov, "the army headquarters' nightingale," was juxtaposed to the hyper-liberal, anti-Russian essentialism of the self-defined magazine's "main politextremist," the former dissident Valeriya Novodvorskaya.[18]

Two of *Novyi vzgliad*'s contributors in particular—the provocative émigré writer Eduard Limonov and the poet, journalist, and queer multimedia artist Yaroslav (Slava) Mogutin—combined discourses on violence, sexuality, and transgression as part of a new paradoxical conception of politics and national identity. Limonov, who had then just repatriated, was becoming a celebrity in Russia, both because of the popular success of his novel *Eto ia—Edichka* (It's Me, Eddie, 1979/1991), which focused on the author's queerness, marginality, and sense of despair in New York in the 1970s, *and* because of his public celebration of masculinity, war, and even fascism as part of a kind of "revolt against the modern world." On the pages of *Novyi vzgliad*, Limonov published his first *limonki*—article-grenades directed at his political opponents, the government, and the Russian intelligentsia in its entirety—and soon thereafter, *Limonka* became the name of the cult newspaper released by his own radical political organization-cum-punk movement, the National Bolshevik Party (NBP).[19]

Mogutin—one of the first openly gay authors in Russia, and one of the first who made writing about his sexuality, and about homosexuality in general, central to his work—had an essential role in defining *Novyi vzgliad*'s style as a combination of tabloid-like sensationalism and "total pluralism." Mogutin's public persona was based on a mix of defiance, anti-intellectualism, and nationalism—and a fascination with youth and (aggressive) masculinity, young soldiers and lumpen proletarians, and the raw beauty of their muscular bodies. Mogutin considered himself a disciple of Limonov (who was at this point reticent about his own sexuality) and played at the same time an important role in introducing and "explaining" Limonov to the Russian public as a combination of a provincial *gopnik*, opinion maker, and provocateur.[20] As part of what he called a form of "class struggle," he criticized Russian intellectuals for their alleged elitism, cowardice, and physical weakness, and claimed for himself, not unlike Limonov, the role of the tough working-class guy from the (in his case Siberian) province.[21] As a regular contributor of *Novyi vzgliad*, he covered, not without a certain dose of irony, various social and cultural events organized by a nascent LGBT movement in Russia.[22] As part of an art performance of sorts, he publicly celebrated and tried to register his wedding with his male partner, the American artist Robert Filippini—and he was soon thereafter prosecuted and ultimately forced to emigrate to the United States on the accusation of "incitement of interethnic hatred" because of a vehemently anti-Chechen article he wrote in response to the war.[23]

In two of his articles from *Novyi vzgliad*, Mogutin combined the early post-Soviet "coming out" of discourses about sexuality and fascination with violence with a self-deprecating and self-exoticizing form of national pride. In one, "Orgy as a Way of Thinking," he argued that Russians had gotten so used to living in crowds—amassing against each other in lines, in the metro during rush hour, and in collective apartments—that they started to find these experiences sexually arousing. In these situations, deep-seated taboos, including taboos against homosexual relationships, could be violated: in dorms and communal apartments strangers could fulfill the roles of "voyeurs and exhibitionists," and in prison camps they "were ready to fall into the ranks of sadists-torturer and masochists-victims."[24] In the second piece, "Boobs Coated in Flour," Mogutin claimed that violence and sadism were an essential component of Russia's everyday life, its literature, and its identity—and of his own generation's relationship with sex. In both texts, a (self-)critical attitude toward this pervasive horror and "lack of boundaries" (*bespredel*) was mixed with a somewhat ironic pride for the country's seeming descent into barbarianism.[25]

Mogutin's pieces and the style of *Novyi vzgliad* more generally offer a good example of the way in which in the early post-Soviet period *stiob* (in Aleksei Yurchak's definition, a "parody based on overidentification") becomes increasingly associated with politics and dark irony, with the result of producing somewhat "shifty" political statements and positions—a tendency that has become pervasive during the Putin era. At the same time, the kind of moral unmasking or revealing (*razoblachenie*) that characterized *chernukha* during perestroika turns into, and overlaps with, a twisted and paradoxical form of national pride—and with a sense of belonging and identity connected with the experience of violence itself.[26]

In different Russian media, the categories of *chernukha* and *bespredel* are related to the act of documenting and, at the same time, magnifying everyday experiences of violence and degradation that become common during the first Soviet decade.[27] These experiences, in their turn, are often associated with a form of social Darwinism that becomes an essential component of hegemonic discourses, in part as a result of a rejection of the formally collectivist Soviet ethos in favor of radical neoliberalism.[28] In response to this state of affairs, two tendencies emerge within both mainstream and countercultural/independent media. On the one hand, *chernukha* degenerates into sheer surrealism and turns into a parody of documentary truth in the form of conspiracy theories and mystifications. On the other hand, violence and pain are associated with authenticity, and, as a consequence, they come to represent the ultimate form of resistance against a post-Soviet reality that is perceived as illusory and alienating.

FROM SOCIAL DARWINISM TO PSYCHEDELIC NAZISM

The TV show *Kriminal'naia Rossiia*, first conceived as a loose adaptation of the American true crime series *Cops*, was one of the main incarnations of 1990s *chernukha* on Russian TV, often criticized for its sensationalism and ostentation of violence. Its first episode,

"The Murylev Case. Death for Apartments," is revealing of the ruthlessness and banalization of violence characterizing the new post-Soviet reality (and its media coverage) and is closely related to the new meanings assigned to private property within said reality (Artifact 00184[c]).[29]

The episode opens with a nostalgic digression about the dream of a state-assigned home for all after the October Revolution and under Khrushchev—and goes on to explain the unique situation of Soviet citizens who suddenly turned into homeowners after the fall of the Soviet Union in 1991. From there, it moves to the specifics of the case of Murylev—the son of a Russian counter-intelligence agent in Germany and a former student at a Moscow medical institute who murdered several destitute homeowners and unemployed alcoholics after tricking them into transferring the property of their apartments to him under the promise of a later payment. Once he is caught and confesses, Murylev (who is clearly seen, in contrast with his victims, as a solidly middle-class and "proper" individual) walks the cameras through the crime scenes detailing the gruesome ways in which he murdered his victims in an absolutely matter-of-fact way. In the close to the episode, the voiceover relates a statement that perfectly captures the darkest forms of social Darwinism pervading Russian society at this time. During questioning, Murylev famously claimed that his actions (his "privatization method," as the commentator mockingly calls it) were justified, because by killing "drunks and degenerates" he was freeing up living space that would be transferred to "far more deserving people." By doing so, he explained, he was acting like "Yeltsin's orderly" or "cleaner" (*sanitar Yeltsina*), in that he was "helping the president purge" Russian society of its "marginal elements" (see Figure 1).

The "Murylev case" is a good example of what could be perceived as the fundamental absurdity of the "bare truth" that the proverbial unmasking of perestroika has revealed. Everyday experiences of violence are widely accessible and publicly exposed, but are also seemingly deprived of any interpretative framework and, as a consequence, of any substance and meaning. And Murylev's remarks convey an even stronger sense of powerlessness and humiliation if one looks at them from the perspective of disadvantaged and marginalized viewers (the majority) who had lost their property and any sense of security as a result of privatization.

Discourses surrounding identity and *chernukha* in the nascent post-Soviet mediascape generally also reflect an underlying dialectic tension between virtual reality and manipulation on the one hand, and the authenticity of physical experience and true belief on the other. A perfect example of this is the trajectory of the experimental musician and performer Sergey Kuryokhin, who can be seen as the quintessential postmodern artist and practitioner of *stiob*. Kuryokhin was generally fascinated with *totalitarian* artforms—as in artforms or actions that would involve a radical transformation of reality, resulting in either a fascination with mass manipulation *or* a romantic

[c] https://postsoviet90s.com/artifacts/yeltsin-s-orderly-sanitar-yeltsina

FIGURE 1 Video from Artifact 00184.[d] Excerpt from "The Murylev Case. Death for Apartments [*Delo Muryleva. Smert' za kvartiry*]," June 24, 1995, TV. First episode of the true crime show *Kriminal'naia Rossiia* (NTV, 1995–2002, with various later versions on TVS, Pervyi kanal, and others).

impulse toward sincerity, belief, and absolute commitment. After experimenting with music performances, film, radio, and television, Kuryokhin decided, in his own words, "to experiment with radical politics" by joining the NBP, the radical organization led by Limonov and the far-right fringe philosopher Aleksandr Dugin.[30]

In one of the last interviews that he gave before dying prematurely of a rare heart disease, Kuryokhin elaborated on the tension between belief and the postmodern commodification and "virtualization" of reality that he thought was becoming predominant after the fall of the Soviet Union. Here, he distinguished between a "vulgar" and an authentic, "elitist" postmodernism. Vulgar postmodernism was the cheap irony of mainstream television, which was devoid of any seriousness or commitment. In contrast, "authentic postmodernism" was an attempt at "joking about the revolution, while maintaining the desire to be revolutionary"—whereas fascism was a radical form of romanticism and the

[d] https://postsoviet90s.com/artifacts/yeltsin-s-orderly-sanitar-yeltsina

quintessential form of militancy, seemingly in the sense of a total commitment to an artistic or political vision. For Kuryokhin, if one is a romantic—truly committed to an aesthetic vision—one will inevitably "become a fascist" (Artifact 00193[e]).[31]

But things were not as clearly defined as Kuryokhin described them in his provocative piece: within post-Soviet media, the boundaries between highbrow and popular, counterculture and mainstream, authenticity and mystification, were—and in many respects still are—fundamentally blurred. Dugin himself had "normalized" psychedelic Nazism and elaborate conspiracy theories on mainstream television when he participated in the show *Tainy veka* (The Mysteries of the Century), broadcast on the main Russian state channel, Pervyi kanal "Ostankino," (First channel Ostankino) in the fall of 1993 (Artifact 00191[f]). The show, hosted by Yuri Vorobevsky, was a clear parody of perestroika's typical *razoblachenie* or unmasking of "top secret" materials. It included fake or deceivingly edited visits to the KGB archives and interviews with self-styled academic experts, former American and Russian spies, and freemasons—and it focused on such topics as vampires, psychotronic weapons that international intelligence services would have allegedly used for mind control, and the murder of the Romanov family.[32] The main group of episodes, co-hosted with Dugin, focused on the mystical undercurrents of Nazism and the activity of *Ahnenerbe*—the pseudoscientific archeological society tasked to prove and support the ancient origins and intrinsic superiority of the Aryan race.

The show had an hallucinatory quality, with haunting jaw harp sounds and mantra, and an endless chain of far-fetched connections between seemingly unrelated historical events. Take, for instance, an excerpt from the episode "Mistika Reikha: taina zelenogo drakona" (The mysticism of the Reich: the mystery of the green dragon). In it, Vorobevsky sits in a dark room, with a green light projected on his face and hands, placing cards with "mysterious" esoteric symbols on a table. "With each episode of *Tainy veka*"—he explains—"more and more questions come up." The "missing card," he continues, may be the elusive "Society of the Green Dragon": Hitler's deputy Rudolph Hess said that the theorist of German expansionism, Karl Hausofer, was a magician, and Hausofer was a member of "The Secret Society of the Green Dragon"—a Japanese secret society; Rasputin, who was a German spy, used to receive messages from Stockholm, signed in green ink; in the 1930s in Berlin there was "a mysterious man from Tibet who used to wear green gloves"; Heinrich Himmler had a "strange liking" for "the green book of the Quran" and always kept his favorite green pen on his desk; the Tsarina Aleksandra Fedorovna, the wife of Nikolay II, used to draw a swastika in her correspondence with the Tibetan healer Pyotr Badmaev; the mystical "crazy Baron" Ungern-Sternberg, a

---

[e] https://postsoviet90s.com/artifacts/romantics-and-fascists

[f] https://postsoviet90s.com/artifacts/the-mysteries-of-the-century-post-truth-and-mystical-nazism-on-russian-tv

White Army commander known for his ruthlessness, used to decorate the epaulettes of his soldiers with a swastika...*and so on and so forth*. The episode resembles a dark version of the famous Lenin-Mushroom TV prank, in which Kuryokhin had "proved" that Lenin had become a mushroom by showing a mushroom-shaped ashtray on his desk, along with unrelated interviews with biologists explaining the scientific characteristics of mushrooms in general—with no specific connections with Lenin and the Bolsheviks.[33] *Tainy veka* follows the same shimmering or shifting logic of *stiob* by covering it with an additional patina of mystery and academic solemnity. In the sequence following Vorobevsky's semi-delirious monologue about the "Society of the Green Dragon," almost as a way of revealing the show's surreal essence, Dugin explains that "it doesn't really matter if [a conspiracy] is real. If it exists in people's consciousness, if it exists in the social sphere, if it exists as a conspiracy, as a sociological fact, as a model used to understand what is happening, the conspiracy is already real."

In other words, *Tainy veka* exploits the late Soviet and early post-Soviet widespread thirst for truth, mystery, and transgression. And not unlike sex and violence, Nazism constituted at the time the ultimate discursive taboo that could be violated as a way of rejecting the well-intended hypocrisy of both Soviet calls for tolerance and equality, and the soon-to-be-broken neoliberal promises of prosperity and freedom dominating the post-Soviet media landscape. The show denies the possibility of truth by mocking perestroika's obsession with it. But it also surreptitiously reclaims the dark, surreal essence of post-Soviet reality as a source of identity and hints at the possibility of exploiting the radical cynicism and skepticism of the dominating neoliberal ethos for reactionary (or, from the point of view of its creators, revolutionary) purposes—that is, to turn "the society of the spectacle" against itself.

Another remarkable example of this tendency is one of the most popular tabloids of the 1990s, *Megapolis-ekspress* (Artifact 00203[g]). *Megapolis-ekspress* started as a classical "perestroika magazine" on politics and society (often described as occupying the same niche as *Ogonyok* and *Moscovskie novosti*), but changed drastically in 1994, when Igor Dudinsky took over the magazine—at the time on the verge of bankruptcy—as editor-in-chief. With Dudinsky—like Dugin a former member of postmodern writer Yuri Mamleev's "metaphysical" underground circle—*Megapolis-ekspress* turned into an extreme parody of the cheapest and most salacious Western tabloids. Its slogan and subheading was "The Exotics of Urban Life"; its typical stories were cases of (self-)cannibalism, sexual encounters with werewolves, interviews with retired "babushki of Russian porn," travels to the afterlife, and "space brawls."[34] Like other former members of Mamleev's circle, Dudinsky had a particular taste for black magic, witchcraft, satanism, and "mystical Nazism"—and for the absurd sadism and the gratuitous violence of Lautréamont's *Songs of Maldoror* that had served as an inspiration for the Surrealist Movement.[35]

---

[g] https://postsoviet90s.com/artifacts/megapolis-ekspress-urban-exoticism-and-national-pride-52bb8047-7159-4f5e-9d80-5236142523bc

And although *Megapolis-ekspress* was clearly a commercial and highly lucrative enterprise (at its peak, its print run got close to 1 million copies), Dudinsky himself used a quasi-populist, patriotic argument to justify his decision to experiment with the genre. The fact that his publication was commercially successful, he explained, allowed it to be free from financial and political pressure, in contrast with more "elitist" and arguably more serious Russian periodicals that did not earn any profit and owed their existence to various oligarchs. *Megapolis-ekspress*—Dudinsky argued—provided a popular, highly accessible form of entertainment. At the same time, he continued, the main targets of the magazine's grotesque irony were capitalism, consumerism, and the decadence of "the Western way of life"—to which Russians had turned after the fall of the Soviet Union. In this sense, the tabloid had been conceived, paradoxically, as a fundamentally "popular," anti-Western, and patriotic project.[36]

A similar tendency, in the sense of a reclaiming of the dark, surreal essence of the 1990s as a paradoxical source of identity and pride, can be observed in the nascent post-Soviet youth and music culture and media industry. Two examples are indicative of this trend: the phantasmagorical musical radio program *Transil'vaniia bespokoit* (Transylvania Speaking) and the equally extravagant TV show *Dryoma* (Doze), which started as "the Russian MTV" and developed into a short-lived but highly influential artistic experiment on mainstream television. *Transil'vaniia bespokoit*, advertised as "the only radio program whose host doesn't have a shadow," was aired weekly on Radio 101 FM, at nighttime, throughout the second half of the 1990s, and was the product of its host, Garik Osipov—a singer, musician, archivist, and "collector," with an encyclopedic knowledge of both niche and mainstream music and film. Osipov, who hosted the show in the guise of his character, Count Khortitsa or Count Dracula—with a deep, hypnotic voice and a maleficent laughter and demeanor—had a unique style of presenting and almost deliriously digressing on a wide variety of themes related to pop music and alternative rock, politics, horror B-movies and spy stories, counterculture, Satanism, occultism, mysticism, and conspiracy theories (Artifact 00204[h]). The musical selection reflected the highly eclectic tastes of its host, including hard rock, heavy metal, funk, and psychedelic music, as well as lesser known or forgotten genres and performers—primarily old-time variety songs from Russia and Eastern Europe, France, and Italy. The result, through Osipov's commentaries and explanations, was an alternative musical canon in which the music of the host's own Soviet youth was invariably better than its Western/American counterpart—and where the (again, Western) countercultures of the 1960s had ended up confirming and reinforcing the neoliberal world order. Osipov also celebrated and included in his selection the most extreme, violent, uncompromising, and anti-systemic musicians

---

[h] https://postsoviet90s.com/artifacts/transilvania-is-bothering-you-on-radio-101-fm-40e4a7e9-8aed-42f2-8dab-61c744b5f23d

and performers, either from the perspective of ideology and lyrics or sound, or both—from Charles Manson to Motörhead and GG Allin.

In terms of politics, Osipov was decisively on the right, with frequent invectives against the New World Order and the "Zionist Occupation Government," political correctness, tolerance and egalitarianism, consumerism, and post-Soviet Russia's material and cultural decline. And through his program he produced a counterpublic of listeners, or, as he occasionally addressed them throughout the show, the "Children of Eurasia": young marginals barely surviving the post-Soviet mayhem but largely defined by it, at various points described as perceiving the grey, bleak reality of post-Soviet life through heroine-induced dreams, buried underneath the sheets in their tiny rooms, surrounded by the squalor of city slums.[37] Significantly, in Osipov's nightmarish, apocalyptic descriptions of post-Soviet reality—intermingled with fantastic stories about vampires, werewolves, and the living dead—the recurring image of the "Empire of Evil"—as in, the United States and the neoliberal "World Order"—becomes superimposed with that of the "Empire of Evil"—as in, post-Soviet Russia itself, the locus where the ultimate late-capitalist decadence is manifested at its worst. See, for instance, *Transil'vaniia*'s 1997 New Year's Eve episode:

> Another year spent vegetating in the liberal pigsty, where everything has a price and nothing has value, where everyone knows prices and no one knows worth, is coming to an end. A disgusting frost is settling on the needles of the imperial pine trees. The deadly, fetid exhalation of the West, with its tourists mincing on thin ice and its agents of influence spreading like mold on a derelict school, from which they took all the students out, because some unexplained incidents have started happening...in the suspicious, incomprehensible, and odious magical Empire of Evil...[38]

Although the TV show *Dryoma* had very little in common with *Transil'vaniia bespokoit* in terms of the latter's support of conspiracy theories, fringe right-wing ideas, imperialism, and "mystical Nazism," it shared with it a similar way of turning violence and *chernukha* into sheer surrealism and the post-Soviet mayhem into a specific source of identity. Initially conceived as "the Russian MTV" and broadcast for only five months between 1997 and 1998, *Dryoma* ended up being an extreme version of its Western counterpart (Artifact 00185[i]). Along with music videos and interviews with Western pop stars, it combined striptease, BDSM performances, Greek tragedy, classical philosophy, and parodies of TV commercials degenerating into absurd scenes of grotesque violence. It systematically violated Soviet and post-Soviet taboos while capturing and embracing the chaotic essence of the 1990s. It appropriated the language of Western popular culture while inventing a specifically post-Soviet one. And, as is often the case

---

[i] https://postsoviet90s.com/artifacts/the-russian-extreme-version-of-mtv

with the work of its main host and creator, Vladimir Epifantsev (spanning from independent theater, film, and art performance to action movies, TV series, and reality shows), it represented an extreme and primarily physical way of challenging commonly accepted norms and beliefs.[39]

The more or less explicit targets of *Dryoma*'s cynical provocations included the absurdity of the post-Soviet experience, the violence and corruption of the Soviet bureaucratic system, the ingenuity and immobility of older generations, and the newly discovered idiocy of mass consumerism. In some instances, post-Soviet decadence was associated with the deeply ironic invention of a countercultural identity. This was the case with the show's "fake commercials" and of Epifantsev's fake or misdubbed interviews with international stars like Einsturzende Neubauten, Elton John, and Aphex Twin. *Dryoma*'s commercials parodies followed the classical scheme, "choose X brand vs. the usual stuff"—except that in this case the usual stuff—detergent, toothpaste, migraine pills—was much better than the brand name. In the sketches, a desperate young man complained that his "brand name stuff" was not doing anything for him—until his girlfriend called in "Dr. Epifantsev," who saved the day by bringing in the usual non-brand product—which magically removed all the stains, rid the character from his toothache, treated his migraine. As was often the case, Epifantsev infused his performance with an element of surreal physicality: in the toothpaste commercial, he came in explaining that he used to have no teeth at all, but then—after he started using "the usual toothpaste"—he got a Hollywood smile. In the migraine pills one, he wore a fake hunchback, saying that since he started taking the "usual pills" he not only completely got rid of his headache, but even started growing a second head.

The interviews with international guests reflected the concept of a late-Soviet imaginary West, and the phenomenon—not uncommon in post-Soviet Russia—of a misreading, reinvention, or reappropriation of Western counter- and pop cultures. In the sense that they were mostly entirely made up or manipulated. Epifantsev did try to interview the members of the German industrial band Einsturzende Neubauten (literally, Collapsing New Buildings) while they were in Moscow—but the latter ended up refusing to answer his questions because, in a surprisingly "bourgeois way," they did not deem the place he had chosen for the interview—the muddy backyard of an abandoned building's construction site—an appropriate location for a television broadcast. As a result, Epifantsev decided to edit together some footage of him discussing the value of avant-garde art in the contemporary context, some other footage with him asking some questions in fake German—misdubbed into Russian—and a sequence in which the band members demanded to be brought back to their hotel room. In another case of misdubbing, Epifantsev turned Elton John into a *pochvennik*, a Russian nationalist writer. The thing he loved to do the most when visiting Moscow, Elton John explained in the Russian version—was to jump on an *elektrichka* and go spend some time in the Russian forest and look at the elks. Even better, he explained, he liked Russian *chipsy* and ate enormous amounts of them, and fed them to the elks—although the last time he did that the elks started biting voraciously the veins in his ankles, he lost an enormous amount of blood, almost died, and ended up in the hospital.[40]

The fake commercials in *Dryoma* undermined the idealization of anything Western or foreign and the obsession with brand names that characterized the early post-Soviet period; at the same time, the commercials parodies ridiculed the opposite tendency—that of nostalgic, uncritical views of the "good old Soviet times"—as the good old generic products had magical but ultimately grotesque effects. The "fake interviews" series reclaimed some of the symbols of late-Soviet and post-Soviet decadence and marginality related to alcoholic, drug, and youth subcultures—the crumbling building, the *elektrichka*—as marks of a certain comical form of "toughness" or authenticity.[41]

Both in Epifantsev's *Dryoma* and in Osipov's *Transil'vaniia bespokoit*, in different ways, a narrative about a "tougher," "more authentic," and more inaccessible homegrown counterculture, related to the bleakness and brutality of post-Soviet life, emerges. Indeed, *chernukha* and *bespredel* turn into paradoxical sources of identity as part of broader discourses of resistance and dissent associating these concepts with forms of authenticity and belief—in direct contrast to a post-Soviet reality that is perceived as increasingly virtual and inhuman as a result of the widespread commodification that the post-Soviet transition to capitalism and "Westernization" has seemingly brought about.

GORE AS A SOURCE OF AUTHENTICITY: DISCOURSES OF RESISTANCE

Chernukha—and more generally, violence and pain—becomes even more clearly associated with ideas of authenticity and identity in the context of new post-Soviet discourses of resistance and practices of dissent. This is particularly true for communities and ideas gravitating around Limonov's (and, up to 1998, Dugin's) NBP, which had a pioneering role in the shaping of post-Soviet protest culture. A good starting point to describe this dialectic tension between authenticity and virtual reality or manipulation is punk and alternative rock, with a specific focus on three iconic songs of the period: Egor Letov's "Moia oborona" (My Defense), Natalia Medvedeva's "Poedem na voinu!" (Let's Go to War!), and "Moskve ne khvataet krovi" (In Moscow There's Not Enough Blood) by the punk band Banda chetyryokh (Gang of Four). Letov's "Moia oborona" is a desperate, at the same time tender and dissonant, hymn to the possibility of seeking refuge in the untainted world of imagination and childhood in order to escape a reality that has been irretrievably reduced to pure materialism and appearance (Artifact 00199[j]).[42] Medvedeva's song is a paradoxical celebration of war as an escape from the mediocrity of modern life. With a deep, heart-wrenching voice, Medvedeva evokes romanticized

---

[j] https://postsoviet90s.com/artifacts/the-world-made-of-plastic-has-won

visions of recent conflicts, celebrating war as absolute freedom and a "beautiful way to die." From there, the lyrics seamlessly move to the post-Soviet *bespredel*—"the lawless streets of Moscow," with "dirty snow" and "danger in one's own house"—where the only way back to reality and meaning is embracing arbitrary violence and chaos as a new (quintessentially masculine and heroic) way of life (Artifact 00200[k]).[43] The third song, "Moskve ne khvataet krovi," by Banda chetyryokh, could be seen as a nasty development from the first two, or the third step of this post-Soviet dialectic of violence. Here, Letov's melancholy and desperate clinging to childhood dreams has turned into detached cynicism vis-à-vis the hopelessness of Moscow's working-class peripheries, and Medvedeva's dark, paradoxical romanticism has turned into raw anger. In a song that not by chance became the hymn of skinheads and soccer hooligans, "blood and fire" become the only possible tools for improving life conditions in a city that has become inhospitable and unrecognizable.[44]

This way of seeing *chernukha* and *bespredel* as a source of identity develops within countercultural communities and extends to mainstream media discourses. Letov, the lead singer of the Siberian punk band Grazhdanskaia oborona, who had cult status in the underground scene across Russia and beyond, joined Dugin and Limonov in 1994 as one of the founders of the NBP and started attacking Yeltsin's reforms and arguing for using the methods of the Italian Red Brigades to overthrow the government on mainstream TV.[45] Medvedeva was Limonov's third wife and, in addition to writing songs that became iconic for rebellious youths gravitating around the NBP and beyond, was also a media personality in her own right, invited as a guest on all of the main talk shows emerging in the early post-Soviet TV broadcasting system and regularly asked to comment on matters of culture, fashion, and taste.[46]

Limonov himself, in addition to being the leader of a radical political organization who eventually ended up spending two years in prison for illegal arms trade and alleged plans to overthrow the government, was a celebrity, a bestseller writer, and a media personality. And in his writing and public appearances he celebrated the beauty of street fighting, revolution, and war—while also advocating for turning the old dusty Russian literary tradition into punk and counterculture (Artifact 00192[l]; Artifact 00197[m]). *Limonka*, the independent newspaper released by the NBP—which was primarily sold in the same record stores where alternative kids bought their hard rock, punk, and heavy metal tapes—appropriated and discussed the aesthetics of the historical avant-gardes, Soviet propaganda, German Nazism, and Italian Fascism, and of all possible musical, artistic, and political countercultures that Russia arguably needed to catch up on (Artifact 00188[n]). While doing that, the newspaper encouraged its readers to create

---

[k] https://postsoviet90s.com/artifacts/let-s-go-to-war
[l] https://postsoviet90s.com/artifacts/novyi-vzgliad-violence-political-irony-and-national-pride
[m] https://postsoviet90s.com/artifacts/limonov-becomes-a-post-soviet-nationalist-rock-star
[n] https://postsoviet90s.com/artifacts/rise-you-cursed-people-the-aesthetics-of-limonka

their own counterculture, largely based on their everyday experience with violence and chaos (Artifact 00187[o]). On *Limonka*'s pages, Dugin called for creating a political avant-garde that would disregard ideological differences in order to unite all radicals who were ready to fight (and die) to put an end to the current systems. And while doing that, he advocated for continuing the legacy of Guy Debord and the Situationist International and their struggle against "the society of the spectacle" (Artifact 00186[p]).[47]

As far as the actual "direct actions" organized by the *natsboly* and their media coverage go, this paradoxical style translated into two opposite trends. On the one hand, the NBP aggressive rhetoric was used as proof that a "red-brown" (i.e., "fascist-communist") threat existed, an argument which, in its turn, was frequently used to dismiss any form of opposition to Yeltsin's radical economic reforms. On the other, the NBP direct actions soon acquired a component of heroism and martyrdom. A good example of this is the coverage of two famous actions organized by the *natsboly* in the 1990s. The first was the "attack" on the main architect of the shock therapy, Egor Gaidar, in January 1999. In the middle of Gaidar's speech at his party's yearly convention, in the exact moment in which he talked about the "real threat" to democracy coming from the national–communist alliance, a group of *natsboly* in the audience stood up and, while pointing their fists up, started yelling the slogan "This is how we will implement our reforms: Stalin! Beria! Gulag!"—until the security intervened and a struggle ensued. In the coverage of the incident on the main Russian news channel, the anchorman described what the viewers saw as "a brilliant confirmation that Gaidar was right," claiming that any weakening of Yeltsin's presidential power would result in a "red-Nazi" totalitarian state with widespread political repressions (Artifact 00202[q]). The second, a few months later, was the action against the film actor and director Nikita Mikhalkov, who was targeted by the *natsboly* for his support of the president of Kazakhstan, Nursultan Nazarbayev, whom they in turn accused of discriminations against the country's Russian minority. In this case, two NBP activists threw rotten eggs at Mikhalkov, who ran into the audience and proceeded to kick one of them in the head while two security guards held him down. The *natsboly* involved in the incident were sentenced to a few months in prison and the one who was assaulted by Mikhalkov suffered serious injuries—but this time the brutality of the director's reaction produced great scandal and won the two activists some public sympathy (Artifact 00202[r]).

Both tendencies—the dismissing of any form of opposition as a red-brown, communist–fascist "plague," and the heroic/self-sacrificing style of Russian protests—remained a defining feature of Russian public culture throughout the Putin era. Examples of the former include the delegitimization, in the early 2000s, of the anti-Putin coalition The

[o] https://postsoviet90s.com/artifacts/an-armed-paradise
[p] https://postsoviet90s.com/artifacts/a-conservative-revolutionary-avant-garde
[q] https://postsoviet90s.com/artifacts/stalin-beria-gulag-natsboly-against-gaidar-and-mikhalkov
[r] https://postsoviet90s.com/artifacts/stalin-beria-gulag-natsboly-against-gaidar-and-mikhalkov

Other Russia and the Dissenters' Marches by pro-government media and organizations, which frequently labeled them—and, as a consequence, any independent media and political groups—as a Western-funded anti-Russian "liberal-fascist" alliance. The "Nazi-communist" or, in its newer incarnation, the "Nazi-liberal," label was used to justify systematic political repressions and was later applied, as part of an anti-political ethos, to the 2011–13 Movement for Fair Elections, Aleksey Navalny, Euromaidan, and, most recently, to Ukraine in its entirety. As far as heroism and martyrdom go, these became a trademark of the *natsboly*'s political style, who became the protagonists of a "tragic street theater" by making themselves victims of state violence to prove that Putin's Russia was indeed a police state—and who later went on to fight as volunteers in Eastern Ukraine as part of a paradoxically similar (from their point of view) "search for authenticity." And this heroic/self-sacrificing tendency had a larger impact on other prominent forms of artistic protests, from the art collective Voina, to Pussy Riot and Pyotr Pavlensky.[48]

Finally, recurring references to gore and violence as sources of authenticity are also present in mainstream media discourses. A telling example of this is the making of an "anti-bourgeois hero"—the actor Sergey Bodrov Jr. (and his main cinematographic alter ego, the tender baby-faced sociopath Danila Bagrov from Aleksei Balabanov's blockbusters, *Brother 1 and 2*)—on Russian television (Artifact 00189[s]). It is an excerpt from the second episode of the new version of the popular talk show *Vzgliad*, which Bodrov co-hosted with Aleksandr Liubimov, one of the show's co-founders, in 1996–99. With the addition of Bodrov, *Vzgliad* started a new format, in which Liubimov, in a business suit, hosted from the desk of a traditional TV studio in the Ostankino tower, while Bodrov hosted a more "down-to-earth," informal, and overall youthful section of the show from a Moscow bar.

Vzgliad covered stories related to topical issues of violence, identity, and social inequality. In this context, Bodrov appeared to act as the voice of an "unfiltered" common sense and resentment, making frequent despising remarks about the "bourgeois" and the wealthy and tacky "new Russians"—and barely resisting the temptation of "cussing" at the injustices described in the various interviews and reportages. In contrast, Liubimov acted as the representative of a different—more middle-class, middle-aged, or bourgeois—type of common sense.

Bodrov's "populism" was devoid of the chauvinism and xenophobia later associated with his character Danila from the *Brother* saga. But like Danila, "Bodrov-the-TV-personality" stood for a kind of "new sincerity" or strive for authenticity. The excerpt included in my selection is preceded by interviews with a young Belorusian political activist who left the country to escape repressions and with a former leader of

[s] https://postsoviet90s.com/artifacts/the-making-of-an-anti-bourgeois-hero

FIGURE 2 Video from Artifact 00189.[1] Excerpt from an early episode (the second) of a new version of the popular talk show *Vzgliad*, co-hosted by Aleksandr Liubimov and Sergey Bodrov Jr., which aired weekly on the TV channel ORT in 1996–99.

the student democratic movement at Moscow State University—with comments from Liubimov and the musician Andrey Makarevich. The conversation revolves around the ideas of "romanticism" and youth rebellion, and at the end, Bodrov remarks that there is something "touchingly old-fashioned" about this idea, because being "romantic" or "rebellious" is not fashionable among young people anymore: what is really "stylish" now is "to be a bourgeois." The next story shifts, somewhat unexpectedly, to a different kind of "romanticism" or authenticity: that of a guy who cut his finger off in order to convince his girlfriend to quit heroin. From there, the participants end up discussing, among other things, the idea of resisting other forms of addiction, like the then emerging "computer networks." Strikingly, here the Internet stands as a quintessential embodiment of the pervasive "virtualization of reality" that the post-Soviet transition appears to have brought (see Figure 2).

CONCLUSION

In various media throughout the 1990s, *chernukha* and *bespredel*, gore and mayhem, play a crucial role in the definition of collective values and identities in post-Soviet Russia—either in the form of a paradoxical embracing of the dark, surreal essence of the

[1] https://postsoviet90s.com/artifacts/the-making-of-an-anti-bourgeois-hero

decade, of its demonizing—or as part of a search for the authenticity of extreme bodily experiences that are seen as a form of resistance to capitalism and commodification. This has, in turn, important consequences for the shaping of Russian public culture during the Putin era, including the normalization of transgression and "anti-PC" in mainstream media and more recent forms of "anti-globalist imperialism" at the levels of both official and popular culture.

Indeed, the episode that symbolically marks the end of the decade and establishes Putin as a new strong leader chosen to bring order and stability to the country has a lot to do with the manifold meaning ascribed to these categories. During a press conference in August 1999, soon after being nominated prime minister, and still relatively unknown, Putin stated that the Russian authorities would chase Chechen terrorists everywhere and, if necessary, would "waste them in the outhouse" ("*my i v sortire ikh zamochim*"). This infamous stylistic fall was considered highly inappropriate for the context and the official role that Putin held, and at the same time had a crucial role in establishing his popularity and paved the way for his first presidency a few months later—in that with this crass, violent expression Putin was perceived to have successfully channeled, "without mincing words," a dominant sense of despair among the Russian public (Artifact 00211[u]).[49] Furthermore, by using an expression belonging to the prison underworld, Putin surreptitiously (if not consciously) established himself as a "strongman" who could bring the lawlessness and chaos of the 1990s to an end *precisely* because he was a typical product of that reality and was able to master its criminal code.

According to Ilya Kukulin, Putin's "dual identity"—which survives in the eye of the public opinion today—is connected to cultural mythologies surrounding such diverse phenomena as the performances of the rock band Lyube, Limonov's prose, and Vladimir Vysotsky's performance as Gleb Zheglov, the detective/"strongman"/outlaw from the popular TV series *Mesto vstrechi izmenit' nel'zia* (The Meeting Place Cannot Be Changed, 1979).[50] This duality extends to more or less officially sanctioned forms of patriotic transgression and fierce "anti-PC" that include the performances and public statements of the writer Zakhar Prilepin, the rap collective 25/17, and the leader of the pro-Putin bikers gang *Nochnye volki* (Night Wolves), "Khirurg" ("The Surgeon")—as well as those of more institutional actors like Russia's foreign office press secretary Maria Zakharova and the Minister of Foreign Affairs Sergey Lavrov.[51]

Finally, these paradoxical forms of transgressive or countercultural nationalism involve quite literal appropriations of cold war tropes from Western fantasy and sci-fi literature, film, and role-playing games like *Lord of the Rings* and *Star Wars*—which also more or less explicitly consolidated a pop culture vision of the Soviet Union or Russia as a stereotypical "Evil Empire." These include some of the performances of the

---

[u] https://postsoviet90s.com/artifacts/vladimir-putin-brings-criminal-slang-and-attitude-to-mainstream-russian-tv

patriotic postmodern writer and "punk-bard" Mikhail Elizarov, who in one of his songs calls, ironically, for recuperating a typically Soviet or Russian "Orc identity"—as well as discussions within online fan clubs and conservative groups about the possibility of self-identifying, as Russians, with one or the other breed of supervillains from said fantasy or sci-fi universes.[52] This plethora of cultural mythologies contributes to creating, both locally and globally, a widespread (self-)orientalizing view of Putin's Russia, and Russians more generally, as obscurantist "agents of chaos" rebelling against the definitive triumph of "Western values."[53] In this regard, through the categories of *chernukha* and *bespredel*, the foundation myth of the "tumultuous 1990s" (*likhie devianostye*) helps define post-Soviet identity as a paradoxical form of hegemonic, and officially sanctioned, countercultural nationalism.

Notes

1 *Chernukha* is a derogatory term used to label graphic, morbid, or sensationalistic portrayals of sex and violence in Russian literature, film, and television in the 1980s and 1990s.

2 See Agamben, *Homo Sacer*, 119–88 (here: 119).

3 See Reddaway and Glinski, *The Tragedy*.

4 On this matter, see Vernant, "Ambiguity."

5 See Prozorov, *The Ethics*, 38–197 (here, 42). *Bespredel*—"mayhem" or "chaos"—means, literally, "lack of boundaries" or "lack of limits" and has become commonly associated in Russia with the lawlessness, absurdity, and unpredictability of the 1990s and the post-Soviet experience more broadly.

6 See Borenstein, *Overkill*, 1–23 (here 2; 23).

7 On "revolutionary negativity" and its possible devolution into imperialism, see: Magun, *Negative*; "Imperializatsiia."

8 See Belekhov, "Gazeta." Current and historical print runs and editors are available at www.sovsekretno.ru/editors/.

9 *Detektiv i politika* was only published through 1992.

10 See "Taina kutuzovskogo."

11 See Semyonov, "Sovershenno otkryto" and artifact discussion.

12 Semyonov, "Sovershenno otkryto."

13 See: Kapustsinskii, "Usazhivaias"; Berdiaev, "O russkom"; Zamiatin, "Iz bloknotov." In later issues throughout the 1990s, the number of more salacious or sensationalist materials about UFOs, impotence, prostitution, and vitamins for "sexual and intellectual performance" grew exponentially.

14 On these issues, see: Borenstein, *Overkill*; Goscilo, *Dehexing*; Lovell, *The Russian Reading*.

15 See Bykov, "Osnovnye"; Gorham, *After Newspeak*. As an example of this, Eduard Limonov explains how two of his short stories published in the first issue of *Detektiv i politika* had to be reprinted because the publication's editors, following a common practice, had entirely rewritten them in a neutral style deprived of the author's specific idiosyncrasies and, as a consequence, of any originality or wit. See Limonov, *Kniga mertvykh*, 190–91.

16 See Dodolev, "Belyi tanets"; "Belyi tanets, samoi gromkoi"; "Pervaia publikatsiia."

17 See Dodolev, "Sud"; "O narushenii." In 1994, *Novyi vzgliad* became the subject of a government investigation and was accused of publishing materials that constituted "a serious threat to the moral interests of children and youths."

18 In her articles, Novodvorskaya argued that Russia, Uzbekistan, and Turkmenistan were uncivilized countries that did not deserve independence, that segregation, colonization, and the genocide of indigenous people are justifiable, and that civilized nations (like England and the United States) should be allowed to invade uncivilized ones (like Iraq). She claimed that Russians were, after Ivan the Terrible, a naturally "manic depressive" people, and argued that the 10 million free people left should secede from

the rest of the country in order to avoid cohabitating with "the triumphant red-brown majority." Because of her articles, Novodvorskaya was prosecuted for "advocating for civil war" and "fomenting interethnic hostility." In response to these accusations, she explained that in *Novyi vzgliad* "all journalists were ironically assigned a role: they presented me as the main extremist and Limonov as the main grenade launcher—and we were required to write only in a paradoxical way." See: Novodvorskaya, "Ne otdadim"; "Rossiia"; "Gore"; "Valeriia Novodvorskaia."

19 See: Limonov, "Psy." Dodolev, *Limoniana*. *Limonka* is a slang word for "grenade," and, in this case, a wordplay on the writer's pseudonym, derived from the word "lemon" in association with the "sourness" of his writing.

20 Mogutin, "Vospominaniia"; "Eduard." On Limonov's early reception in post-Soviet Russia, see also: Wakamiya, *Locating*; Essig, *Queer*, 3–25, 123–61. On Mogutin's trajectory more generally, see: Slavamogutin.com; Mogutin, "The Queer"; Gessen, *Dead*, 165–85. A *gopnik* is "a member of a delinquent subculture in Russia, Ukraine, Belarus, and in other former Soviet republics—a young man (or a woman, a gopnitsa) of working-class background who usually lives in suburban areas and comes from a family of poor education and income" ("Gopnik"). Some of the *gopnik*'s distinguishing features and behaviors starting in the 1980s include: wearing Adidas tracksuits, squatting to avoid sitting on the cold ground, eating sunflower seeds (*semechki*).

21 See: Mogutin, "Bez intelligentov."

22 Mogutin, "Griaznye"; "Alla"; "Mogutin zhiv'em."

23 See Gessen, 165–85; Mogutin, "Chechenskii"; Dodolev, "Delo Mogutina"; "1995. Chechenskii uzel." Like Novodvorskaya, Mogutin was prosecuted for "fomenting interethnic hostility."

24 See Mogutin, "Gruppovukha"; "Sis'ki."

25 Mogutin, "Sis'ki."

26 On *stiob* and its evolution in the post-Soviet period, see: Yurchak, *Everything Was*; Lipovetsky, *Paralogii*; Gabowitsch, "Fascism"; Hemment, *Youth Politics*; and Fenghi, *It Will Be Fun*.

27 See note 6.

28 See Magun, *Negative*.

29 See "Delo Muryleva."

30 See: "Politologi"; "Referendum." On Kuryokhin: Yurchak, "A Parasite"; Kan, *Kurekhin*; Kushnir, *Sergei Kurekhin*.

31 See "Esly vy romantik," 82.

32 See "Tainy veka"; Vorob'evskii, "Dugin i brat"; "A. Dugin. O Vorob'evskom i o programme."

33 See Yurchak, "A Parasite."

34 See: "Riskovannye puteshestviia"; "Ded Moroz"; "Khochu prodat'"; "Spasaite zhen"; "P'ianaia draka"; "Ispoved' babushki"; "Antonov kormitsia."

35 See Dudinskii, "Desiat' dnei." On the Iuzhinskii circle, see: Laruelle, "The Iuzhinskii"; Clover, *Black Wind*, 151–75.

36 See "Bul'varnaia pressa."

37 On counterpublics, see Warner, "Publics."

38 See: *Transil'vaniia bespokoit*; "Georgii Osipov: 'My strazhi poroga imperii'"; "Garik Osipov: 'Ia vosprinimal.'"

39 See "Vladimir Epifantsev Kak vse nachinalos' (Telekanal Dozhd')." Epifantsev's work as an actor reflects a kind of performative obsession with violence, grotesque physicality, and aggressive masculinity. He can be seen in this sense as a kind of Meierkhol'dian, highly physical actor who was able to embody some of the main contradictions of the post-Soviet experience.

40 See "The Russian (Extreme) MTV."

41 Literary echoes of this "mythology of marginality" can be found in authors like Venedikt Erofeev, Eduard Limonov, Yuri Mamleev.

42 Letov, "Moia oborona."

43 Medvedeva, "Poedem na voinu!"

44 Banda chetyrekh, "Moskve ne khvataet."

45 See Letov, "Moia oborona": Artifact commentary.

46 See, for instance: "Akuly pera"; "Nataliia Medvedeva. 'Pro eto pri svechakh s Elenoi Khangoi.'" For an example of *chernukha* as a source of identity and "provincial romanticism" from pop music, see Mumiy Troll, "Utekai."

47 See: Dugin, "Novye"; "Gi Debor"; Tsvetkov, "Skinkhedy."

48 On Limonov, Dugin, Tsvetkov, Letov, Medvedeva, and on the NBP more generally, see Fenghi, *It Will Be Fun*.

49 See Gorham, *After Newspeak*, 131–65.

50 See Kukulin, "Longing for"; on the combination of machismo and "tricksterism" characterizing Putin's public image, see also Goscilo, *Putin as Celebrity*.

51 Kukulin, "Cultural Shifts" (here: 230). See also: Borenstein, *Plots*, 133–79; Lipovetsky, *Paralogii*, 247, 490–91, 499, 502–3, 526–27; Hemment, "Satirical strikes."

52 Borenstein, *Soviet Self-Hatred*, 121–53. A less-known albeit striking example of this patriotic reclaiming of Western subcultures is the symbol of Dugin's staunchly imperialistic Eurasia movement, the eight-pointed star, which is said to have been inspired, among other things, by the symbol of chaos from Moorcock's multiverse and *World of Warcraft*.

53 See Borenstein, *Soviet Self-Hatred*, 121–53; Budraitskis, *Dissidents*, 7–30.

Works Cited

"1995. Chechenskii uzel. Mogutin." *Artprotest.org*. Accessed October 21, 2024. https://web.archive.org/web/20180317041340/http://artprotest.org/cgi-bin/news.pl?&id=3430.

"A. Dugin. O Vorob'evskom i o programme Tainy veka." *Arcto.ru*. May 21, 1999. Accessed October 21, 2024. https://arctogaia.org.ru/article/862/.

"Akuly pera. Gost' v studii – Nataliia Medvedeva." TV-6. December 1995.

Agamben, Giorgio. *Homo Sacer: Sovereign Power and Bare Life*. Stanford, CA: Stanford University Press, 1998.

"Antonov kormilsia sobsvennym telom." *Megapolis-ekspress* 50, no. 277 (November 27, 1995).

Banda chetyrekh. "Moskve ne khvataet krovi." *Banda.lenin.ru*. 1997. Accessed October 21, 2024. http://banda.lenin.ru./texts.htm.

Belekhov, Leonid. "Gazeta, kotoraia tak nikomu i ne poklonilas'." *Sovsekretno.ru*. Accessed October 21, 2024. https://www.sovsekretno.ru/history/.

Berdiaev, Nikolai. "O russkom natsional'nom soznanii." *Sovershenno sekretno*, no. 3 (December 1989): 14–15.

Borenstein, Eliot. *Overkill: Sex and Violence in Contemporary Russian Popular Culture*. Ithaca, NY: Cornell University Press, 2007.

Borenstein, Eliot. *Plots against Russia: Conspiracy and Fantasy after Socialism*. Ithaca, NY: Cornell University Press, 2019.

Borenstein, Eliot. *Soviet Self-Hatred: The Secret Identities of Postsocialism in Contemporary Russia*. Ithaca, NY: Cornell University Press, 2023.

Bykov, Dmitry. "Osnovnye tendentsii SMI v 1987 godu." *Novyi vzgliad* 34 (December 27, 1997).

Budraitskis, Ilya. *Dissidents among Dissidents: Ideology, Politics and the Left in Post-Soviet Russia*. New York; London: Verso, 2022.

Clover, Charles. *Black Wind, White Snow: The Rise of Russia's New Nationalism*. New Haven, CT: Yale University Press, 2016.

"Ded Moroz soshel s uma. A Snegurochka zaberemenela." *Megapolis-ekspress*, no. 50 (328): December, 1996. 5.

"Delo Muryleva. Smert' za kvartiry" (The Murylev Case. Death for Apartments), June 24, 1995, TV. First episode of the true crime show *Kriminal'naia Rossiia* (NTV, 1995–2002, with various later versions on TVS, Pervyi kanal, and others). Artifact 00184.[v]

Dodolev, Evgenii. "Belyi tanets, istoriia samoi gromkoi stati o prostitutkakh." *Moskovskii komsomolets* (December 3, 2019).

Dodolev, Evgenii . "Belyi tanets." *Moskovskii komsomolets* (November 19, 1986). Artifact 00191.[w]

[v] https://postsoviet90s.com/artifacts/yeltsin-s-orderly-sanitar-yeltsina

[w] https://postsoviet90s.com/artifacts/the-first-article-on-prostitution-in-the-soviet-union

Dodolev, Evgenii . "Delo Mogutina." *Novyi vzgliad*, no. 35 (September 23, 1995).

Dodolev, Evgenii . "Pervaia publikatsiia pro sovetskikh prostitutok v "Moskovskom komsomol'tse." YouTube. January 10, 2009. https://www.youtube.com/watch?v=BcOfVdy5RFw. [Originally broadcast on NTV+, "Kto est' kto."]

Dodolev, Evgenii . "Sud da delo." *Novyi vzgliad*, no. 30 (August 6, 1994).

Dodolev, Evgenii . *Limoniana, ili neizvestnyi Limonov*. Moscow: Zebra-E, 2012.

Dudinskii, Igor. "Bul'varnaia pressa i natsional'naia ideia." *Zavtra* (August 7, 2000). [Interview with Igor Dudinsky conducted by Liudmila Serova].

Dudinskii, Igor. "Desiat' dnei v ob"iat'iakh ved'mi: Ira Trubina iz bezimiannoi mogily prishla v odnu iz moskovskikh kvartiry." *Megapolis-ekspress* 17, no. 244 (April 26, 1995): 12. Artifact 00203.[x]

Dugin, Aleksandr. "Gi Debor mertv. Spektakl' prodolzhaetsia." *Limonka* 14 (May 1995).

Dugin, Aleksandr. "Novye protiv starykh." *Limonka* 1 (November 1994). Artifact 00186.[y]

"Esli vy romantik, vy—fashist! Rassuzhdeniia o postmodernizme. Interv'iu s Sergeem Kurekhinym." *Elementy*, no. 8 (1996/97): 83–6. Artifact 00193.[z]

Essig, Laurie. *Queer in Russia: A Story of Sex, Self, and the Other*. Durham, NC: Duke University Press, 1999.

Fenghi, Fabrizio. *It Will Be Fun and Terrifying: Nationalism and Protest in Post-Soviet Russia*. Madison: University of Wisconsin Press, 2020.

Gabowitsch, Mischa. "Fascism as Stiob." *Kultura*, no. 4 (December 2009).

"Garik Osipov: 'Ia vosprinimal Krouli kak kosmicheskoe telo.'" *Thelema.ru*. 2011.

"Georgii Osipov: 'My strazhi poroga imperii,'" *Zavtra* 3, no. 268 (January 19, 1999).

Gessen, Masha. *Dead Again: The Russian Intelligentsia after Communism*. London: Verso, 1997.

"Gopnik." Wikipedia. Accessed October 21, 2024. https://en.wikipedia.org/wiki/Gopnik#:~:text=A%20gopnik%20(Russian%3A%20гопник%2C,man%20(or%20a%20woman%2C%20a.

Gorham, Michael. *After Newspeak: Language Culture and Politics in Russia from Gorbachev to Putin*. Ithaca, NY: Cornell University Press, 2014.

Goscilo, Helena. *Dehexing Sex: Russian Womanhood during and after Glasnost*. Ann Arbor: University of Michigan Press, 1996.

Goscilo, Helena. *Putin as Celebrity and Cultural Icon*. New York: Routledge, 2013.

Hemment, Julie. *Youth Politics in Putin's Russia: Producing Patriots and Entrepreneurs*. Bloomington: Indiana University Press, 2015.

Hemment, Julie. "Satirical Strikes and Deadpanning Diplomats: Stiob as Geopolitical Performance in Russia–US Relations." *PoLAR: Political and Legal Anthropology Review* 45, no. 2 (2022): 201–23.

"Ispoved' babushki russkogo porno." *Megapolis-ekspress* 3, no. 435 (January 27, 1999): 13.

Kan, Aleksandr. *Kurekhin. Shkiper o Kapitane*. St. Petersburg: Amfora, 2012.

Kapustsinskii, Ryshard. "Usazhivaias' za party…" *Sovershenno sekretno*, no. 1 (June 1989): 5.

"Khochu prodat' kusok sebia." *Megapolis-ekspress* 39, no. 317 (October 1996): 4.

Kukulin, Ilya. "Cultural Shifts in Russia since 2010: Messianic Cynicism and Paradigms of Artistic Resistance." *Russian Literature* 96–98 (February–May 2018): 221–54.

Kukulin, Ilya. "Longing for Fear and Darkness: 'Oppositional Grassroots Stalinism' of the 1970s–1980s and Its Influence on Legitimizing Political Elites in Today's Russia." In *Post-Soviet Nostalgia: Confronting the Empire's Legacies*, edited by Otto Boele, Boris Noordenbos, and Ksenia Robbe, 89–114. New York: Routledge, 2019.

Kushnir, Aleksandr. *Sergei Kurekhin. Bezumnaia mekhanika russkogo roka*. Moscow: Berstel'man Media Moscau, 2013.

Laruelle, Marlène. "The Iuzhinskii Circle: Far-Right Metaphysics in the Soviet Underground and Its Legacy Today." *Russian Review* 74, no. 4 (2015): 563–80.

Letov, Egor. "Moia oborona." *Gr-oborona.ru*. 1989. gr-oborona.ru/texts/1056898718.html. Artifact 00199.[aa]

[x] https://postsoviet90s.com/artifacts/megapolis-ekspress-urban-exoticism-and-national-pride-52bb8047-7159-4f5e-9d80-5236142523bc

[y] https://postsoviet90s.com/artifacts/a-conservative-revolutionary-avant-garde

[z] https://postsoviet90s.com/artifacts/romantics-and-fascists

[aa] https://postsoviet90s.com/artifacts/the-world-made-of-plastic-has-won

Limonov, Eduard. *Kniga mertvykh*. Saint Petersburg: Limbus Press, 2000.

Limonov, Eduard. "Psy voiny." *Novyi vzgliad*, no. 19 (May 22, 1993).

Lipovetsky, Mark. *Paralogii. Transformatsii (post)modernistskogo diskursa v russkoi kul'ture 1920–2000-kh godov*. Moscow: Novoe literaturnoe obozrenie, 2008.

Lovell, Stephen. *The Russian Reading Revolution: Print Culture in the Soviet and Post-Soviet Eras*. New York: St. Martin's Press, 2000.

Magun, Artemy. "Imperializatsiia (Poniatie imperii i sovremennyi mir)." *Polis: Politicheskie issledovaniia* 2 (2007): 63–80.

Magun, Artemy. *Negative Revolution: Modern Political Subject and Its Fate after the Cold War*. New York: Bloomsbury Academic, 2013.

Medvedeva, Nataliia. "Poedem na voinu!". YouTube, July 29, 2011. Original recording: 1995. https://www.youtube.com/watch?v=4v7TPPJGayo. Artifact 00200[bb].

"*Megapolis-ekspress*: The Exotics of Urban Life." Artifact 00203[cc].

Mogutin, Iaroslav. "The Queer Russian Photographer Who Made Global Headlines in the 90s." *i-D Magazine* November 7, 2022. https://i-d.co/article/slava-mogutin-photography/.

Mogutin, Iaroslav. "Alla Pugacheva liubit golubykh, a sama ona rozovaia." *Novyi vzgliad*, no. 41 (October 9, 1993).

Mogutin, Iaroslav. "Bez intelligentov, utopia." *Novyi vzgliad*, no. 36 (September 30, 1995). [First published in: *Limonka*, no. 1 (November 1994)]

Mogutin, Iaroslav. "Chechenskii uzel. 13 tezisov." *Novyi vzgliad*, no. 3 (January 28, 1992). Artifact 00058.[dd]

Mogutin, Iaroslav. "Eduard Limonov, sovetsko-frantsuzskii natsional'nyi geroi." *Novyi vzgliad*, no. 101 (1992).

Mogutin, Iaroslav. "Griaznye kontsy." *Novyi vzgliad*, no. 34 (September 4, 1993).

Mogutin, Iaroslav. "Gruppovukha kak obraz mysli." *Novyi vzgliad*, no. 129 (1994).

Mogutin, Iaroslav. "Mogutin zhiv'em." *Novyi vzgliad*, no. 42 (October 23, 1993).

Mogutin, Iaroslav. "Sis'ki v teste." *Novyi vzgliad*, no. 117 (1993). Artifact 00192.[ee]

Mogutin, Iaroslav. "Vospominaniia russkogo panka, ili, avtoportret bandita v molodosti." In *U nas byla velikaia epokha*, by Eduard Limonov, 158–87. Moscow: Konets Veka, 1994.

Mumiy Troll. "Utekai." 1997. Artifact 00201.[ff]

"Nataliia Medvedeva. 'Pro eto pri svechakh s Elenoi Khangoi.'" NTV. November 1999. Accessed October 21, 2024. YouTube. https://www.youtube.com/watch?v=iEZvhBR5fDg.

Novodvorskaia, Valeriia. "Gore pobediteliam." *Novyi vzgliad*, no. 24 (June 25, 1994).

Novodvorskaia, Valeriia. "Ne otdadim nashe pravo nalevo!" *Novyi vzgliad*, no. 33 (August 28, 1993).

Novodvorskaia, Valeriia. "Rossiia no. 6." *Novyi vzgliad*, no. 1 (January 15, 1994).

"O narushenii pravovykh i eticheskikh norm v publikatsiiakh ezhenedel'nika *Novyi vzgliad*. Reshenie." Sudebnaia palata po informatsionnym sporam, no. 7(d) (March 17, 1994).

Pelevin, Victor. *Generation P.* Moscow: Vagrius, 1999. Translated into English as *Homo Zapiens* (New York: Penguin Books, 2002).

"P'ianaia draka v kosmose." *Megapolis-ekspress* 3, no. 435 (January 27, 1999): 13.

"Politologi Ibis i Anubis (Dugin i Kurekhin) vybory 1995." YouTube. September 17, 2016. https://www.youtube.com/watch?v=cdiLQLEeLUs. Artifact 00194[gg].

Prozorov, Sergei. *The Ethics of Postcommunism: History and Social Praxis in Russia*. Basingstoke, Hampshire: Palgrave Macmillan, 2009.

[bb] https://postsoviet90s.com/artifacts/let-s-go-to-war

[cc] https://postsoviet90s.com/artifacts/megapolis-ekspress-urban-exoticism-and-national-pride-52bb8047-7159-4f5e-9d80-5236142523bc

[dd] https://postsoviet90s.com/artifacts/the-chechen-knot-13-theses

[ee] https://postsoviet90s.com/artifacts/novyi-vzgliad-violence-political-irony-and-national-pride

[ff] https://postsoviet90s.com/artifacts/mumiy-troll-s-breakthrough-utekai-take-off-becomes-the-song-of-the-year-1997

[gg] https://postsoviet90s.com/artifacts/what-is-concealed-will-be-revealed-kurekhin-s-and-dugin-s-post-ironic-political-campaign-in-saint-petersburg

"Referendum 1993: The "Yes Yes No Yes" campaign." Artifact 00039.[hh]

Reddaway, Peter, and Dmitri Glinski. *The Tragedy of Russia's Reforms: Market Bolshevism against Democracy*. Washington, DC: United States Institute of Peace Press, 2001.

"Riskovannye puteshestviia: V Moskve poiavilis' pervye nekronavty." *Megapolis-ekspress* 18, no. 245 (May 1995): 12.

"The Russian (Extreme) MTV." ["Drëma." TV-6. 1997–98. Selection.]. Artifact 00185.[ii]

Semyonov, Iulian. "Sovershenno otkryto." *Sovershenno sekretno*, no. 1 (June 1989): 2. Artifact 00190.[jj]

Slavamogutin.com. [Yaroslav Mogutin's website, focusing primarily on his photography and on his work as a multimedia artist in NYC starting in 1995 ca.]

"Spasaite zhen ot oborotnei." *Megapolis-ekspress* 23, no. 301 (March (?) 1996): 14.

"Taina kutuzovskogo prospekta." *Sovershenno sekretno*, no. 1 (June 1989): 1. Cover included in Artifact 00190.[kk]

"Tainy veka. Mistika Reikha: taina zelenogo drakona." Pervyi kanal, Chetvertyi kanal. 1992–1993 (?). YouTube. March 1, 2013. https://www.youtube.com/watch?v=jHg-fhNSe1Y&list=PLrdZBfBRFMoL8XyNsjyWBqPKxghGaYMqz&index=4. Artifact 00191.[ll]

"Transil'vaniia bespokoit." *Radio 101 FM*. December 31, 1997. New Year's Episode. Artifact 00204.[mm]

Tsvetkov, Aleksei. "Skinkhedy." *Limonka* 61 (March 1997). Artifact 00187.[nn]

"Valeriia Novodvorskaia: 'Da zdravstvuet Ukraina, potomu chto ia vam ochen' zaviduiu.'" Newzz.in.ua. July 14, 2009. https://web.archive.org/web/20120522112725/http://newzz.in.ua/main/1148831211-valerija-novodvorskaja-da-zdravstvuet-ukraina.html.

Vernant, Jean-Pierre. "Ambiguity and Reversal: On the Enigmatic Structure of Oedipus Rex." In *Myth and Tragedy in Ancient Greece*, edited by Jean-Pierre Vernant and Pierre Vidal-Naquet, 113–140. New York: Zone Books, 1990.

"Kak vse nachinalos' Vladimir Epifantsev." YouTube. April 12, 2022. https://www.youtube.com/watch?v=GrThlJA898Y.

Vorob'evskii, Iurii. "Dugin i brat Markion." Livejournal.com. March 8, 2019. https://swinopes.livejournal.com/258569.html.

Wakamiya, Lisa Ryoko. *Locating Exiled Writers in Contemporary Russian Literature: Exiles at Home*. New York: Palgrave Macmillan, 2009.

Warner, Michael. "Publics and Counterpublics." *Public Culture* 14, no. 1 (2002): 49–90.

Yurchak, Aleksei. "A Parasite from Outer Space: How Sergei Kurekhin Proved That Lenin Was a Mushroom." *Slavic Review* 70, no. 2 (2011): 307–33.

Yurchak, Aleksei. *Everything Was Forever, Until It Was No More: The Last Soviet Generation*. Princeton, NJ: Princeton University Press, 2005.

Zamiatin, Evgenii. "Iz bloknotov 1914–1928 godov." *Sovershenno sekretno* 1, no. 8 (1990): 26–7.

[hh] https://postsoviet90s.com/artifacts/referendum-1993-the-yes-yes-no-yes-campaign

[ii] https://postsoviet90s.com/artifacts/the-russian-extreme-version-of-mtv

[jj] https://postsoviet90s.com/artifacts/top-secret-investigative-journalism-and-true-crime-during-perestroika

[kk] https://postsoviet90s.com/artifacts/top-secret-investigative-journalism-and-true-crime-during-perestroika

[ll] https://postsoviet90s.com/artifacts/the-mysteries-of-the-century-post-truth-and-mystical-nazism-on-russian-tv

[mm] https://postsoviet90s.com/artifacts/transilvania-is-bothering-you-on-radio-101-fm-40e4a7e9-8aed-42f2-8dab-61c744b5f23d

[nn] https://postsoviet90s.com/artifacts/an-armed-paradise

CHAPTER 4
The Rock-and-Roll State: Popular Music, Print Media, and Soviet Bureaucracy

Rita Safariants

Shocking much of the civilized world with its unrelenting brutality, Putin's invasion of Ukraine in February 2022 has polarized virtually every faction of Russian cultural life. One surprising byproduct of the war has been the ideological division within the popular music and entertainment industries, which, for the most part, have remained largely apolitical since the collapse of the USSR. The political polarization that has materialized in Russian popular music in the wake of the war has not followed the predictable formula of traditional mainstays on state-controlled television accepting Russia's position, while performers in more "underground" genres oppose the official narrative. Just like many Russian families,[1] Russian popular music split into two distinct camps: those who support, and those who oppose, the war and the actions of the Russian Federation, disrupting the implicit political spectrum of post-Soviet popular culture, in which mainstream genres like pop, patriotic rock, and comedy toe the Kremlin line, while the more transgressive rock, punk, and rap present as liberal and Western leaning.

Arguably the most dramatic inversion of the above schema came from an Instagram post by popular Soviet performer Alla Pugacheva, the ultimate diva of Russian pop music, in which she asked the Russian government to officially brand her a "foreign agent" in support of her husband, the comedian Maksim Galkin, who has publicly criticized the war.[2] Having enjoyed continued support from audiences and government structures for most of her career, Pugacheva has since been shunned by official media for her position on the war and for her choice to leave Russia. In March 2022 the pop legend publicized her decision to relocate to Israel with her family, which spurred an astonishing onslaught of negative publicity for the couple in official Russian media, given Pugacheva and Galkin's previous positions as decades-old household names and media darlings.[3]

On the other side of the spectrum, previously outspoken and irreverent rock musicians like Sergei Shnurov, Oleg Garkusha, Viacheslav Butusov, and Garik Sukachev, who established their creative voices in opposing the ideologically suffocating Soviet regime, have been, if not outright supporting, then, at the very least, condoning their country's military actions in Ukraine. On July 7, 2022, Sukachev, the politically controversial lead singer of the Moscow-based rock band Brigada-S, released a music video tribute to the 1994 song "I am staying" ("*Ia ostaius*'") by the Russian heavy metal band Black Obelisk (*Chernyi Obelisk*), whose lead singer Anatolii Krupnov died of a heart attack twenty-five years prior. Sukachev rolled out the commemorative project on the anniversary of Krupnov's passing but considering the mass emigration of Russians following Putin's invasion of Ukraine, the tribute acquired an increasingly aggressive political tone. The project, for which Sukachev recruited close to two dozen Soviet-era and contemporary rock musicians along with the VGTRK children's choir, has been described as a "manifesto" of those choosing to remain in Russia in the wake of the war, as well as a reproach of those who chose to flee.[4] The use of the hashtag *#Яостаюсь* (*#IAmStaying*), which is featured prominently in Sukachev's music video, characterizes the participating musicians as loyal patriots of their country, further stratifying Russia's sharply divided popular media and entertainment community. The timing of Sukachev's release is furthermore not accidental: coming on the same day as Russia's official list of banned musical artists, published by St. Petersburg's online news source *Fontanka*.[5] The message of the Black Obelisk cover is unmistakably clear: the aging members of the late-Soviet rock underground are voicing their support for their country, government, and president in their decision to wage war on a peaceful neighbor.

At first glance it may seem surprising that a large swathe of the late-Soviet underground community that made rock music a symbol of freedom and change for the perestroika generation is aligning itself with a totalitarian and ideologically isolationist political leader. The genre of rock music itself, with its Anglo-American countercultural roots, may seem an unlikely vehicle for encouraging nationalist militaristic fervor. However, the sociocultural conditions under which rock music flourished in the Soviet Union have consistently worked to temper its politically transgressive potential, framing Sukachev's rock-infused pro-war propaganda as an historical inevitability, rather than an anomaly. Moreover, Sukachev's choice to patriotically resurrect a musical text that originated in the early post-Soviet 1990s, a time of political tumult, economic scarcity, violence, and uncertainty, is another manifestation of the meticulously calculated political message that *#IAmStaying* is meant to impart. The project reflects the historical imperative for both the war and the rock community's patriotic position as an antidote to Russia's collective trauma following the collapse of the USSR. *#IAmStaying* stages a semblance of patriotic unity, an unchanging love of country, and warns any potential dissenters that change and cultural progress are best achieved in collaboration with government power structures. Ultimately, Sukachev's project advertises the same trajectory that Soviet rock music had followed from its inception. In investigating the bureaucratic mechanisms behind the mainstream ascent of rock culture during perestroika, this chapter will argue that Russo-Soviet popular music, no matter how clandestine or ideologically transgressive, has always existed in connection to the official state in both the Soviet and post-Soviet spheres of cultural production, often projecting the dominant governing structure's priorities and values.

THE SOVIET ROCK CLUB

Russia carries with it a long history of uniquely positioning itself against Western cultural, intellectual, and ideological trends, and routinely manifesting its exceptionalism through literature, art, and music. Just as the nineteenth-century Russian novel often served as a vehicle for national identity formation while polemicizing with Western trends, in the late-Soviet period it was replaced by popular culture, and particularly rock music, by way of its transnational character and mass appeal. By engaging a rapidly growing global genre while targeting the mainstream working-class consumer, the history of rock music in Russia is marked by galvanizing the attention of a wide array of sociopolitical institutions in the USSR. The end of the Second World War was instrumental in bringing new forms of popular culture into the Soviet Union, with Red Army troops returning home from Europe with Western jazz records and other scarce consumer goods, which were highly coveted by the war-weary and severely deprived Soviet public. The demand for Western popular music only grew with the following decades just as Soviet authorities continued to control the import of Western goods and media. Soon, a highly successful and vibrant black market and bootleg music industry developed in the USSR, infiltrating the material culture of post-war Soviet life. One of the most metaphorically poetic manifestations of this was the production of bootleg records. In the early 1960s and 1970s, musical recording equipment was hard to come by for the average consumer while the USSR was in the throes of a largescale plastic shortage. Out of sheer necessity, clandestinely circulated musical records smuggled from abroad were imprinted on used x-ray film, quite literally inscribing rock-and-roll on the images of Soviet corporeality, earning the widespread practice the evocative name "rock on bones".[6]

This thriving bootleg industry presented both an ideological, and more importantly, commercial threat to Soviet officials, who tried everything in their power to undermine the growing popularity of rock music. One strategy was public shaming and media censorship. A well-known satirical cartoon from the 1970s depicted a hippie youth as a drug and rock-and-roll fueled loafer, impeding Soviet ideological and economic progress while taking advantage of his aging parents. In his anthropological study of the last Soviet generation, Alexei Yurchak cites excerpts from Soviet databases that list the names of British and American rock bands that were to be banned from official public media. Some of these lists contained specific designators of moral and ideological corruption attached to each band. For example, according to the transcribed tables in Yurchak's book, the American rock band The Talking Heads were flagged for "myth of the Soviet" and "military threat" while Black Sabbath was cited for "violence" and "religious obscurantism."[7] To curb the profits of the growing black-market system that the demand for foreign popular music helped sustain, Soviet officials routinely made arrests for "speculation" (*spekuliatsiia*), any form of illegal commerce which was considered a criminal offense. As both a cultural and commercial commodity, Western rock, as well as its homegrown domestic variant, thrived under the conditions of being bureaucratically marked an ideological foe to the central values of the Soviet Union.

There were also many systemic and logistical barriers for rock music production and consumption in the USSR. Soviet amateur rock musicians who were not registered with local composers' unions were banned from performing in public, marginalized, and persecuted by the authorities in official media outlets. Amateur rock bands in Russia were not played on the radio or shown on television and therefore had to rely on bootlegging, unofficial apartment concerts, and simple word-of-mouth to sustain their makeshift recording and performing careers.[8] Yet despite being effectively banned by the state, by the early- to mid-1980s underground rock communities were flourishing across the USSR. It was therefore only a matter of time before the local municipal officials in large urban centers caught on to this trend and, gradually, instead of fighting the rapid proliferation of unofficial rock music culture in quotidian Soviet life, chose to work with it to maintain control of rock music's ideological and commercial potential. This dynamic challenges the general assumption that alternative culture was forced underground until Gorbachev's perestroika reforms, which encouraged a more collaborative approach between the state and unofficial art. As Sergei Zhuk has illustrated in his book *Rock and Roll and the Rocket City*, late-Soviet life was inundated with Western cultural products to such an extent that "the Westernization of Soviet popular culture and ideological discourse [occurred] not only in the capital cities, but also in the provinces."[9] The traditionally accepted model of Soviet institutional sabotage of fledgling proto-Western artistic movements shifted much earlier than the official policies of glasnost, providing infrastructural support to new trends in art, private business, and media. These practices existed in the decade leading up to perestroika, often in the most surprising places. One such place was the late-Soviet rock club, where the KGB played a well-documented role in its support and formation. The first rock club was formed in Leningrad in 1981, but by the late 1980s, most mid-size cities across the USSR had an analogous organization. The most culturally significant of these clubs were the Leningrad Rock Club (LRC) (Artifact 00171[a]; Figure 1), the Moscow Rock Laboratory, and the Sverdlovsk Rock Club, whose official organizational structures varied by geopolitical location.

But what were these organizations designed to do? And why would members of the seemingly countercultural movements like the late-Soviet rock and punk scenes want anything to do with the KGB? Serguei Oushakine in his study of Soviet *samizdat* makes the point that Soviet dissident culture, to which unofficial rock music was adjacent, "in a sense shared the symbolic field with the dominant discourse: it

---

[a] https://postsoviet90s.com/artifacts/leningrad-rock-club

FIGURE 1 Image from Artifact 00171.[b] A crowd waits to enter the Leningrad Rock Club at 13 Rubinstein Street in Leningrad sometime in the mid-1980s, likely before a rock performance.

echoed and amplified the rhetoric of the regime, rather than positioning itself outside or underneath it."[10] This essay will argue that the desire for this type of discursive collaboration was bilateral—with musicians and Soviet security agencies maintaining symbiotic interests in cooperating to support the rock music industry in the USSR.

The historical development of the late-Soviet rock club relied on a contradictory and symbiotic relationship with government control in the years leading up to perestroika, continuing up until the collapse of the Soviet Union in 1991. The Soviet underground rock community regularly encountered protective and collaborative policies from government agencies, including the KGB, standing in sharp contrast to today's relationship between the Russian state and independent media, which remains effectively banned. This dynamic baffled even the most weathered of Soviet rock connoisseurs. In 1981 Soviet rock critic Artemy Troitsky was incredulous to learn from Boris Grebenshchikov, leader of the Russian rock band Aquarium and one of the first Soviet rock stars, that municipal agencies in Leningrad were planning to allow a rock club to exist:

> Boris Grebenshchikov handed me two documents to read entitled "Proposal for a Rock Club" and "Charter of The Rock Club." There in the most official language imaginable, I read a point-by-point outline of goals and tasks, rights, and obligations, privileges and violations,

[b] https://postsoviet90s.com/artifacts/leningrad-rock-club

> hierarchy, and functions for the newly proposed organization. The word "rock" appeared infrequently and seemed preposterous in such a context. Take this phrase, for instance: "The rock club sets itself the goal of attracting youth to a wide range of amateur creative activities, of raising the cultural level of visual presentation and ideological artistic content in such performances, and likewise of portraying and propagandizing the best examples of national and international music in the given genre.[11]

The jarring bureaucratese that Troitsky ridicules in the above excerpt reveals rock musicians' strategic compliance with the official rituals of Soviet institutional discourse. Despite being expelled from the Komsomol (the USSR's official Soviet youth organization that was a gateway to party membership) after Aquarium's performance at the Tbilisi Rock Festival in 1980,[12] the enthusiasm with which Grebenshchikov lobbied for the LRC's establishment that surprised Troitsky is indicative of the general ideological ambivalence of the underground rock community, which relied on established infrastructural frameworks to achieve a modicum of creative self-determination. In fact, the rock club's governance retained a decidedly complex and rigid bureaucratic structure, which was enforced not by the municipal authorities, but by the club's council, made up of rock musicians. As Grebenshchikov's friend and Aquarium cofounder Anatoly Gunitsky phrased it, "the rock club was its own state within a state with its own microclimate."[13]

For the Soviet authorities the functional purpose of the LRC was to provide venues, oversee creative activities, and control the monetary exchanges in amateur rock circles during the last Soviet decade. In fact, both musicians and concert organizers maintain that the municipal bodies, including the KGB, were mostly interested in monitoring the financial transactions of the rock club to prevent illegal commercial activity, likely pocketing much of the profit from amateur rock performances.[14] The rock clubs were therefore established under the auspices of the KGB with allotment for local governance and suffrage by the musicians themselves. These organizations stood in direct contrast and competition to the long-established Unions of Composers and Youth Councils that required any amateur musician that sought access to instruments, performance venues, and recording equipment to pass a stringent vetting process, including the censorship of song lyrics as well as general judgments of aesthetic and ideological legitimacy. The clubs sought to streamline these procedures while also keeping them intact, giving young musicians an official space to audition, and offering Soviet rock music cultural legitimacy in its immediate community. Since the members of the so-called Soviet rock counterculture did not see themselves as an ideological threat, they were mostly happy to cooperate, welcoming the authorities' efforts to regulate and infrastructurally support amateur rock performers.

Troitsky has characterized rock music as having a "sacred significance in the Soviet Union,"[15] leading its practitioners and fans to see their cultural role as one, which transcended ideological and political prescriptions. On the level of official engagement with rock music in the late-Soviet period, the curating government agencies often saw their work as a service of fostering security while simultaneously facilitating the cultural vibrancy of its urban centers. In a 1992 interview, former KGB general Oleg Kalugin admitted the following,

> The KGB created in Leningrad a Rock Club, was its sponsor, and its immediate organizers were our agents. Yes, the committee did aim to place under control the anarchist tendencies of the city's musical life, but the creation of the rock club was objectively good for the city! Why, then, do we need to blow the whistle on these jazz boys now?...Many of them have become famous people today...[16]

The model of the Soviet rock club offered a radically different mechanism for cultural production during a time of sociopolitical transition: allowing amateur musicians and artists a significant amount of ideological and thematic self-determination while maintaining logistical and financial control over the underground rock music community. In other words, musicians were allowed to have venues and freely make and perform their music on government property with state-owned equipment as long as the local KGB authorities received regular reports on club activities and were able to patrol the premises. Given that during the Soviet period it was virtually impossible to independently procure access to professional recording equipment, stage lighting, and soundboards, the rock club served as a perfect logistical and ideological compromise for both the musicians and the Soviet state. Artists were enabled to write, record, and perform, while local municipal government agencies were able to monitor as well as market and promote a highly coveted cultural product: rock music. The KGB functioned as the unlikely analogue to the modern-day music producer and PR agent, overseeing the organization of performances and music festivals as well as ticket sales and advertising. The organizational structure of the late-Soviet rock club therefore created an unprecedented, paradoxical symbiosis between Soviet security agencies and the rock music subculture in the last Soviet decade. This process of collaboration between official government organizations and unofficial rock communities led to the post-Soviet model of censorship in the Russian arts, political activism, and social and news media, redefining and challenging the traditionally held assumption that late-Soviet musical counterculture existed in direct confrontation with the communist state. The Soviet rock club was a site of ideological ambivalence, in which traditionally anti-establishment or transgressive cultural milieus associated with and benefitted from existing power structures—an entrenched dynamic that has been revealed within Russia's entertainment industry by the war in Ukraine.

Gena Zaitsev, the first president (1976–81) of the LRC before Nikolai (Kolya) Mikhailov took his place in 1981 and oversaw operations until the club's official dissolution in 1992, initially established the organization with his brother in his Leningrad flat some years before Grebenshchikov's involvement. Zaitsev belonged to the Soviet hippie subculture, which was perceived as being decidedly anti-establishment, and, as Julianne Fürst has demonstrated, prefigured much of post-Socialist countercultural practices after the collapse of the USSR.[17] Nevertheless, Gena was a card-carrying member of the Komsomol Youth Organization. Zaitsev's "Komsomol Member Activities Card" was an official party document that allowed him to ascend to his post at the rock club. Zaitsev, Grebenshchikov, and many others, willfully cooperated with the authorities to establish the LRC as a culturally significant and ideologically legitimate late-Soviet institution. It was eventually housed in the Theatre of People's Art (*Teatr Narodnogo Tvorchestva*), at the legendary address of 13 Rubinstein Street in St. Petersburg, becoming a pilgrimage site for an entire generation of late-Soviet youth. The theatre employed a ticket system for their events, the so-called "invitations," to preserve the semblance of socialist non-commercialism. In reality, of course, the KGB closely monitored all financial transactions of the club to curb bootlegging and black-market activities that the agency had been fighting for at least two decades. Another perk of the municipal engagement with the rock-and-roll subculture was its highly professional model of concert promotion: official posters, concert tickets, and other publicity materials. In a poster for the Leningrad band Rossiane ("Russians"), for example, the venue is advertised as "The Leningrad Rock Club," neither hiding nor masking the musical genre being advertised, as was the general practice at the time in other spheres of cultural production, like the Soviet film industry.[18]

Cooperating with the Soviet national security agency did come at a cost for many rock musicians and the rock club's administrative staff. Musicians and club personnel were subject to trips to their local KGB offices, from which they received regular summonses. According to Zaitsev and others, however, these were often routine check-ins to make sure that the club was not engaging in unlawful financial operations. And in many cases, the musicians and their assigned KGB curators were on relatively friendly terms. Zaitsev has recalled that most of these meeting were mere formalities to show the higher administration that the agency was performing its job in accordance with regulations. At other times, to fulfill their quotas of preventing ideologically dangerous activity that Kalugin has described above, KGB "curators" would routinely cancel rock club shows, leaving fans disappointed and musicians frustrated. Rashid Nugmanov, in his 1986 documentary film *Yahha* (Artifact 00128[c]), captures this dynamic perfectly in a scene where a concert by the popular Leningrad band Kino is cancelled at the last minute. To cheer up his fan base, the benevolent Viktor Tsoi (Artifacts 00123[d], 00124[e],

---

[c] https://postsoviet90s.com/artifacts/yahha-documentary-film-excerpts
[d] https://postsoviet90s.com/artifacts/red-wave-4-underground-bands-from-the-ussr
[e] https://postsoviet90s.com/artifacts/kino-s-last-concert-luzhniki-stadium-moscow

00131[f], 00132[g], 00138[h], 00139[i], 00170[j]), who soon became the USSR's most celebrated and enduring rock star, invites his fans to come to a boiler room where he worked, and which functioned as an unofficial space for rock performances. Nugmanov's film demonstrates the rock community's precarious balance of reliance and cooperation with government agencies while projecting creative autonomy for its emerging musical personalities. The film highlights the shifting position of the underground musician in relation to the Soviet regime, its structures, representatives, and the rock subject's individual identity that was inevitably defined and established through these various tensions.

This often-precarious balance of both censorship and validation in many ways essentialized perestroika-era cultural production, spearheading a pervasive pattern of unlikely symbiotic relationships between officialdom and dissent that endured from the Soviet Cold War period to the Putin regime, serving as a precursor to today's trends in Russian popular culture, which have coerced popular performers into ideological compliance. Originating in the late 1980s and developing throughout the post-Soviet 1990s, many of these trends follow the characteristics of late-Soviet culture as outlined by Alexei Yurchak. One such trend is the almost ubiquitous reliance on what Yurchak terms "dead irony" or *stiob*, a discursive practice that was pervasive during the perestroika era[19] and the early post-Soviet period. In fact, several chapters in this volume describe *stiob* in a variety of contexts (see Fabrizio Fenghi's, Thomas Keenan's, and Daniil Leiderman's essays in this volume for further illustration of the ubiquity of this practice).

With regard to the late-Soviet rock community, the use of irony supported the bilateral cooperation described above by virtue of its overidentification with Soviet rituals, and in many ways guaranteed the oft-maligned musical genre's survival in ensuring its bureaucratic and cultural legitimacy. Soviet rock consistently sought to position itself as an authentic extension of the Russian literary canon, foregrounding its "literary" potentiality.[20] In his study of the use of *stiob* in Soviet rock music, Mark Yoffe describes the practice as "a form of ironic mockery, parodic double-talk engaged in by the initiated" that followed Bakhtin's model of the carnivalesque.[21] Therefore, in retracing the satirical footsteps of Pushkin and Gogol, whose works often poked fun at social elites and government bureaucracies while inscribing both writers into the national literary pantheon, many rock performers deliberately foregrounded the excessive bureaucratese of the logistical infrastructures that supported the late-Soviet rock music industry.

---

[f] https://postsoviet90s.com/artifacts/alexei-uchitel-s-1992-documentary-film-posldenii-geroi

[g] https://postsoviet90s.com/artifacts/sovetskii-ekran-with-tsoi-on-cover

[h] https://postsoviet90s.com/artifacts/interview-with-viktor-tsoi-and-natalia-razlogova-conducted-by-sergei-sholokhov-at-the-golden-duke-film-festival-in-odessa-1988

[i] https://postsoviet90s.com/artifacts/1992-1993-school-math-calendar

[j] https://postsoviet90s.com/artifacts/tsoi-s-wall-on-arbat

FIGURE 2 Video from Artifact 00137.[l] An excerpt from a February 1987 episode of the perestroika-era television program *Muzykal'nyi Ring* (Musical Ring), which was dedicated to showcasing new musical talent. Here, a group of Leningrad rock musicians performs a piece by composer and avant-garde jazz pianist Sergei Kuryokhin, who is also the show's host.

This strategy fashioned a form of artistic expression, which ensured ideological compliance by way of veiled mockery. To achieve their goals, Soviet rock musicians relied on the so-called aesthetics of *stiob*, which in Yurchak's definition is a form of parody that relies upon overidentification with its object. *Stiob*'s essential feature is that it is often impossible to tell where earnest reverence ends, and the parodic mockery begins and vice versa. Rock club members, therefore, were not simply grateful beneficiaries of the KGB protectorate, they were also expert jokesters with an iron poker face, which sought to subvert the authority of official state institutions by utilizing excessive bureaucratic language in rock club documents and policies.

One example of this practice can be found in the answers to the LRC's official band survey by the experimental art rock band Pop Mechanics (*Pop Mekhanika*) (Artifact 00137[k], Figure 2) written by its leader, the rock and jazz composer Sergei Kuryokhin. Kuryokhin was a legendary figure within the Soviet rock art scene for his artistic versatility and innovative approaches to performance—he was a celebrated jazz musician

[k] https://postsoviet90s.com/artifacts/musical-ring-television-program-musical-guest-sergei-kuryokhin-and-pop-mekhanika-february-1-1987

[l] https://postsoviet90s.com/artifacts/musical-ring-television-program-musical-guest-sergei-kuryokhin-and-pop-mekhanika-february-1-1987

and composer, most notably of film music, and was the leader of a band that performed impromptu avant-garde musical "happenings" that featured Leningrad's rock musicians. Kuryokhin's performances sometimes included interpretive dance and found object noise art, as well as unorthodox stage elements, such as farm animals brought on stage to assist the performing musicians, a rotating roster of the Leningrad rock music community's most celebrated stars. Kuryokhin, who aptly went by the nickname "The Captain," applied the same whimsical approach to official rock club business and documentation. The LRC band survey (Artifact 00153[m]) included a prompt with the following question:

> Do you see the Rock Club as...
> (a) a place for artistic expression;
> (b) a place for social protest;
> (c) a place for active rest; or
> (d) a place for social self-expression.

The reply to the survey prompt rendered in Kuryokhin's handwriting reads, "a place for active socially professional rest," crafting an ironic amalgamation of the multiple-choice question, which compromises the official utility of Pop Mechanics' answer, while retaining and complying with the document discursive form. The pattern continues throughout the rest of the document, in which Kuryokhin subverts Soviet official language through *stiob*-infused overidentification with the bureaucratic task at hand:

> **Question 4:** What qualities do you believe rock club committee candidates should have?
> **Answer:** Brains
> **Question 5:** How do you see the rock club committee? (*Kakim vy vidite sovet rok-kluba?*)
> **Answer:** I don't see it at all (*voobshche ne vizhu*)
> **Question 8:** With which organizations do you think the Rock Club should work?
> **Answer:** The KGB

Kuryokhin's answer to survey question 8, in which he directly implicates the KGB in having a role within the organizational and operational framework of the rock club, is particularly indicative of the type of discursive cooperation that occurred within the late-Soviet rock music milieu. Kuryokhin's statement relies on both the Soviet ritual of venerating its governing power structures, and on humorously subverting the bureaucratic tone of the official utterance. Its humor is accessible only to the *stiob*-conscious reader, and neither rejects nor condones the rock club's well-documented connection to the KGB. The semantic ambivalence of Kuryokhin's *stiob* maintains the

[m] https://postsoviet90s.com/artifacts/band-survey-from-the-leningrad-rock-club-completed-by-sergei-kuryokhin-of-pop-mekhanika

ideological integrity of the Soviet security forces as a legitimate institution, while retaining Pop Mechanics' position as practitioners of a nonconformist underground culture. Kuryokhin, who shortly after the collapse of the USSR became linked to the formation of the far-right National Bolshevik Party (Artifact 00186[n]), headed by Eduard Limonov, was also responsible for the so-called "Lenin Was a Mushroom" televised hoax (Artifact 00205[o]), in which Kuryokhin asserted on Leningrad television that Vladimir Lenin, the leader of the Bolshevik revolution, was, in fact, a fungus. Both phenomena are expertly described by Fabrizio Fenghi in the previous chapter of this volume. Kuryokhin's use of post-Socialist *stiob* in its overidentification with the "Lenin-mushroom" thesis was so compelling that many viewers of the program were thoroughly convinced of the veracity of its highly improbable claim. When this became apparent to the television show's creators, neither Kuryokhin nor his co-host Sergei Sholokhov hurried to clarify their project's ironic intent; on the contrary, defending their position with added conviction.[22]

Directly adjacent to the operations of the LRC in the late-Soviet and early post-Soviet period was another municipal project, which merged newly sanctioned access to Western popular music and media with newfound perestroika-era religious freedoms. A petition for the construction of the so-called "John Lennon Temple of Rock-n-Roll" ("*Khram Rok-n-rolla imeni Dzhona Lennona*") in St. Petersburg (Artifact 00179[p]) was spearheaded by Kolya Vasin, Leningrad's longtime devoted curator of Beatles-related memorabilia and a major figure behind the formation of the LRC. The temple's official charter is written in ironic bureaucratese:

> Citizens-entrepreneurs, holders of meetings, and thinkers! Be prescient! You have the opportunity to take part in the foremost spiritual event of our time—the construction of the John Lennon Church of Rock-n-Roll in St. Petersburg! Be the first! Join us.

The document bears an official-looking stamp in the shape of a heart with a peace sign drawn through it along with the words "All You Need Is Love," referencing the famous Beatles song. Moreover, the phonetic similarity between the names of John Lennon and Vladimir Lenin, were, of course, not lost on Vasin, who managed to establish his own Beatles museum that is still open to the public in St. Petersburg, positioning himself as Russia's preeminent "Beatleologist." As a self-proclaimed Soviet hippie, rock music fan, and vocal pacifist, Vasin believed that The Beatles were deities considering their colossal influence on Soviet society and its underground rock music. Vasin also maintained that perestroika was only possible with the aid of The Beatles and Soviet

---

[n] https://postsoviet90s.com/artifacts/a-conservative-revolutionary-avant-garde

[o] https://postsoviet90s.com/artifacts/lenin-was-a-mushroom

[p] https://postsoviet90s.com/artifacts/kolia-vasin-s-petition-for-the-john-lennon-church-of-rock-n-roll-khram-rok-n-rolla-imeni-dzhona-lennona-in-st-petersburg-april-1992

rock-and-roll. Emboldened by the surge of novel religious practices and organizations flooding Russia immediately following the collapse of the USSR, Vasin took advantage of the free-market economy and the freedoms of religious expression to solicit support for his temple. The wording of Vasin's appeal is rendered with irony, *stiob*, and elements of parody of Soviet official jargon, which, in turn, also functioned to legitimize the petition for St. Petersburg's municipal authorities, since the creation of the John Lennon temple would become the bulk of Vasin's life's work. The project never came to full fruition, despite a mural and a plaque dedicated to Vasin's efforts being installed at the Pushkinskaya 10 Art Center in St. Petersburg (Artifact 00179[q]), where Vasin housed his Beatles museum before his death of an apparent suicide in August of 2018, having left a note that read, "it's impossible to live in a country where nobody supports a Temple of John Lennon."

The tragic fate of Vasin's mission highlights the vast consequentiality of the underground rock music's discursive cooperation with government and municipal authorities. The seemingly lighthearted irony used by the rock community in its official dealings with power structures in many ways reflected a tacit acceptance of the existing bureaucratic and ideological policies—allowing figures like Vasin, Kuryokhin, Grebenshchikov, and many others, to effectively operate within the government system while still maintaining their nonconformist identity. The semantic and inflective ambiguities inherent within the *stiob* aesthetic precluded the necessity to exist in strict opposition to the state in the form of the outright rejection of its frameworks, relying instead on overidentification to both maintain the structure of the Soviet ritual while expanding its range of interpretative modalities and cultural identities. This approach allowed for Soviet rock music's infrastructural survival and development, while effectively projecting for the authorities an attitude of ideological compliance. Nikolai Mikhailov, the second and longest-serving president of the LRC, saw the role of the KGB as a generally positive one for late-Soviet rock culture, stating the following,

> The authorities believed that "it wasn't feasible trying to catch them in basements and attics, but if they could be gathered in one place, then it would be possible to monitor them, educate them, guide them, and so on...They said that it was pointless trying to crush all of this, or regulate it in some way, but that "it is necessary to help them so that they get on their feet and move forward...[23]

By supporting a cultural force they could no longer ignore nor fully control, the late-Soviet state implemented the ideologically pluralistic values of glasnost in order to sustain its own legitimacy in the face of a rapidly modernizing and Western-looking

---

[q] https://postsoviet90s.com/artifacts/kolia-vasin-s-petition-for-the-john-lennon-church-of-rock-n-roll-khram-rok-n-rolla-imeni-dzhona-lennona-in-st-petersburg-april-1992

society. The model of the late-Soviet rock club as a product of cooperation between disparate cultural elements of Western-style popular music and the Soviet state apparatus reveals larger trends within late- and post-Soviet cultural production. It closely predated the vastly transformative 1988 economic reform known as the Law of Cooperatives that for the first time since Lenin's New Economic Policy allowed for small-scale private business ownership. The process of government regulation of unofficial popular culture during perestroika reveals a precarious process of simultaneous censorship and validation of novel forms of cultural expression. It created new pathways for the formation of a post-Soviet identity, which are indelibly linked to its regimented totalitarian past. A similar dynamic can also be observed in unofficial print culture devoted to rock music, a critical organizational and discursive mechanism within the Soviet underground rock music community.

SOVIET ROCK *SAMIZDAT*

Rock music was a formidable force during the late-Soviet and early post-Soviet period in providing a new mode of creative expression for a new generation, which began to view Soviet totalitarianism through a skeptical lens. As an alternative model of mainstream cultural production and a highly coveted form of mass entertainment with roots in the capitalist West, the rapid growth of rock music communities across the vast expanses of the USSR acted as a harbinger for the collapse of the Soviet Union. The gradual process of rock music culture's assimilation into the quotidian Soviet media landscape was accompanied by the rapid proliferation of rock music-inspired material culture.

In addition to recorded albums (Artifacts 00123[r], 00148[s]), performance footage (Artifacts 00124[t], 00125[u], 00137[v], 00144[w], 00146[x]), and the budding industry of late-Soviet and post-Soviet celebrity culture, many unofficial rock music communities also left behind an extensive collection of *samizdat* artifacts in the form of self-published music periodicals (Artifacts 00134[y], 00140[z]), which illuminate not only rock musicians' Western-leaning musical tastes, but also their philosophical, literary, and political proclivities. From the last Soviet decade through the early 1990s, the unofficial music

[r] https://postsoviet90s.com/artifacts/red-wave-4-underground-bands-from-the-ussr

[s] https://postsoviet90s.com/artifacts/mat-bez-elektrichestva-profanity-without-electricity-a-ska-punk-rock-album-by-leningrad-cover-art-and-excerpts

[t] https://postsoviet90s.com/artifacts/kino-s-last-concert-luzhniki-stadium-moscow

[u] https://postsoviet90s.com/artifacts/auktsyon-s-performance-at-the-8th-leningrad-rock-club-festival

[v] https://postsoviet90s.com/artifacts/musical-ring-television-program-musical-guest-sergei-kuryokhin-and-pop-mekhanika-february-1-1987

[w] https://postsoviet90s.com/artifacts/roksi-music-journal-samizdat-vol-15-1990

[x] https://postsoviet90s.com/artifacts/lyube-performing-atas-during-a-televised-concert

[y] https://postsoviet90s.com/artifacts/roksi-music-journal-samizdat-vol-15-1990

[z] https://postsoviet90s.com/artifacts/urlait-music-journal-samizdat-1985-1992

zine culture was a flourishing underground industry, giving rise to countless *samizdat* newspapers, magazines, leaflets, and newsletters, which have inspired Soviet rock historians to engage in efforts of encyclopedic collection and annotation.[24] In contrast to the largescale municipal visibility of running a rock club or promoting rock music concerts, Soviet rock journalism, like much of Soviet *samizdat*, was an ideologically risky yet relatively clandestine industry, capable of routinely evading official censorship while providing and circulating coordinated information about performances, record releases, and other related events. All the more crucial is the fact that rock *samizdat* was a necessary feature of every rock music community across the Soviet Union and served a variety of informational and community-building functions.[25] The rock zines reflected the ideological attitudes, tastes, genre preferences, and lifestyles of their corresponding region, documenting a wide range of diverse positions of rock music production and consumption.

Regional rock clubs, which were often modeled after the administrative structure of the LRC, had flourished in number across the USSR by the late 1980s, and were accompanied by a prolific unofficial zine industry, which was indispensable for providing centralized up-to-date information and music journalism to rock music fans throughout the eleven Soviet time zones.[26] Local municipal authorities, including the KGB, were left with the challenge of enforcing order and ideological control on this unofficial publishing industry, which was rapidly outnumbering the officers assigned to its individual cases. As we saw in our discussion of the LRC, toward the latter years of Gorbachev's perestroika, government authorities radically shifted their approach to underground rock music from a policy of strict censorship to one of a protective symbiotic collaboration. In setting up a predictable editorial program of regular vetting with the collaboration of zine publishers, the Soviet security agencies provided a modicum of creative and ideological autonomy for the budding print culture of late-Soviet popular music criticism. The official policies regarding rock music *samizdat* journalism were not monolithic, but rather reflected specific regional priorities. A survey of several geographically disparate rock-*samizdat* publication models, from Leningrad's *Roksi* (Artifact 00134[aa]) and Moscow's *Urlait* (Artifact 00140[bb]) to its Siberian peer publications (*Blagim Matom*, *Kvadrat*, etc.), demonstrates that late-Soviet geopolitics played a significant role in negotiating the extent to which ideologically sensitive content could be proliferated. And since the study of underground music culture cannot be effectively undertaken without recourse to understanding *samizdat* and its cultural and material significance, the following discussion will attempt to provide a sketch of the diverse thematic and ideological elements embedded within Soviet underground rock music journalism, which foregrounded a system of ideological reciprocity between officialdom and

---

[aa] https://postsoviet90s.com/artifacts/roksi-music-journal-samizdat-vol-15-1990
[bb] https://postsoviet90s.com/artifacts/urlait-music-journal-samizdat-1985-1992

the nonconformist musical entertainment industry, a pattern that in large part persists in Russia to the present day.

While a prolific underground industry, Soviet rock *samizdat* very often appeared side by side with officially sanctioned printed documents in existing Soviet rock archives. These collections often include rock club posters, venue tickets or invitations, and festival programs, as well as officially vetted rock club governance documents. The *samizdat* materials, in the form of rock zines, were often compiled and designed by the same people that were active in regional rock club governance, who were under tight surveillance by the KGB. The standard narrative of *samizdat* as existing on the periphery and outside of official control at the level of production seems to be very unlikely within the context of late-Soviet self-published materials relating to rock music culture. In fact, the KGB appeared to support the circulation of supposedly "uncensored" (*netsenzurnye*) manuscripts, which is the accepted definition of Soviet self-publishing. The phenomenon of rock *samizdat*, therefore, seems to challenge and break down its very definition, since it blurs the line between autonomous self-circulation and officially sanctioned and censored materials.

As established earlier, the KGB was primarily interested in controlling the financial side of the underground rock community's activities to prevent and prosecute illegal commerce. The rock club structure allowed the authorities to monitor any such activity by providing the musicians a centralized physical location that allowed for easy surveillance. The members of the rock club were highly active in the production of not only musical performance, but also "self-published" print materials in the form of "musical journals" or "zines," which were sporadically vetted by the KGB during routine check-ins.[27] And since Soviet rock-and-roll was also a highly successful black market and bootleg industry, the "rock on bones" makeshift records constituted the musical equivalent of *samizdat*—a veritable industry of *samozapis'*, which by the mid-1980s was in wide circulation across the USSR.

The organizational structure of Soviet rock clubs created an unprecedented symbiosis between official government organizations and the rock-and-roll subculture, giving rise to its reliance on irony in perestroika-era unofficial media to negotiate the paradox of simultaneously depending on and subverting official ideology and its bureaucratic mechanisms. Irony was also an enduring artistic and representational trope of Soviet *samizdat* literary culture during late Socialism. As Ann Komaromi notes, Soviet *samizdat* often exhibited "the more ironic and self-reflexive trends" in literature and other print media.[28] These practices directly connect to Yurchak's definition of *stiob* and reflect a mainstay trope of late-Soviet rock culture, including both rock *samizdat* and the bureaucratic process of rock club management described earlier. Since these activities were undertaken largely by, and for the benefit of, the same artistic community and subculture, they must be considered one cultural mechanism that operated within the same discursive conventions. To this end, Soviet underground rock music journals fully followed the aesthetic prescription of irony that Komaromi describes, making it their central stylistic feature. Sergei Gur'ev, the head editor of the Soviet rock zine *Urlait*, gives the following characterization of late-Soviet unofficial rock print culture:

> ...rock-*samizdat* became an extract of *samizdat* as a whole, its sphere, where spontaneous experiments with language and journalistic form were most pronounced. In contrast with *politizdat*, the notion of freedom was based entirely on the stylistic aspect. Musical slang and colloquial speech were the central foundations of rock journalism and stood in opposition to the pompous "academese" of the official Soviet press.[29]

Gur'ev moreover posits that rock *samizdat* was a coded form of hermeneutic play, which stratified its readership according to their ability to interpret a given text as ironic *stiob* or earnest music journalism. Gur'ev summarizes the dynamic as discursive play:

> Having destroyed the genre boundaries between art and text, rock-samizdat simultaneously raised and brought down informational language. Facts are transformed into semi-abstract thought sketches, designed to continue the game of intellectual ornamentalism. At the same time the principle of "the fool will take this at face value" worked [alongside the dynamic described above].[30]

In describing the practice of rock *samizdat* as a game with a set of clandestine rules, Gur'ev essentially proves Komaromi's claim that late-Soviet *samizdat* "began to value, or fetishize the samizdat text, a phenomenon later profiled by younger generations of samizdat users, who directed critical attention toward the form of the characteristic samizdat page."[31] The strategy Gur'ev outlines is readily apparent on the pages of his own zine *Urlait*, which often merged political treatises with descriptions of concerts and latest record releases. For example, Issue 4 (22) from 1988 of the magazine features caricatures of Brezhnev, Khrushchev, and Stalin dressed in punk rock-style clothing on its cover with a caption that reads "punk rock *i ego mesto v nashei zhizni*" ("punk rock and its place in our life"), while including a treatise on the perils of nationalist attitudes in Soviet society in the editorial column (2–4), a full reprint of the ideological manifesto of The People's Front of Latvia (5–11), and an ode in verse to Kim Il Sung (18), as well as more traditional rock zine fare like a review of Alexey Uchitel's 1988 documentary film *Rock* (61–64). Oushakine, in his study of late-Soviet *samizdat*, reveals its function of ideological mimicry, which followed the dominant regime's rhetorical and discursive conventions.[32] The rock zine print culture is no exception to this model, and, as Yoffe has shown, the Soviet rock zine, which he attributes to late-Soviet youth culture, exhibits "the tendency toward what Mikhail Bakhtin called the carnivalesque and folk humorous tendencies...often represent[ing] a parody of adult forms of magazine/newspaper publications."[33] While the ironic, self-conscious aesthetic of Soviet rock *samizdat* fully adheres to the uncensored print culture's genre prescriptions, it also reveals a series of striking contradictions regarding the extent to which these publications were factually monitored by local municipal offices of the KGB. In fact, it is entirely possible that the self-referential, prescriptively humorous, and highly esoteric style of rock *samizdat* was a symptom of self-censorship and functioned as a way to preserve its existence by duping the uninitiated KGB operatives through "the fool principle" that Gur'ev describes. Yet despite outlining the ironic Aesopian discourse that was inherent to late-Soviet underground rock journalism, both Gur'ev and his long-term collaborator Aleksandr Kushnir, who compiled the most comprehensive encyclopedia of Soviet rock *samizdat* to date, continue to maintain that the industry was not subject to official censorship:

> There was no censorship in samizdat. It is just that the internal freedom of Siberian journalists was higher, than in the metropolitan centers. They just weren't afraid of anything. In Moscow there was some pressing in 1984–1985, but by 1987 there was complete freedom.[34]

At the same time, their writing on the subject consistently makes references to KGB interference in the self-publishing process. For instance, Gur'ev has stated that "the history of the major rock journals in Moscow was inseparably tied to the sharpest quasi-political confrontation, which was problematized by the pressure and intrigues from the KGB until 1988."[35] Kushnir, in turn, characterizes the early efforts of Soviet *samizdat* in Russia and Eastern Europe as an ideological battle: "just as *Beat Echo*, the rock journal *Ear* (*Ukho*) was crushed at the end of 1983 by KGB forces in accordance with all of the rules of the art of war."[36] Kushnir even goes as far as coining a pun to describe this unfavorable period for rock *samizdat* as "rock-phobic repressions" ("*rokofobskie repressii*"). By 1987, as policies of Gorbachev's glasnost picked up speed and as rock clubs became a normalized part of urban cultural life, some of the most prominent rock zines, *Roksi* (Leningrad) and *Urlait* (Moscow), reestablished their publishing activities, despite the KGB's presence within the rock community.

There is evidence that Soviet geopolitics played an outsized role in determining the extent to which the authorities enforced their tactics of censorship and ideological control on self-publishing output of regional rock communities. Certain geographical locations across the USSR were more privileged than others to engage in countercultural activities. For example, in remote Siberian strategic locations, which bore high concentrations of scientists and intellectuals due to the region's high-profile nuclear research and technological infrastructures, rock *samizdat*, as well as its accompanying underground music community, was flourishing in spite of, and with the participation of, municipal government agencies. In fact, Siberian towns with leading scientific research institutions like Akademgorodok, Novosibirsk, and Tiumen' served as the cradles of the late-Soviet punk movement. Vladimir Kozlov's documentary film *Traces in the Snow* (*Sledy na snegu*, 2014) chronicles Siberian punk's development in the last years of the

USSR. The film connects the punk community with the region's highly prolific *samizdat* rock zine industry. In one scene Valerii Murzin, a Siberian aviation technician and legendary rock journalist, talks about his experience in making *samizdat* rock journals, citing the relatively liberal and privileged environment of the Siberian academic elite. Murzin mentions having to periodically submit his publications to the local security office, which he considered a formality. Moreover, according to Kushnir, Murzin was not simply being a "good citizen" in following KGB's vetting protocols, but was, in fact, one of their agents. As Kushnir writes,

> Murzin smartened up quickly. When he was subtly invited to go into an inconspicuous door for an intimate conversation, he was internally prepared to carry out a warning strike. "It was a bit terrifying to make that decision, but as the clever French say, it's only the first step that is difficult. So, I quickly made my move by expressing a burning desire to cooperate, to the KGB agent's great amazement."[37]

Murzin eventually took up the post of director of the Novosibirsk Rock Club, where, in addition to organizing performances, he continued publishing the *Tusovka* music journal. His status as an alleged KGB operative was likely the primary reason that he was able to continue his *samizdat* activities.

What we see here is evidence of not only complacency on the part of the authorities, but also a form of a protectorate for budding Soviet rock journalists, which follows the same model of bilateral collaboration that we saw in the rock club infrastructure. The fact that in Murzin's case his recruitment to serve as a KGB informant was not met with resistance also demonstrates a level of pragmatism and ideological pliancy on the part of the Siberian rock community. Murzin, among many others, seemed to understand that collaborating with the authorities would ultimately work to undermine the system—whether through semantic ambiguity provided by the discourse of *stiob*, or through direct ideological confrontation. Siberian bands like Egor Letov's Civil Defense (*Grazhdanskaia Oborona*) (Artifact 00126[cc]), which Murzin helped promote, were among the first to produce politically subversive song lyrics, which were neither ironic not metaphorical, as was the case with most late-Soviet rock compositions, inviting the conclusion that the geographical peripheries allowed for greater political activism within the underground music community. In a 2016 correspondence, Aleksandr Kushnir admitted as much, commenting that "in Siberia there were many punk bands with cult-followings and this punk aesthetic was much more revolutionary than, for example, in conservative Petersburg."[38]

Geopolitical location was a key element governing the self-determination of rock music communities in the USSR, with regions further geographically removed from the

---

[cc] https://postsoviet90s.com/artifacts/vse-idet-po-planu-audio-recording-by-grazhdanskaia-oborona/

Kremlin enjoying a higher level of autonomy and occupying the opposing side of ideological spectrum from the Soviet political establishment, while refusing to conform to the ubiquitous "apolitical" stance of most bands located in Leningrad and Moscow. Of all late-Soviet underground popular music, it was indeed Siberian punk that contained the most articulated political stance, which was often reflected in song lyrics and performance style, positioning its members as anti-establishment dissidents. Letov, as Fabrizio Fenghi has documented in the previous chapter of this volume, joined Kuryokhin in the early formation efforts of the abovementioned National Bolshevik Party. The paradoxical effects of the administrative collaboration with Soviet security agencies on the part of the rock community therefore suggest that the formation of this late-Soviet bu-*rock*-racy allowed the rock subculture to coopt their socio-economic reality into an artistic (and political) statement while enabling its growing popularity among the youth.

ROCK MUSIC AND LATE-SOVIET CINEMA

By the latter years of perestroika, the rock club and rock-*samizdat* model of pragmatic collaboration with the Soviet establishment infiltrated many more fields of cultural production. Most notably this is apparent in perestroika-era cinema. The interplay of rock-and-roll culture and its emerging heroes with the late-Soviet film industry fostered a similar symbiotic relationship.[39] Precisely at the point when rock music infiltrated the movies, the film industry began to decentralize both in terms of how it functioned economically and on the level of government control. The production of Soviet rock films not only worked to further popularize the music and canonize a new cohort of perestroika-era celebrities (Artifacts 00129[dd], 00132[ee]) but also reified the subversion of the ideological status quo while following its discursive conventions. The trend of both colonizing and parodying Soviet official discourse is readily apparent in Sergei Solov'ev's film *Assa* (1987) (Artifact 00127[ff]), which propelled Leningrad musician Viktor Tsoi to legendary rock stardom. In its very famous last scene, Tsoi, who is playing himself, clashes with a stereotypical bureaucrat, and after cavalierly walking out on her mid-sentence comes out on top as the voice of the perestroika generation, metaphorically ripping the proverbial microphone out of the hands of the establishment. In this iconic scene Solov'ev masterfully subverts the socialist realist tropes of collective cooperation and the motifs of enduring class struggle in establishing Tsoi as the Soviet Union's last hope and unlikely yet enduring hero,[40] a position the rock star has maintained for more than three decades since his death in 1991.

After the collapse of the Soviet Union, in the interim years of Yeltsin-era liberalism, the culturally transformative potential of rock music faded into the background,

---

[dd] https://postsoviet90s.com/artifacts/sovetskii-ekran-with-k-kinchev-on-the-cover

[ee] https://postsoviet90s.com/artifacts/sovetskii-ekran-with-tsoi-on-cover

[ff] https://postsoviet90s.com/artifacts/assa-motion-picture-excerpts/

and instead became a vehicle of nascent post-Soviet nationalism.[41] The emergence of the "patriotic rock" genre exemplified by the band Liube and its military-uniform-clad lead singer Nikolai Rastorguev cemented the discursive and ideological pliancy of rock music as a consumer product (Artifacts 00146[gg], 00147[hh]). The rapid shift from rock music as a symbol of change to a form of folklore foregrounds late-Soviet and early post-Soviet entertainment culture as operating alongside the mainstream ideological agenda rather than against it, with points of subversion largely embedded within ambivalent discursive practices, such as *stiob*, irony, and overidentification. Sukachev's seemingly government-appeasing *#IAmStaying* project, which opened our discussion, is therefore yet another manifestation of the bilateral cooperation practices that supported the underground rock community from its inception. This well-traveled pattern of ambivalent discourse can also explain the lack of a unified anti-war stance among Russia's popular musicians, with most choosing against publicly articulating a clear position. Moreover, this ambivalence can most compellingly be observed in Alexey Balabanov's films *Brother* (1997) and *Brother 2* (2000) (Artifacts 00150[ii], 00151[jj], 00152[kk]), which have been coopted by Russia's official propaganda to justify Putin's invasion of Ukraine. State media has made it a practice to identify with the nationalist, xenophobic, and militaristic utterances of the film's protagonist Danila Bagrov, who became a national symbol of the post-Soviet 1990s, while styled as an anti-hero by the film's director.[42] Danila's obsession with Russian rock music at the expense of Western electronica develops a compelling portrait of post-Soviet patriotism throughout the film. The music of the Sverdlovsk band Nautilus Pompilius (Artifact 00144[ll]) provides the soundtrack for Danila's misadventures, using the film's soundscape to subtly comment on his decisions and actions. Balabanov uses the diegetic modalities of Nautilus Pompilius's songs to differentiate the moral positions of the director and his protagonist, casting the latter as morally flawed.[43] Balabanov, who was no stranger to the discursive mores of late-Soviet rock counterculture, infuses his films with the same ironic conventions that allow for interpretative ambiguity and ideologically pliant hermeneutic play that constituted a major cornerstone of late-Soviet unofficial culture. It is therefore unsurprising that his films have the capacity to be interpreted as both nationalistic master narratives of Russian imperialist exceptionalism and simultaneously its most biting critiques. Through his use of *stiob*-like overidentification, Balabanov engineers an ideologically and hermeneutically ambivalent hero that an audience unfamiliar with the timestamps

---

[gg] https://postsoviet90s.com/artifacts/lyube-performing-atas-during-a-televised-concert

[hh] https://postsoviet90s.com/artifacts/lyube-stop-fooling-around-america-ne-valiai-duraka-amerika-music-video

[ii] https://postsoviet90s.com/artifacts/brother-motion-picture-dir-aleksei-balabanov-excerpts

[jj] https://postsoviet90s.com/artifacts/brother-2-motion-picture-dir-aleksei-balabanov-excerpts/

[kk] https://postsoviet90s.com/artifacts/interview-with-sergei-bodrov-jr-1997-selections

[ll] https://postsoviet90s.com/artifacts/nautilus-pompilius-performing-last-letter-poslednee-pis-mo-gudbai-amerika/

and diegetic valences of Nautilus's discography could readily interpret as the moral compass of the narrative, falling prey to Gur'ev's "fool principle", a dynamic that Putin's propagandists eagerly employ.

CONCLUSION

The late-Soviet period ushered in a seemingly unlikely process of economic and ideological collaboration between official government bodies and unofficial culture. This occurred on the level of perestroika-era artistic and literary production and is most poignantly reflected within the development of late-Soviet rock music and its paradoxically symbiotic relationship with official government agencies. The development of rock in the USSR and Russia should therefore be considered as thoroughly interconnected with state policies, agencies, bureaucratic practices, and, above all, with official discourse. While this unlikely symbiosis did, indeed, often result in ideological subversion, the rock community's steady commitment to employing bureaucratic vocabulary and discursive practices, engaging in what Yurchak terms "ideological rituals,"[44] connects directly to the contemporary trend of Russia's musical entertainment industry's participation in propaganda production. In Sukachev's case, the *#IAmStaying* project contains many of the elements of ideological collaboration described above, including the potentiality for subversive doublespeak in its allusions to fear and danger, however muted, that appear in Krupnov's original text. Sukachev, who in his past was a lauded political activist for organizing the 1991 anti-police-brutality music festival "Rock Against Terror" ("*Rok protiv terrora*") in Moscow (Artifact 00145[mm]), is aiding Russia's official government propaganda in many of the same ways that late-Soviet rock counterculture worked to ensure its survival within the confines of a totalitarian regime. The faction of rock performers who have emigrated abroad and publicly rejected Russia's official position on the war in Ukraine can therefore be seen as a deviation from the established patterns of bilateral ideological cooperation between rock music and the Soviet state. Rapper Oxxxymiron, for example, has been actively using his concerts abroad to protest the Putin regime while raising money for Ukrainian refugees, and in the process gaining exposure in Western media,[45] while Boris Grebenshchikov rallied his Western musician friends to produce and release *Heal the Sky* (2023), a compilation album of British and American rock artists to raise funds for the Ukrainian children's hospital Ohmatdyt.[46] For their efforts, the Putin regime has branded both musicians foreign agents, a practice that targets anti-war opposition.

Among those who, like Sukachev, have stayed, Russia's domestic geopolitical context tends to inform their political posturing, policing even their private lives, just as it did during the Soviet period, and sending some to complete military service for perceived

[mm] https://postsoviet90s.com/artifacts/rok-protiv-terrora-music-festival-april-6-1991-moscow

transgressions.[47] Similarly, Soviet-era foreign policies and military conflicts were also indelibly linked to the country's musical entertainment landscape. Perestroika-era unofficial culture tended to support the political trajectory of domestic demilitarization enabled by Gorbachev, who allowed open criticism of the USSR's invasion of Afghanistan. Hence, the fact that a large swathe of ageing Soviet rock personalities that once rallied for peace are suddenly engaging in collaborative ideological rituals that directly support the destruction of innocent lives in Ukraine is unspeakably unsettling and carries with it devastating consequences. The trend of government appeasement that has been revealed since February 24, 2022 within Russia's music entertainment industry is therefore a direct symptom of the late-Soviet and post-Soviet process of cultural modernization, which does not conform to the traditional Cold War-style view of late-Soviet unofficial popular culture as existing in direct confrontation with government ideology. Instead, highly pragmatic mechanisms of collaboration and mutual reliance paved the way for the development of Russian mass media from the Khrushchev years to the present day. The late-Soviet period, therefore, should be seen not in terms of political or ideological binaries, but rather as a system of creative and ideological compromises that offers a model of cooperation rather than confrontation. The perestroika decade in large part created the foundational structures of modern-day Russia with its adoption of economic and ideological diversification of semi-privatized entertainment cooperatives and cultural organizations. And since the Soviet period helped develop Russia's business structure for the arts and popular media as largely funded and often curated by government subsidies, the late-Soviet collaborative model in alternative media production is therefore crucial to understanding the post-Soviet trend of government regulation of not only culture, but all domestically produced industries. This fact leads to the inevitable conclusion that only when positioned outside of Russia's informational and ideological infrastructure can traditionally transgressive genres of musical entertainment obtain unobstructed self-determination.

Notes

1 Andrei Loshak. *Broken Ties* (*Razryv Sviazi*, 2022), film.

2 Alla Pugacheva [@alla_orfey], Instagram, September 18, 2022.

3 Margarita Simon'ian, "About Maksim Galkin," Vecher s Vladimirom Solov'evym. Rossiia 1 (April 26, 2022).

4 Aleksei Mazhaev, "Retsenziia na klip: Garik Sukachev i dr. – 'Ia ostaius'. Spisok razreshennykh muzykantov," InterMedia, July 10, 2022, https://www.intermedia.ru/news/371608.

5 "Ne tol'ko DDT i Manizha. "Fontanka" publikuet spisok zapreshchennykh muzykal'nykh ispolnitelei," Fontanka, July 7, 2022, https://www.fontanka.ru/2022/07/07/71472080/.

6 Artemy Troitsky, *Back in the USSR: A True Story of Rock in Russia* (London: Faber & Faber, 1988), 19.

7 Alexei Yurchak, *Everything Was Forever Until It Was No More: The Last Soviet Generation* (Princeton, CA: Princeton University Press, 2006), 214–15.

8 Polly McMichael, "'A Room-Sized Ocean': Apartments in the Practice and Mythology of Leningrad's Rock Music," in *Youth and Rock in the Soviet Bloc*, ed. William Jay Risch (Lanham, MD: Lexington Books, 2015), 182–208.

9 Sergei Zhuk, *Rock and Roll in the Rocket City: The West, Identity, and Ideology in Soviet Dnepropetrovsk* (Baltimore: Johns Hopkins University Press, 2010), 9.

10 Serguei Oushakine, "The Terrifying Mimicry of Samizdat," *Public Culture* 13, no. 2 (2001): 192.

11 Artemy Troitsky, *Back in the USSR: A True Story of Rock in Russia* (London: Faber & Faber), 71.

12 Troitsky, *Back in the USSR*, 55–59.

13 Dmitrii Glukhov, "Anatoly Gunitsky: 'Rok-klub byl gosudarstvom v gosudarstve so svoim mikroklimatom,'" Rokklult, December 10, 2021, https://rockcult.ru/interview/gunitskiy-2021/.

14 Gennadii Zaitsev, interview. Conducted in August 2015. Luga, Russia; Nikolai Mikhailov, interview. Conducted in June 2018. St. Petersburg, Russia.

15 Svetlana Nikul'shina, "Artemii Troitskii o Leningradskom rok-klube: 'Muzyka ne imeet seichas takogo sakral'nogo znacheniia, kak v SSSR,'" Sobaka (March 11, 2021), https://www.sobaka.ru/entertainment/music/125343.

16 A. Broido, "'Sviatoi' apostol Oleg," *Argumenty i Fakty* 9, no. 20 (April 17, 2003): 18–19.

17 Julianne Fürst, *Flowers through Concrete: Explorations in Soviet Hippieland* (Oxford: Oxford University Press, 2021).

18 Rita Safariants, "'Thank God We're Not Alive': The Rock Star in Soviet and Post-Soviet Cinema," in *Ruptures and Continuities in Soviet/Russian Cinema*, ed. Birgit Beumers and Eugenie Zvonkine (London: Routledge, 2017), 92.

19 Yurchak, *Everything Was Forever*, 249–51.

20 Troitsky, *Back in the USSR*, 40–41.

21 Mark Yoffe, "The Stiob of Ages: Carnivalesque Traditions in Soviet Rock and Related Counterculture," *Russian Literature* 74, no. 1–2 (2013): 209.

22 Dima Mishenin, "Tikhii Sholokhov," Krest'ianka (December 2008), https://web.archive.org/web/20100113143904/http://www.krestyanka.ru/archive/year2008/dec/dec_349.html.

23 Viktor Rezunkov, "Rok, KGB, Komsomol," Radio Svoboda, April 14, 2016, https://www.svoboda.org/a/27675500.html.

24 Aleksandr Kushnir, *Zolotoe podpol'e: polnaia illiustrirovannaia entsiklopediia rok-samizdata, 1967–1994* (Nizhnii Novgorod: Dekom, 1994).

25 Mark Yoffe, "Why Collect Zines?: Notes on the Soviet and Russian Rock Zine Collection in the Global Resources Center of George Washington University Libraries," *Slavic and East European Information Resources* 22, no. 3–4 (2021): 276–86.

26 Polly McMichael, "'After All You're a Rock and Roll Star (At Least That's What They Say)': Roksi and the Creation of the Soviet Rock Musician," *The Slavonic and East European Review* 83, no. 4 (October 2005): 664–84; Yngvar Bordewich Steinholt, *Rock in the Reservation: Songs from the Leningrad Rock Club 1981–86* (Mass Media Music Scholars' Press, 2005), 47–53.

27 Kozlov, 2014.

28 Ann Komaromi, "The Material Existence of Samizdat," *Slavic Review* 36, no. 3 (2004): 589.

29 Kushnir, Zolotoe podpol'e, 5.

30 Kushnir, Zolotoe podpol'e, 1994, 6.

31 Komaromi, "The Material Existence of Samizdat," 600.

32 Oushakine, "The Terrifying Mimicry of Samizdat."

33 Yoffe, "Why Collect Zines?" 281.

34 Aleksandr Kushnir, personal message (correspondence), November 1, 2016.

35 Kushnir, Zolotoe podpol'e, 7.

36 Kushnir, Zolotoe podpol'e, 8.

37 Kushnir, Zolotoe podpol'e, 151.

38 Kushnir, 2016.

39 Safariants, "'Thank God We're Not Alive'; Safariants, "The School of Rock: Sergei Solo'vev's Workshop and Its Legacy for the Popular Music Film," *Studies in Russian and Soviet Cinema* 13, no. 2 (2019): 208–16; Safariants, *Soviet Rock on Screen: The Life, Death, and Resurrection of a Film Genre* (Madison: University of Wisconsin Press, forthcoming).

40 Safariants, "'Thank God We're Not Alive,' 97–100; Birgit Beumers, 2017; Boris Barabanov, *ASSA: Kniga Peremen* (St. Petersburg: Amfora, 2008).

41 Mark Yoffe, "Conceptual Carnival: National Elements in Russian Nationalist Rock Music," in *Rock 'n' Roll and Nationalism: A Multinational Perspective*, ed. Mark Yoffe and Andrea Collins (Newcastle: Cambridge Scholars Press, 2005), 96–119.

42 Anthony Anemone, "About Killers, Freaks, and Real Men: The Vigilante Hero of Aleksei Balabanov's Films," in *Insiders and Outsiders in Russian Cinema*, ed. Stephen Norris and Zara Trolone (Bloomington: Indiana University Press, 2008), 127–41; Ira Osterberg, *Aleksei Balabanov: Brother* (Bristol: Intellect, 2022), 33–135.

43 Ira Osterberg, *What Is That Song: Aleksej Balabanov's Brother and Rock As Film Music In Russian Cinema* (Helsinki: Unigrafia, 2018), 114–99; Osterberg, *Aleksei Balabanov*.

44 Yurchak, *Everything Was Forever*, 15.

45 Ed Cunningham, "Meet Oxxymiron, the Russian Rapper Railing against Putin's Regime," *TimeOut*, March, 17, 2022, accessed January 16, 2024, https://www.timeout.com/news/meet-oxxxymiron-the-russian-rapper-railing-against-putins-regime-031722.

46 Ludovic Hunter-Tinley, "Russian Rock Star Boris Grebenshikov: 'Millions Are Afraid to Think, Afraid to Speak Out,'" *Financial Times*, September 16, 2023, accessed January 18, 2024, https://www.ft.com/content/ef51acbd-cbbc-45eb-80b6-f5794d7486be.

47 Anastasiia Astakhova, "Raskryto mesto sluzhby Vacio posle aresta," Lenta.ru, January 16, 2024, accessed January 18, 2024, https://lenta.ru/news/2024/01/16/raskryto-mesto-sluzhby-repera-vacio-posle-aresta/.

Works Cited

Anemone, Anthony. "About Killers, Freaks, and Real Men: The Vigilante Hero of Aleksei Balabanov's Films." In *Insiders and Outsiders in Russian Cinema*, edited by Stephen Norris and Zara Trolone, 127–41. Bloomington: Indiana University Press, 2008.

Astakhova, Anastasiia. "Raskryto mesto sluzhby Vacio posle aresta." *Lenta.ru*. January 16, 2024, accessed January 18, 2024. https://lenta.ru/news/2024/01/16/raskryto-mesto-sluzhby-repera-vacio-posle-aresta/.

Barabanov, Boris. *ASSA: Kniga Peremen*. St. Petersburg: Amfora, 2008.

Beumers, Birgit. "Waiting for Change: Sergei Solov'ev and the Dreams of the Young Generation." In *Ruptures and Continuities in Soviet/Russian Cinema*, edited by Birgit Beumers and Eugenie Zvonkine, 51–68. London: Routledge, 2017.

Broido, A. "'Sviatoi' apostol Oleg." *Argumenty i Fakty* 9, no. 20 (April 17, 2003): 18–19.

Cunningham, Ed. "Meet Oxxymiron, the Russian Rapper Railing against Putin's Regime." *TimeOut*, March 17, 2022, accessed January 16, 2024. https://www.timeout.com/news/meet-oxxxymiron-the-russian-rapper-railing-against-putinsregime-031722.

Fürst, Julianne. *Flowers through Concrete: Explorations in Soviet Hippieland.* Oxford: Oxford University Press, 2021.

Glukhov, Dmitrii. "Anatoly Gunitsky: 'Rok-klub byl gosudarstvom v gosudarstve so svoim mikroklimatom.'" *Rokklult*, December 10, 2021. https://rockcult.ru/interview/gunitskiy-2021/.

Hunter-Tinley, Ludovic. "Russian Rock Star Boris Grebenshikov: 'Millions are Afraid to Think, Afraid to Speak Out.'" *Financial Times*, September 16, 2023, accessed January 18, 2024. https://www.ft.com/content/ef51acbd-cbbc-45eb-80b6-f5794d7486be.

Komaromi, Ann. "The Material Existence of Samizdat." *Slavic Review* 36, no. 3 (2004).

Komaromi, Ann. *Uncensored: Samizdat Novels and the Quest for Autonomy in Soviet Dissidence*. Evanston, IL: Northwestern University Press: 2015.

Kushnir, Aleksandr. *Zolotoe podpol'e: polnaia illiustrirovannaia entsiklopediia rok-samizdata*, 1967–1994. Nizhnii Novgorod: Dekom, 1994.

Loshak, Andrei. *Broken Ties* (*Razryv Sviazi*, 2022), film.

Mazhaev, Aleksei. "Retsenziia na klip: Garik Sukachev i dr. – 'Ia ostaius'. Spisok razreshennykh muzykantov." *InterMedia*, July 10, 2022. https://www.intermedia.ru/news/371608.

McMichael, Polly. "'A Room-Sized Ocean': Apartments in the Practice and Mythology of Leningrad's Rock Music." In *Youth and Rock in the Soviet Bloc*, edited by William Jay Risch, 182–208. Lanham: Lexington Books, 2015.

McMichael, Polly. "'After All You're a Rock and Roll Star (At Least That's What They Say)': *Roksi* and the Creation of the Soviet Rock Musician." *The Slavonic and East European Review* 83, no. 4 (October 2005): 664–84.

Mishenin, Dima. "Tikhii Sholokhov." *Krest'ianka*, December 2008. https://web.archive.org/web/20100113143904/http://www.krestyanka.ru/archive/year2008/dec/dec_349.html.

"Ne tol'ko DDT i Manizha. "Fontanka" publikuet spisok zapreshchennykh muzykal'nykh ispolnitelei." *Fontanka*, July 7, 2022. https://www.fontanka.ru/2022/07/07/71472080/.

Nikul'shina, Svetlana. "Artemii Troitskii o Leningradskom rok-klube: 'Muzyka ne imeet seichas takogo sakral'nogo znacheniia, kak v SSSR.'" *Sobaka*, March 11, 2021. https://www.sobaka.ru/entertainment/music/125343.

Osterberg, Ira. *Aleksei Balabanov: Brother.* Bristol: Intellect, 2022.

Osterberg, Ira. *What Is That Song: Aleksej Balabanov's Brother and Rock as Film Music in Russian Cinema.* Helsinki: Unigrafia, 2018.

Oushakine, Serguei. "The Terrifying Mimicry of Samizdat." *Public Culture* 13, no. 2 (2001): 191–214.

Pugacheva, Alla [@alla_orfey]. *Instagram*, September 18, 2022.

Rezunkov, Viktor. "Rok, KGB, Komsomol." *Radio Svoboda*, April 14, 2016. https://www.svoboda.org/a/27675500.html.

Safariants, Rita. *Soviet Rock on Screen: The Life, Death, and Resurrection of a Film Genre* (Madison: University of Wisconsin Press, forthcoming).

Safariants, Rita. "'Thank God We're Not Alive': The Rock Star in Soviet and Post-Soviet Cinema." In *Ruptures and Continuities in Soviet/Russian Cinema*, edited by Birgit Beumers and Eugenie Zvonkine, 90–107. London: Routledge, 2017.

Safariants, Rita. 2019. "The School of Rock: Sergei Solo'vev's Workshop and Its Legacy for the Popular Music Film." *Studies in Russian and Soviet Cinema* 13, no. 2 (2019): 208–16.

Simon'ian, Margarita. "About Maksim Galkin." *Vecher s Vladimirom Solov'evym. Rossiia* 1 (April 26, 2022).

Steinholt, Yngvar Bordewich. *Rock in the Reservation: Songs from the Leningrad Rock Club* 1981–86. New York and Bergen: Mass Media Music Scholars' Press, 2005.

Troitsky, Artemy. *Back In the USSR: A True Story of Rock in Russia.* London: Faber & Faber, 1988.

Yoffe, Mark. "Conceptual Carnival: National Elements in Russian Nationalist Rock Music." In *Rock 'n' Roll and Nationalism: A Multinational Perspective*, edited by Mark Yoffe and Andrea Collins, 96–119. Newcastle: Cambridge Scholars Press, 2005.

Yoffe, Mark. "The *Stiob* of Ages: Carnivalesque Traditions in Soviet Rock and Related Counterculture." *Russian Literature* 74, no. 1–2 (2013): 207–25.

Yoffe, Mark. "Why Collect Zines?: Notes on the Soviet and Russian Rock Zine Collection in the Global Resources Center of George Washington University Libraries." *Slavic and East European Information Resources* 22, no. 3–4 (2021): 276–86.

Yurchak, Alexei. *Everything Was Forever Until It Was No More: The Last Soviet Generation.* Princeton, NJ: Princeton University Press, 2006.

Zhuk, Sergei. *Rock and Roll in the Rocket City: The West, Identity, and Ideology in Soviet Dnepropetrovsk.* Baltimore: Johns Hopkins University Press, 2010.

CHAPTER 5

B. U. Kashkin: The Underground Seeking the Public in the 1990s

Daniil Leiderman

The changing media of the post-Soviet 1990s has unavoidable archival gaps, especially where the artists involved made conscious decisions to avoid both Soviet-era artistic institutions, and emerging means of circulating and selling their art. Such artists made art, but neither sold it, nor attempted to institutionalize it, instead adapting tactics closer associated with the Soviet artistic underground to the new era. B. U. Kashkin (b. Evgenii Malakhin), a self-proclaimed "punk-skomorokh," relied upon such tactics, and his changing practice articulates the problems with which the Soviet artistic underground approached the epochal shift into the 1990s. I will argue that the legacy of B. U. Kashkin's playful and silly performances is alive in the work done by contemporary artists like Katrin Nenasheva to knit together Russian society and community where the state cannot or will not help.

B. U. Kashkin's changing work and philosophy exemplifies the search for a path alternate to both the Soviet model of the underground artist, and the new post-Soviet models oriented to the capitalist art market. I argue that this aspect of B. U. Kashkin's work reveals an underexamined philosophical and artistic current that is still apparent in the work of contemporary artists in Russia. As I will show, B. U. Kashkin was responding not only to the end of the Soviet Union, but the rise of a new neoliberal regime, characterized significantly by the willful erosion or neglect of previously upheld social fabrics and communities. This trend was exemplified by factors described earlier in this volume, for instance, the newspaper disappearance of reader-generated content, and its replacement with advertising. I consider B. U. Kashkin's turn to socially positive activity as an attempt to compensate for such erosions, treating his practice as a key precedent to the work of contemporary artists and activists like Katrin Nenasheva, who also turned to community organizing over traditional art.

B. U. Kashkin's turn towards absurdist collective gift-giving performances articulates a shifting relationship to the commercialization of art. His turn seeks new communities to pick up the legacy and the slack, but not the baggage of those collective social organizations no longer supported by the greater society after the dissolution of the USSR. B. U. Kashkin's project relocates artistic practice from the production of either artworks or concepts to the weaving of communities, socially positive activity, and performances closer to social work than to traditional art or even 1990s actionism.

One consequence of this turn is a certain precarity: artists leave behind artworks for art historians to examine, social fabrics remain in the possession of those they bond. To compensate for this archival problem, the article uses the photographs, interviews, and recollections gathered within *Б.У. Кашкин (1938–2005): Жизнь и творчество уральского панк-скомороха*, edited and compiled by Alexander Shaburov for a 2015 exhibit at the Ural branch of the Government Center for Contemporary Art.[1] Shaburov, an artist who is best known for his work with Vycheslav Mizin in their artistic collaboration as the "Blue Noses," met B. U. Kashkin while he was still a teenager and consequently participated in his collective performances. In the 2000s, he first organized the collection of artworks, essays, and recollections on B. U. Kashkin into a book, and supplemented my questions raised by the book with an interview conducted over the phone in September 2022, and further comments left as voice messages discussing an earlier draft of this essay in May 2023. In many ways, this article both structurally relies on Shaburov's account of B. U. Kashkin and is in active debate with it, as, for instance, Shaburov's generous comments on this article criticized the idea that there was any sort of art market to reject on B. U. Kashkin's part, either during or after perestroika in the city of Yekaterinburg (Sverdlovsk under the USSR), making my point moot. If Moscow's unofficial circles were fundamentally changed by some of the involved artists becoming millionaires overnight in 1988, the same situation never repeated in Yekaterinburg. Nevertheless, I still insist that B. U. Kashkin's work does respond to the changing economic situation of the artist during perestroika, even if sudden wealth at a Sotheby's auction never threatened him.

Shaburov also disputes my labeling of B. U. Kashkin as a member of the "underground," emphasizing that neither B. U. Kashkin nor his circle, the "Kartinnik Society," ever opposed the Soviet state or called themselves dissidents, functioning openly within the framework of socially positive activity supported by officially approved clubs. I use the term "underground" to mean all artists whose works and activities were not directly sanctioned by the Soviet State, with the full awareness that it doesn't represent a rigid oppositional break with officialdom. The "underground" is a peculiarly slippery term in this context. As Lipovetsky, Glanc, Engström, Kukuj, and Smola argue in the *Oxford Handbook of Soviet Underground Culture*:[2]

> many underground artists earned their daily bread by contributing to official culture, and not all works banned by the state were truly innovative and radical. Although the rigid binary opposition between the official culture and the underground does not hold water, the coexistence of the two cultures remains a historical fact. Insomuch as Soviet political ideology orchestrated a utopian project of communism, the cultural underground presented a counter-utopia.

It is precisely the presence of such a "counter-utopia" in B. U. Kashkin's work that fuels his naïve populist intimacy. However, if the preceding chapter shows that members of the cultural underground were skilled at adopting and adapting the language of officialdom to achieve their ends, it also shows that the authorities were equally skilled at coopting elements of the "underground" under their wing, with "KGB [functioning] as the unlikely analogue to the modern-day music producer and PR agent, overseeing the organization of performances and music festivals as well as ticket sales and advertising" (Safariants, this volume).

In B. U. Kashkin's case, cooperation with the authorities seems solely discursive and parasitic on B. U. Kashkin's end. Much of his activities and the activities of his art circle "Kartinnik" took place at a basement apartment provided by officialdom, but not accompanied by any sort of agreed-upon surveillance. According to the interview I conducted with Shaburov in September 2022, B. U. Kashkin had managed to obtain the basement space through Uraltekhenergo either officially or using favors, ostensibly for a photography studio. This studio was not B. U. Kashkin's home, as he shared an apartment with his spouse. The studio was for his art and engaging in various apparently socially positive ventures, such as making numerous posters promoting sobriety and warning about the dangers of alcohol to accompany the 1985–88 temperance campaign initiated by Gorbachev. This made B. U. Kashkin's activities comparable to those of a normal, officially sanctioned photography enthusiasts' club, or something similarly innocuous, even though close scrutiny to the kinds of photographs and posters the studio created would raise the eyebrows of any official body. B. U. Kashkin clearly used officialdom to his benefit, but there is no evidence that officialdom benefitted in turn.

Despite the impossibility of cleanly separating officialdom and its discontents, cases like B. U. Kashkin's still show that some artists consciously structured their practice in such a way as to make it hard to coopt, and difficult to confuse with officially sanctioned artworks. There is a world in which B. U. Kashkin seems like the ideal Soviet community organizer—a sort of fictional Timur-and-his-gang leader, organizing disaffected Soviet youth (minds rotten with postmodernism) into socially positive campaigns to fight alcoholism and revitalize urban blight. In this regard, B. U. Kashkin performs what in the preceding chapter Safariants called "the jarring bureaucratese that…reveals rock musicians' strategic compliance with the official rituals of Soviet institutional discourse." However, B. U. Kashkin was really having his collective make posters to fight alcoholism and later painting trash bins to revitalize urban blight. It is just that the approach B. U. Kashkin took verged on graffiti, was never formally sanctioned, and operated precisely as the inappropriate appropriation of official rituals to unexpected and unpredictable ends. What is paradoxical about him, and his work in the early 1990s, is that he was all this and more, while at the same time presenting and being understood as an artist leading a provocative underground lifestyle as a "Punk-Skomorokh." Had B. U. Kashkin asked the Artists' Union of the USSR for membership or permission to work as he saw fit, he would have been rejected. Consequently, B. U. Kashkin was never a member of any artists' union. He was primarily an engineer who made art as a hobby until losing his job, and then continued making art as a janitor, sharing this art publicly and in a way that clearly didn't fit the stylistic norms of 1970s and 1980s socialist realism. In my view this qualifies him as an underground artist.

A typical work from 1988–92 by Kartinnik showing both B. U. Kashkin's own artistic approach and both its affinities and incongruencies with socialist realism is a painting on a kitchen cutting board. The specific artist responsible for such a board is not identified.[3] In this case, the board depicts a cartoonishly childlike image of an athletic man flexing his muscles, surrounded by written slogans. The text is indicated to be by B. U. Kashkin, while the side label identifies its genre as a "morally-mundane edu-cutting board" and reads, in the present author's translation: "If you want to be the best, don't you dare forget the rest! [*Samym-prisamym khochesh' byt' ty ne vzdumai togda nichego pozabyt'*!]" The crudely painted man is apparently in the process of self-improvement (perhaps flexing while smiling), with a semi-correct (or correct after corrections apparent within the image) multiplication table written on his chest. Nothing about this work is overly anti-Soviet, or even controversial. At the same time, it is not a typical work of socialist realism, and could not ever be confused for a work of socialist realism even despite its positive message and optimistic address. It feels like a parody of a socialist realist address to the audience, but it is not an overt parody. With B. U. Kashkin and his "Kartinnik" circle we see a model of an artistic nonconformism or even underground that is alternative and distinct from those typically discussed in the context of the Moscow art scene: neither esoteric, not confrontational, not even obviously critical, but structurally communal and oriented towards community-based play.

B. U. KASHKIN'S "KARTINNIK"

B. U. Kashkin was born Evgenii Malakhin in 1938, and spent most of his life working as an electrical engineer at Uraltekhenergo. His earliest artistic experiments were with photography in the 1970s.[4] At some point Malakhin assumed the pseudonym "K. Kashkin," which could be translated as "P. Oopy." His photographic work involved thermally modifying photographic images and negatives (for instance, by leaving film near a hot stove, causing deformations) and painterly works Shaburov expressly compares to Jackson Pollock's "drip paintings" for their use of dripping and paint-throwing.[5] Malakhin's use of abstraction involved some degree of play: Shaburov's recollection has Malakhin comparing one of his works with Kazimir Malevich's *Black Square*.[6] The work in question is a photograph purposefully overdeveloped into blackness, which Shaburov describes as an attempt to capture everything, overlaid over everything else. This means that while irony is definitely present, it is not self-purposeful irony or irony-for-irony's sake. Instead, irony here is incorporated into a broader avant-garde project where experimenting with the frontiers of art is a worthy and meaningful endeavor, and irony is a required and privileged tool, associated with *stiob* "overidentification with the target of criticism by mimicking its style and form…that kind of exposure to mockery that leads to an irreversible and permanent profanation."[7]

Irony features strongly in Malakhin's literary texts from the 1970s and early 1980s, when he writes parodies of avant-garde classics, Soviet cliches, and public slogans as his primary poetic form.[8] All this changes at the height of perestroika, in 1989, when K. Kashkin suddenly dramatically adjusts his practice, even assuming a new pseudonym—B. U. Kashkin, which can be translated as "B. Uggy." The name shift should be considered notable, for if "K. Kashkin" was both child-like and confrontationally fecal, "B. U. Kashkin" doubles down on the child-like, evoking both innocence and vulnerability, without the provocation implicit in the previous pseudonym.

A new artistic practice came along with the name change. B. U. Kashkin's previous experiments, however serious or ironic, still fell within the familiar avant-gardist archetype of the individual artist pursuing autonomous artistic experiments. Instead, Malakhin adopts a new persona with a matching costume of the "punk-skomorokh": combining Western tropes of the rebellious subculture and the skomorokh, a kind of pre-modern Slavic harlequin. It is at this point that Malakhin consolidates a friendly collective called "Kartinnik" around his leadership. The term "Kartinnik" is understandable as either an incorrect neologism for "painter" (approximately translating as "Paintingman"), or for a painting-industry (like a pig farm or *svinnarnik* for paintings, or Andy Warhol's "Factory"). With Kartinnik, as B. U. Kashkin, Malakhin gives up making autonomous art. From this point on, B. U. Kashkin no longer makes art with his own hands, delegating the task to friends and strangers instead. Both possible meanings of "Kartinnik" apply in this regard, describing the willfully amateurish character of the work and its focus on collective mass production.

Kartinnik grew organically out of a circle of young engineers and other colleagues and friends from Uraltekhenergo, Malakhin's son's friends, and young artists like Shaburov, who gathered around the already mature B. U. Kashkin. Members of Kartinnik would meet at B. U. Kashkin's basement studio and make artworks at his command. His authority should be noted as significant and perhaps surprising: B. U. Kashkin had no real institutional power or privilege beyond the aforementioned basement space. Several recollections semi-jokingly, semi-seriously represent the common experience of walking into B. U. Kashkin's basement and being immediately handed art supplies and a directive. While B. U. Kashkin himself no longer painted, the artworks were all prompted by his texts, slogan deconstructions, poems, and jokes written throughout the 1980s. These were drawn from B. U. Kashkin's numerous books, typewritten by B. U. Kashkin for a fictive publishing house called "Kashkin Books" under the equally fictive "World Kashkin Books" publishing company.[9] It is as if in the absence of actual institutional power, B. U. Kashkin created his own fictional institutions, which then functioned as canons for his circle—becoming a legitimate source of quotes and sources, however comical and ludic. This is a key point to consider: even under the Soviet Union, B. U. Kashkin chose to set up alternate and unsanctioned institutions, however absurd. This practice becomes even more significant when established Soviet institutions become derelict during perestroika.

Kartinnik's artworks were painted on improvised surfaces like used kitchen cutting boards, and after a significant number had been assembled, B. U. Kashkin would take the whole Kartinnik society into public spaces for comical, non-professional performances where they would display and distribute the art they made to strangers. All Kartinnik artworks and performances seem evocatively and playfully "bad," in the sense of willfully rejecting skill as a prerequisite to making art. This "badness" is an important aesthetic characteristic of the nonconformist underground, as noted by Boris Groys in his 1993 article "The Artist as a Curator of Bad Art" and as the subject of a chapter in Ekaterina Bobrinskaia's book *Other? Unofficial Art: Myths, Strategies, Concepts*,[10] as well as by Ilya Kabakov, in his 2008 essay "The Bad Thing," which Bobrinskaia uses as a foundational source.

Despite the apparent similarity, B. U. Kashkin's "bad things" differ from Kabakov's "bad things" in a major way. Kabakov's analysis centers the decay of the "bad thing": "... for a minute it must tell us something, or rather it has to seem to us that it is 'speaking,' but it is still constantly drifting away with them, with the things of our meager daily life, into a collective heap of garbage and dust."[11] For Kabakov, garbage metaphorizes an exegesis through entropy, where the disintegration of the meager object reveals the truth of daily life. B. U. Kashkin's work reverses Kabakov's trajectory: he declares garbage to be a joyful gift, actually gifting it to a stranger, and then making even the sites of garbage into festive gifts to the collective (if unauthorized and thus illegal like any work of graffiti). If Kabakov's "bad thing" is pessimistic about the collective, presenting it as a "heap of garbage and dust," B. U. Kashkin's is comically exuberant, to the point of near parody. If Bobrinskaia and Groys understand Kabakov's "bad thing" to also mean historically "unsuccessful art," accentuating the outsider status of nonconformist "artworks that fell out of the big history of art," B. U. Kashkin and Kartinnik don't present themselves as unsuccessful at all.[12] As a notable example, B. U. Kashkin frequently performs in a custom T-shirt declaring himself to be a "Great Russian Poet"!

Effectively, B. U. Kashkin's late-1980s and early-1990s practice earnestly takes up the obligations of the "Great Russian Poet": organizing a collective towards a socially positive project, transforming life into art, even creating canons and institutions. All of this activity is nevertheless presented in a consistently parodic way that strips poetic power from B. U. Kashkin's persona, putting it into the hands of the Kartinnik circle, and then into the hands of the strangers that Kartinnik involves in passing. Others paint his paintings and recite his words: B. U. Kashkin acts as a dynamic catalyst for their artistic expression and community.

In 1989, B. U. Kashkin wrote a supplementary samizdat volume called *Devices for Maximizing Communication* offering basic skeletons of rhyming, catchy, and child-like poems to involve the public, so as "any passer-by could join in and sing along by changing out, say, the last word."[13] This directly highlights how his practice balances on the edge between the playful and the serious—*Devices for Maximizing Communication* and its overly officious title resembles official discourse, but is certainly tongue-in-cheek, and serves Kartinnik's direct aims. They really were meeting strangers and trying to rope them into playing along with their songs and poems and dances.

B. U. KASHKIN AFTER PERESTROIKA

It is apparent that a tectonic shift had happened in B. U. Kashkin's artistic practice, and yet not in a way we might associate with the typical narratives of perestroika. For instance, Matthew Jesse Jackson presents the arrival of the capitalist art market in the form of Sotheby's first auction of contemporary art in the Soviet Union on July 7, 1988, as a nearly apocalyptic event for the Moscow artistic underground: "The [Moscow] Conceptualists understood that their rituals of unofficial creation and communal discussion has been rendered void by the art world and its auction. The artists' struggles for accurate consciousness seemed overblown and trite when encountered in a commercial context."[14] Presumably, if we accept the idea that artists like B. U. Kashkin were also engaged in a similar artistic struggle for "accurate consciousness," they too would find themselves "rendered void" as an artistic community of the like-minded. However, as far as the recollections suggest, the situation was different in Sverdlovsk, not the least because Sotheby's never ever came to turn members of the local art scene into internationally recognized millionaires, as was the case in Moscow. This is not to say that Sverdlovsk and the surrounding region did not have a significant amount of unofficial art. Rather, it is that nonconformist artists on the peripheries received none of the attention or glamour we might associate with artists near the centers of Moscow and St. Petersburg in the wake of the Sotheby's auction.

B. U. Kashkin nevertheless involved himself in a significant artistic debate that seemed key to his shifting practice. Shaburov recounts a specific episode from 1988, as a kind of structural parable explaining B. U. Kashkin's practice. The account must be taken with a grain of salt, as it does not appear that Shaburov was present, recalling and retelling B. U. Kashkin's own narrative, with whatever distortions it already contained. The story is of a heated argument B. U. Kashkin had with a long-term friend and fellow artist, the metalworker Alexander Lysiakov, around the exact problem identified by Jackson: the relevance of the nonconformist artist in a global capitalist art market.

Lysiakov, who even today sells hand-forged traditional metalwork in Yekaterinburg, became financially successful during the perestroika period. Shaburov links the conflict between B. U. Kashkin and Lysiakov to B. U. Kashkin's artistic turn to profitless gift-giving:

> B. U. Kashkin made up his first gift handouts to illustrate his ideals and spite his friend the blacksmith Lysiakov, with whom he'd go to the sauna every Thursday. Until they broke off their friendship over art...At the time, the first cooperatives sprung up, Lysiakov's metalworking business was booming and he declared: art—is that which brings profit. That which is made well and for the centuries! A material thing that can and should be sold! B. U. Kashkin countered: art—is not a thing, it is an idea! An act of communication, of freely renewing the experience of the world in the mind of another person...[15]

This debate is curious: even though Sotheby's is nowhere in sight, as Shaburov himself insists, the stakes remain the same, and hardly specific to the perestroika context. In Shaburov's retelling, B. U. Kashkin and Lysiakov spar over conceptual art, and the central issue of whether true art is materially embodied and finely made, or primarily conceptual and deeply thought, is much more acute precisely due to the new possibility of profiting from art. This possibility changes the situation of older, self-organized communities of unofficial artists like Kartinnik, which made a lot of material objects by inclination, but sold none of them by necessity.

Lysiakov's point can be restated as follows: before, artists like B. U. Kashkin had the excuse of the USSR's limiting notions of what an official professional artist could be or could create to justify their unofficial artistic activities remaining unofficial. In the perestroika era, anyone not offering their art for sale to the public, and making money from the endeavor, should consider themselves a don't-quit-your-day-job amateur, and leave the spotlight to true professionals. This is why B. U. Kashkin's response is so provocative and interesting—he embraces the spotlight, but in a way that uplifts and glorifies the amateurish.

If Lysiakov imagines capitalism rewarding professional artistic enterprise (and ignoring the unprofessional amateur), B. U. Kashkin's approach seems closer aligned to the popularizing moves of American Pop Art—only if Warhol hypothesizes a future where everyone has their fifteen minutes of fame, B. U. Kashkin earnestly attempts to give everyone involved in his performances the "Great Russian Poet" experience. Everything he does artistically following his fight with Lysiakov seems calculated to make it impossible to make a profit from his artworks, and to emphasize the greatness of the unskilled and non-professional.

This is a nuanced decision: B. U. Kashkin could easily stop at arguing that his art is about ideas, embracing the conceptual over the material. In the 1990s, plenty of prominent nonconformist artists like Andrei Monastyrski adopted a certain artistic esotericism and ignored the art market entirely. B. U. Kashkin doesn't do this, embracing the "act of communication" instead, by opening his practice to a circle of young people, letting them paint for him and misbehave with him in public, making a fool of himself in front of anonymous crowds for their pleasure. Between 1989 and 1991, B. U. Kashkin and the whole Kartinnik society tour through dozens of USSR cities and music festivals, including Moscow, Leningrad, Odesa, Tallinn, Omsk, Novosibirsk, Krasnoyarsk, Barnaul, Chelyabinsk, Perm, and others, involving as many as 500 different performers, and handing out more than 5,000 artworks.[16]

These performances follow a stable pattern. For example, Shaburov describes a Kartinnik performance held at a festival in Narva in 1989. There B. U. Kashkin's circle set up a tent designed by B. U. Kashkin and covered in painted boards, and began to rile up the crowd with chants, loud instruments, and playful poems. B. U. Kashkin played the master of ceremonies, dressed in his "Great Russian Poet" shirt (the text in English, not Russian, B. U. Kashkin claiming that "otherwise people wouldn't understand"), a jester's cap, and a jacket covered in dozens of buttons with the face of Lenin, all the Lenins facing in one direction on one side of the jacket, and the other direction on the other side. He recited a cute poem about a sad crocodile, afterwards, calling out asking if any crocodiles were in attendance, until someone volunteered themselves as a crocodile in response. B. U. Kashkin then gifted the volunteer-crocodile a painted board with the poem.[17]

Shaburov notes that although apparently innocent, B. U. Kashkin's performances could swiftly turn subversive, the harmless poems joined by much more provocative ones. When one poem referenced the CheKa—the organization that preceded the KGB in the early years of the USSR—B. U. Kashkin's friendly back-and-forth with the public becomes much more tense: "I said 'Any Chekists in the crowd?' Awkward silence. 'C'mon', I said, 'Any KGBists around? Informants, snitches, anyone? No? No one?' Finally, someone got it and said 'Me!' And just a few months later, this would get laughs from people."[18]

B. U. Kashkin's approach differs from the kind of shock tactics one might associate with post-Soviet actionism in Moscow, especially with Oleg Kulik and Alexander Brener. Their approach is most different in how the artists relate to their own power: both Brener and Kulik necessarily rely on the hierarchical privilege of the artist over their audience. B. U. Kashkin's approach mocks that privilege, or destabilizes it: the punk-skomorokh doesn't and can't demand respect or compliance. He uses laughter as preferable to shock—getting people to laugh along, as though the old cruelties of the state could be made irrelevant through mutual play. Conversely, the bodily and demeaning character of their actions does nothing to destabilize Brener's and Kulik's power and authority. Brener (accompanied by Anton Litvin and Bogdan Mamonov) gets away with public defecation as an artist in *Plagiarism* (1993). Kulik violates social and human norms, becoming a dog in the name of art in *Mad Dog or the Last Taboo, Guarded by a Lone Cerberus* (1994).[19] In both cases, what would otherwise be base criminality is re-contextualized as a critique that overrides the criminal element with philosophical and artistic motives. As a consequence, both artists exploit a hierarchical relationship wherein artists are entitled to subject an audience to various non-consensual experiences, from a position of authority where their privilege to do so is philosophically assured and validated by artfulness. Anatolii Osmolovsky states this directly, writing:

> In the 1990s, power was the main ambition of the artist. Brener would open a show at the Government Center for Contemporary Art and declare: "I am going to seize power". He'd march to the Red square to take the Kremlin. By the Spasskaya tower the guard would tell him to get lost and the performance would end.[20]

The audience, conversely, are imagined as either passive or actively traumatized observers with no real rights within the action, other than to accept their lot as subject to the artist's abuses—e.g., Brener leaves his feces for the museum staff to clean, Kulik is only a dog when it suits him, and benefits from the legal protections of a human otherwise.

Nothing of the sort is true in B. U. Kashkin's work. His authority seems as serious as it is playful: his "Kartinnik" society obeys his directives, but his directives are silly and never threaten violence. His performances are not traumatic for the audience, they are purposefully popular, not esoteric. Most people take them as good fun, and numerous pictures show parents letting their children play along (something unimaginable with either Brener or Kulik's performances). Kartinnik actions do not attempt to change the audience through the shock and the artist's power to subject the audience to something traumatic. At the same time, B. U. Kashkin's provocations still pull the audience into his silly "Great Russian Poet" project, still directly evoking prior avant-garde efforts to radically transform the consciousness of the audience through art—winking all the while, and yet doing it.

B. U. Kashkin's performance has obvious parallels with the more playful actions of the Collective Actions group. For instance, the 1979 action *Pictures*, when the action organizers, including Monastyrski, led their participant friends (which included Boris Groys and Ilya Kabakov) into a snowy field and gave them instructions for creating abstract artworks out of colorful construction paper. Having thus distracted their audience, the organizers then documented the "true" action of the organizers quietly leaving the group and disappearing into the snow, unnoticed by anyone.[21] Like many other Collective Actions, *Pictures* relies upon several registers of play and deception, and fundamentally, upon a selective audience primed to play along, informed about performance art and expecting an unusual experience. If the organizers of *Pictures* tricked their friends, it was with kindness and play, and the clear understanding that the prank was not a cruel one—not even accidentally cruel as the 1981 *Ten Appearances*, when Vsevolod Nekrasov didn't realize he was to return to the start of the action to end it, and went home instead, scaring his friends who feared him lost in the snowy woods (Nekrasov in *Collective Actions: Audience Recollections*[22]). Kabakov even directly describes his experience of the same action as a gift: "…the effect of this gift produces a staggering impression, as though we had been present at the production of this gift, as though we had made our own day" (Kabakov in *Collective Actions: Audience Recollections*[23]).

B. U. Kashkin's performances are even more precarious—Kartinnik doesn't choose their audience, and although the recollections and images seem uniformly positive, as apparent in photographs documenting the performances (see Figure 1), there were obvious risks of strangers taking offense, or just being destructive or disruptive.[24] Compared to the Collective Actions group, B. U. Kashkin's Kartinnik is taking conscious steps to open itself to hostility and even violence—it is vulnerable more than it is violent or experimental, and nothing expresses this vulnerability more than their principled dedication to gift-giving. In this regard, Kartinnik anticipated contemporary radical works by artists like Katrin Nenasheva, who in 2020 staged a series of works entitled *Argue with Me*, where she opened herself up to the public in a way that expressly invited both violence and vulnerability:

> Wearing an Edwardian wedding dress, Nenasheva set up a small folding table in the middle of a street or a residential courtyard. When someone approached to ask what she was doing, she invited the stranger to take a seat. She would then offer them three options: to have an argument with her, to discuss a conflict from their personal lives, or to do something for a loved one such as knit a handkerchief with a word or phrase on it.[25]

According to Hanukai, Nenasheva's work "sought to address the troubling uptick in domestic violence during the initial period of [COVID-19] state-imposed lockdowns."[26] Three decades earlier, Kartinnik seemed to be doing the same in response to perestroika: setting themselves up for arguments, personal revelations, and gift-giving as a means of intimately, rather than authoritatively, repairing the damage wrought to the social fabric of post-Soviet society.

Kartinnik performances always culminate in gifts—when B. U. Kashkin asks for someone to identify with one of his silly poems, and someone yells out in response, they always receive the painted board with no expectation of payment. There is no question of honesty or dishonesty—only of play—if someone truthfully admitted to being a KGB officer, they'd still get a cute little poem on a painted board to keep or throw away, just as if they'd playfully admitted to being a KGB officer. Indeed, this proves a challenge to archiving B. U. Kashkin, perhaps purposefully on B. U. Kashkin's end, for if Shaburov's book and collection are the most authoritative collection of the works made by Kartinnik between 1988 and 1992, it still offers only a small portion of the total output which was anonymously given out to strangers all around the USSR. This is a notable and significant decision at a time when there is neither institutional economic support for artists from the state, nor from wealthy capitalist donors or art patrons, and

FIGURE 1 Image from Artifact 00055.[a] B. U. Kashkin and other members of Kartinnik perform for a small crowd at the Sverdlovsk Dam boardwalk in 1989.

when the precarity of B .U. Kashkin's work is acute, and frankly, when people might be quite willing to pay a token amount for an original artwork. It made perfect sense for Kartinnik to sell art, however cheaply, yet they chose not to. Their focus on gifts must be considered as a disciplined choice on B. U. Kashkin's part—his own strategy of eliding both the heroic stereotype of the nonconformist artist-philosopher, and the new capitalist virtues of self-promotion and marketeering. The act of gift-giving here both escapes and structurally neglects the systems that would curb or control it, neither caught up in a capitalist marketplace, nor a Soviet ideological convention, nor even nonconformist philosophical critique, and instead appealing to a kind of populist, naïve intimacy structured around gifting silly drawings and silly poems as a source of meaning and community.

In 1993, he and Kartinnik expanded their gift-giving practice further, beginning what was to become a whole series of projects focused on garbage bins. In such works, B. U. Kashkin and the rest of Kartinnik would take over a derelict public area. Kartinnik would clean up the site, and paint the entirety of it in their characteristically

[a] https://postsoviet90s.com/artifacts/the-kartinnik-picture-man-society-at-the-dam-boardwalk-in-sverdlovsk-1989

FIGURE 2 Image from Artifact 00059.[b] B. U. Kashkin stands in front of painted Ural Electro-Technical Institute rubbish bins. Featured in Alexander Shaburov, *B. U. Kashkin (1938–2005). The Life and Work of a Ural Punk-Skomorokh* (Ekaterinburg: Ural Branch of the Government Center for Contemporary Art, 2015). Used with the permission of A. Shaburov.

optimistic amateurish style. The first such work is visible the background of the photograph in Figure 2.[27] The photograph depicts B. U. Kashkin standing in the garbage yard of Uraltechenergo, where he worked as an engineer in his civilian life, and where he became a janitor when he retired (Artifact 00059[c]).

The dereliction of the site, with puddles of mud, odd bottles, and scavenging pigeons, contrasts with the bright butterflies and flowers painted by Kartinnik. Notably, both in this case, and later, the work was done for free and without any apparent leave from either the authorities or the daily users of the bins, and thus technically constituted illicit graffiti, with a side of cleaning. Kartinnik's interventions thus do not leave behind an artwork to circulate. The bins would be preserved only by community consensus,

[b] https://postsoviet90s.com/artifacts/the-collective-society-kartinnik-picture-man-let-s-turn-trash-bins-into-flowers-and-put-those-flowers-round-our-heads
[c] https://postsoviet90s.com/artifacts/the-collective-society-kartinnik-picture-man-let-s-turn-trash-bins-into-flowers-and-put-those-flowers-round-our-heads

and ruined or at least sullied by necessity, in the course of daily use. They are site-specific public artworks directly reminiscent of the sort organized by community beautification projects—and within the USSR by the state and organizations like the Young Pioneers. Is this to say that B. U. Kashkin's project is in continuity with the socially positive projects of Soviet socialist realism and collectivism? On the surface, there is some connection to the socialist realist artwork's desire to galvanize the audience into socially positive action, or make the audience accept a glowing (and illusory) image of reality. Surprisingly, B.U. Kashkin's own narrative, at least as recounted by Shaburov, seems to directly address postmodernism instead:

> That's how we are different from today's avant-gardist-postmodernists…they want to turn the museum into rubbish and we want to turn rubbish into the museum! The rubbish bin is an indicator of social changes in governance, a measure of the level of civilization! "Our art belongs to the people" this is why we are painting trash bins, to bring this whole "art" to the people, to make it pleasant to throw something into it, or grab something out of it.[28]

Joking as it is, the response is densely woven: the opposition to postmodern excess comes from the Soviet avant-garde's (and particularly the Constructivists') project to turn all of life (the rubbish bin) into art, and to do it for "the people." It also paradoxically sounds like a socialist realist denunciation of bourgeois Western art, with "Our art belongs to the people" functioning as almost a direct quote from socialist realist discourse. B. U. Kashkin is processing both the socialist realist and Soviet avant-garde legacies through their deconstruction within the nonconformist generation of the 1960s, as in Oscar Rabin's numerous works using trash and trash bins as metaphors for Soviet life—*Trashbin #8* (1959), among others. If in such works, Rabin used trash to signify the collapse of Soviet society, placing symbolic objects like religious icons adjacent to garbage to accentuate the tragedy of this collapse, B. U. Kashkin's trash is unambiguously hopeful, even caring.

Rather than treating the avant-garde project to turn life into art as unsuccessful and literally trashed, B. U. Kashkin treats trash as a source of potentiality and vibrancy—a kind of fecund zone where the stuff of life circulates. This is why he concludes with the suggestion that the transformed trash bins are not removed from the world into the realm of "art," but instead engaged and heightened in their ability to recirculate and rejuvenate existence, "to throw something into it, or grab something out of it."[29] In this regard, B. U. Kashkin's practice obviously resonates with Kabakov's, while remaining quite different from it. Throughout the 1980s, Kabakov too frequently uses trash as a grand source of meaningful metaphors for daily life and Soviet experience, as described at length in Amei Wallach's *Ilya Kabakov: The Man Who Never Threw Anything Away* (1996), and according to Shaburov, B. U. Kashkin and Kabakov had mutual acquaintances, and B. U. Kashkin knew of the Moscow-based artist at least by reputation.

However, B. U. Kashkin's use of trash seems related to his own parallel collecting and bricolage practices. Photographs and recollections of B. U. Kashkin's studio basement show a literally packed space: walls pasted with images, corners stuffed with boards and canvasses. The gifting of garbage and its transmutation into art is less an associative response to Kabakov and more a direct answer to Lysyakov. Instead of producing well-made things for sale in a nascent capitalist marketplace, B. U. Kashkin recuperates and revitalizes the ruined Soviet and post-Soviet present. In many ways, this is the same theory of therapeutic honesty and care that characterized the Kartinnik "who here is KGB?" performance. B. U. Kashkin doesn't seem to believe that any aspect of life and history deserves to be cast aside as shameful, preferring to directly air everything. He chooses to use art and performance as mere premises or devices for throwing a prophylactic yet loving spotlight on what is otherwise repressed and shameful and ruined.

A key question arises around the problem of artistic power. The problem of power, after all, was crucial for the prior generation of artists—Collective Actions, for instance, structurally designed their performances so that even the organizers didn't know how exactly they were going to play out. It also remained crucial for the current generation of artists, as Brener's and Kulik's actions were conversely fixated on the artist's control—with no metaphor more obvious than that in *The Mad Dog, or, The Last Taboo, Guarded by Lone Cerberus* (1994). There Kulik, chained like a dog, colluded with Brener, who held the chain, over how to best terrify and provoke their audience: completely in control of being out of control. B. U. Kashkin, conversely, seems perpetually in control, but always precariously: as powerful (and as weak) as whoever is seeking during hide-and-seek, or any other game. He seems to be a pretend leader, rather than an absolute one, whether he is leading a procession of youths as their punk-skomorokh elder, or trolling new guests to his studio with unreasonable and uncomfortable demands (some joking, some not: he almost always told guests to make art, and expected them to play along, but also enjoyed telling particularly respectable-looking guests to "strip and get in bed," and similarly inappropriate directions intended only to provoke).

The paradox of B. U. Kashkin's approach revolves around the permissiveness of perestroika—nothing was suddenly true, and everything was permissible, so long as it sold—as the blacksmith Lysiakov argued. B. U. Kashkin's radicalism consists of totally rejecting this idea, insisting on social unity and collectivism like an old-fashioned communist: insisting that socially positive acts like Kartinnik's loving painting of trash bins were also permissible, because no one forbade them either (even though, in the strictest legal sense, painting public property was equally forbidden before and after perestroika). B. U. Kashkin acted with none of the baggage and certainly no love for the opportunistic and mercenary models offered by the encroachment of neoliberalism. B. U. Kashkin's artistic approach is structurally dissimilar from that of a "proper" Soviet artist, and yet unexpected for a nonconformist. His art bleeds into life, which in turn resembles the life of a fictional character from Soviet inspirational literature—like Lenin, but not the historical Lenin, rather the Lenin of the many Soviet children's books about Lenin organizing a snowball fight or a New Year's Eve party for orphans. It is this parodic and yet naïvely earnest anti-leadership that renders B. U. Kashkin's authority appealing and palatable to the young people that by rights should have rejected both his authority and peculiarity, and that allowed B. U. Kashkin to exercise the power that he exercised despite lacking a supporting institution, fame, and wealth.

CONCLUSION

B. U. Kashkin's paradoxical shift to social activism deserves extra focus, as it resonates powerfully with contemporary radical artists. Contemporary actionism is inseparable from social activism: for instance, Katrin Nenasheva, whose early work was actionist in character, has in recent years increasingly turned her practice to social organizing and community service. Maxim Hanukai directly characterizes her work as addressing an "ethic of radical care."[30] In early works like *Punishment* (2016), where Nenasheva cleaned city streets while strapped to a prison bed, or in *Between Here and There* (2017). In *Between Here and There*, Nenasheva first gained access to an asylum for children, where they are confined indefinitely without meaningful treatment, and photographed the desperate conditions within. Her documentation showed the asylum as an inheritor of the Soviet Union's legacy of punitive mental care, arguing that many of the children locked within were there because their parents found it convenient to be rid of them. Then Nenasheva played her photographs in a sequence within a virtual reality helmet that she wore through Moscow's streets, blinded by the helmet to the world outside the asylum playing before her eyes. Part of the action was the obligation to stop and share the helmet and the images within it with any passerby that requested it. In a dramatic twist, Nenasheva was arrested in the course of the action, because she joined an ongoing protest against the regime while blindly following the noise of the crowd through the helmet. In this action, Nenasheva directly engaged the actionist politics described by Jacques Rancière as the "distribution of the sensible" in his book *The Politics of Aesthetics* (2000).[31] Her actions contested the possible and imaginable as presented by society through direct interventions that "call into question the distribution of roles, territories, and languages...contribut[ing] to the formation of political subjects that challenge the given distribution of the sensible."[32] Hanukai characterizes Nenasheva's work as building on the dissolution of binary oppositions:

> Every time Nenasheva stepped out onto the street in her VR glasses, she appeared to passersby as someone outside the norm. Some thought she was blind and offered to help, others reacted aggressively, while others still sought to initiate a conversation. As a result, different

> kinds of "betweenspaces" arose in the course of the action: between the outside world and the psychiatric ward, strength and vulnerability, social work and artistic practice, "norm" and "not norm."[33]

Hanukai's reading emphasizes how this dissolution of binaries creates a "betweenspace" for Nenasheva to both confront, mitigate, and suffer pent-up social violence, and to provide the kind of "radical care" she sees as desperately lacking in contemporary Russian society.

However, in the wake of Russia's invasion of Ukraine in 2022, Nenasheva has almost completely abandoned art-making in favor of social organizing. While representing this as a personal crisis in social media posts, she has nevertheless dedicated her efforts to projects like "Teens and Kittens," a support and group-therapy space for teenagers suffering from addiction, marginalized for their sexual or gender orientation, or otherwise unrepresented and maligned within mainstream Russian society. She is also running a support group for opposition artists who chose not to emigrate and to remain as outsiders in Putin's Russia called "We Remain." More and more, Nenasheva's practice abandons the production of individual artworks for circulation, instead privileging radical care as an end in itself, but an end necessarily driven underground, if only because Putin's regime refuses to support or nurture the groups with which Nenasheva interacts most—marginalized and vulnerable youth.

Nenasheva's work builds on the legacy of such feminist artists as Mierle Laderman Ukeles' *Washing/Tracks/Maintenance: Outside* (1973), where Ukeles reclaimed the invisible and unappreciated labor of maintenance and cleaning for art, via photography and documentation. Writing in her 1969 Maintenance Art Manifesto, Ukeles draws a distinction between "Development" and "Maintenance," writing by way of an explanation: "The sourball of every revolution, who's going to pick up the garbage Monday morning?"[34] Ukeles' critique of radicalism in art focuses on this obligation to pick up garbage as crucial, identifying it with a gendered and marginalized labor: "The culture confers lousy status on maintenance jobs=minimum wages, housewives=no pay."[35] Ukeles realized her critique through a series of performances, which typically involve performing janitorial labor like washing the steps of the Wadsworth Atheneum in 1973 for *Washing/Tracks/Maintenance: Outside*, or in the 1974 *Transfer: The Maintenance of the Art Object*, cleaning a case displaying an Egyptian mummy, and donating the act of cleaning as her artwork for the collection. In Ukeles' case, the feminist critique also relied on the redistribution of the sensible, shifting the audience's focus to invisible and marginalized labor, whose marginalization has clear markers of sexism, classicism, and racism that Ukeles exposed and examined through her actions. B. U. Kashkin's and Nenasheva's works resonate with Ukeles', not only in explicit parallels, such as the performance of cleaning in public, but in the overall effort to reclaim the valuable but neglected and marginalized labor of the subaltern through art, drawing it into focus and appreciation. However, Nenasheva's reclamation is not specifically of cleaning and maintenance labor, but of socially beneficial labor as such—of witnessing suffering and doing all the necessary and unpleasant work of facing it, from taking care of derelict public spaces, to nurturing mentally ill castaways, maligned children, and vulnerable addicts—all work that Russian society either fails to do, or delegates to underpaid or unpaid and neglected women.

This effort is profoundly kindred to B. U. Kashkin's project—an alternative to the pursuit of artistic power and the shock methods of actionism, embracing a socially positive communal practice of maintenance, of improving and beautifying those zones of society that seem structurally neglected, causing decay and suffering. Furthermore, if Ukeles' work was pro-social to an extreme, ultimately resulting in Ukeles becoming the official artist of the NYC department of sanitation, both Nenasheva and B. U. Kashkin do their socially positive activity without official sanction, as though setting up institution parallel or perpendicular to those already existing in their society. Their maintenance activity is on the edge of open criminality, suggesting that the decay they challenge is not a product of neglect, but willful design.

This means that both retain one key element of actionist politics: their socially positive acts are in direct confrontation with their society. The legacy initiated by B. U. Kashkin and carried by Nenasheva is powered by their fundamental ambivalence about artistic power and authority. Both experimented with an artistic practice where the artist's ability to subject their audience to an undesirable experience for their own good is an important (or even necessary) formal component. Both went on to methodically eliminate the role of violence and power instead, reducing their own authority to merely facilitating the artistic and affective dimensions of an audience's self-guided liberation, but directing this effort to the greater society. In B. U. Kashkin's case the artist's society has no interest in revitalizing anything without a profit, and in Nenasheva's case, it would explicitly have all the people and suffering that she reveals remain silent and invisible instead. In a word, whereas Ukeles is recuperating subaltern labor to the benefit of her society, both B. U. Kashkin and Nenasheva are setting up alternate societies—byways and underpasses, patching up the holes in the social fabric left by both the institutional neglect and neoliberal callousness of the 1990s.

Notes

1 Materials for this volume were also presented at an exhibition organized by Shaburov for the Garazh Exhibition of Contemporary Art in 2010. The volume itself was published to accompany the 2015 exhibition "Lived a life, still alive: a tribute to B. U. Kashkin" in the Ural branch of the Government Center of Contemporary Art. There was also a 2019 exposition of the B. U. Kashkin Museum at the Ural State Federal University in Yekaterinburg.

2 Mark Lipovetsky et al., eds., *Oxford Handbook of Soviet Underground Culture* (New York; London: Oxford University Press, 2024), 2.

3 Alexander Shaburov, ed., Б.У. Кашкин (1938–2005) Жизнь и творчество уральского панк-скомороха [B. U .Kashkin (1938–2005) *The Life and Work of a Ural Punk-Skomorokh*] (Ekaterinburg: Ural branch of the Government Center for Contemporary Art, 2015), 328.

4 Shaburov, *Б.У. Кашкин*, 37.

5 Shaburov, 37–38.

6 Shaburov, 38.

7 Lena Jonson, "Introduction," in *Russia—Art Resistance and the Conservative-Authoritarian Zeitgeist* (London: Routledge, 2018), 16.

8 Shaburov, 40–41.

9 Shaburov, 46.

10 Ekaterina Bobrinskaia, Чужие? Неофициальное искусство: мифы, стратегии, концепции [*Others? Unofficial Art: Myths, Strategies, Concepts*] (Moscow: Shalva Breus, 2012), 332–70.

11 Ilya Kabakov, 60-е-70-е...Записки о неофициальной жизни в Москве [*The 60s–70s...Notes on Unofficial Life in Moscow*] (Wien: Wiener Slawistischer Almanach, 1999), 55.

12 Bobrinskaia, *Чужие? Неофициальное искусство*, 334.

13 Shaburov, 48.

14 Matthew Jesse Jackson, *The Experimental Group: Ilya Kabakov, Moscow Conceptualism, Soviet Avant-Gardes* (Chicago: University of Chicago Press, 2010), 243.

15 Shaburov, 47.

16 Shaburov, 372.

17 Shaburov, 381.

18 Shaburov, 382.

19 Andrei Kovalev, ed., Российский Акционизм 1990–2000 [Russian Actionism 1990–2000] (Moscow: World Art Museum (#28–29), 2007), 12, 163–64.

20 Kovalev, *Российский Акционизм1990–2000*, 157.

21 Andrei Monastyrsky, ed., Поездки за город [*Trips out of Town*] (Moscow: Ad Marginem, 1998), 29.

22 Yelena Kalinsky, ed. and trans., *Collective Actions: Audience Recollections from the First Five Years, 1976–1981* (Chicago: Soberscove Press, 2012), 70.

23 Kalinsky, *Collective Actions*, 24.

24 The "Kartinnik"/ "Picture-Man" Society at the Dam Boardwalk in Sverdlovsk, 1989, in Alexander Shaburov, ed. Б.У. Кашкин (1938–2005) Жизнь и творчество уральского панк-скомороха [B. U. Kashkin (1938–2005) *The Life and Work of a Ural Punk-Skomorokh*] (Ekaterinburg: Ural branch of the Government Center for Contemporary Art, 2015), 376–77.

25 Maksim Hanukai, "Russian Actionism as Biopolitical Performance: Shifting Grounds and Forms of Resistance," *Russian Literature* 141 (2023): 127.

26 Hanukai, "Russian Actionism as Biopolitical Performance," 127.

27 Shaburov, 448.

28 Shaburov, 452.

29 Shaburov, 452.

30 Hanukai, 125.

31 Jacques Rancière, *The Politics of Aesthetics: The Distribution of the Sensible*, trans. G. Rockhill (New York: Continuum International, 2004), 12–19.

32 Rancière, 40.

33 Hanukai, 126.

34 Mierle Laderman Ukeles, *Maintenance Art Manifesto*, 1969. Accessed June 30, 2023, https://queensmuseum.org/wp-content/uploads/2016/04/Ukeles-Manifesto-for-Maintenance-Art-1969.pdf, 1.

35 Ukeles, *Maintenance Art Manifesto*, 2.

Works Cited

Bobrinskaia, Ekaterina. *Чужие? Неофициальное искусство: мифы, стратегии, концепции* [*Others? Unofficial Art: Myths, Strategies, Concepts*]. Moscow: Shalva Breus, 2012.

Groys, Boris. *Утопия и Обмен* [*Utopia and Exchange*]. Moscow: Znak, 1993.

Hanukai, Maksim. "Russian Actionism as Biopolitical Performance: Shifting Grounds and Forms of Resistance." *Russian Literature* 141 (2023): 111–42.

Jackson, Matthew Jesse. *The Experimental Group: Ilya Kabakov, Moscow Conceptualism, Soviet Avant-Gardes*. Chicago: University of Chicago Press, 2010.

Jonson, Lena. "Introduction". In *Russia—Art Resistance and the Conservative-Authoritarian Zeitgeist*, 1–25. London: Routledge, 2018.

Kabakov, Ilya. *60-е-70-е... Записки о неофициальной жизни в Москве* [*The 60s–70s...Notes on Unofficial Life in Moscow*]. Wien: Wiener Slawistischer Almanach, 1999.

Kalinsky, Yelena, ed. and trans. *Collective Actions: Audience Recollections from the First Five Years, 1976–1981*. Chicago: Soberscove Press, 2012.

Kovalev, Andrei, ed. *Российский Акционизм 1990–2000* [*Russian Actionism 1990–2000*]. Moscow: World Art Museum (#28–29), 2007.

Lipovetsky, Mark, Maria Engstrom, Tomas Glanc, Ilja Kukuj, and Klavdia Smola, eds. *Oxford Handbook of Soviet Underground Culture*. New York; London: Oxford University Press, 2024.

Monastyrsky, Andrei, ed. *Поездки за город* [*Trips out of Town*]. Moscow: Ad Marginem, 1998.

Nenasheva, Katrin. *Катрин Ненашева: документация акций 2015–2020* [*Katrin Nenasheva: Documentation of Actions 2015–2020*]. Google doc shared by the artist, 2022.

Rancière, Jacques. *The Politics of Aesthetics: The Distribution of the Sensible*, trans. G. Rockhill (New York: Continuum International, 2004), 12–19.

Shaburov, Alexander, ed. *Б.У. Кашкин (1938–2005) Жизнь и творчество уральского панк-скомороха* [*B. U. Kashkin (1938–2005) The Life and Work of a Ural Punk-Skomorokh*]. Ekaterinburg: Ural branch of the Government Center for Contemporary Art, 2015.

Ukeles, Mierle Laderman. *Maintenance Art Manifesto*, 1969. Accessed June 30, 2023. https://queensmuseum.org/wp-content/uploads/2016/04/Ukeles-Manifesto-for-Maintenance-Art-1969.pdf.

CHAPTER 6
Russia's Gay (and Not-So-Gay) Nineties: Sexual and Gender-Expression Pluralism in the First Post-Soviet Decade

Thomas Keenan[1]

In 2013, Vladimir Putin signed into law legislation providing steep penalties for "propaganda of nontraditional sexual relationships in the presence of minors," effectively outlawing any public expression of LGBTQIA identities in any venue where people under the age of eighteen might be present. In 2014 Russia annexed Crimea and began the current war on Ukraine. In January 2018—right in the middle of the ten-year arc described in this paragraph—what looked like an enormously disproportionate reaction of Russian authorities to a homoerotic parody video produced by some Russian air-transport cadets occasioned a flood of similarly homoerotic sympathy videos, in which homoerotism appeared in fact to be simply a trope for resistance to authoritarian limitations of individual self-expression.[2] In February 2022 Russia launched its full-scale invasion of Ukraine. In December 2022 Putin enacted a law prohibiting any and all "propaganda" of "nontraditional" sexual orientations or relationships, and of transgenderism and transsexualism, via any means of mass communication (this has been broadly understood to include social media). "Propaganda" has been broadly interpreted to mean any material that presents "nontraditional" sexual relationships or gender expressions in a positive or neutral way, or is seen to represent them as legitimate alternatives to those of the heterosexual cis-gendered male/female binary. Between the Ukraine invasion and the further anti-LGBTQIA screw-tightening, in a September 2022 speech Putin committed a complex of brazen acts of rhetorical deflection and inversion in an attempt to cast the West as dictatorial suppressor—and Russia as the stalwart defender—of people's right to self-determination (*samoopredelenie* and *voleiz'iavlenie*).[3] That speech was centered around the delegitimization and rhetorical erasure of a curious dyad of identities: the Ukrainian national identity, and LGBTQIA identities. These have been two throughlines of Putin's narrative of a clash between a decadent Western civilization and an ascendent Russian civilization: that Ukraine is part of extended Russian territory on which the West is trying to encroach by sponsoring separatist extremists and promoting the fiction of a separate and distinct Ukrainian nation, and that expressions of sexual and gender pluralism in Russia represent the insidious contaminations of a dissolute Western culture.[4]

The first, however distorted and riddled with fallacies, has an evident internal logic and geopolitical-strategic function within Putin's larger Russia–West scheme. The function of the second is less obvious. How did pluralism of sexuality and gender expression become so prominent an element in this campaign and such a lightning rod for the Putin regime's anti-Western animus?[5] What is at the root of the violent phobia of public expression of LGBTQIA identities that views this as a threat to the Russian state somehow related to the threat of an autonomous Ukraine? The answer appears to be that both of these phenomena are, to the Putin regime, emblematic of a dangerous tendency of lower-stratum free agency and spontaneous self-determination, an atomizing, disaggregating momentum that poses a direct challenge to the imperial, patriarchal model of great-power statehood that the Putin regime has pursued for twenty-first-century Russia. In the shape of the Putinist historiography of the Soviet and post-Soviet eras, LGBTQIA belongs to the same category of destructive Western forces that sowed the chaos of the 1990s in Russia and, per Putin's September 2022 speech cited here, very nearly destroyed it. It is a part of the same anti-Russian Western force responsible for Euromaidan, a "neo-Nazi coup" sponsored by "Western masters." This is a historiography that reactivates the improbable association between LGBTQIA and Fascism,[6] as well as Great Patriotic War-history tropes of traitorous Ukrainian Nazi collaborationists, in a grand narrative wherein the West emerges as the anti-Russia. The post-Euromaidan era has produced portmanteaus such as "homofascism" and "homofascists" (*gomofashizm*, *gomofashisty*), ostensibly denoting forceful imposition of an LGBTQIA agenda on unwilling populations, but, on a deeper level, representing an instance of the Putin regime's decoupling of the words *Fascism* and *Fascist* from their original meanings and conversion of them into floating signifiers, the immense emotional force of which for the collective Russian consciousness can be mobilized against any entity the regime deems hostile to Russia (or to itself as coterminous with the Russian state and the Russian nation).

The thirty LGBTQIA-related artifacts in the Sourcebook show a cross-section of media responses to the novelty of public expression of sexual and gender pluralism in the 1990s—the crucible in which Russia's twenty-first-century political culture was forged. The artifacts' analysis in this essay finds that, in the dizzyingly unstable first post-Soviet decade—immediately following the glasnost experiments with openness and the collapse of the Soviet state, and immediately preceding Putin's introduction to the Russian public—tolerance or intolerance for publicly declared "nontraditional" sexual and gender identities functions as an eloquent index of post-Soviet Russia's identity crisis, its fraught rapprochement with the West, and Russia's tolerance for pluralism and individual self-determination in general. The 1990s are a historical moment of exhilarating but also frighteningly chaotic and often destructive lawless freedom that paved the way for Putin's rise to power on a promise to restore order and stability. This is a moment of many different imaginary Wests and imaginary Russias[7]—past, present, and future. In this moment, the responses to pluralism of sexual and gender identities in the public sphere are a kind of barometer of the extent to which Russians imagine pluralism and freedom of individual self-determination in general are possible in a hypothetical near-future Russia conceived not as a phenotype of a Western model of statehood, but as an expression of some uniquely Russian essence, as a polity and culture apart from the West.

The analysis of these artifacts and the wider phenomena they document finds that, broadly speaking, in the 1990s in Russia public expression of what in contemporary Western terminology are referred to as LGBTQIA identities proved incompatible with emergent post-Soviet Russian national identities that insisted on a vision of Russia as a distinct political and cultural entity outside the Western world.[8] The 1990s in Russia are a time of radical political, social, and cultural instability, crises of identity from the national down to the individual level, and a flooding-in of new, primarily Western, foreign influences. In this moment of experimenting with new identities and models of self-conception and self-presentation, the West's relatively recent social, political, and cultural integration of LGBTQIA people occasioned a range of responses in Russia, both from people experiencing homosexual desire and/or gender dysphoria, and in the wider cultural and political arena. Some, who saw the end of the Soviet experiment as an occasion for Russia to be reintegrated with a Western civilization from which it had been violently severed in 1917, advocated unmodified adoption of the LGBTQIA categories. For those insisting on a non-Western Russian national identity, public declarative sexual or gender self-presentations outside the cis-gendered, heterosexual model tended to be seen as at odds with that national identity. Same-sex erotic desire and struggles with gender identity are viewed here as things that must submit to the limitations imposed by that national identity in the social and public spheres, including but not necessarily limited to mass communication. On the part of many subjects of homosexual desire and/or gender dysphoria themselves there is a sense that open expression of "nontraditional" sexual and gender identities is somehow un-Russian. They express a voluntary submission to, even comfort with, limitations imposed by an authoritarian structure that requires social and public performance of the heterosexual cis-gender binary, and they recognize insistence on social or public expressions of other sexual and gender identities as affrontive excesses of idiosyncrasy and selfish demands for individualistic freedom that challenge the very valuable stability and rigor of a distinctly Russian social and political structure. There is a comfort with taboos enforcing a discursive silence of sexual desire and gender expressions outside of these rigidly restrictive norms, and with relegation of those experiences beyond the margins of social, public, and political life.

All of this seems to anticipate the Putin regime's intense phobias around sexual and gender-expression pluralism as dangerously anarchical elements that threaten the stability of Russian society, phobias that turned them into a synecdochic target for righteous invective in the ideology of an ascendent Russian civilization opposing a decadent Western civilization, and phobias that occasioned the regime's efforts to legislate those pluralisms out of rhetorical existence. These phobias are foreshadowed in a 1990s media landscape that exhibits particular patterns of presence and absence, declarative expression and silence around LGBTQIA. There are a number of new periodical titles (mostly with very limited circulation) produced by and for mostly West-oriented LGBTQIA Russians who openly self-identify as such. There is the more or less total absence from the mainstream media sphere of a category documented in sociological studies: 1990s Russians who preferred to persist in late-Soviet patterns of performing cis-gendered heterosexuality while indulging same-sex erotic desire and/or fluidity of gender expression in clandestine ways that insulated these behaviors from their social and public identities. Mainstream media picks up some of the activities of a very small number of LGBTQIA rights activists—some who adopt those Western-styled sexual and/or gender identities, some who resist them and continue to search for distinctly Russian ways of doing sexual and gender-expression pluralism—and a variety of responses to this from the wider contemporary society. Finally, an interesting performance-silence pattern is documented in early post-Soviet mass-consumed artistic culture: a *stiob*-like aesthetic play at authorial identification and non-identification with, or proximity to and distance from, artistic personas or alter-egos that extravagantly perform homosexual desire and/or ambiguous gender expression.

THE LGBTQIA PRESS IN 1990S RUSSIA

In the immediate post-Soviet years, a number of limited-circulation periodicals aimed directly at an LGBTQIA (to use contemporary Western terminology) readership are inaugurated.[9] This novel niche corner of the rapidly evolving Russian 1990s media sphere at-large documents a number of interesting trends among the authors and publishers who produced this material and among their readership (at least as those authors and publishers envisioned it). Several different imaginary Wests and imaginary Russias are represented in this material, as are different categories of LGBTQIA identities representing different postures vis-à-vis Russia and the West—past, present, and future.

A rush to adopt Western modes of public expression of "nontraditional" sexual and gender identities, as well as Western LGBTQIA mass-media genres, is well documented in the periodical output of the early 1990s. After the acknowledged failure of the Soviet project, some quotient of the Russian population lurched into an individualist, consumerist societal model where entertainment of personal desires and ambitions were seen as the primary economic and cultural engines, and there were LGBTQIA dimensions of this heady swing from the Soviet command-economy system to the free-market one. For part of the emergent community of people of unconventional sexual and/or gender identities, this new centering of individual desire manifested as an unrestrained erotic hedonism. Desires repressed as deviant and socially dangerous in the Soviet era are expressed and indulged on the pages of these titles in a celebratory way that seems not to brook inhibition of any kind. These issues imply an imagined contemporary Russia that is essentially indistinguishable from a Western imaginary of post-Stonewall "Pride" sexual identities centered around a festive homoerotic sensuality largely unencumbered by any grander political, social, or intellectual ambitions. This ethos is documented in 1990s Russian versions of 1980s and 1990s Western LGBTQIA periodical genres: glossy magazines presenting an LGBTQIA culture defined by emphatic sexuality and glamor. The issues are made up of nude photographs of young, athletic men (less often women); erotic fantasy fiction; pieces on figures from the realms of cinema, popular music, television, and fashion; and advertisements for products and services (frequently sex-related).[10] They represent an uncritical adoption of modes of LGBTQIA communal-identity expression from the post-Stonewall West, modes where the defining features of a collective gay identity and the basis for community cohesion were first and foremost the specificities of sexual desire and practice themselves, and secondarily preferences and tastes in the areas of clothing style, recreation, and popular culture. These publications tended to adopt Western lexicon as well, using the word "gay" (*гей*)—at the time a neologism in Russian—instead of more familiar Russian expressions such as "sexual minorities," "homosexuals," "sexually exceptional people."

Some of these publications made rather superficial attempts at rooting the LGBTQ culture they represented in a deeper history, often via references to an august Greco-Roman antiquity in which homosexual relationships were commonplace.[11] In general, though, the publications in this category were concerned exclusively with the here-and-now, and could be described as not having any serious political, intellectual, or cultural agendas.

There were also periodicals proposing distinct collective LGBTQIA identities that insisted on deeper roots and more dimensions than just the specificities of sexual desire and practice, recreation, and entertainment, including but not limited to a political dimension. They asserted a distinct communal gay and lesbian identity that was the collective subject of a long, rich, and complex history and a legacy of much longer endurance and deeper cultural consequence than more of-the-moment popular-culture entertainments. The emphasis on a deeper diachronic dimension of the collective LGBTQIA historical and cultural identity seems motivated at least in part by an imperative to dismantle the perception that gay men and lesbians were no more than a category of scattered isolated deviants leading marginal lives and leaving no appreciable lasting effect on the societies they inhabited. A group of publications worked to promote a view of gay men and lesbians as categories that had been a distinct but integral part of Western culture from its earliest beginnings.[12] Like their more hedonistic and consumerist contemporaries, this category of LGBTQIA periodical also tended to have a distinctly Western cultural orientation, albeit one of greater diachronic scope and intellectual ambition. There appears to be a broadly shared view here of Russia as a participant in the larger project of Western civilization up to the moment when it is artificially isolated from that cultural evolution by the Soviet experiment. On the other side of that failed experiment in the early 1990s, these proponents of LGBTQIA identities pursue an agenda to rejoin post-Soviet Russian culture with the West, and to repair the rupture in twentieth-century Russian LGBTQIA history and culture by regathering the fragments of that history and culture that were scattered into the West by the violence of the Bolshevik Revolution and the Soviet order's hostility toward diversity of sexual identities and gender expressions. The representation of the West presented in these periodical issues is, of course, a very selective one. It is an idealized, chronologically generalized vision that refers often to a pantheon of canonized figures (Michelangelo, DaVinci, Oscar Wilde, Marcel Proust, Thomas Mann, Andre Gide, Pier Paolo Pasolini) and implies an organic integration of LGBTQIA elements into Western culture, eliding the more troubled aspects of that legacy. There is scant reference to, for example, Wilde's persecution.[13]

A number of gay and lesbian periodicals from the early post-Soviet era document efforts to reconnect with a lost pre-Soviet Russian LGBTQIA artistic and intellectual legacy from what is cast as a present moment akin to a Renaissance after the dark middle age of a repressive, obscurantist Soviet regime that did not tolerate open declaration of anything resembling non-hetero or non-binary sexual or gender identities in the historical record or public sphere. Numerous contributions to these titles go about the business of restoring essential LGBTQIA dimensions to the identities of canonical figures, such as those of the nineteenth-century writer Nikolai Gogol, nineteenth-century composer Pyotr Ilich Tchaikovsky, and the early twentieth-century poets Marina Tsvetaeva, Sergei Esenin, Viacheslav Ivanov, Zinaida Gippius, Sophia Parnok, and Soviet cinema auteur Sergei Eisenstein. There were also pieces aimed at restoring figures unfairly effaced or sidelined by the Russian cultural canons as inherited from the Soviet era: the likes of the poet and prose writer Mikhail Kuzmin and poets Nikolai Kluyev and Valery Pereleshin.[14]

Several of these periodical titles present a sort of idealized pre-Soviet, extra-Soviet (émigré), and a hoped-for post-Soviet Russia that is a distinctly Western category, a Russia that, but for the aberration of the Soviet era, would have continued to partake of Western political and cultural evolution. This Western Russian identity implies a postulated Western normalization of sexual and gender-expression pluralism. A vignette on the relationship between Marina Tsvetaeva and Sofia Parnok (Artifact 00023),[a] for example, adumbrates an early-twentieth-century Russian society that responds

[a] https://postsoviet90s.com/artifacts/tsvetaeva-and-parnok

to romantic relationships between people of the same sex as matters of course, focusing as it does very narrowly on the milieu of Tsvetaeva and Parnok, which included Mikhail Kuzmin. For the Soviet era, there is a sort of reassembling of pieces of a Russian LGBTQIA culture dispersed into the West by the Bolshevik political and cultural violence, both at the level of Russian cultural figures whose creative output was realized or distributed largely or only in the West (Diahghilev, Tsvetaeva, Vicheslav Ivanov, Zinaida Gippius, Eisenstein), and at the level of the reconstruction of LGBTQIA Russian cultural history via the scholarly work of Russian émigrés based in the United States, scholarly work that could not have been undertaken in Soviet Russia. The latter category, again, presents only a very fragmentary picture. Represented almost exclusively by the work of Simon Karlinsky, it prescinds from accounts of the fierce resistance from others in the international Russian émigré community to his work on LGBTQIA elements in Russian culture.[15]

These periodicals also present another variety of Russian LGBTQIA identity predicated on a view of Russian culture as a subcategory of Western culture from which it was artificially severed through the Soviet period. Unlike the model already discussed, where sexual, gender, and cultural identities derive primarily from pre-Soviet and/or extra-Soviet origins, this model presents distinctly post-Soviet identities defined first and foremost by Soviet experience. The imaginary Russia here is primarily a particular memory of the Soviet past, a kind of revisionist history that is an LGBTQIA facet of a broader social phenomenon of the early post-Soviet moment. That broader phenomenon is the process of national soul searching at the end of the Soviet era, involving excavation of a Soviet legacy that had until then been studiously hidden from the public, a process perhaps best instantiated in the work of the organization Memorial (liquidated by order of the Russian Supreme Court in 2021) and new Russian editions of the memoiristic accounts of former political prisoners of the Soviet penal system such as Alexander Solzhenitsyn and Varlam Shalamov.[16] The imaginary West in these texts is that of the democratic vision of the WWII Allies, seen in opposition to the antidemocratic, totalitarian vision of the Axis powers. In spite of its official WWII allegiances, the Soviet Union is paired in this model with the Fascist regimes as a retrograde, patriarchal, totalitarian state.

There is a very forceful challenge here to a crucial Soviet historiographic orthodoxy, the officially shaped national memory of an identity-defining Russian confrontation with the West: the official Soviet history of the clash between the Soviet Union and Nazi Germany, which casts Russia as a just force for social progress pitted against the evil retrograde tyrannical German oppressor. Some publications in LGBTQIA periodicals in 1990s Russia present accounts of sexuality and gender in the Soviet Union as, like so many other areas of Soviet life, a backslide into a patriarchal authoritarianism and into a social and aesthetic conservatism that rendered Soviet life and culture counterintuitively similar to life and culture under the Soviet system's arch-antagonist far-right order—Fascism and Nazism. They document a legacy of virulent and oppressive sexual and gender conservatism that was an aspect of the Soviet order's pervasive hypocrisy: the de facto retrograde patriarchy of the ostensibly ultra-progressive Soviet system. LGBTQIA victims of Soviet oppression give first-hand accounts of a totalitarian apparatus that regarded their private erotic desires as incompatible with its grander societal plan, and one that pathologized or criminalized and brutally punished pursuit of those desires.

Women found to have been involved in same-sex relations were considered to be mentally ill and often compelled to submit to treatment by a Soviet state whose emancipatory program for women, at least in its ultimate application, did not accommodate this kind of self-determination or expression and pursuit of a female sexuality beyond the male–female sexual relations that advanced larger political imperatives such as population expansion.[17] The post-WWII Soviet state's response to male homosexuality was both more violent and more complex. Sexual relations between men was a criminal offense, and men discovered to be engaged in homosexual activity were sentenced to terms in penal colonies and prisons. Inside those facilities, sexual activity among the all-male inmates was widespread and functioned as part of the mechanism that regulated the social hierarchy and an economy of masculine dominance and a feminoid submission. Men known to have been receivers of penetrative sex acts were referred to as *opushchennye*, as fallen, demeaned, or humiliated. They occupied the lowest point in the social hierarchy. The quotidian experience of these inmates was so unrelentingly horrific that often they chose suicide as an avenue of escape. Their persecution was often compounded by the authorities in charge of the penal facilities who singled out inmates witnessed in the receptive position of penetrative sex acts for prosecution under the Soviet Union's sodomy laws (Article 121 of the Criminal Code), which had the effect of prolonging their sentences and therefore also their abuse. The inmates on the delivery end in these sex events—including aggressors in acts of rape—often enjoyed total impunity. These testimonies belie the myth of the Soviet ultra-progressive leftist policy of gender equality through exposure of the most intensely primitive patriarchal hierarchy of gendered values. Masculinity was by definition aggressive, domineering, and predatory, and a priori superior to femininity, which was by definition submissive. Manifestation by an anatomically male person of attributes understood as feminine was, in this paradigm, viewed as an abomination that rendered that person subhuman.

Addressing an early post-Soviet audience as eyewitnesses of these abuses, these commentators report that, as a rule, their non-LGBTQIA fellow victims and resisters of Soviet oppression were, at worst, complicit in the state's persecution of "sexual dissidents," and, at best, indifferent to their plight. They also report that the ostracism of "sexual dissidents" or "sexual non-conformists" (*seksual'nye dissidenty, seksual'nye inakomysliashchie*) has continued in post-Soviet life.

These accounts were published at a time when discussion of the horrific injustices of the Soviet penal system was a crucial part of larger efforts to reveal darker elements of Soviet history that had been concealed from the Soviet public. This was an essential part of post-Soviet Russia's new public sphere. LGBTQIA people, however, were excluded from these wider processes of post-Soviet Russians' discovery of their own recent historical legacy, and from rehabilitative and healing processes of acknowledged injustice and redeemed suffering that elevated and commemorated victims of Soviet-era abuses. Worse, the ostracism and persecution of LGBTQIA Russians was being perpetuated in the new post-Soviet social and cultural reality. Any men engaging in sexual activity with other men through 1993 were criminals and subject to prison sentences per in-force Russian law.[18] Several early post-Soviet documenters of the plight of LGBTQIA people under the Soviet regime (among them Gennady Trifonov, Valery Klimov, and Yaroslav "Slava" Mogutin) decry the indifference, disdain, or worse, approval vis-à-vis the vicious persecution of men labeled as passive homosexuals in the works of newly lionized Soviet dissidents. At best the abuses of these men (*opushchennye*) are passed over in silence in these testimonies. At worst, the sense of their abject degradation and even subhumanity is justified and perpetuated by accounts that seem to share the Soviet system's disgust for this category of person. Although these non-conformist thinkers railed against the Soviet system's dictatorial intolerance of pluralism and exposed that system's similarity to its ostensibly antithetical arch-conservative adversaries—Fascism and Nazism—they showed themselves to be intolerant of pluralism in the area of sexual identity or gender expression. In this respect they appear to be not at all at odds with the patriarchal sensibility that prescribes rigidly defined gender roles, imposes narrow limits on sexual behavior, and views deviation from this by men as a descent from masculine dignity. In addition to the memoiristic accounts of prisoner-chroniclers like Solzhenitsyn and Shalamov, this posture of celebrated Soviet-era dissidents vis-à-vis their sexually different non-conformist fellows is instantiated in remarks made by Elena Bonner in a 1991 interview with Masha Gessen (Artifact 00025).[b]

The swift upheaval of these early post-Soviet years to some extent elevated dissidents and rehabilitated victims of Soviet repression to a new élite martyr-hero status in a sort of inversion of Soviet-era hierarchies. Some exponents of LGBTQIA identities in this moment present those identities as part of that new post-Soviet élite category. This was a moment of shedding received social identities determined by a now defunct political apparatus, and expressing social identities representative of individual sensibilities. It was a moment that exalted the dissidents—those who in the pre-perestroika, preglasnost Soviet era had suffered terribly for having the courage of their convictions and declaring positions that represented grave political and social liabilities. Commentators

---

[b] https://postsoviet90s.com/artifacts/elena-bonner-nothing-interests-me-less-than-this-problem

like Trifonov, Klimov, and Mogutin present post-Soviet gays and lesbians as not just sexually different, but sexually dissident.[19] To denote what would now be termed differences of sexual orientation, these commentators use the phrases "sexual dissidents," "sexual dissidence," "sexual non-conformism," and "sexual non-conformists" ("*seksual'nye dissidenty,*" "*seksual'noe dissidentstvo,*" "*seksual'noe inakomysliashchie,*" and "*seksual'noe inakomyslie*").[20] In the Russian language the latter two phrases have a strong connotation of non-conformist *thinkers* and non-conformist *thought*. These exponents of LGBTQIA identities in early post-Soviet Russia appended the qualifier "sexual" to these distinguished late-Soviet and early post-Soviet categories, categories enjoying a certain reverence for their noble resistance to authoritarian powers and martyrdom for the cause of diversity of thought, plurality of perspectives and subjectivities, and liberties to express the same in the social and public spheres. These distinctly late-Soviet and post-Soviet models are deployed here with the "sexual" qualifier to signal belonging to this Soviet legacy of righteous suffering. In fact, to some extent Soviet and post-Soviet LGBTQ people are represented here as dissidents par excellence, as dissidents among dissidents, dissidents who were disdained by the other dissidents, and whose persecution persisted into the post-Soviet political and social reality.

In one of the artifacts in this project's Sourcebook, an article from the journal *Gay, Slavs!* by Gennadii Trifonov (Artifact 00178),[c] the author expresses a profound pessimism regarding the future of tolerance of sexual and gender-expression pluralism in Russia, and regarding the future of democracy and individual freedoms of self-determination in Russia generally.

> It is unthinkable that something like the uniquely English phenomenon of Oscar Wilde could appear in Russia anytime in the next three hundred years. For, even as the number of Moseses ready to lead us out of the Egypt of our own making increases by the day, our soul continues to cherish our native darkness, where we stumble and trample each other and into which we sink ever deeper with a wanton, admirable abandon.[21]

Trifonov refers in this article to a centrality of criminal culture in post-imperial Russian politics—the fact that, after the tsars, ultimate responsibility for the administration of the state was assumed by rebels and revolutionaries who had spent time in prisons and penal camps. He adduces this as an origin of Russia's patriarchal attitude toward (male) homosexuality, concluding that attitude is derived from the brutally enforced hierarchies of all-male prisoner populations. He observes that a persistent pervasiveness of homophobia in Russia is one of the few things that unites a Russian population deeply divided after the collapse of Soviet power. Comparing Soviet treatment of homosexuals to that of the Soviet Union's sworn enemies—Nazis and Fascists—Trifonov dismantles

---

[c] https://postsoviet90s.com/artifacts/soviet-homosexuals-yesterday-today-tomorrow

the paradigm in which a purely Western Fascism emerges as the anti-Russia and vice versa. He also calls out a long-time Russian tendency to represent homosexuality as a disease of Western origin, citing a dissociative Soviet-era canard about Nikolai Ezhov: that he was infected by homosexuality through his contact with Fascists on a visit to Nazi Germany. Trifonov, finally, makes a point that will be made many times again by many different commentators in the first two decades of the twenty-first century: that post-WWII Germany should in at least one sense be regarded as an exemplar for post-Soviet Russia; that Russia needs a public programmatic reckoning with the atrocities committed by its citizens and authorities in the twentieth century, including its systematic persecution of homosexuals, and that without this, there is no way forward.[22]

SPEECH AND SILENCE IN MAINSTREAM PRINT MEDIA

At the end of the 1980s people in Russia living with homosexual desire or nontraditional gender identities had, as a rule, never seen these experiences documented in the Russian historical record or Soviet mass media. A noteworthy exception in the later 1980s is scattered discussion of "homosexuals" in the mainstream Soviet press in connection with the new global epidemic of HIV/AIDS. These were generally profoundly alienating and unsympathetic representations that emphasized homosexuals' pariah status in late-Soviet society. Articles appearing in major journalistic publications lumped homosexual men in with other groups defined solely on the basis of abhorrent deviant behaviors, groups such as drug addicts and criminals. Indeed, sexual relations between men constituted a criminal offence through the end of the Soviet era and into the first years of the post-Soviet era.[23] Russia's legal and social intolerance of sexual relations between men was frequently lauded in late-Soviet public discourse as a morally correct posture that was also functioning as a critical defense against the epidemic, a posture that would ensure the AIDS crisis would be far less dire than in Western countries where homosexuality had been normalized. "Homosexuals" were largely dehumanized in these pieces, treated as disease vectors that were bringing the plague home to Russia and endangering the Russian population, vis-à-vis which they represented a fringe or outside element.[24] Gay men's own welfare and access to treatment are generally at best secondary considerations in these pieces.

If the new, post-Soviet LGBTQIA print channels discussed in the preceding section were not illicit in the sense of being officially prohibited, they operated distinctly outside the mainstream media. They had limited circulation aimed more or less exclusively at LGBTQIA readers, and were conscious of operating in an inhospitable wider environment.[25] Indeed, until 1993, any of their male authors, editors, publishers, or readership who pursued fulfillment of same-sex desire were by that very fact criminals. These publications were produced within a broader social reality that was perceived to be at best unreceptive and at worst actively hostile to the elements of an exiled Russian LGBTQIA culture and history that they were in a sense repatriating via Western channels, as well as to the novel (from an early post-Soviet Russian perspective) Western-modeled sexual identities they were asserting on behalf of their editors, authors, and readers. Some of these titles relied heavily on the samizdat practices developed over the second half of the Soviet era for effective distribution,[26] and some of them, or at least some subset of their issues, had an improvised appearance and formatting reminiscent of samizdat publications of the late-Soviet period. Whether this was the product of design or circumstances, it would seem to have had the effect of conferring a samizdat aura of stubbornly resilient truth that the unjust, backward public sphere could not tolerate, a category of some prestige in late-Soviet unofficial intellectual culture.

One new book publisher did attempt to package sexual pluralism (primarily male homosexuality and bisexuality) for a mass 1990s Russian audience. The Moscow publisher Glagol, founded in 1990 by Alexander Shatalov, a gay writer, critic, and editor, published Russian translations of Western works by LGBTQIA authors and/or with LGBTQIA themes or motifs. It also published previously unpublished (at least in Russia) works by Soviet and post-Soviet LGBTQIA authors and/or Soviet and post-Soviet Russian works having LGBTQIA subject matter.[27] From 1990 to 2002 Glagol published works by William S. Burroughs, James Baldwin, and Edmund White, alongside the first editions of works by the late Soviet gay author Evgenii Kharitonov. In her 1999 monograph *Queer in Russia*, sociologist Laurie Essig observes that Glagol's selection of material for publication itself stands as a document of the peculiarities and limits of the broader 1990s Russian public's tolerance for homosexuality, at least as envisioned by Glagol's editors. Glagol, per Essig, specifically favored works in which homoerotic experiences were depicted as anomalous or altered-state episodes. Either these experiences occurred in alternate, specially demarcated dimensions spatially, temporally, or ontologically distant from the rest of the diegetic realities (dreams or hallucinations, states of intoxication, memories),[28] and/or they occurred in exotic locales geographically, chronologically, and/or culturally remote from the social reality of the 1990s Russian readership. This containing of homoerotic experience in zones from where it can have no appreciable effect on social and public life or social and public self-presentations aligns with broadly shared 1990s Russian modes of homosexual experience and behavior explored at length in Essig's 1999 book, and discussed later in this section.

The Sourcebook includes an excerpt from an interesting cinematic instantiation of this from 1993: *Creation of Adam* (*Sotvorenie Adama*) directed by Yuri Pavlov.[29] The film features a male protagonist whose childless marriage is faltering, and a series of homoerotically suggestive scenes between that protagonist and a mysterious stranger (Figure 1). Ultimately that stranger is identified as something of a guardian angel for the protagonist, and through their encounters the protagonist's relationship with his wife is restored. Finally, he and his wife conceive a child. The scenes between the two

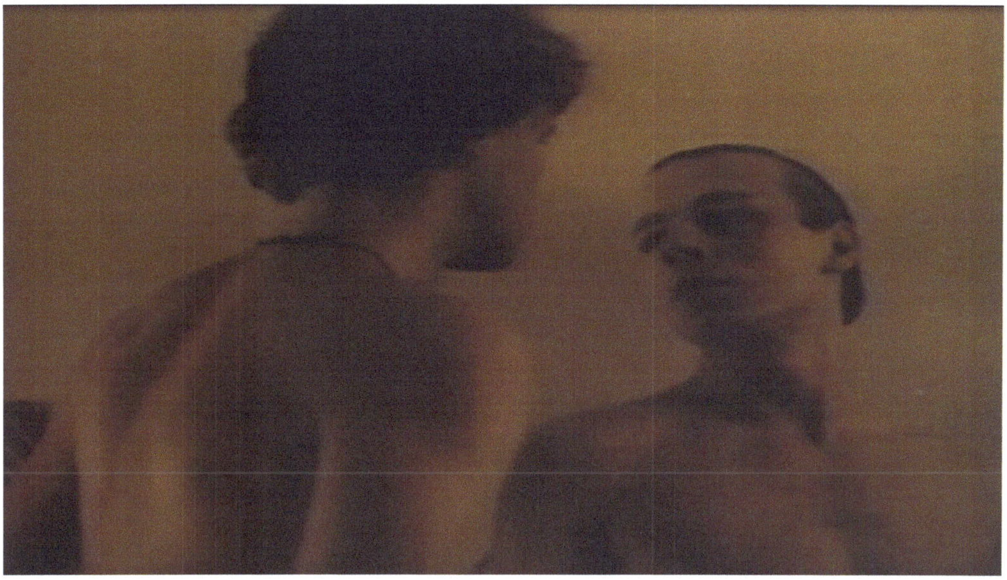

FIGURE 1 Image from Artifact 00027.[d] Still from a scene between the film's protagonist, Andrei, and his guardian angel, Phillip.

men are crafted in such a way that the homoerotic elements are demarcated from the wider diegetic reality of the film, and their ontological status is irresolvably ambiguous; the viewer cannot definitively determine whether they are wholly real, wholly imaginary, or both in part. In the film, like in the James Baldwin novel *Giovanni's Room*, published in Russian translation by Glagol, the ultimate resolution of the anomalous homoerotic encounter is restoration of the heterosexual, procreative relationship. The fact that *Creation of Adam* and the literary works published by Glagol are works representing fictional narrative worlds is also significant. As will be discussed in the next section of this essay, there was some tendency in the 1990s in Russia of freer, widely broadcast public exploration of homoeroticism safely contained within aesthetic modes of representation, where, it was understood, there was always the possibility to claim that homoerotic elements were tropes obliquely signifying something other than their apparent literal meaning of homoerotic experience.

To whatever extent Essig's assessment of the significance of Glagol's selection of material is or is not accurate, there is direct evidence of the press's editors resorting to longstanding Soviet techniques of peritextual framing in the packaging of ideologically or otherwise problematic literary works for a Soviet readership. In at least one case (the first Russian edition of Eduard Limonov's *It's Me, Eddy*) a prefatory text was used to neutralize and/or contain a novel's homoerotic elements, as will be discussed in the next section.

---

[d] https://postsoviet90s.com/artifacts/the-creation-of-adam-1993-dir-iu-pavlov

The mass-media sphere in 1990s Russia sporadically registers the very small number of actors working to effect broader societal change related to sexual and gender-expression pluralism, actors addressing broader audiences including but not limited to "sexual minorities" themselves. In the 1990s media sphere at large, not only patterns of speech and action, but also of silence around sexual and gender-expression pluralism document a tension between different imaginary Wests and imaginary Russias—past, present, and future—and within these differing models the concept of Western freedom has different valences.

One model that seems to be implicit in some of the speech and actions recorded in the broader post-Soviet media is the one, already discussed, of a pre-Soviet Russia that is in essence a European political and cultural entity. In that paradigm, with the definitive failure of the Soviet experiment, the presumed path forward for post-Soviet Russia is to rejoin the West and participate in Western political and cultural evolution, meaning that Western individualist freedoms, including the relatively new Western model of a pluralism of sexual and gender identities, should be transferable to post-Soviet Russia.

Another model is one in which pre-Soviet Russia is conceived of as a culture and even civilization apart, distinct from the West. An essential constitutive property of this imaginary Russia is a tradition of authoritarian rule and more rigidly structured society whose constituents are more tightly bound together by networks of interdependencies, a society that requires execution of assigned functions and performance of codified roles. For proponents of this model, Western individualist "freedoms," apart from being simply un-Russian, connote anarchical, ungovernable forces that threaten to destabilize valuable, identity-constituting traditions. The disorienting and frightening cultural, economic, and political instability that followed the collapse of the Soviet state was seen by many Russians as the result of the introduction of the Western phenomena of democracy and privatization, the Russian-language equivalents for which—*demokratiia* and *privatizatsiia*—produced pejorative neologisms like *der'mokratiia* and *prikhvatizatsiia*. *Der'mokratiia* replaces the first part of the word meaning "democarcy" (demo) with *der'mo*, a word for "shit." In *prikhvatizatsiia*, the addition of a single letter adds the verb "to grab or snatch away" (*prikhvatit'*) to the word for "privatization." It appears that for many, the Western model of sexual and gender-expression pluralism, which meant socially and politically integrated sexual and gender identities outside the cis-gendered heterosexual male/female binary, stirred similar anxieties around socially disintegrating, anarchic, individualistic Western intrusions, here one that attacked a binary that had been one of the most basic structural elements of the fabric of society since time immemorial.

The same nostalgia and craving for stability and order that gave rise to Vladislav Surkov's concept of "sovereign democracy" in the early 2000s seems to have occasioned a search for a kind of sexual pluralism *po-russki* in the 1990s. If for some the concept of Western freedoms represented emancipation from oppressive structures and strictures, for others these unfamiliar and foreign freedoms were themselves oppressive, inasmuch as the onus of free agency and individualistic self-determination in the absence of a stable, comprehensible, and predictable external structure was paralyzing. Like the process that led to a "sovereign democracy" that was not democracy at all, a nostalgia for a lost sense of belonging to something grand, and the stability and predictability of an assigned role in a larger social and public structure, makes those structures and strictures seem freeing, and leads some to seek a *po-russki* sexual pluralism that includes conforming to one's prescribed role in the traditional heterosexual male/female binary in one's social and public life, while relegating expression and pursuit of any impulses at odds with that role to zones outside social and public life. In other words, a sovereign Russian sexual pluralism that means no pluralism at all in the social or public spheres. Many Russian subjects of same-sex erotic desire and/or gender dysphoria in the 1990s seem to discern a kind of distinctly Russian freedom in a familiar institutionalized duplicity where all socially and politically troublesome desires are pursued in clandestine ways that don't compromise a person's social and/or public identity. There is an evident momentum of a model in which mutually contradictory thoughts and impulses can be simultaneously entertained by being isolated from each other in a compartmentalized existence, allowing one to persist indefinitely in unresolved dichotomies, privately engage in behaviors deeply at odds with one's social or public self-presentation, and embrace paradoxes such as simultaneously wanting freedom and authoritarian structure, and even seeking the former in the latter. These apparently widespread tendencies result in enormous silences in the Russian media sphere of the 1990s.

Individuals with activist agendas to effect change in the broader social and political reality in order to improve the lives of Russian subjects of homosexual desire and/or gender dysphoria had some inevitable investment in some manner of publicly visible alternative sexual and/or gender identities, because they required a visible minority population on whose behalf they could speak and act. Some of them felt the Western models of LGBTQIA sexual and gender identities should be applied unmodified to the Russian population. Others resisted what they perceived as undue Western influence and looked for indigenous versions of tolerance of sexual and gender diversity.

The journalist and activist Masha Gessen themselves embodied a kind of Russian reunion with the Western world. Born in Moscow in 1967 and émigrated to the United States in 1981, where they wrote for LGBTQ publications such as *The Advocate*, Gessen moved back to Russia in 1991 to continue their career in journalism and LGBTQIA activism. For some in the 1990s Gessen represented a link between Russia and the West, a hybrid half-Russian half-American. The article "Lesbian Masha Takes on the Bureaucrats" (Artifact 00068)[e] from the Moscow weekly *Megapolis ekspress* views Gessen in precisely this kind of light.[30] It presents them as a member of a sexual minority who,

---

[e] https://postsoviet90s.com/artifacts/lesbian-masha-attacks-the-bureaucrats

as a result of their time in the United States, has developed a self-assuredness and resolve in their assertion of rights entitlements for "sexual minorities" uncommonly encountered in Russia. It is their formative American experience, the article seems to suggest, that allows them to unflinchingly do battle with Russian bureaucrats.

There are other activists speaking to the mainstream Russian media who convey the sense that post-Soviet Russia is joining the Western Pride-era movement of integration of sexual and gender-expression pluralism into broader society and culture. The essential reference point here is the 1969 Stonewall Riots in New York City. In a 1992 interview (Artifact 00221[f]) published in the Tver' newspaper *Smena*, the director of an activist group called The Tchaikovsky Fund discusses a "Christopher Street Festival" organized in Russia (there were also Russian "Stonewall" events mounted in Moscow and St. Petersburg) with extensive collaboration of Western partners. The name of the organization is also suggestive of a vision of Russia as an essentially European or Western culture in which LGBTQ figures have historically played impactful roles, to whatever extent their sexuality or gender identities are or are not widely discussed. Tchaikovsky looks to have been chosen as a namesake for this organization inasmuch as he is a pre-Soviet Russian cultural figure who is an integral part of a Western cultural canon, and also a figure whose homosexuality was something of an open secret in Russia.

Within the category of activists representing a kind of anxiety of influence vis-à-vis the West and a somewhat defensive assertion of a distinct un-Western Russian identity, Yaroslav ("Slava") Mogutin is something of an anomaly.[31] Along with figures like Masha Gessen and Evgenia Debryanskaya (about whom more to follow), Mogutin was one of the few specimens of a very rare bird in the early 1990s media sphere in Russia: a media personality of some visibility loudly declaring their own non-heterosexual orientation. Mogutin quickly emerged as something of an épateur and savvy media manipulator in the 1990s. Among his more impactful publicity stunts were the 1993 publication in *Still: An Independent Erotic Newspaper* (*Eshche: nezavisimaia eroticheskaia gazeta*) of his piece "Komsomols' Dirty Peckers" (*Griaznye kontsy komsomol'tsev*) in which the pop star Boris Moiseev claimed to have performed sexual favors for male Komsomols,[32] and Mogutin's attempt in 1994 to register his marriage to his partner, American artist Robert Fillippini.

While leading his own provocative campaign for a kind of sexual liberation in post-Soviet Russia, Mogutin was at the same time in many senses anti-liberal. His was an unusual, from a twenty-first-century Western vantage point, mixture of fierce nationalism and libertinism.[33] While expressing an intensely nationalist view of Russian identity that was not only entirely apart from Western culture, but also not in any sense ethnically or religiously diverse or tolerant, he nonetheless appeared to envision a near-future Russia with some kind of enfranchisement of exponents at least of his own type of

[f] https://postsoviet90s.com/artifacts/gays-and-lefties-comrades-in-misfortune

sexual difference: male homosexuality. He was deeply disdainful of political liberals in post-Soviet Russia, whom he accused of virulent homophobia, and indicted the hypocrisy of celebrated Soviet dissidents who exhibited a backward conservatism when it came to male homosexuality. A 1993 two-part piece in *The New Times* (Artifact 00174,[g] co-authored with Sonja Franeta) calls out the failure of figures like Solzhenitsyn and Shalamov to make the imaginative leap to empathize with, and recognize the injustice of the persecution of, a category of non-conformists with whom they themselves did not identify.[34] Very shortly after this article was published, however, Mogutin displayed his own chauvinisms and the limitations of his own empathetic capacity vis-à-vis minority populations in Russia to which he himself did not belong. In 1995, a year into the First Chechen War, Mogutin published an article in the newspaper *New View* (*Novyi vzgliad*) which was essentially a frenzy of Russian nationalist sentiment and a hateful orientalist attack on the Chechen nation.[35] In it Mogutin's proud sense of an essentialist Russian national identity seems inextricably involved with a Christian religiosity. To some extent the piece seems animated by an idea of an epochal clash of civilizations, or rather between civilization, Christian by definition, and the uncivilized non-Christian (here Muslim) world. At the same time the text expresses some anti-Western or specifically anti-American sentiments. From a Western, third-decade-of-the-twenty-first-century perspective, Mogutin's marriage of aggressively countercultural sexuality with the kind of nationalist and religious jingoism that now tends to be associated with conservative currents may seem counterintuitive. But even at the end of the Soviet era, religiosity and nationalism (and identities based thereon) were subversive from the perspective of the official ideology.[36] Mogutin seems in this text to be trying to fashion a personal identity at the intersection of his aggressively asserted unconventional sexuality, and the nationalist and religious dimensions of a pre-Soviet Russian national identity, all three of which would have been an affront to the official values of the late-Soviet society in which Mogutin came of age.[37] His view of the identity Russia was about to manifest as a polity and national culture seemed almost to eroticize the patriarchal, militaristic view of masculinity traditionally promoted by the authoritarian state. He is adamant that erotic relations between men be sanctioned in the new Russia, but seems less concerned with women and even hostile to ethnic and religious minorities. Ultimately, Mogutin's vision of a nationalist Russia incorporating broad tolerance of male homoerotism did not achieve traction in any wider arena.

The activist Evgenia Debryanskaya in some ways represents an even more improbable combination of seemingly even less compatible elements, but in fact her vision combining a sense of Russian exceptionalism and nationalism with a distinctly Russian version of sexual and gender-expression pluralism is much more broadly representative. A vociferous and highly visible advocate for Russians pursuing fulfillment of same-sex

---

[g] https://postsoviet90s.com/artifacts/homosexuality-in-soviet-prisons-and-camps

erotic desire, and one who very publicly declared her own sexual preference for women, by 1997 she had been married to two different men, one of them the arch-conservative, arch-nationalist ideologue Alexander Dugin.[38] Dugin and Debryanskaya's marriage predates somewhat the solidification of the former's neo-Eurasianist philosophy, which is extremely inhospitable to any notions of sexual or gender-identity pluralism in Russian society. Nonetheless, she continued to express admiration for his work after they divorced, and also voiced her support for nationalist politician Vladimir Zhirinovsky, while acknowledging that, if he came to power, it would spell doom for "open queers."[39]

One of the points on which Essig's book focuses most regarding Debryanskaya is the latter's insistence that sexual desire and behavior are not a basis for identity formation, or at least cannot be in Russia. Debryanskaya vigorously defended—often at no small risk to herself—what she believed to be the right of Russian citizens to express sexual difference, including the expression and fulfillment of same-sex erotic desire. At the same time, she asserted a belief that public identities based on sexuality or gender expression were and would remain impossible in Russian society, that LGBTQIA identities in Russia were malapropos Western transplants or impositions. For her, some Russian national identity was primary and absolute for all Russian people, and that Russian national master identity could not tolerate competing identities, particularly ones of foreign (here Western) origin, like LGBTQIA identities.[40] Russians, per Debryanskaya, had to find their own uniquely Russian way of doing sexual pluralism, one that had of necessity to contend with a likely hostile conservative Russian national ethos that was itself essential, beautiful, and worth preserving.

Debryanskaya at moments expresses admiration for the Western models—publicly declared LGBTQIA identities and enfranchised groups representing them—but ultimately she concludes that this is somehow un-Russian. She postulates certain unspecified traditions as fundamentally constitutive of Russian nationhood, traditions that are incompatible with publicly demonstrated sexual and gender-expression pluralism, and traditions that cannot, and should not, be compromised. The objective of her activism on behalf of Russia's sexual minorities is first and foremost their protection against active persecution. The distinctly Russian freedom she tries to claim for herself and other sexually different Russians is a freedom to embrace indeterminacy and an existence of irresolvable contradictions and inconsistencies. This includes demonstrating sincere reverence for valuable Russian traditions and institutions—be they patriarchal and/or authoritarian—while availing oneself of the affordances of a Russian tolerance for contradiction and mercuriality in order to entertain other dimensions of one's personality, including socially and politically inconvenient erotic desire. Hers is a freedom to participate in Russia's familial institutions by marrying members of the opposite sex and having children, while still finding ways to indulge same-sex erotic desire; to contradict oneself from one act or speech event to the next; to resist stability. In the 1997

Arguments and Facts interview (Artifact 00022),[h] Debryanskaya has already somewhat retired from activism on behalf of sexual minorities in Russia.[41] The main message that can be distilled from her responses to the interviewer's questions there is a defense of a modular and protean existence including same-sex romantic relationships; heterosexual marriages; selective, intermittent, provisional commitments to spouses, romantic partners, causes.

In some sense Debryanskaya serves as a public exponent of a phenomenon that is otherwise only negatively represented by silence in the 1990s Russian media. In *Queer in Russia*, sociologist Laurie Essig registered similar positions in her many 1990s anonymous interviews with Russians who pursued sexual relationships with people of the same sex, many of whom told her that these were behaviors anyone might engage in at any time, and as such were incidental to, and not definitive of, a person's identity. These subjects, per Essig, viewed the specificities of erotic desire and its gratification as fluid and also private, and as such aspects of a person's life that need not be reflected in the identity they present to social or public spheres. This is a posture very much at odds with that of the West-oriented "sexual dissidents" discussed in the preceding section, for whom LGBTQIA people were a distinct population with its own distinct intellectual and cultural subjectivity and its own historical legacy. For them, social or public expression of distinct LGBTQIA identities was crucial to achieve recognition as a cohesive, legitimate, and valuable human category having, in addition to its own historical and cultural legacy, specific rights entitlements (among them the right to present their sexual and gender identities without fear of persecution). As a group the "sexual dissidents" were not especially invested in preserving a specifically Russian identity, although the specific Soviet legacy of oppression was a crucial part of their self-definitions as post-Soviet LGBTQ people living in Russia.

As far as notions of Russian national identity as primordial and the incompatibility of that primary national identity with unconventional sexual identities, it appears there were at minimum two things going on. One was a more general early post-Soviet Russian identity crisis in the disorienting sense of mid-air suspension in the 1990s. The Soviet order and the ideology that had defined Russia's national identity for more than seventy years had suddenly dematerialized and the Soviet Union's arch-enemy (the United States) had become the new, post-Soviet Russia's ally or even exemplar, seemingly overnight. This produced some anxiety of influence vis-à-vis the United States and the West more broadly. Many Russians living through this jarring reversal struggled with a sense of being absorbed into a foreign world (and one they had long been instructed to regard as hostile) without any residue of their earlier formative experience as Soviet citizens.

Some Russians rejected what they perceived to be a tabula-rasa repudiation of their prior sense of identity to become nothing more than newcomers to a foreign culture, and

[h] https://postsoviet90s.com/artifacts/evgenia-debryanskaya-i-don-t-give-a-damn-about-public-opinon

looked for organically and distinctly Russian versions of new modes of being adopted from the West.[42] Debryanskaya presents an example of this response to the 1990s in the area of sexual identity. She resisted what she saw as undue imposition of Western models on an emerging sexual pluralism in post-Soviet Russia. She boycotted a 1991 event advertised as the "Russian Stonewall" because of what she perceived as a slavish imitation of an American model. She worked to achieve a kind of Russian national purity at a subsequent event by sidelining foreign participants.[43] On that occasion Masha Gessen was deemed by Debryanskaya to be too American or insufficiently Russian. For many 1990s Russians, it seems, private pursuit of same-sex erotic desire in a way that did not affect a person's social or public identity was the Russian way of doing sexual pluralism, and social or public identities like "lesbian" or "gay" were artifacts of Western culture that were malapropos in the Russian social reality.

There were certainly anxieties of a more urgent and practical nature at work here as well. Incorporating open expression of same-sex erotic desire into one's social or public self-presentation was literally unthinkable throughout nearly all of the Soviet era. It is easy to see why, in the dizzying social and cultural instability of the Russian 1990s, many people who experienced same-sex erotic attraction worried that this could be a serious social and political liability, and therefore preferred to engage in homosexual behaviors in a private way, to insulate those behaviors from their wider social involvements such that those private behaviors would not affect their public identities. It appears to have been an all too deeply ingrained pattern to relegate those socially inconvenient parts of themselves to a kind of shadow dimension beyond social and public life and, actually, beyond public discourse and even language. These people seemed inclined to persist in a status quo where there were no current linguistic tokens to reify, in a neutral or non-disparaging way, people who experienced same-sex erotic desire and/or differences of gender identity into distinct social entities and categories. This apparently widespread model and experience of "nontraditional" sexuality is therefore completely unrepresented in the mass media of the 1990s, apart from in the figure of Debryanskaya.

POPULAR CULTURE

Other patterns of performance, speech, and silence at the level of mass-consumed popular culture suggest another order of responses to postulated collective Russian subjectivities; inhibitions stemming from internalized authoritarian strictures around sexuality and gender expression; and processes of individual-identity formation and self-presentation to a mass audience. Specifically, there is a tendency observed on the part of several 1990s Russian cultural figures with mass audiences to provocatively perform homoeroticism and/or ambiguities of gender expression as an element of broadcast personas, while studiously avoiding any declarative statements of "nontraditional" sexual and/or gender identities on their own behalf, and also avoiding any definitive acknowledgements of identity with their performative personas or alter-egos. Likely to some degree a response to an intuition that the lawless freedom of self-expression in Russia at that moment could only be a transitory anomaly, and to anxieties about hypothetical present and/or future enforcements of some dictates around sexual and gender identity, there is a *stiob*-like disjunct between the aesthetic and discursive modes in these figures' self-presentation. The aesthetic mode is treated as one of semiotic instability where it is possible to more or less safely indulge in aggressively provocative performance of same-sex erotic desire or transgressive gender expression, in the sense that it is possible to do this in a way that will be accepted by a Russian mass audience.

There is a *stiob*-like problematizing of the relationship between performance, performative persona, and performer, as well as of the relationship between signifier and signified. There is also a purported non-indexical, semiotic, encoded nature of the homoerotic and/or gender-transgressive elements of these personas and performances, an assertion that these are tropes not subject to literal interpretation, tropes having more oblique meanings or referents. In the starker discursive mode, conversely, there appear to be some deeply internalized immovable barriers preventing unequivocal declarations of sexual or gender identities outside the cis-gendered heterosexual male/female binary. The result is narratives of sex between men, patently homoerotic images, men dressed in lingerie, lamé blouses, makeup, wigs, with their authors resisting, sometimes even vigorously rejecting, designations such as "gay" or "queer."

In the somewhat rarefied but still robust art scene on the cusp of the late-Soviet and post-Soviet periods, homoerotic and gender-transgressive motifs are actually quite prominent. Scholarship has observed that, in some milieus, these elements became broader tropes for a countercultural aesthetics, tropes used quite independently of the actual sexual and/or gender identities and/or orientations of the artists themselves.[44] This may have later helped embolden some popular-culture artists who were subjects of same-sex erotic impulses and/or fluid gender identities to feel they could incorporate expression of this into their works or public personas in a way that preserved plausible deniability of their own homosexuality and/or nontraditional gender identity. This will be discussed further along vis-à-vis figures such as Sergei Penkin, Vladimir Vesyolkin, and, to a lesser extent, Boris Moiseev.

Apart from their use as an element of the transgressive aesthetics of groups like the Necrorealists, where they generally do not appear to have been directly representative of the sexualities or gender identities of the creators,[45] aspects of homoerotism and unconventional gender expression are also characteristic of the work of some actively gay and/or gender-variant artists. Two of the most impactful art-scene figures in this category were, much like Slava Mogutin, proponents of the bourgeoning and ultimately moribund vision of post-Soviet Russianness that wedded a new sexual and gender-expression pluralism to an otherwise conservative, nationalist, and religious program. The negative image of the USSR's similarly incongruous combination of a de facto patriarchal sexual and gender conservatism with a declared ultra-progressive political program that was aggressively antinationalist and atheist, these reactions against the Soviet ethos saw a way forward for Russia that celebrated an intersection of sexual and gender fluidity and plurality with a distinctly Russian nationalist and religious identity. The gay artist Timur Novikov—leader of the New Academy group of artists in St. Petersburg—combined artworks including variously implicit or explicit homoerotic elements with a largely neo-conservative aesthetic program,[46] and, later, with a nationalist and religious orientation that intensified toward the untimely end of his life.[47] Vladislav Mamyshev-Monroe, a close associate of Novikov's whose most impactful works involved photographs of him assuming the appearances of historical and contemporary public figures, both men and women,[48] made erotic involvement with men a crucial part of his own public image.

In a sense functioning as his own medium and artwork, Mamyshev-Monroe made declarative homosexuality and gender fluidity essential elements of his boundary-challenging artistic philosophy and practice, as well as of his own boundary-challenging self-presentation. This was, again, however, combined with a conservative philosophical and aesthetic agenda including Russian nationalist and national-religious components and, especially counterintuitively, elements of male chauvinism. He expressed ideas of a messianic mission for Russia as the locus of an achievement of a kind of spiritual synthesis and unification (reminiscent of Dostoevsky's ideas of *sobornost'*), including a merging of the genders and manifestation of a divine feminine essence (reminiscent of Vladimir Solov'ev).[49] Mamyshev-Monroe saw a central role for himself and his artistic practice in all of this, and asserted that the divine feminine ideal was something that could only be apprehended and manifested by a man.[50]

In terms of the reach of artistic groups of this order and their amplification via broadly distributed media, one magazine bears mention here: *Ptiuch*, published in Moscow beginning in 1994. Reaching a peak circulation of 80,000 copies in 1996, *Ptiuch* achieved a substantial newsstand presence in Moscow and St. Petersburg, but was very far from the category of mass-distributed titles such as *Ogonek* or *Krokodil*, which had circulations in the millions. *Ptiuch* was a somewhat more rarefied glossy magazine aimed at a metropolitan élite—members of the boundary-pushing art and culture scenes and club scenes.[51] Sexual and gender-expression pluralism were prominently featured elements of that vanguard culture as represented on *Ptiuch*'s pages, which covered subjects like Mamyshev-Monroe, transvestitism, gender fluidity, LGBTQIA Pride events, etc.

As a rule, when these elements (sexual pluralism and gender variance) migrated to the realm of truly mass-consumed popular culture, they did so in a modulated and attenuated form. There seems to be broad consensus among scholars that the lesbian-erotic elements of the performances of the popular singing duo t.A.T.U. in the 1990s were in essence gratuitous flourishes intended to lend their performances a touch of scandalous provocation, and were not in any way representative of the sexual subjectivities of the performers, or any other position or agenda.[52] Pop star Philipp Kirkorov appears to have cynically used homoerotic and to some extent gender-fluid elements in his performances and self-presentation to signal the kind of rebellious audacity that gives pop-music performers a certain transgressive edge.[53] He was, though, always careful to do this in a way that avoided anything that could read as even an implicit declaration of his own homosexuality or gender fluidity. Indeed, the relationship of these elements of his public persona to Kirkorov's own sexual and gender subjectivity remains undetermined. This non-committal mode of homoerotic and/or gender-fluid elements as ostensibly purely aesthetic tropes or devices is also the default for a number of performing artists whose personal homoerotic desire and/or gender-expression fluidity are more or less well documented.

Boris Moiseev is in some sense the outlier that helps to define broader tendencies here, in that he did, in the 1990s themselves, make more or less explicit declarations of his homosexuality. For example, in an interview (printed in a Riga paper with limited circulation, it should be noted) Moiseev told Slava Mogutin that he had performed oral sex on numerous men in the Komsomol.[54] Moiseev was a classically trained dancer who toured with Alla Pugacheva for a number of years before emerging as a pop performer in his own right, and one with an outsize outrageous persona that was emphatically extravagant in its performance of unconventional sexuality and gender expression. Under the Putin regime, he will claim any statements of his own homosexuality were just part of the larger épatage performance that was his public persona—an aesthetic construct that did not necessarily reflect in all its aspects the identity of its creator.[55] He will do the same vis-à-vis the essential sexually and gender-transgressive aspects of that persona: feminine accoutrements and performance of a provocative effeminate (at least by 1990s Russian standards) sexuality.

In his performances, Moiseev frequently appeared in traditionally feminine dress and heavy makeup. The music video for Moiseev's song "Egoist" (Artifact 00216)[i]—shows him in full maquillage and eighteenth-century women's costume: a bustier, powdered wig, strands of pearls. In the 2000s he will, owing to whatever combination of genuine sensibility and pragmatism, speak about Russian public life as a sphere that could not, and should not, countenance public displays of sexuality and gender expression beyond the traditional cis-gendered heterosexual male/female binary. While he defended a right for people to privately pursue "nontraditional" relationships, he defended with equal or greater tenacity some postulated reverend laws of decency in Russian public and social life to which public expression of nontraditional sexual and gender identities was an affront.[56] The purported traditional Russian values and institutions must, he will say, take precedence over personal desires or impulses at odds with them, at least in public and social life. Per twenty-first-century Moiseev, while the minority of Russians

---

[i] https://postsoviet90s.com/artifacts/boris-moiseev-egoist

experiencing same-sex erotic desire should have the right to pursue fulfillment of those desires privately, they also had a duty to defer to the traditional sensibilities and institutions of a Russian majority in their public and social self-presentation. They owed this public silence on their desires and private selves to a venerable Russian moral majority. Moiseev was therefore a vociferous opponent of Pride demonstrations or festivals and of same-sex marriage.

In general, by the late 2000s, less than ten years after Putin's rise to power, any visions of a post-Soviet distinctly Russian national identity having sexual pluralism and/or gender fluidity as defining characteristics were dead. Slava Mogutin had been forced to leave in the Yeltsin years, in 1995. Roman Kalinin, an openly gay RSFSR presidential candidate of 1991, had retreated from public life by the end of the 1990s. Timur Novikov had died of AIDS in 2002. Vladislav Mamyshev-Monroe left Russia to live abroad around 2007.[57] Boris Moiseev was denying his own homosexuality (loudly declared a decade earlier), and speaking out against same-sex marriage, against public LGBTQIA demonstrations and Pride celebrations, and in defense of Russian religious conservatism and authoritarian political power. Philipp Kirkorov had secured the blessing of the Russian authorities, which he continues to repay with unreserved, reverent support, and in his performances he uses homoerotic and/or gender-transgressive innuendo within limits and in ways that are acceptable to, and perhaps in some ways even serve the agendas of, the Putin regime.[58]

In the 1990s, many highly visible popular-culture figures seem to sense this coming. As a rule, artists playing with homoerotic or gender-transgressive elements in works aimed at a mass audience tend in the 1990s themselves to isolate these elements in aesthetic dimensions of presumptive semantic and semiotic indeterminacy and, while they might tease their audience with innuendo about the relationship between those elements of their works and their own identities as those works' creators, they are careful to avoid anything definitive or declarative in the discursive mode. These figures, operating and to some degree reveling very publicly in the social, political, and cultural wilderness of the 1990s, seem nonetheless to intuit that some immovable, if invisible, barriers remain when it comes to unequivocal self-announcement or self-presentation, that there are points of no return one might regret having passed in some still undiscernible future Russia, and that certain kinds of definitive public declarations of identity might be dangerous, if not there and then, then in the long term.

This appears to be the case of Vladimir Vesyolkin. Like Moiseev, Vesyolkin was a classically trained dancer performing with an A-list pop-music act—the band Auktsyon—until he broke away to headline his own act in 1992. While on tour with Auktsyon in 1989, he was invited by almost certainly the most famous gay Russian expatriate and pre-eminent dancer on the world stage Rudolph Nureyev to relocate to Paris and dance with the company at Palais Garnier (of which Nureyev was then director). Vesyolkin passed up this opportunity to relocate to the West and opted instead to return to Russia, and a few years later addressed an early 1990s Russian mass audience with the album "Impossible Love" (*Nevozmozhnaia liubov'*) with his newly founded group "Vova and the Organ of Internal Affairs" (*Vova i organ vnutrennykh del*).[59]

The group's name is something of a double entendre, with the vaguely bureaucratese phrase "organ of internal affairs" having the secondary meaning of a bodily organ used for penetration. The album's title song "Impossible Love," performed by Vesyolkin, addresses some masculine object of an impossible love (the unidentified object has masculine verb forms applied to it).[60] The front album cover (Artifact 00182)[j] features one of Tom of Finland's homoerotic paintings, and the back cover—a photograph of Vesyolkin in a long-haired wig and lingerie. The inside sleeve shows a photograph of three nearly naked men sitting on top of one another, with what appears to be an almost naked woman lying on the floor below them. The images are plainly meant to be provocative and represent a challenge to sexuality and gender-expression conventions, but, because they are images, it is impossible to determine a precise, stable, or unequivocal significance of those provocations.

When it comes to the somewhat more definitive medium of verbal language, Vesyolkin skates on the edge of the utterable in a way that emphatically gestures at an intuited boundary between it and the unutterable. There is the unnamed masculine (at least grammatically) object of the title song's "impossible love," and the insistence on polysemy in the name of the group, not only in the double entendre (government agency, anatomical organ for penetration), but in the question of whose organ (in the second meaning) is referenced. Is it Vova's own? Someone else's? Is the organ one that penetrates or one that is penetrated? This semiotic and semantic indeterminacy will allow Vesyolkin to ascribe a safer meaning to this multi-media utterance in the 2000s when the climate has radically changed. In no measure expressions of homosexual desire or ambiguous gender expression on the part of their author, he claimed, these words and images were more oblique tropes for grander and less concrete signifieds: freedom of self-determination and expression themselves, broadly construed.[61]

Popular-music star Sergei Penkin presented his 1990s Russian mass audience with a persona whose accoutrements were typical of what at least at that time would have been a distinctly feminine glamour: bejeweled and fur-lined garments and accessories, ostentatious jewelry. The cover image for Penkin's 1993 album *Holiday* (Artifact 00219)[k] featured a head shot of him dressed in an outsize lamé garment with a wide collar and puffed-out shoulders, and decorated with pearls and feathers. He is also wearing what appears to be a diamond (or faux-diamond) brooch under a bow tie. Penkin claimed his feminine accoutrements and overall presentation were nothing more than a general assertion of artistic license and were in no way representative of his own sexuality or

[j] https://postsoviet90s.com/artifacts/impossible-love

[k] https://postsoviet90s.com/artifacts/sergei-penkin-holiday-album-cover

gender expression. He, in fact, fought legally to control the public interpretation of his extravagant self-presentation in his performances, and on at least one occasion sued journalists for suggesting he was gay.[62]

To lend greater authority to his prescribed reading of his own performative persona, he adduced the fact that this was (or surely must have been) how his persona was read by high-level political authorities who treated him as an honored guest on his performance tours around Russia. In the offstage persona Penkin projects in interviews it seems to be almost a point of pride that he is an initiate into rarefied circles in a Russia where, he implies, it would have been impossible for a man who presented as gay to achieve any kind of legitimate status at all.[63] Penkin's strategy here seems to belong, as to some extent do other examples in this section, to a slim Russian tradition of "open secrets," including figures such as the Soviet and post-Soviet estrada artist Valery Leont'ev.[64] This open-secret practice of obedient discursive silence attending audacious provocative performance of sexual or gender-expression difference would appear to have the function of confirming and reinforcing the power of the discursive taboo and the force of the unspoken control over public discourse.

Then there is the case of the literary author turned nationalist political figure Eduard Limonov. Limonov in some ways had much in common with Slava Mogutin (of whom he was a close associate).[65] They shared an emphatically nationalist vision of the future of the post-Soviet Russian state and both projected a militant, aggressive masculinity. Limonov was, however, packaging himself for a much larger mass audience. Demonstrative, declarative homosexuality was an essential element of Mogutin's aggressive épateur personality and he never tried to distance himself from it. Limonov, having written a novel full of autobiographical details and featuring a protagonist with his own name ("Edichka"), a protagonist who has numerous sexual encounters with men,[66] did actively distance himself from the homoerotic aspects of the narrative. He stated that those elements of Edichka (a Limonov creation) were not directly representative of authorial life experience, but rather a literary device for figurative representation of other, more abstract categories (representation of the abject degradation of the protagonist using the conceptual language of the Soviet penal system: *opushchenie*).

The first Russian edition of the work was published by Glagol Press in 1991. The Glagol edition of *Edichka*, released the year of Limonov's return to Russia after living in the West since 1974, was packaged for a broad post-Soviet Russian audience. A thirteen-page preface by Alexandr Shatalov (Artifact 00217)[1] does a sort of nervous dance around the question of whether or not—or the extent to which—the author and his protagonist can be considered coterminous, and studiously avoids any explicit mention of the book's homoerotic dimension, alluding instead to a "hypersexuality" (emphatically the character's and not the author's) and drawing seemingly gratuitous parallels

[1] https://postsoviet90s.com/artifacts/eduard-limonov-it-s-me-eddy-glagol-press

with Walt Whitman.[67] Addressing an imagined immediately post-Soviet Russian readership regarding a returning émigré who was to become a prominent figure in Russian nationalist politics, Shatalov places a lot of emphasis on the perception that Eddy (the character) resists becoming American and, through the émigré experience there, locates and consolidates his own Russian identity ("Russianness").[68] There are even notes of defensive irony in observations that the denizens of "the promised land of America" cannot comprehend how Eddy cannot want to become one of them.[69] In this preface by a gay editor of a new press publishing primarily gay literature, a preface to a book featuring multiple scenes of sexual encounters of the male protagonist with other men, assertion of a Russian national identity for that protagonist seems to push that protagonist's homosexuality from text into subtext. Limonov remained in Russia until his death in 2020. To the end he was a conservative, nationalist public figure, a vocal opponent of the Euromaidan protests in Kiev and supporter of the annexation of Crimea in 2014.

The performative and discursive behaviors described in this section almost seem to anticipate the audacious rhetorical strategies of the Putin regime: doing Fascism in plain view of the whole world while strenuously rejecting the label. Authors of emphatically extravagant performances of homoerotism and/or gender-norm transgression, in the discursive sphere vigorously deny that those performances mean what they appear to mean. Putin's administration maintains an authoritarian, proudly anti-liberal, antiprogressive, and antidemocratic state embodying "traditional values," while attempting a complete decoupling of the very powerfully charged words *Fascism* and *Nazism* from their original meaning.

Putinist rhetoric attempts a bold conversion of those words into versatile labels whose potent poison can be weaponized against any opponent by the authorities of what has become the quintessence of the contemporary Fascist state.[70] And in fact, the vaguely defined, abstract referent of some of the sexually or gender-transgressive elements of their works and personas alluded to by celebrated public performers in the 1990s—broader freedoms of self-determination and self-expression—are in essence the same value the Putin regime appears to ascribe to publicly expressed sexual and gender-identity pluralism. And this is precisely the reason for the aggressive limitation of this kind of "speech" under Putin's regime, whether literal, discursive speech, or the much slipperier expressions of art and performance. They are regarded as the very essence of an impermissible radical freedom of self-determination.

***

For many 1990s Russians who were not content to have post-Soviet Russia simply become a Western country, and there were many, the introduction of the Western model of socially integrated, publicly acknowledged sexual and gender-expression pluralism, like *demokratiia* and *privatizatsiia*, appears to have represented a frighteningly destabilizing intrusion. This feeling was shared by many Russian subjects of same-sex erotic desire and gender dysphoria, as well as among the wider public. Performance of conventional gender roles determined by birth sex, including mandatory heterosexuality, was perceived as one of the basic elements of the implicit contract whereby the individual agrees to suppress certain of their idiosyncrasies and impulses and conform to certain conventional standards in exchange for living as a member of the ordered collective of a society.[71]

In the frighteningly unstable political, social, and cultural climate of the 1990s, dissolving the fundamental organizing principle of the conventional heterosexual gender binary appears to have seemed to many to have the potential to undo the social fabric. There was a common perception that sexual or gender-expression impulses that deviated from that binary model were to be entertained, if at all, through whatever affordances were incidentally offered by status-quo social structures, usually in clandestine ways to avoid compromising a person's social or public identity.[72] The heterosexual sex between cis-gendered persons sanctioned by society since time immemorial was itself a private matter in Russia up through the end of the Soviet era, and there appears to have been some understanding in the 1990s that homosexual behavior happening out of public view (including in the penal system and the military, where it was almost institutionalized as a regulator of all-male hierarchies) was tolerable. If allowed to emerge into public life and compete with or subvert age-old fundamental orthodoxies, however, these rogue, anarchic tendencies had the potential to sow chaos and to attack the integrity of the social fabric at the cellular level. These anxieties around LGBTQIA as a foreign (Western) force of significant destructive potential were there in a massive quotient of the Russian population throughout the 1990s. They were there ready to be exploited as a synecdochic target of the Putinist proudly anti-liberal ideology of Russia as an ascendent civilization and bastion of stability, order, and tradition, and the West as a decadent civilization and a dissolute, degenerate force for anarchy. They were available to be attached, in the historiographic dimension of Putinist propaganda, to the anti-Russian Western existential threat from the most identity-constituent military contest for Soviet and post-Soviet Russia: the Fascists of Nazi Germany in the Great Patriotic War.

The deep psychological barriers to broad-based tolerance of sexual and gender-expression pluralism in post-Soviet public life are evident even in the lawless, (seemingly) anything-went media sphere of the 1990s. These deeply internalized boundaries between private impulses or sensibilities and public self-presentation, and anxieties around maintaining—and never misjudging—those boundaries, are reified on the macro scale in the 1990s media landscape. They are evident in what is and isn't said there, what is and isn't performed, how, and through which particular channels aimed at which particular audiences. Given the specificities of how they have been exploited by the Putin regime, those barriers appear to be emblematic of even deeper and broader anxieties around pluralism in general, anxieties about pluralism vis-à-vis stability, pluralism vis-à-vis predictability, and a predilection for a sense of stability inside Russia and an external global stability (via preservation and exercise of Russian geopolitical strength), at whatever cost to private, personal freedoms.

Notes

1 Thanks are due to Maya Vinokour and the reviewers of earlier drafts of this essay for their many suggestions that helped me substantially improve it. I would also like to thank Rita Safariants for introducing me to the fascinating figure of Vladimir Vesyolkin.

2 Gessen, "How Russia's Hilarious, Homoerotic 'Satisfaction' Became a Nationwide Meme of Solidarity."

3 "And this is, of course, their right, their inalienable right, established in the first article of the UN Charter, where the principle of equality and self-determination of peoples is explicitly stated...We will always remember the heroes of the 'Russian Spring,' those who in 2014 could not abide the neo-Nazi coup in the Ukraine...I want the authorities in Kiev and their true masters in the West to hear me, and for all to take note: the people living in Lugansk and Donetsk, Kherson and Zaporozhye are becoming our citizens once and for all...And today's authorities in Kiev have to respect these peoples' free expression of will...Our compatriots, our brothers and sisters in the Ukraine—an integral part of our single nation—have witnessed with their own eyes what the ruling élites of the so-called West have in store for all of humanity...After the collapse of the Soviet Union the West decided the whole world, all of us, would have to submit to its dictates. Back then, in 1991, the West thought Russia wouldn't come through such trials, that it would disintegrate all on its own. And this almost happened. We all remember the 90s, the fearsome 90s, hungry, cold, and hopeless...the West itself...feels it can be the arbiter of who has the right of self-determination and who does not, who is not worthy of that...Their hegemony has the unmistakable character of totalitarianism, despotism, and apartheid...The Western countries for centuries have spouted that they are bringers of freedom and democracy to other peoples...They have drowned truth in an ocean of myths, illusions, and fakes, using propaganda that is aggressive in the extreme, they lie recklessly, like Goebbels. The more outlandish the lie, the faster they'll buy it, that's how they work, that is their principle...And those who legitimately ask 'how so?' are immediately labeled enemies, extremists, and radicals...do we really want in our country, in Russia, to have mom and dad replaced by 'parent number one,' 'number two,' 'number three'...Do we really want perversions leading to degradation and degeneration foisted on our schoolchildren? Do we want it hammered into them that, apart from men and women, there are supposedly some other genders and that they can have operations to change their sex? Is this what we want for our country and our children? For us all of this is unacceptable. We have another future, our future." Translation mine. "И это, конечно, их право, их неотъемлемое право, которое закреплено в первой статье Устава ООН, где прямо сказано о принципе равноправия и самоопределения народов... Мы всегда будем помнить героев "русской весны", тех, кто не смирился в 2014 году с неонацистским государственным переворотом на Украине...Хочу, чтобы меня услышали киевские власти и их реальные хозяева на Западе, чтобы это запомнили все: люди, живущие в Луганске и Донецке, Херсоне и Запорожье, становятся нашими гражданами навсегда... И сегодняшние киевские власти должны относиться к этому свободному волеизъявлению людей с уважением...Наши соотечественники, наши братья и сестры на Украине – родная часть нашего единого народа – своими глазами увидели то, что правящие круги так называемого Запада готовят всему человечеству... После распада Советского Союза Запад решил, что миру, всем нам навсегда придется мириться с его диктатом. Тогда, в 1991 году, Запад рассчитывал, что Россия от таких потрясений уже не оправится и дальше развалится сама по себе. Да это почти и произошло – мы же помним 90-е, страшные 90-е годы, голодные, холодные и безнадежные... Именно так называемый Запад... сейчас по своему собственному усмотрению решает, кто имеет право на самоопределение, а кто нет, кто его недостоин... Их гегемония имеет ярко выраженный характер тоталитаризма, деспотизма и апартеида...Западные страны веками твердят о том, что они несут другим народам и свободу, и демократию... Правду утопили в океане мифов, иллюзий и фейков, используя запредельно агрессивную пропаганду, врут напропалую, как Геббельс. Чем

невероятнее ложь, тем быстрее в нее поверят, вот так и действуют, по этому принципу…А тех, кто начинает задавать справедливые вопросы: "Собственно говоря, почему так?" – немедленно объявляют врагами, экстремистами и радикалами… разве мы хотим, чтобы у нас, здесь, в нашей стране, в России, вместо мамы и папы был "родитель номер один", "номер два", "номер три"… Разве мы хотим, чтобы в наших школах с начальных классов детям навязывали извращения, которые ведут к деградации и вымиранию? Чтобы им вдалбливали, что кроме женщин и мужчин якобы существуют еще некие гендеры и предлагали сделать операцию по смене пола? Разве мы всего этого хотим для своей страны и своих детей? Для нас все это неприемлемо, у нас другое, свое будущее." "За нами – правда!"

4 There appeared to be an echo of this in the November 30, 2023 Supreme Court decision to declare some entirely undefined "international LGBT movement" as an "extremist organization" whose operation within the Russian Federation is unlawful. See: "Верховный суд признал ЛГБТ «экстремистской» организацией."

5 This kind of conservatism around sex and gender expression is, of course, by no means unique to the Russian case. There is a long history of virulent phobia around sexual and gender-expression pluralism or fluidity in patriarchal and authoritarian regimes, likely at least in part because it interferes with the masculine prestige on which patriarchy is predicated. Social integration and political enfranchisement of LGBTQIA people in Western democracies is itself a development of the most recent two or three decades, and those developments continue to be contested by some groups in those countries. Still, a non-Western Russia could in theory have gone further faster with sexual and gender-expression pluralism than the West had.

6 Russian, or perhaps more properly Soviet, association of homosexuality and fascism dates to before WWII. In an article published in *Pravda* and *Izvestiia* on the same day in 1934, Maxim Gorky named homosexuality in an enumeration of the ills unleashed on humanity by the Fascist world, and quoted what he called a contemporary "sarcastic saying:" "destroy homosexuals, and fascism will vanish." Горький, "Пролетарский гуманизм." A dissociative tendency to look for external origins for any manifestations of homosexuality on Russian territory and to blame foreign, Fascist agents for them is instantiated in the trope that Nikolai Ezhov, head of the NKVD during the purges, was infected with homosexuality through his contact with the Nazis. See p. 149.

7 The "imaginary West" is a category often invoked by Alexei Yurchak in his 2006 monograph *Everything Was Forever, Until It Was No More* to talk about different ideations of "the West" observed in different groups of Soviet citizens during "late Socialism."

8 A few exceptions—in the form of fledgling visions of a distinctly, essentially Russian national identity and political future, a crucial part of which is plurality of sexualities and fluidity of gender expression—are discussed further down. Ultimately, all are very short-lived.

9 To some extent this gets started earlier, during the last years of glasnost and perestroika. See Roldugina, "Dissidents of Love," 239–40.

10 The main tiles in this category are *Dimka*, *Argo* or *Argot* (*Арго*), *Stag Party* (*Мальчишник*), and *You* (*Ты*).

11 For example, the title of the magazine *Арго* was seemingly a double entendre having both the meaning of argot or esoteric slang, and that of the ship of the Argonauts in the Greek legend of the Golden Fleece—a legend featuring homosexual love (of Heracles for Hylas). That legend also recounts a voyage of Hellenic heroes to the eastern shores of the Black Sea, and in this context could also imply a migration of the culture of Western Classical Antiquity to Russia.

12 Examples of publications in this category include *1/10* and its literary supplement *9/10*, *Gay, Slavs!* (*Gay, Славяне!*), *Risk*, and *Theme* (*Тема*).

13 One of the exponents of a Russian gay identity in the 1990s, Gennadii Trifonov, notes this trend in an essay included as Artifact 00174. "Amongst Soviet homosexuals there's a widely shared idea regarding Western freedoms, namely that their Western counterparts have enjoyed a peaceful and harmonious existence there since Adam. This despite the fact that the long, often tragic, frequently even bloody history of sexual minorities' fight for their rights in Western countries has its chroniclers." ("В среде советских гомосексуалистов применительно к западным свободам бытует расхожее мнение о том, что их западные единомышленники благоденствуют со времен Адама. Длительная, часто трагическая, зачастую даже кровавая история борьбы сексуальных меньшинств в странах Запада за свои права имеет своих летописцев.") Трифонов, "Советские гомосексуалисты: вчера, сегодня, завтра," 12.

14 Homoerotic elements were pronounced in the early-twentieth-century works of Kuzmin and Kluyev, and their works were not published in Soviet Russia from the late 1920s through the late 1970s and early 1980s, though they continued to be published by Western European and North American presses publishing Russian literature in the original. Kluyev was executed in 1937. The official reason for his arrest and exile in 1934 and 1936 were composition and distribution of antirevolutionary literary works and association with antirevolutionary religious groups. One of the documents in this Sourcebook ("Two Lives, Two Destinies"), however, suggests that he was destroyed by the Soviet regime primarily because of his homosexuality (Юрлов, "Две жизни, две судьбы," Artifact 00054). After 1929 Kuzmin would not be published in Russia until 1989, when his works begin to reappear with Современник in Moscow, and Верхне-Волжское кинжное издательство in Yaroslavl. He is published extensively in the 1970s and 1980s by Prideaux Press in England, Ardis Press in Ann Arbor Michigan, Berkeley Slavic Specialties in Berkeley California, Russica in New York, and W. Fink in Munich. Kluyev somehow fares somewhat better. After 1928 he is published only abroad from the 1950s to the 1970s: by Издательство им. Чехова and Мост in New York, A. Neimanis in Munich, and Prideaux Press in England. At the end of the 1970s begins an almost steady trickle of Russian editions from Советский писатель (1977) and Советская Россия (1981) in Moscow; from Северно-Западное книжное издательство in Arkhangelsk (1986); Правда (1988) and Современник (1989) in Moscow; Карелия (1990) in Petrozavodsk; from Moscow publishers Столица, БОК, and Художественная литература, Правда, and Молодая гвардия in 1991; from Ставропольское книжное издательство in Stavropol in 1992. I assume Kluyev's more overtly homoerotic works were not selected for the Soviet editions, but I did not examine them in my research for this article. Pereleshin was a gay poet raised in the Russian émigré enclave of Harbin in northeast China who published often homoerotic poetry in Russian in the 1960s, 1970s, and 1980s through Western European and North American presses publishing literature in the Russian language (Posev in Frankfurt, Leuxenhoff in the Hague, Al'batros in Paris, New England Publishing in Holyoke Massachusetts).

15 Karlinsky devoted much of his scholarly career to LGBTQIA elements in Russian culture, particularly Russian literary culture. He published two books on Tsvetaeva: *Marina Cvetaeva: Her Life and Art* and *Marina Tsvetaeva: The Woman, Her World, and Her Poetry*. He published a book on Zinaida Gippius in 1980: *A Difficult Soul: Zinaida Gippius*. His 1976 book *The Sexual Labyrinth of Nikolai Gogol*, which asserts that Gogol was gay and that his suppressed homosexuality is an enormously determinant force in his oeuvre, raised a scandal among Russian émigré scholars.

16 Shalamov's prose was not published in the Soivet Union until 1989. Solzhenitsyn's *One Day in the Life of Ivan Denisovich* had a somewhat more complex history. It was authorized for publication under Khrushchev and appeared in the journal *New World* (*Новый мир*) in 1962, and then was published monographically that same year. Shortly thereafter there was a reversal of official attitudes (after Khrushchev's ouster) and all copies of the text were recalled and removed from libraries. From that point on it circulated in Russia only in tamizdat and samizdat copies of Western editions, until it was published in multiple editions in Russia beginning in 1990.

17 See Artifact 00215, "Olga. Love and Faith Are Not Dead" ("Ольга: Любовь и вера не изчезли").

18 Article 121 of the Criminal Code of the Soviet Union, essentially a law against "sodomy" (*мужеложство*) or sexual relations between men, became Article 121 of the Russian Republic after the fall of the Soviet Union. It remained in force until 1993, when it was repealed.

19 Slava Mogutin (about whom more to follow) had a much wider audience than the other authors mentioned here, and is the only author who (along with co-author Sonja Franeta) published on these topics in a mainstream print publication. See Artifact 00174, "Homosexuality in Soviet Prisons and Camps" ("Гомосексуализм в советских тюрьмах и лагерях").

20 See Artifact 00178, "Soviet Homosexuals: Yesterday, Today, Tomorrow" ("Советские гомосексуалисты: вчера, сегодня, завтра"). Irina Roldugina observes that one of the earliest post-Soviet mainstream-press articles on the lot of homosexuals in Russia, an article from the November 29, 1991 issue of *Комсомольская правда*, used the word "repressed" (*репрессированные*) in reference to homosexuals, thereby including them in the category of rehabilitated victims of persecution at the hand of the Soviet state apparatus. Roldugina, "Dissidents of Love," 238.

21 "Такое чисто английское явление как Оскар Уайльд в России немыслим ещё в ближайшие триста лет, ибо количество Моисеев, готовых вывести нас из собственного Египта, хотя и увеличивается каждодневно, нашей душе все ещё любезны родимые потемки, блуждая в

которых и давя друг друга, мы утверждаемся с завидным самозабвением." Трифонов, "Советские гомосексуалисты: вчера, сегодня, завтра," 12.

22 Broader consideration of memory politics in 1990s Russia, and their Putin-era legacy, is given in Maya Vinokour's chapter in this volume.

23 See note 18.

24 An example of this kind of article is Artifact 00053, "AIDS: More Questions Than Answers." For other examples, see Мороз, "СПИД у нас дома;" Куликовская, "Обратного хода нет."

25 In his chapter in this volume Bradley Gorski refers to a scarce exception to the general rule from the very end of the Soviet era: a cartoon published in *Izvestia* in 1990 that suggests that public opinion vis-à-vis a number of longstanding taboos, including "sexual relations between members of the same sex," is changing.

26 See on this: Gessen, "Moscow Activists Push for Gay *Glasnost*;" Roldugina, "Dissidents of Love."

27 Glagol also published scholarly works related to LGBTQ aspects of Russian cultural history, such as Познанский, *Самоубийство Чайковского: миф и реальность*; Жук, *Русские амазонки: история лесбийской субкультуры в России, XX век*.

28 Essig, *Queer in Russia*, 93–97.

29 See Artifact 00027, *Сотворение Адама* (*Creation of Adam*).

30 The history and character of *Megapolis express*, and its evolution over time, is discussed in Fabrizio Fenghi's chapter in this volume.

31 Mogutin, and in particular his relationship with Eduard Limonov (discussed further along in this essay), is also discussed in Fabrizio Fenghi's contribution to this volume.

32 Могутин, "Грязные концы комсомольцев."

33 In her 1999 monograph *Queer in Russia* sociologist Laurie Essig groups Mogutin in a category she calls "nationalist queers." Essig, *Queer in Russia*, 143–6.

34 Могутин и Франета, "Гомосексуальность в советских тюрьмах и лагерях," 46. This was one of the very few publications on this subject in the mainstream media, in the monthly *The New Times* (*Новое время*).

35 Interestingly, Irina Roldugina points to the First Chechen War (1994–96) as something of a turning point for the fledgling LGBTQIA movement in post-Soviet Russia. See Roldugina, "Dissidents of Love," 246. The re-militarization of Russian society and the resurgence of nationalist sentiment brought with them, per Roldugina, promotion of a rigidly defined model of masculinity (physical strength, valor, conformity to a shared code of behavior of the tribe), and this stymied any progress toward a more fluid, pluralistic view of sexuality and gender expression. Mogutin seemed in many ways to embrace this aggressive, militarized masculinity, while seeming to want to introduce the novelty of accommodations for male homosexuality. Curiously, Mogutin would be forced out of Russia, ostensibly because of nationalistic speech verging on hate speech, though many believe he was in fact being persecuted for his open, even deliberately provocative homosexuality. In any event, his vision of a nationalist, militaristic Russia that embraced homosexuality proved not to be a viable one.

36 This Sourcebook contains a document of another instance of conceiving a uniquely Russian gay male identity via connection to old Russian religious (Christian) traditions. In Юрлов, "Две жизни, две судьбы" ("Two Lives, Two Destinies," Artifact 00054). The author writes about the poet Nikolai Kluyev as an exponent of a Russian homosexual spirituality related to the Khlysty Christian sect. Evgenii Kharitonov, whose homoerotic prose works were, evidently, "written for the drawer" during the second half of the Soviet era, also had a profound Orthodox Christian religiosity bound up in very problematic ways with his homosexuality. For anyone persuaded by the arguments in Simon Karlinsky's monograph *The Sexual Labyrinth of Nikolai Gogol*, Kharitonov would in some sense appear to have continued a Gogolian precedent.

37 Mogutin was born in 1974 and was seventeen years old when the Soviet era ended in 1991.

38 Dugin is discussed at greater length in Fabrizio Fenghi's chapter in this volume.

39 Essig, *Queer in Russia*, 143. Essig also summarizes rumors about Zhirinovsky's own sexuality, which included allegations of a sexual appetite for very young men.

40 Essig, *Queer in Russia*, 139–43.

41 Masha Gessen wrote that by 2007, Debryanskaya had, "like many activists of old," changed gears and become an entrepreneur. Gessen, *The Future Is History*, 257.

42 The attraction–repulsion relationship to Western culture is discussed at length in Rita Safariants's contribution to this volume.

43 Essig, *Queer in Russia*, 140–41.

44 Campbell, "Homosexuality as Device."

45 Campbell, 68.

46 Discussion of the various philosophies and positions of figures like Novikov and others mentioned in this section is inevitably vexed by layered irony and seemingly endlessly fluctuating critical distance from their own personas, their own works, and from any subject they treated discursively or aesthetically. This phenomenon, broadly denoted by the word *stiob*, whether purely strategic, purely sincere, or somewhere in between, was widely characteristic of cultural and public figures in the late-Soviet and early post-Soviet periods. Julie Cassiday, Helena Goscilo, and Jonathan Brooks Platt write about the New Academy artists as "arch-ironic" and intensive practitioners of *stiob*. See Casssiday, Goscilo, Platt, "Introduction: The Allure of Retro: Neoacademism after the Fall," 190.

47 Novikov's turn toward an increasingly nationalist and religious conservativism, even Fascism, coincided with his declining health after infection with HIV. HIV/AIDS was seen by many as a gay plague and, by some, as divine retribution for the sin of homosexuality. See Stodolsky, "A Multi-Lectic Anatomy of Stiob and Poshlost';" Stodolsky, "A 'Non-Aligned' Intelligentsia," 40.

48 See note 50. Ironic layering combined paradoxically with an over-identification with may-be-or-may-not-be parodic targets, characteristic of 1990s *stiob*, makes definitively determining Mamyshev-Monroe's affective posture vis-à-vis his subjects, and his own unstable identity, difficult.

49 Casssiday, 228, 233–35.

50 Mamyshev-Monroe made a number of remarks about the necessity for a male subjectivity to access and manifest the divine feminine ideal or essence, because of women's pedestrian preoccupation with petty interests. An exception was made for Marilyn Monroe, who was so central to Mamyshev-Monroe's worldview and aesthetic program that he added her name to his own. Monroe's Americanness, and therefore non-Russianness, troubled him, however, and he made attempts to claim her as a de facto Russian figure based on her physiognomic features. See Cassiday, "Vladislav Mamyshev-Monroe, Frog-Princess of Neoacademism," 228–29, 234–35.

51 *Ptiuch* also attracted numerous Western advertisers, among them Absolut Vodka, Seagram's, Gitanes, Pall Mall, L'Oréal, Adidas, Diesel, Guess, Sony, Lufthansa, and Jaguar.

52 Cassiday, "Post-Soviet Pop Goes Gay." Cassiday also suggests that the lesbian-erotic elements were part of a strategic appeal to Western sensibilities to secure advantage in the Eurovision competition.

53 Brock and Miazhevich, "From High Camp to Post-Modern Camp."

54 Могутин, "Грязные концы комсомольцев."

55 "Я лгал, что я гей! А мне верили! Это грех;" Моисеев, *Птичка живой звук*, 57–8, 113–4.

56 "Певец Борис Моисеев: "По поводу геев у нас с Лужковым одинаковое мнение";" "Борис Моисеев не согласен с настойчивостью московских геев;" "Борис Моисеев: ...Половая свобода не важна;" Моисеев, *Птичка живой звук*, 57–8, 87–9, 113–4, 305–7. In that book Moiseev also writes about his support of Putin and the United Russia party (see pp. 180–3).

57 Mamyshev-Monroe's untimely demise occurred in somewhat troubling circumstances. A few weeks before he was found dead, drowned in a pool in Bali, he reported having been approached by the Oligarch Sergei Polonsky and Sergei ("Afrika") Bugaev, who asked him, seemingly on behalf of Russian state authorities, in the person of Vladislav Surkov, to weaponize his own brand of homoerotic and gender-variant impersonative art against the Kremlin's detractors, including creating a photograph depicting Alexei Navalny anally penetrating Boris Akunin. Mamyshev-Monroe refused, and said he had been disturbed by the incident, in which, he said, Bugaev had communicated that from that point forward, those who openly opposed the Kremlin would be "killed, maimed, or starved." Mamyshev-Monroe had been openly critical of the Putin regime. See Lipovetsky, "A Trickster in Drag: Vlad Mamyshev-Monroe's Aesthetic of Camp;" Троицкий, "На дне. Пролог."

58 Brock and Miazhevich, 1004. Kirkorov was named *narodnyi artist Rossiiskoi Federatsii* in 2008, and has vociferously supported the war on Ukraine, as well as Lukashenko's repression of the uprisings in Belarus in 2020–21. There are resonances and continuities here with the phenomenon of ostensibly transgressive or countercultural elements being harnessed by state authorities as described in Rita Safariants's account of the KGB's sponsorship of late-Soviet rock in her chapter in this volume.

59 The non-standard spelling *внутренных* (standard would be *внутренних*) is a nod to the pop-music band with which Veselkin was initially associated. "Auction" spelled its name with a non-standard *ы* in place of the *и*: *Аукцыон*.

60 "*Как же так ты обманул меня.*"

61 Бояринов, "Танцор риска;" Веселкин, "Вова Веселкин: жизнь и трагедия рок-фавна."

62 Essig, *Queer in Russia*, 118; Кучкина, "Кто снимает ПЕНКина. Теленеделя."

63 There is some similarity here between Penkin and Kirkorov, who appear to play at homoerotic and gender-fluid innuendo from a place of privileged safety as artists enjoying the patronage of the political authorities. Vladislav Mamyshev-Monroe, who was to become an outspoken critic of the Putin regime and refused an invitation (allegedly from Vladislav Surkov, delivered through the oligarch Sergei Polonsky and Sergei "Afrika" Bugaev) to allow his sexuality, gender expression, and artistry to be instrumentalized by the regime weeks before his mysterious demise, is said to have despised Penkin. See: Cassiday, "Vladislav Mamyshev-Monroe, Frog-Princess of Neoacademism," 231. The role of the probably gay and/or gender-variant man who signals homosexual desire and gender fluidity only in strategic and circumspect ways in an effort to secure both public popularity and the protection of tyrannical authorities—this role seems to have been repugnant to Mamyshev-Monroe, who once remarked vis-à-vis Kirkorov's marriage to mega-star Alla Pugacheva that Pugacheva had married "herself with five o'clock shadow." Cassiday, "Vladislav Mamyshev-Monroe, Frog-Princess of Neoacademism," 229.

64 See on this Brock and Miazhevich, "From High Camp to Post-Modern Camp."

65 For more on the association between Mogutin and Limonov, see Fabrizio Fenghi's chapter in this volume.

66 Эдуард Лимонов, *Это я — Эдичка* (Москва: Глагол, 1991). In fact, the homoerotic episodes were so salient to several early translators of the novel in the 1980s that they rendered the title as "The Russian Poet Likes Big Black Guys:" Eduard Limonov, *Le poète russe préfère les grands nègres*, trans. Emmanuelle Davidov (Paris: Éditions Ramsay, 1980); Eduard Limonov, *De Russische dichter houdt van grote negers*, trans. Mieke Lindenburg (Amsterdam: Uitgeverij Bert Bakker, 1981); Edward Limonov, *Il poeta russo preferisce i grandi negri: Romanzo*, trans. Marina Marrazza (Milan: Frassinelli, 1985).

67 Лимонов, *Эдичка*, 11, 20.

68 Лимонов, *Эдичка*, 15.

69 Лимонов, *Эдичка*, 10.

70 Of course, the roots of this go deeper into the Soviet period and the cognitive contortions it required of its citizens, often referred to as "double-think" after George Orwell via Yuri Levada. The 2010s neologisms *gomofashizm*, *gomofashisty* themselves have something of a fringe-culture or counterculture 1990s precedent. The concept of gayness was sometimes coupled with the quintessentially anathema, anti-Soviet (anti-Russian?) concept of Fascism in the scandalizing self-styling of 1990s punk bands as an extreme anti-establishment provocation. Laurie Essig quotes one of her interviewees as having said in 1994, "My brother is part of a neofascist punk band, and of course they're all gay and they're all for Zhirinovskii. I thought that homosexuals were always connected with fascism," Essig, *Queer in Russia*, 124.

71 It should be observed here that this, of course, was also true of most if not all Western societies until the end of the twentieth–beginning of the twenty-first century.

72 This is to some extent an extension of phenomena of late-Socialism described by Yurchak in *Everything Was Forever*: finding loopholes or affordances in established structures and conventions that allow one to creatively reinflect, or find private freedoms within, those structures and conventions. There are some anecdotal accounts of LGBTQIA facets of this in the late-Soviet era, for example, gay men and lesbians marrying each other, securing the benefits contingent on married status (such as housing allotments), and then carrying on relationships with their respective same-sex partners.

Works Cited

Bakich, Olga. *Valerii Pereleshin: Life of a Silkworm*. Toronto: University of Toronto Press, 2015.

Brock, Maria, and Galina Miazhevich. "From High Camp to Post-Modern Camp: Queering Post-Soviet Pop Music." *European Journal of Cultural Studies* 25, no. 4 (2022): 993–1009.

Campbell, Thomas. "Homosexuality as Device: Necrorealism and Neoacademism." In *Russian Art in Translation*, edited by Nicholas Herman, Eugene Raikhel, and Elena Sorokina, 68–79. Brooklyn, NY: Ante, 2007.

Cassiday, Julie A. "Post-Soviet Pop Goes Gay: Russia's Trajectory to Eurovision Victory." *Russian Review* 73, no. 1 (2014): 1–23.

Cassiday, Julie A. "Vladislav Mamyshev-Monroe, Frog-Princess of Neoacademism." *Russian Review* 78, no. 2 (2019): 221–44.

Casssiday, Julie A., Helena Goscilo, and Jonathan Brooks Platt. "Introduction: The Allure of Retro: Neoacademism after the Fall." *Russian Review* 78, no. 2 (2019): 183–200.

Essig, Laurie. *Queer in Russia: A Story of Sex, Self, and the Other.* Durham, NC: Duke University Press, 1999.

Gessen, Masha. *The Future Is History: How Totalitarianism Reclaimed Russia.* New York: Riverhead Books, 2017.

Gessen, Masha. "How Russia's Hilarious, Homoerotic 'Satisfaction' Became a Nationwide Meme of Solidarity." *The New Yorker*, January 22, 2018. https://www.newyorker.com/news/our-columnists/how-russias-hilarious-homoerotic-satisfaction-became-a-nationwide-meme-of-solidarity.

Gessen, Masha. "Masha Gessen and David Remnick on Putin." Interview with David Remnick. *The Vault*, 2014. https://newbooksnetwork.com/masha-gessen-and-david-remnick-on-putin.

Gessen, Masha. "Moscow Activists Push for Gay *Glasnost*." *The Advocate* 566 (1990): 50–51.

Gessen, Masha. *Surviving Autocracy.* New York: Riverhead Books, 2020.

Karlinsky, Simon. *A Difficult Soul: Zinaida Gippius.* Berkeley: University of California Press, 1980.

Karlinsky, Simon. "A Hidden Masterpiece: Valery Pereleshin's *Ariel*." *Christopher Street* 2, no. 6 (December 1977): 37–42.

Karlinsky, Simon. *Marina Cvetaeva: Her Life and Art.* Berkeley: University of California Press, 1966.

Karlinsky, Simon. *The Sexual Labyrinth of Nikolai Gogol.* Cambridge: Harvard University Press, 1976.

Limonov, Edward. *Il poeta russo preferisce i grandi negri: Romanzo.* Translated by Marina Marrazza. Milan: Frassinelli, 1985.

Limonov, Edward. *Le poète russe préfère les grands nègres.* Translated by Emmanuelle Davidov. Paris: Éditions Ramsay, 1980.

Limonov, Edward. *De Russische dichter houdt van grote negers.* Translated by Mieke Lindenburg. Amsterdam: Uitgeverij Bert Bakker, 1981.

Lipovetsky, Mark. "A Trickster in Drag: Vlad Mamyshev-Monroe's Aesthetic of Camp." *Arts* 11, no. 5 (2022): 87–106.

Roldugina, Irina. "Dissidents of Love: The Politics and Practice of Russian LGBTQ Samizdat after the Fall of the USSR." In *In Defense of the Mainstream*, 237–49. Moscow: V-A-C Press, 2021.

Stern, Mikhail. *Sex in the USSR.* New York: Times Books, 1980.

Stodolsky, Ivor A. "A Multi-Lectic Anatomy of Stiob and Poshlost': Case Studies in the Oeuvre of Timur Novikov." *Laboratorium* 3, no. 1 (2011): 24–50.

Stodolsky, Ivor A. "A 'Non-Aligned' Intelligentsia: Timur Novikov's Neo-Avantgarde and the Afterlife of Leningrad Non-Conformism." *Studies in Eastern European Thought* 63 (2011): 135–45.

Yurchak, Alexei. *Everything Was Forever, Until It Was No More: The Last Soviet Generation.* Princeton, NJ: Princeton University Press, 2006.

Берберова, Нина, Малькольм Браун, Симон Карлинский. "Пересмотр версии самоубийства Чайковского: Опровержение." *Gay Славяне* 1 (1993): 6–8.

"Борис Моисеев не согласен с настойчивостью московских геев." *Росбалт*, 2 июня (2008). https://rosbalt.ru/moscow/2008/06/02/490146.html.

"Борис Моисеев: ...Половая свобода не важна." *XGAY.RU*, 6 февраля (2006). https://xgayru.info/art/music/singer/russian/moiseev/bmoiseev2006.html.

Бояринов, Денис. "Танцор риска." *Такие дела*, 16 октября 2015. https://takiedela.ru/2015/10/veselkin/.

"Верховный суд признал ЛГБТ «экстремистской» организацией." *Новая газета*, 30 ноября 2023. https://novayagazeta.eu/articles/2023/11/30/verkhovnyi-sud-priznal-lgbt-ekstremistskoi-organizatsiei-news.

Веселкин, Владимир. "Вова Веселкин: жизнь и трагедия рок-фавна." Интервью Андрея Королева. *Настоящее время*, 17 декабря 2015. https://www.currenttime.tv/a/27429551.html.

Гессен, Маша. “Елена Боннэр: Меньше всего на свете меня интересует эта проблема.” *Тема* №2–3 (1992): 9.
Горький, Максим. “Пролетарский гуманизм.” *Известия* 23 мая 1934 г.: 2.
Горький, Максим. “Пролетарский гуманизм.” *Правда* 23 мая 1934 г.: 3.
Жук, Ольга. *Русские амазонки: история лесбийской субкультуры в России, XX век.* Москва: Глагол, 1998.
“За нами – правда!” *Российская газета* (№. 221) 1 октября, 2022: 1–2.
Карлинский, Симон. “Гомосексуализм в русской истории и культуре.” *Тема: издание Ассоциации сексуальных меньшинств* 2 (1991): 1–3.
Кузнецов, Эдуард. *Мордовский марафон.* [Иерусалим]: Москва-Иерусалим, 1979.
Куликовская, Галина. “Обратного хода нет.” *Огонёк* 23 (1987): 18–20.
Кучкина, Ольга. “Кто снимает ПЕНКина. Теленеделя.” *Комсомольская правда*, 24 мая, 1994.
Лимонов, Эдуард. *Это я — Эдичка. Роман.* Москва: Глагол, 1991.
Маркман, Владимир. *На краю географии.* [Иерусалим]: Москва-Иерусалим, 1979.
Могутин, Слава. “Грязные концы комсомольцев.” *Ещё* 4/16 (1993).
Могутин, Слава, Соня Франета. “Гомосексуализм в советских тюрьмах и лагерях.” *Новое Время* 35 (1993), 36 (1993): 44–47, 50–54.
Моисеев, Борис. *Птичка живой звук.* Москва: АСТ, 2007.
Морозов, Олег. “СПИД у нас дома.” *Литературная газета* 14 декабря 1988: 12.
Мурадов, Борис. “Евгения Дебрянская: «Мне плевать на общественное мнение».” *Аргументы и факты* 19 ноября 1997: 20.
“Ольга: Любовь и вера не исчезли.” *Риск* январь 1991: 6.
“Певец Борис Моисеев: “По поводу геев у нас с Лужковым одинаковое мнение.”” *Известия* 6 июня (2006). https://iz.ru/news/314384.
Познанский, Александр. *Самоубийство Чайковского: миф и реальность.* Москва: Глагол, 1993.
Павлов, Юрий, реж. *Сотворение Адама*, 1993; Киностудия Борчалы, 1995. VHS.
“Птюч.” *Большая российская энциклопедия.*
“СПИД: вопросов больше, чем ответов.” *Литературная газета* 6 мая 1986: 15.
Стомахин, Игорь. “Лесбиянка Маша атакует чиновников.” *Мегаполис экспресс* №24 (1994): 8.
Трифонов, Геннадий. “Советские гомосексуалисты: вчера, сегодня, завтра.” *Gay славяне* 1 (1993): 9–15.
Троицкий, Артемий. “На дне. Пролог.” *Новая газета*, 14 апреля 2013. https://novayagazeta.ru/articles/2013/04/15/54350-na-dne-prolog.
Федеральный закон “О защите детей от информации, причиняющей вред их здоровью и развитию” Статья 6.21. Пропаганда нетрадиционных сексуальных отношений среди несовершеннолетних.
Хроника «Мемориала». https://www.memo.ru/ru-ru/memorial/history/.
“Цветаева и Парнок.” *Риск*. Январь (1991): 8–9.
Юрлов, Борис. “Две жизни, две судьбы.” *1/9: литературное приложение к газете 1/10* 1 (1992), 2 (1992): 2–7, 3–8.
“Я лгал, что я гей! А мне верили! Это грех.” *Cosmopolitan* 169 (2010). https://web.archive.org/web/20110130053740/http://tnt-online.ru/Cosmopolitan/169/v01.htm.

CHAPTER 7

The Revolution of the New *Narod*: Perestroika, the 1991 *GKChP* Coup, and the Televised Post-Soviet Subject at *Vzgliad/ViD*

Pavel Khazanov

> "If it is true that there's no *narod* without song, then it is here that the backbone of a new *narod* is taking shape, or perhaps a new stratum, bearing within itself a post-*narod* truth and a post-*narod* song.
>
> —Grigory Pomerants, 1968

> "Here are our guests. Famous writers, poets...drug addicts, telepaths, psychopaths, and some other people who don't do much in particular..."
>
> —A parody of *Vzgliad*, 1989

> "Racketeers with wads of cash came and took our agitation sheets and went to distribute them among all the army units. The bourse gave us food, poets gave us verses, Afghan vets gave us weapons. The banks hauled over a bunch of Xerox machines and printing equipment...the factory next door came over and brought us gas masks for a possible attack."
>
> —*Vzgliad*, August 21, 1991

In 2015, on the twenty-fifth anniversary of one of post-Soviet Russia's most popular TV gameshows, *Kapital shou "Pole chudes"* (*Capital Show "Field of Miracles"*), its production company *ViD* (literally, *View*, originally an acronym of "*Vzgliad* and others") released a celebratory TV documentary, *Est' takaia bukva (There Is Such a Letter)*[a]. In it, many of the original creators and producers give interviews, explaining the show's concept origin, but the emphasis of the documentary is undoubtedly on the *narod*—the folk audience of *Pole chudes* and its inimitable folkish host, Leonid Yakubovich. The show, according to the documentary, is driven neither by the intellectual thrill of the trivia question (borrowed from *The Wheel of Fortune*), nor the excitement of watching people haggle over sometimes highly lucrative mystery prizes (borrowed from *Let's Make a Deal*). Rather,

[a] https://www.1tv.ru/doc/pro-shou-biznes/est-takaya-bukva

the *real* core of *Pole chudes*, "the secret of its success," we are told, is its special bond to a *narod* that arrives in Moscow with pickled vegetables to give to Yakubovich; a *narod* that has dispensed presents and wisdom on the host over twenty-five years, a *narod* that celebrates its financial lucky breaks in a genuine, everyman style. The documentary culminates this narrative with a visit to the inauguration of the *Pole chudes* museum for displaying the *narod*'s gifted handywork. Vis-à-vis this institution, Yakubovich appears as the people's perfect media leader, a "kind, adult, smart, bright man, welcoming his guests—it is a little like a VDIaKh—an Exhibit of the Achievements of the Yakubovich Economy."[1]

As I write this essay in 2022–24, in the midst of Russia's bloody invasion of Ukraine, initiated in the name of defending the interests of Russian-speakers in the "near abroad," the documentary's references to the *narod* sound especially sinister, especially in moments when we learn that representatives of "43 countries" have attended this show's "feast for the soul"—as one former contestant calls it, citing the famous 1974 Village Prose film *Kalina krasnaia* (*The Red Snowball Tree*), by the Russian nationalist writer/filmmaker Vasily Shukshin.[2] As is often the case with Russian state discourse regarding the populace over which it seeks to extend its dominion, the term *narod* in *Est' takaia bukva* does not describe a collective bearer of political will—if it did, then this word would be entirely inappropriate for the post-Soviet foreign nationals who have appeared on the show. Rather, Yakubovich's *narod* should be understood in terms of "demotic identity"—it is an amalgam of post-Soviet regional identities still happily subordinating themselves to the gaze of the unchanging Russophone imperial center.[3] We can think of it as an updated version of "national in form, socialist in content" for an era in which "socialism" as a referent has disappeared but its old imperialist meaning has been recoded into the term *Russkii mir* (Russian world). At the time of the 2015 documentary's filming, this ideology already powered the first stage of Russia's assault on Crimea and the Donbass.

In addition, quite apart from its not-so-latent imperialism, *Est' takaia bukva* is a historically insidious film, because of how it entirely eviscerates the sense of post-Soviet liberatory potential that informed the creation of *Pole chudes* in late perestroika. The documentary mentions that the show was made by a team of media producers who first came together in 1987 to make the show *Vzgliad* (*A Look*). However, as far as Putinist 2015 hindsight is concerned, *Vzgliad*'s great achievement in the late 1980s lay in its ability to disrupt the staid, officious Soviet aesthetics of programming like the evening newscast *Vremia* (*Time*), but nothing substantially more than that. Unlike prim and proper, soporific Soviet anchors, we are told, "the *Vzgliad* guys used to speak with the audience in a human and honest way…And thus it is no surprise that the *Vzgliad* guys came up with a new, unheard of game on Soviet television, in which a person could easily receive money."[4] What exactly it was that the "*Vzgliad* guys" wanted to speak *about*, in that "human and honest way," and what political meaning the use of "human honesty" meant in the late Soviet decades, is deliberately downplayed. The former

Vzgliad lead and present-day *ViD* exec Alexander Liubimov does note that in 1991, flush with advertisement cash as a result of the popularity of *Pole chudes*, *ViD* was able to field twelve camera crews during the *GKChP* (Committee for the State of Emergency) attempted coup that August, at a time when the coup leaders shut down the Ostankino TV station.[5] "So yes, freedom is independence, and thus a new era began," Liubimov concludes.[6] But a vague belief in financially independent, aesthetically "free" media was hardly the reason the *Vzgliad/ViD* team spent days holed up in the Russian republican parliament building (known in Moscow as the White House), along with the rest of the pro-democracy activists, armed with weapons, awaiting what seemed to them like imminent storming by *GKChP*'s security forces. And aesthetic freedom fails to explain why *Vzgliad* spearheaded cutting-edge perestroika-era political programming, which included muck-racking journalism, hard-hitting discussions and townhalls with USSR's leading political actors, and exposés on various aspects of previously censored Soviet and Russian history and culture.

In 2015, the reduction of *Pole chudes* to an imperialist celebration of the post-Soviet folk and the reduction of its origin story to some vague notion of a fresh new free style go hand in hand. In fact, in this telling, the *ViD* team looks as if all along they always had been like the subservient elite flipside of their own post-Soviet mediatic *narod*—freewheeling, enjoyable to watch, definitively post-socialist, and at the same time never claiming an independent political subjectivity. Instead, the Putinist *ViD* and the Putinist *narod* are happy to perform their joint role in what Sergei Guriev and Daniel Treisman have termed a "spin dictatorship," in which the state presents itself as an outcome of popular will, even as it rigs all institutions, especially the media, against actionable expressions of collective discontent.[7]

Other contributors to this volume examine various aspects of this pro-authoritarian acclamatory role-playing dynamic, as well as the willingness of ostensibly independent-minded elites to take part in it, and at times, their ability to justify their actions by relying on jingoistic discourse on the *narod*.[8] For my part, despite the obviously nefarious potential present in all rhetoric pertaining to the people and their will, I do not think that in Russia the use of such constructs has always amounted merely to an arrow in the authoritarian quiver. On the contrary, this chapter will contend that perestroika-turned-early-post-Soviet Russian mass media's political imaginary of a "new *narod*"—which the makers of *Vzgliad* inherited from the post-Stalin field of consensus between a haltingly reformist state, the intelligentsia, and the middle class "ITR workers"—drove these media actors into the thick of the battle against Soviet authoritarianism in the late 1980s–early 1990s, and also into the thick of the capitalist transition, which they embraced at first not as an elitist opportunity, but as a popular revolution. I will argue that their implicit conception of popular will in late-Soviet USSR/Russia underwrote their commitment to values like spontaneity, discursive pluralism, and private ad hoc association for open-ended mutual gain. I will try to show why throughout the late-Soviet era, inclusive of perestroika, these values felt self-evident, irreproachably humanist, and democratic. And ultimately, I will try to explain why from the vantage point of the team at *Vzgliad* and *ViD*, their post-Soviet "new *narod*" seemed to have united in triumph against the *GKChP* forces in August 1991, only to lose the plot afterwards, by becoming a useful tool for the formation of a post-Soviet dictatorship.

A BRIEF SKETCH OF THE "NEW *NAROD*" AS THE SUBJECT OF POST-STALINIST HISTORY

To begin thinking about the political imaginary of the *Vzgliad/ViD* team, let us start with a 1988 broadcast of *Vzgliad*, celebrating the show's one-year anniversary (Artifact 00003[b], Figure 1). At this point, the show's format and style had already coalesced enough to be mocked. As the regular *Vzgliad* hosts look on, drinks in hand, a sketch comedy group summarizes the show in a nutshell. For three minutes, actors playing Vladislav Listyev, Alexander Liubimov, and Dmitry Zakharov interrupt each other constantly, ask the audience to call in, while not knowing where the phone is, and watch a music

FIGURE 1 Video from Artifact 00003.[c] The hosts of *Vzgliad* look on as a sketch comedy trio puts on their outfits and mocks their informal style.

---

[b] https://postsoviet90s.com/artifacts/early-vzgliad-parodies-itself
[c] https://postsoviet90s.com/artifacts/early-vzgliad-parodies-itself

video on a portable TV that the audience cannot see. Finally, they end the act with the following conversation:

> **Mock-Zakharov:** Today, on our show, we've got stories that aren't happening, produce that isn't edible, houses that are unfinished, promises that aren't kept, frozen building plans and poor harvests...
> **Mock-Listyev:** Sorry, just to interrupt, also, our traditional live broadcast of the Olympic games in Seoul. [*To Mock-Liubimov*] You're going to be there, right?
> **Mock-Zakharov:** Just bring back a t-shirt, mate!
> **Mock-Listyev:** You remember? A blue one with a bit of green, size 52. [*They give each other high-fives and Mock-Liubimov leaves.*] By the way, about the t-shirt [*to Mock-Zakharov*], our regular viewer from Karaganda is wondering, what does it say on your t-shirt?
> **Mock-Zakharov:** Well, actually, I guess you could say my t-shirt has the slogan of our social services, in English. [*Reads in English*] "By the people for the people." Which in translation means, "nothing, ever for normal human beings!" [*laughs*].
> **Mock-Listyev:** Sorry, you know, it's true, we'll definitely get back to that in our next show. In the meantime, here are our guests. Famous writers, poets...
> **Mock-Zakharov:** Drug addicts, telepaths, psychopaths, and some other people who don't do much in particular...
> [...]
> **Mock-Listyev:** Ok, well, of course, we'll get back to that, for sure. You know, we've already talked about a lot of issues today, there are still some issues we haven't discussed. But you know, if we haven't discussed them, then we haven't discussed them, right? So, we're saying goodbye now, our show today was hosted...
> **Mock-Zakharov:** ...just hosted by normal guys. And now, for whoever isn't asleep yet, a music video.[9]

The parody treatment of *Vzgliad* is driven by a radicalized performance of its hosts' seemingly freewheeling interpersonal relationship, which the comedy troupe defines along two prongs. The first prong is the logic of informal semi-private exchange of all sorts of social and cultural capital, which can range from the circulation of underground culture to the distribution of sought-after material goods, in this case Olympic t-shirts from South Korea. The other prong, related to the first one, is the informal circulation of late-Soviet semi-private political discourse, in this case represented by Mock-Zakharov's joke about the meaning of his shirt—a typical perestroika kitchen-table lament, "never anything for normal people in this country."[10] Both of these forms of exchange turn the hosts of *Vzgliad*—and the troupe mocking them—into "normal guys," as Mock-Zakharov puts it, who have ended up on Soviet television as if by accident. This, in turn, indicates a certain belief on the part of *Vzgliad* in the truth of the English message on Mock-Zakharov's t-shirt, "by the people, for the people." The *Vzgliad* guys' performative, dressed-down informality, their spontaneity, and their acting as a typical private network of Soviet friends exchanging gray-market goods and cultural capital, are altogether meant to tell viewers that they are coextensive with them, that this show is "by" and "for" them. But are these viewers really "the people"? How should we think about them as a collective?

At times, *Vzgliad* addresses its audience as the majority of the "Soviet people" consuming glasnost journalism, in which *Vzgliad*'s reports do not really differ from the muckraking on primetime Central Television news shows, such as *Prozhektor perestroiki* (*Perestroika Floodlight*) (Artifact 00029[d]). At other times *Vzgliad* implies its ideal viewer to be a member of the urbanized, educated "junior intelligentsia" mass elite, constrained more or less to the 12% of the population with college degrees. Or, finally and most self-evidently, the fact of *Vzgliad*'s production at the Central Television Youth Desk suggests that the show's ideal viewer is the Soviet "youth"—also a kind of countercultural elite, self-defining not by formal education, but by snobbish interest in various supposedly non-conformist "writers, poets…telepaths and psychopaths," such as Alexander Gradsky, the semi-underground "father of Russian rock," whose ironic performance of a song about insipid Soviet television opened *Vzgliad*'s very first broadcast in 1987[e] and served as a key part of this show's strategy of mass viewerly appeal (which was, of course, fully vetted with the Soviet state censorship apparatus, as were Soviet rockers like Gradsky, as Rita Safariants explains in the present volume).[11] However, I would like to suggest that none of these three collective constructs quite captures the full political capaciousness of the construct "normal guys," as Mock-Zakharov puts it. And to understand that capaciousness, we should briefly recall the 1960s–1970s political conjuncture that gave birth to post-Stalinist mass media programming, as well as everyday informal social habits modeled by *Vzgliad*.

As Christine Evans has noted in her study of Soviet Central Television, commitment to an aesthetic of informality and spontaneity played a major role in the early formation of the medium in the USSR. Evans has traced these commitments to the first theorization of television by the Thaw-era critic, Vladimir Sappak (1921–61); for my part, in my previous work I have tried to explicate the political imaginary implied in Sappak's theory.[12] Sappak's text, *Television and Us*, written in 1960–61 on the critic's deathbed and published posthumously, does not simply aim to understand what looks good on TV, but rather, albeit not entirely explicitly, makes an argument for television to treat its viewership as an anti-Stalinist political community, which has come into being as a matter of inevitable evolution of the Hegelian Spirit of History on Soviet soil. Thus, he explains that in the 1920s–1930s, "people didn't yet want to become viewers,"

---

[d] https://postsoviet90s.com/artifacts/putting-the-spotlight-on-an-experimental-three-hour-line-for-soviet-luxury-clothes

[e] https://www.youtube.com/watch?v=AWPcU0rn4w8

and instead used to relate to one another through "spontaneous meetings" and "naïve 'mass actions'" in public squares, or through "Komsomol construction sites." Today, that "naïve" collectivism no longer appeals to "us." And yet the TV era fulfills the destiny of those early collective actions better than they themselves ever could, because this medium accentuates "the most characteristic quality of the 20th century: communication, nonalienation, interdependence of all human lives."[13] The paradigmatic made-for-TV moment that encompasses all of these socialist-humanist values is Yuri Gagarin's parade after his successful return from space. In Sappak's view, Gagarin best fits the role of "our" epochal hero when we just *see* him on our private TV screens, without paying attention to the "pathos of radio announcers, the crowdedness of press conferences, the arm-high portraits on the front pages of newspapers." Television allows us "to understand this human, to grasp him, to get at something internal, trustful, intimate inside of him," and as a result of this encounter, "millions of eyes are becoming kinder," thus "rais[ing] the *moral potential* of our era in the eyes of history" (all italics in the original).[14] But "we" do not only like Gagarin—other "positive heroes of the TV screen" in Sappak's account involve the American pianist Van Cliburn, pre-Stalin intelligentsia figures, such as Kornei Chukovsky and Viktor Shkolvsky, the aging Spanish Communist Dolores Ibarurri, and a young attentive man named Felix, who reminds Sappak of his brilliant friend who died in the war. Thus, ideal "TV screen heroes" are sometimes young and sometimes old, sometimes elite cultural icons and sometimes random passersby, sometimes Soviet and sometimes foreign. In Sappak's presentation, they do not target specific segments of the Soviet population, but all of us "modern people," who are committed to the socialist-humanist mood of the epoch, which salubriously combines high culture, socialist science, space heroics, youthful exuberance, public intellectualism, sports, and above all—as Sappak notes while talking about Valentina Leontieva, his favorite TV host—an "easygoing," "independent," authentic (and therefore no longer crudely collectivist) mode of behavior.[15]

Another text from the 1960s—Grigory Pomerants's 1967–69 *samizdat* essay, "Man from Nowhere," about which I have also written extensively elsewhere, gives a name to Sappak's "modern people"—the "new *narod*."[16] For Pomerants, this term evolved out of his thinking about the nature of cultural production in post-war USSR. He was impressed by the fact that, unlike in imperial Russia, 1960s culture was being produced by and for "a very wide stratum" of "grandchildren of the old peasant *narod*," which included a "rabble of cosmopolitan…minstrels" like Bulat Okudzhava, Yulii Kim, Vladimir Vysotskii, and Alexander Galich,[17] as well as physicists-turned-unofficial-novelists, and even "taxi-drivers" like the *samizdat* fiction writer Yuz Aleshkovsky. As "Man from Nowhere" considers all of this variegated foment, it articulates a belief in the possibility of a new type of universal collective coming into being through this form of post-industrial, horizontal cultural activity. And the essay chooses the name "new *narod*" for this collective to emphasize its Hegelo-Marxist potential. Forged by the brutality of Stalinist industrial modernization, which has left nothing but "horns and hooves" of the Russian Empire's predominantly peasant society—that is, the original *narod*—the new *narod* now possesses the power and the popular will to overcome the post-Stalin political impasse.

A future scholarly project would have to retrace not just the origins of this faith in the possibility of dialectically overcoming Stalinism by means of a new universal collective, but the extent to which this type of discourse remained effective in late-Soviet culture, and why.[18] For the moment, I only wish to emphasize that a key attribute of this faith lies in its appeal to what Pomerants in his memoirs calls "myth" that can "change everything"—that is, a politically creative rallying cry which derives power simultaneously from materialist and imaginary claims.[19] The new *narod* is appealing because on the one hand it describes the social fact of the existence of a modernized, educated mass polity. At the same time, the new *narod* does not appeal to this polity in a sociological fashion, by seeking to represent the interests of, say, a tenth of the Soviet population with higher education degrees.[20] Rather, the new *narod* appeals to the *future* polity that will inevitably be majority-comprised of enlightened "scientists, engineers [and] teachers," capable of working in the post-industrial economy in the morning, legislating in the afternoon, and reading "Tiutchev" at night (to paraphrase young Marx and young Pomerants himself).[21] It is my contention that the political charge of the socialist-enlightenment myth described above ended up animating *Vzgliad* twenty years later. That is why the show could so easily pivot between interviews with "artists, writers, telepaths and psychopaths," whether young or old, official or semi-underground like Gradsky, *and* stories of "unbuilt roads" and "unkept promises"—precisely because after decades of post-Stalin socialism's consensus about the new *narod* it became easy to link the kind of subject who makes art to the kind of subject who comments on unbuilt roads, to the kind of subject who becomes an elected parliamentarian, as many of *Vzgliad*'s hosts would in 1989. The new *narod* encompassed all of these subjects at once, allowed *all* of them to feel "normal," to not have to reflect on their possible elitism, their vanguardism, their sociological rather than imaginary limits of popularity, and other such specifics of liberal-democratic, rather than Soviet socialist, politics.

Meanwhile, thanks to socialist everyday life practices, studied by scholars like Alexi Yurchak and Alena Ledeneva, while *remaining* the new *narod* "we" can also step into another subject position, in which we can think of ourselves as members of a semi-private, well-connected group with special access to redirected state resources, but also feel like our use of those resources and our informal circles is normative, humane, and even anti-Stalinist. As Evans notes, *Vzgliad*'s broadcasts play with this sensibility when they tell its millions of viewers that they are about to access domains that are normally guarded from them by official doors marked "Do Not Enter, Staff Only."[22] We also see it in the sketch comedy skit, when its "normal guys" ask one another for t-shirts from Seoul. As Yurchak's study of "*svoi*" networks has shown, this sensibility had also been cultivated for decades since Stalin's death, as a kind of post-Stalin anti-political project. Members of semi-private social circles would repeatedly use state resources—for instance, local Komsomol organizations—in order to recruit "good people" into their ranks and to reward one another with perks of the job, while thinking about everyone within the network as fundamentally "normal," in contrast to the *ab*normal pro-Soviet activists, to the extent that anyone ever met such people, which was allegedly quite rarely.[23] In Ledeneva's study of private circulation of those perks, their users repeatedly describe their actions as a matter of "humane" mutual aid.[24] Of course, unlike the perestroika-era *Vzgliad*, neither Yurchak's nor Ledeneva's late Soviet *svoi* claimed to be interested in political speech—in fact, they said they were *dis*interested in it, especially with respect to the dissidents. However, as Benjamin Nathans and Kevin Platt have pointed out, that claim was a necessary stance, requiring psychic effort from people who knew that they had to show their peers that they knew *what* not to say about someone like Andrei Sakharov, and *how* not to say it for the system to work in their favor.[25] Perestroika removed this necessity of performative anti-politics, while otherwise not upending the *svoi* circles, nor the feelings of "normalcy" that these generated among their members. On the contrary, normalcy itself turned into a political slogan, which was circulated through the common late-Soviet and perestroika lament highlighted by Nathans and Platt, "I wish to live in a normal country."[26] In a sense, *Vzgliad* presented itself as a model of that normal country to come, a state for the new *narod*—a normal country's normal body politic.

1991 AND POPULAR WILL ON *VZGLIAD*

Thanks to the development of a post-Stalin new *narod* discourse in the 1960s–1980s, when perestroika entered into full swing *Vzgliad* could present its remarkably omnivorous programming as coextensive with the omnivorousness of its audience. The viewers, like the show's hosts, could simultaneously think of themselves as "normal" people and *also* as members of *svoi* networks, and also as countercultural youth, and also as Soviets. Socialist rhetoric, as well as socialist everyday practices, enabled this state of indeterminacy, while Gorbachev's glasnost enabled political speech to be uttered from that indeterminate, pan-socialist perspective. The parody skit from 1988 captures this dynamic in a joking fashion, but we might also note a more serious example, from one of the earliest broadcasts, aired on October 9, 1987[f].[27] Liubimov starts off with a segment on long lines for scarce goods in Soviet capitals Moscow and Tashkent. After a series of interviews with masses of angry, hopeless everyday Soviet people, the show points out that no one even wants to wear this Soviet manufacture and then cuts to the next segment: a man is selling some kind of clothing on the black market to some woman, although

[f] https://www.youtube.com/watch?v=uxeTrsLF71s

we can hear both of them clearly—thus from the start we know that the encounter is staged. At the end of the transaction, the man gets arrested for speculation. Ten minutes later, we finally meet him—it's the journalist and soon-to-be co-host Alexander Politkovsky, on the show for the first time. First, he gives a tutorial on how to sew a fashionable women's dress out of two pairs of easily purchased, stunningly ugly men's undergarments. Then, he is interviewed by Listyev, Liubimov, and Zakharov. Speaking to his host-friends, Politkovsky shows how much more fashionable his own handmade clothing line is than whatever the Soviet industry produces, and then points out that although the black-market sale we saw earlier was indeed staged, the arrest was real. Finally, he explains with concrete figures how the hawking of clothing works in the Soviet black-market economy. Notably, this whole segment is tucked in between two cultural reports, one on John Lennon and the other on Rachmaninov. Here, we can see a microcosm of *Vzgliad*'s sense of its ideal viewership. The show's fashionable young hosts are in the same boat as the rest of the Soviet populace, both when it comes to the official shortage economy *and* when it comes to the semi-private circulation of unofficial goods. Politkovsky's arrest while engaging in black-market exchange serves as an example of the kind of spontaneous, dangerous social improvisation that *Vzgliad*'s viewers are forced to engage in every day while living in the USSR. Moreover, the hosts and their viewers pay equal attention to Soviet market failures as to Western rock and Russian classical music.

Vzgliad's commitment to omnivorous broadcasting generated the potential for growing tensions, which could result from incongruities within the very concept of the new *narod* as a mass movement made up of very different people, organized around a hazy post-Stalin goal of "changing everything," as Pomerants had put it. I think these tensions were released in several ways on the show. For one, they guided the different emphases of the hosts and fed into their sense of private enmity with one another. Hence, Vladimir Mukusev in his memoir claims that at some point in 1988 *Vzgliad* settled into "essentially two types of shows" and that their seeming friendliness on screen was nothing but a TV trick, that "never once did all of us get together for a cup of tea."[28] The nights hosted by Mukusev (and often also Zakharov and Politkovsky) had less chummy repartee and more hard-hitting journalism. For Mukusev writing in retrospect, this direction was morally correct, as reflected in his chosen career highlights: a 1989 report on Lenin's Mausoleum and the need to bury Lenin, a 1987 exposé on the dubious practices of historical preservation of the revolutionary ship Aurora (1987), and above all, a 1988 report[g] on an impoverished orphanage, which ends with one boy there singing, "O Distance Lovely, Don't Be Cruel." Curiously, twenty years later, this very report would turn into a paradigmatic Russian nationalist memory of perestroika in Vladimir Sorokin's novel, *Day of the Oprichink*.[29]

[g] https://www.youtube.com/watch?v=n38L1DN4USQ

Meanwhile, the nights hosted by Listyev and Liubimov (and, for fairness's sake, also some nights by Mukusev) continued leaning into their distinctive informal *svoi* social style, even as the guests who were invited into their conversations were often not *svoi* in any way—for instance, Marshal Akhromeev, head of the Soviet armed forces and future leader of *GKChP*. This display of humanist communication across political boundaries obviously clashed with the fact of politicization of all life during perestroika, particularly with the rise of the Congress of People's Deputies in 1989, and this clash started having an effect on *Vzgliad*'s core format. That year, the show's bachelor pad setting started receding into the background, whereas the foreground was taken over by a striking orange plus-sign-shaped table, around which hard-hitting discussions with Soviet higherups often ensued. In other episodes, *Vzgliad* explicitly started introducing itself as a talk-show (*tok-shou*) with a studio audience. Thus, at the opening of this new format in September 1989, we hear the following[h] emotionally charged voiceover:

> A talk show [*tok shou*] is an honest conversation about hot-button issues! A talk show is an arena for pluralism! A talk show is disarming questions, a talk show is answers that contain ways to solve the most difficult problems! A talk show is the collective work of minds within the hard boundaries of live broadcasting![30]

This first talk show featured newly elected members of the Congress and was organized around a sportsman-like thrill of rapid-fire political speech (throughout the broadcast, Zakharov, Listyev, and the producers were constantly shown holding sports timers, set to two minutes).

Still, even as *Vzgliad* started airing political bloodsport, it continued interspersing it with rock music videos and performances—that quintessential privately circulated cultural product of the 1980s (and heir to the 1960s "cosmopolitan minstrels" of the new *narod* described by Pomerants). And sometimes, the fourth wall between the music videos and the show would break down. For instance, in one episode, we see several performances by the band *Kino* and then also watch Kino's legendary frontman Viktor Tsoi participate in a two-plus-hour-long discussion about private enterprise—"cooperation"—in Russia[i].[31] Tsoi's participation in the debate is miniscule; this episode mostly airs polemics between the era's public political figures, such as the first Soviet millionaire Artem Tarasov and his adversary, the head of official Soviet trade unions and another future *GKChP* leader Gennadii Yanaev.[32] Still, until its state-imposed closure in December 1990 the producers of *Vzgliad* apparently continued to believe that Tsoi and Yanaev and Tarasov *needed* to share a stage, that Mukusev and Liubimov *needed* to host their different formats under the framework of one TV program. In that way, the show kept trying to model a certain kind of humanist universalism for

[h] https://www.net-film.ru/film-81287/

[i] https://www.youtube.com/watch?v=97DethKxNsE

its audience, derived from the socialist new *narod* ideology, even as it was politically bursting at the seams.

Perhaps the most poignant place where the show reflects on its humanist political project is in the discussion following a bombshell exposé on Nina Andreeva[j], led by *Vzgliad*'s frequent guest-host, the journalist Evgeny Dodolev. Andreeva's letter, "I Refuse to Forsake My Principles," had been published in the newspaper *Sovetskaia Rossiia* in March 1988, and was interpreted by many liberal activists as the first salvo of the Politburo right-wing's war on Gorbachev's reforms. While this was indeed the letter's public effect, it wasn't actually written by a high-level Moscow apparatchik, but by a mid-tier party member and professor of chemistry in Leningrad. Over the course of the USSR's existence, but especially in the late-Soviet era, many thousands of such letters made their way to various media outlets and some were occasionally printed. Both in the present volume and elsewhere, Courtney Doucette has argued that the meaning of glasnost was being negotiated through such public letters by non-public persons.[33] And it is instructive that Dodolev's discussion of his report on Andreeva emphasizes her private Soviet normalcy:

> **Dodolev:** You know, Sasha, when I was going to my meeting with Nina Aleksandrovna, I was getting ready for a conversation with a political actor [*politicheskim deiatelem*]. I mean, there are so many rumors, so many hints about high sources of information. But it turns out that to be a talented publicist and an active Stalinist doesn't yet mean to be a politician. The thing is, the numbers to which Nina Andreeva refers, such as the number of corrupt millionaires and other information, it all comes from the same sources that all of us use. Appearances in newspapers, very often not very objective ones. TV shows, sometimes tendentious ones. Kitchen conversations. You understand? A seminarist's understanding of life, built on this kind of information, cannot possibly pretend to the status of theory. Nina Aleksandrovna is one of our regular compatriots. And, by the way, a hospitable one, and certain of her rightness.
> **Liubimov:** I noticed that, she keeps repeating the phrase, "without a doubt."

From this point of Andreeva's "regularity," Dodolev and Liubimov go on to consider the left and the right of perestroika politics as they see it, and they express fear that those politics are potentially becoming inhuman:

> **Dodolev:** Whatever the case, I am certain than Andreeva was chosen by accident of circumstance, to make a political act. She woke up famous, as they say. And so her name is surrounded by a mysterious halo. And behind it is a regular person. Ok, maybe she's mistaken or doesn't accept something, but let's not turn her into some sort of monster, let us try to be more tolerant of one another. I think it's enough already with mutual recriminations and doomsday prophecies, the Rubicon has been crossed, there's no way

[j] https://www.youtube.com/watch?v=XcxM-w2ZtvY

back. However, Sasha, I am certain that *everyone* will be unhappy with this interview. The left won't like that Andreeva's monologue is ultraloyal to the "stormy petrel of the anti-perestroika forces," as it is called by many publications. Which she, in turn, calls "the loudmouth yellow press."
Liubimov: I think the right is going to be the most unhappy, because Nina Andreeva's television debut has happened on *Vzgliad*. They will see this as an affront to their pure, old-guard standard.

Finally, Liubimov makes a "centrist" appeal:

Dodolev: Yes, perhaps so. But as for centrists? We hardly have any confident centrists. We hardly have people who are afraid of participating in, you know, this mutual act of tipping our union boat on one side. [...]
Liubimov: I don't know, I think the two poles fighting over perestroika are pulling commonsense people away from the center. And also, I think censorship over political life in our country, which I think still exists, is playing a role. It often forces people to commit more radical acts than they might have wanted.
Dodolev: The problem is that with this background of loud battles on the pages of magazines, to admit to one's centrism, in the revolutionary conditions of perestroika, is similar to accepting criminal neutrality.
Liubimov: No, God forbid, centrism and neutrality don't have anything in common. I am ready to declare my centrism and I do not think I am violating my principles when the show *Vzgliad* airs Nina Andreeva's interview.
Dodolev: Of course, your [*vashe*–plural] credo is pluralism, and as everyone knows, one can't have two opinions about pluralism [*laughs*].[34]

What *is* centrism here (leaving Dodolev's quip about pluralism aside for the moment)? It doesn't seem to be a rational calculation of political compromise between the political demands of the "yellow press" and the "stormy petrels." For Liubimov, centrism is defined by a humanist fear of *all* potentially overly antagonistic political discourse. Liubimov yearns for a vaguely defined anti-politics of universal humanist togetherness, to be recovered beyond all of the perestroika political agonism. A fantasy of such togetherness appears to him as an object of great desire, the telos of the "revolution." And curiously, Liubimov and his colleagues (sans Mukusev) will go on to make that same appeal to centrist popular will at the culmination of perestroika, in *Vzgliad*'s final broadcast[k], during the heady days of the 1991 August *GKChP* coup.

For most observers of Russia at the time, the several days of the abortive "Committee for the State of Emergency," with its failure to take power from Gorbachev, isolate Yeltsin, and institute a military regime, retrospectively seem like an unquestionable moment of

[k] https://www.youtube.com/watch?v=pLgetnrHLlo

triumph for what were alternatively referred to as the "pro-Yeltsin" and "pro-democracy" forces.[35] Certainly in the 1990s, this moment seemed perfectly suited to become a foundational state memory for a democratic Russian Federation, its pro-democratic "myth," in Pomerants's sense of the term.[36] Politically speaking, it is indeed the case that the pro-Yeltsin side decisively took charge of the moment, leaving no way back for any Soviet leader, and it is also true that throughout his career in high politics, Yeltsin drew support from people who thought of themselves as democrats. At the same time, it is notable that in August 1991 the RSFSR parliamentarians holed up in Moscow's White House along with their many supporters did not necessarily see their collective action as pro-Yeltsin. *Vzgliad* certainly did not. When the show returned on national airwaves for several days, as *GKChP* quickly lost its grip over Central Television, the hosts of *Vzgliad* were remarkably *wary* about Yeltsin. Neither them nor their correspondents interviewed Yeltsin, nor did they almost ever directly speak about him. And they concluded one of their broadcasts from the *GKChP* days with two statements of warning. One was a demand not to vilify rank-and-file communists (recall Liubimov's and Dodolev's statements about Andreeva). And the other was an admonition against the cynical opportunism of the Yeltsin team, given its frenzy of ad hoc adverse possession of CPSU property on Russia's territory. Liubimov summed up his attitude to this move with the statement: "whoever battles to take the spot of the enemy always reaps defeat."[37] The broadcast then printed these words on screen as the show's last word, against the background of protesters removing the Dzerzhinsky monument at the KGB headquarters.[38]

But if the anti-*GKChP* triumph wasn't pro-Yeltsinist, as far as *Vzgliad* was concerned, then who did they think (or hope!) won instead? And what did *that* collective want? In this regard, two monologues from the coup days stand out (Artifact 00028[1]; Figure 2). One is an interview with Mstislav Rostropovich, the world-renowned cellist, who was holed up in the "White House" during its most uncertain first night, on August 19, 1991, when it seemed like the building would get stormed by the military. In the tense lead-up to a battle that does not actually ensue (thanks to Yeltsin's maneuvering vis-à-vis Soviet army commanders), we see this consummate Soviet *intelligent* holding a machine gun in his lap, a tea cup in his hand, being interviewed by Listyev and Liubimov. Rostropovich explains to them that he is there to support an epochal movement of universal solidarity against a minoritarian militarist junta:

> **Listyev:** If you had an opportunity to speak to a multi-million Soviet audience, what would you want to say to people?
> **Rostropovich:** I would say that I am proud of my country, which hasn't happened to me often. [...] You know, when I was exiled from my motherland, I was struck by how few people supported me here. At those organized meetings at the Moscow Conservatory, even my own

[1] https://postsoviet90s.com/artifacts/vzgliad-at-gkchp/

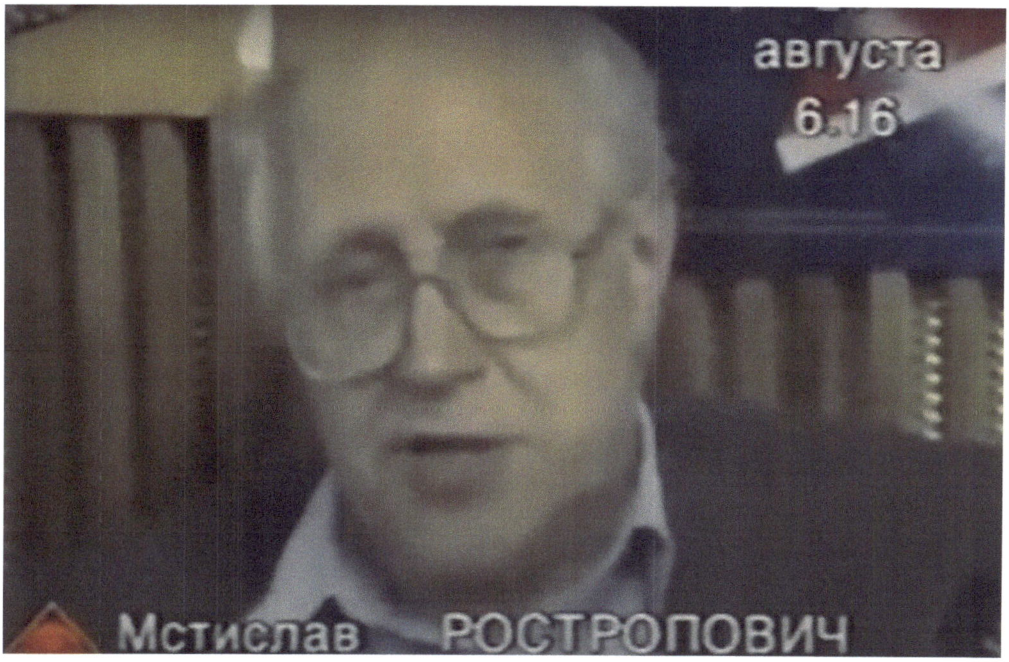

FIGURE 2 Video from Artifact 00028.[m] The cellist Mstislav Rostropovich, along with the hosts of *Vzgliad*, discusses the triumph of democracy against Soviet tanks, during the 1991 *GKChP* coup days.

> students said that they were ashamed of having studied with me. You know, it leaves a trace. [...] But tonight, last night, what I saw, has returned my faith in people, in the *narod*, which gave the world Prokofiev and Shostakovich and Pushkin and Lermontov and Dostoevsky. This night was very significant for me and I am so happy [*schastliv*] that I came here. [...] [*hands the machine gun to Listyev*] Take this away from me!
> **Listyev:** What do you think, does this instrument have anything in common with your cello?
> **Rostropovich:** No, they are opposites, it seems to me that the cello gives life, whereas this takes it away. [...] But when they send tanks against the *narod*, we have to learn how to respond. We must get to the point that it is impossible for these people to send tanks. [...] And I repeat, the danger will remain for as long as the communists continue to try to build their experiment, by way of the most idiotic, anti-humanist slogans.[39]

The *narod* rhetoric comes so easily to Rostropovich, and he so easily becomes a part of it, so much so that he discusses the need to use deadly force on "our" behalf. Listyev, too, links this construct of the *narod* to his viewers, whom he describes as a multi-million *Soviet*—not just Russian—audience, even as the conversation is happening in the "White House," the political heart of Yeltsin's Russian Federation. Meanwhile, as Rostropovich states, the enemies of this *narod* are an anti-humanist, irrational, minority force of retrograde communists. Altogether, this rhetoric perfectly overlaps with the

[m] https://postsoviet90s.com/artifacts/vzgliad-at-gkchp/

new *narod* imaginary discussed earlier, and also with the rhetoric of humanist "centrism" used by Liubimov.

The other telling monologue takes place a bit later in the broadcast, and is filmed a day or two after the frightening night of August 19. Already certain of their victory, Liubimov and Listyev start describing the feeling of "blood brotherhood" that had formed among the defenders of the White House:

> Racketeers with wads of cash came and took our agitation pamphlets [*listovki*] and went to distribute them among all the army units. The bourse gave us food, poets gave us verses, Afghan vets gave us weapons. The banks hauled over a bunch of Xerox machines and printing equipment...the factory next door came over and brought us gas masks for a possible attack.[40]

Once again, we see in this description of solidarity the idea that what was unfolding at the "White House" was a popular uprising of all right-thinking people, except Liubimov's list is a bit more descriptive, and for that reason more interesting. Because, to take just one example, shouldn't the racketeers and the Afghan vets, many of whom worked as muscle for the mob already then, have been in a different category than the poets, or the bourse, or the banks? It is here, I think, that we can start seeing the limits and the vector of future transformation of what throughout the late-Soviet years had been an *oppositionist* discourse on popular will and that was now becoming the discourse of the newly founded state.

THE POST-SOCIALIST LIMITS OF THE NEW *NAROD*

Recall the Andreeva segment, in which Liubimov waxes on about his support of "centrism" and Dodolev responds with a quip: "Of course, your [*vashe*–plural] credo is pluralism, and as everyone knows, one can't have two opinions about pluralism."[41] When examining Liubimov's coalition at Moscow's White House, the smirk takes on its full critical meaning. On the one hand, the panoply of social backgrounds among the defenders of the White House seemed to *Vzgliad* to have been essential to their success. A day later, in the show's last coup-related broadcast[n] (and, in fact, their *very* last broadcast as the original *Vzgliad* team) Gorbachev tells Liubimov, "I am so happy that all of our democracy, that what has happened in these conditions of our society, did not allow this reactionary turn to take place."[42] "All of our democracy," "centrism," "pluralism"—versus "careerists," "anti-humanists," "reactionaries"—all of these phrases describe the kind of unity that the discourse of the new *narod* posits when it imagines popular will and its enemies. And in August 1991 that discourse was powerful enough

[n] https://www.youtube.com/watch?v=pLgetnrHLlo

to hold together a crowd that included Rostropovich, Gorbachev, Yeltsin, Elena Bonner (Sakharov's widow), Liubimov, Listyev, Politkovsky, *and* the racketeers, the manual workers, the bankers, the Afghan vets. Without such broadness, it is not at all clear that the coup would have failed. Certainly, judging by their quite competent appearances on *Vzgliad* in the late 1980s, figures like Yanaev and Akhromeev were capable of taking power and wielding it successfully under the right circumstances. But in this moment, thanks to its widespread adoption over prior decades, the ideologeme of the new *narod* standing off against a small, unrepresentative clique of inherently incompetent, pro-Soviet "reactionary" enemies *felt* true enough on a mass level, such that it could mobilize a lot of disparate people, and to convince even the Party functionaries and the army to switch their loyalties to Yeltsin.

On the other hand, as "our" victory is in the offing, shouldn't one "have two opinions" about the new *narod*, given who's actually in it? Nina Andreeva had certainly been concerned about this matter, with her orthodox Marxist-Leninist warning to Dodolev in 1988 that the country was returning "to the very lowest form of capitalist production, the pre-monopolistic form of primitive accumulation of capital."[43] At the time, Liubimov had responded to these words with a smile: "they try to scare me, but I'm not afraid."[44] Perhaps he *should* have been afraid. As Fabrizio Fenghi points out in his contribution to this volume, Liubimov maintained his "bourgeois" centrist equipoise well into the mid-1990s, when he resurrected *Vzgliad* with co-host Sergei Bodrov Jr. However, the host and producer Mukusev broke with the show in late 1990–early 1991 precisely due to what he saw as the team's reckless willingness to participate in "primitive accumulation." In January 1991, *Ogonek* ran a bombshell interview (which was actually taken a few months prior), in which Mukusev publicly aired his concerns, stating that "the journalistic temple called *Vzgliad*" was being destroyed from within as a result of the rise of *ViD*.[45] For this, within about a week of publication he was kicked out of *Vzgliad* and *ViD* and, according to him, was subsequently blacklisted from Central Television. Retrospectively, Mukusev's principled distaste for *Vzgliad*'s capitalist turn aligns well with the conclusions of Ilya Kukulin and Maria Maiofis regarding a great deal of perestroika-era media structures. In their view, groups like *Vzgliad/ViD,* which seemed to many to epitomize a free press, were easily coopted or shut down by post-Soviet authoritarian leaders because they weren't actually all that idealistic at their core. They were "organized around the basis of 'available resources' and 'advantageous situation[s],'" as opposed to "an idea" or a "project for the future."[46]

I would suggest that while frustration with *ViD*'s apparent readiness to sell out is understandable, the tragedy of the situation is that the "normal guys" at the helm of Russia's first private media enterprise perceived some version of selling out—that is, collaborating with lots of people engaged in "primitive accumulation"—*as* a reasonable "project for the future." It was just an anti-political project derived from the new *narod* ideology.[47] Undoubtedly, plenty of early-1990s actors, including some principled media teams celebrated by Kukulin and Maiofis (such as *Ekho Moskvy* and *Interfax*), thought politically in the agonistic sense of this term, by reflecting on their role, the limits of their coalitional alliances, and their enemies. But *Vzgliad*'s experience in 1991 did not suggest to the team that *they* were supposed to cultivate such a praxis. Instead, the *GKChP* outcome suggested to *ViD* that its original ideology as a universal humanist voice for the "normal" new *narod was* actually valuable in itself, because it was so instrumental in bringing down the old regime. Moreover, without their commercialization, as Liubimov points out in *Est' takaia bukva*, *Vzgliad* probably wouldn't have even had the resources to be a media player at all that August. And finally (and ironically, from the stand-point of socialism), wasn't a fully liberated pursuit of material success in and of itself a part of the implied telos of the new *narod*?

Sappak's ideal TV viewers and Pomerants's "scientists, engineers [and] teachers" were already in the 1960s touted as materially successful products of Soviet modernization, owning their private TV sets and circulating their cosmopolitan new *narod* culture in newly minted private Soviet apartments. Presumably, all of them wanted to get more of those apartments and more of those consumer goods.[48] Moreover, ironically, the Soviet socialist economy, with its crude egalitarianism, its "poverty meted out equally to everyone" as Liubimov quipped in 1988 about Nina Andreeva, convinced the new *narod* that everything they had attained and desired to attain in the future was also normative, equally available for everyone.[49] *ViD* simply followed this vector to its rightful post-Soviet outcome, by turning into a commercial media conglomerate that thought it could comfortably pursue financial success, news programming, and mass entertainment all at once. Perhaps the conceptual divergence among the shows hosted by Listyev in the four years between rise of *ViD* and his murder on March 1, 1995 best expressed that initial sensibility and its eventual sorry outcome.

A combination of "Wheel of Fortune" and "Deal or No Deal," *Pole chudes* was Listyev's first solo project, which he started in late 1990, when *Vzgliad* was still running. The gameshow involved sets of three players at a time spinning a roulette wheel, guessing letters to a word based on a clue, and getting various prizes for many non-word-related reasons, either in the form of money or consumer goods (throughout the 1990s these were typically things like microwaves and televisions). But the televised product, which is still on air today, was always less a guessing game and more a celebration of the liberated social practices of the new *narod*. These at first included the picking apart of fairly intellectual word clues pitched at a reasonably educated public, an unfettered exchange among a mix of guests from all walks of life, and a somewhat taboo-breaking display of desire for money and Western gadgets, which remained financially inaccessible to most post-Soviets in the early 1990s and still do to many players today. Listyev as host was always willing to insert himself into the game by haggling with players about everything, from answers to prizes. And finally, within just a few months of the show's premiere, a culture of *reverse* gift-giving started taking root, as guests *themselves* began indulging the host with presents of their own. The first one was a handmade toy, which Listyev received while joking about potential corruption involved in the "blat" transaction.[50]

Looking over the above description, we might say that *Pole chudes* from the start fulfilled Sappak's greatest hopes for good television and both his and Pomerants's hopes for good post-Stalin socialism: it was full of spontaneity, it centered the humanity of everyone, and in the early 1990s when it first appeared it exuded an ethic of egalitarianism, for several reasons. For one, it hosted people across the whole Russian Federation and soon-to-be former USSR. For another, the distance between the people and the host had shrunk into a playful informal relationship—perhaps this was even, to some extent, a *socialist* relationship, somewhat akin to the one unfolding in the gift-giving performances of the artist B. U. Kashkin, studied by Daniil Leiderman in the present volume. And finally and most importantly, all of the players on early *Pole chudes* appeared to be more or less equally impoverished and equally eager to improve their lot. Perhaps the best example of this "democratism" (as Sappak would have termed it) appears on the show's one-year anniversary broadcast[o], in which top-tier Russian celebrities compete for the same money and prizes as everyone else, and the overall winner, Alexander Abdulov—by then the 1991 People's Artist of the Russian Federation and Best Supporting Actor at the Russian Motion Picture Academy—appears to be genuinely excited[p] about his new vacuum cleaner.[51]

The problem is that the show *wasn't* airing during socialism anymore, and the brief moment of seeming equality and solidarity among an inclusive post-Soviet collective simply could not last. By the end of the 1990s, in a reformed, capitalist movie market Abdulov presumably had vacuum cleaners aplenty, unlike most other every(wo)man participants, whom we meet in *Est' takaia bukva* in 2015 and who are not exactly thriving. Or, to take another example, Listyev, as late as fall 1993, was excited about renovating a relatively modest two-bedroom Moscow apartment with a loud alcoholic down the hall.[52] By this time, he had already passed the job of host of *Pole chudes* to Leonid Yakubovich, and he himself was hosting a new *ViD* program, the talk show *Tema* (*Theme*). Still, already that year, he was appearing across several TV networks in commercials[q] in a tux with a thoroughbred Great Dane, advertising a luxury European cruise on the appropriately named "Fedor Dostoevsky," which among excellent service would also include the filming of a special broadcast of *Tema*. Its topic would be banking, with bankers in attendance.[53] As the informants of *Est' takaia bukva* point out, the audience on such cruise ships was mostly made up of gangsters, who were among the

---

[o] https://www.youtube.com/watch?v=XS_H22rAIKs
[p] https://www.youtube.com/watch?v=XS_H22rAIKs&t=6510s
[q] https://www.youtube.com/watch?v=p3SxVmuMjsU

few for whom primitive accumulation was going sufficiently well.[54] By January 1995, just on the eve of his murder, thanks to the patronage of the oligarch Boris Berezovsky, a far wealthier Listyev quit *ViD* and became the CEO of the *ORT* network, the successor to Central Television and the predecessor to Channel One that exists today.

Meanwhile, the attendees of *Pole chudes* remained as poor as ever, and the show's erstwhile egalitarianism quickly turned into a celebration of the common folk and their ventriloquist Yakubovich, without further appearances by Listyev. By the mid-1990s, what had started as a friendly performance of a post-Soviet middle-class sensibility, reinforced with reverse gift-giving as a meaning-making practice not marked by class differences, looked like Central Television elites pandering to the lowly demotic folk. The latter regaled the host with as much local color as they could muster, including time-intensive amateur performances, ridiculous wardrobes, and above all, complicated rituals of consumption of homemade beverages and foodstuffs. Yakubovich would humor all of them and egg them on with performative excess of his own. Meanwhile, intellectually savvy former Soviets could look onto all of this populist indulgence with disdain, perhaps best articulated by Tatiana Tolstaya in her essay on *Pole chudes*, written at about the same time:

> His show, like all gameshows, is stolen from the Americans and translated into a *sovok* mode [*sovkovyi lad*]...The wheel of fortune barely spins, and the guessing of words—at least some shadow of intellectual labor—has been relegated ten rows back by the participants, who are mostly enthralled in the mutual exchange of edible and inedible objects. These circuses [*zrelishche*] are considered to be "culture"—an entirely proletarian sort of confusion. Before the revolution, a *muzhik* would take a bear with a ring in its nose around a village and tell it, "come on, Misha, dance! Misha, show us how a woman [*baba*] washes clothes!" But no one used to think of the bear or the *muzhik* as a cultural actor. The bear would dance, the bear would bow, the bear would be fed exactly how they feed Yakubovich. The only difference is that they would stick the bear in a stinky lair for the night, while Yakubovich sleeps in a warm bed. Another difference is that the bear wasn't rude and didn't molest children.[55]

In her description, Tolstaya inveighs against the very elements of the show that in 1990–91 had seemed well within the purview of the viewership of *Vzgliad*, i.e. of people like Tolstaya herself. She also uses the word "*sovkovyi*," to signify the sociality on *Pole chudes* as something belonging to an incorrigible people with an incorrigible "proletarian" past that the rest of us living in the post-Soviet times should do our best to break with. That rest of us is addressed in another essay in Tolstaya's collection, "Merchants and Artists," in which she discusses the need to change cardinally Russian high culture's suspicion of money, and attempts to solve this problem by running a literary prize for "best stories about honest capitalists."[56]

Listyev, as far as I know, was never as negative as Tolstaya about his folkish creation or its audience, but her use of the term "*sovok*" does directly connect to one of *ViD*'s last broadcasts with Listyev in it—a memorial edition of his final show, *Chas pik* (*Primetime*), aired just after his murder (Artifact 00130[r]). Andrei Makarevich, the rock star and one-time competitor on *Pole chudes*, opens *Chas pik* with a mournful message and then plays a series of clips of conversations of Listyev and his celebrity guests, all of whom by 1995 think of themselves as winners of the post-Soviet transition, and believe themselves fit to offer pithy summaries of various domains of post-Soviet and former Soviet life. One of these guests is Alexander Gradsky, the rock star whose 1987 performance opened *Vzgliad*'s first broadcast. As it turns out, he claims *he* invented the moniker *sovok* back in the 1970s, while drinking portwine out of a kids' shovel (the literal meaning of the word "sovok"), which was on the one hand a bit gross, but on the other hand could hold a lot of liquid. In Gradsky's telling, this image stands as a metaphor for everyone's collective existence back then: "it was something inevitable and sweet. What can you do, we're all like this—and you'd say it with a smile."[57] Meanwhile, on the same memorial broadcast, in perfect juxtaposition to Gradsky's nostalgic affect, we hear an exuberantly dour celebration of the capitalist present, from the writer Alexander Kabakov, who tells Listyev,

> There's only one kind of freedom—freedom for everyone. I am deeply in agreement with the old Soviet publicists, like Yuri Zhukov, who used to write about Western "so-called freedoms," "so-called democracies," that it's all just freedom to die from hunger. That's right, freedom is always freedom to die from hunger...You know where you can really be sure of what the next day is going to bring? In jail.[58]

Back in the 1960s, the same Yuri Zhukov had inspired Pomerants to write "Man from Nowhere," in which, as we have seen, "freedom for everyone" was supposed to be freedom of communication, cultural circulation, and individual success for an educated, enlightened, potentially universal post-class collective.[59] In the 1990s that collective no longer existed. Or rather, the former hosts and guests of *Vzgliad* could no longer imagine it. Instead of playing hosts to the new *narod*, they preferred to commune with the "honest capitalists," who themselves recalled, sometimes with remarkable pangs of conscience, having once been *sovki*.[60] Or, they were willing to do their part to cordon off those who were *still sovki* into a kind of safe, apolitical TV space, through shows like *Pole chudes*, while also doing their best to make sure that these *sovki* would never have the power to unseat Yeltsin's government. By the 2000s, the two jobs were combined within a single state-media conglomerate, as Konstanin Ernst became head of Channel

[r] https://postsoviet90s.com/artifacts/list-ev-s-russian-liberals-on-chas-pik

One, arguably the most important media player in Putin's system of "managed democracy." Perhaps appropriately, Ernst first came to television in 1988 as a junior member of *Vzgliad*.[61]

AFTERWORD

In his study of the "poetics" of the discourse of the Soviet engineering and technical masses—the so-called "ITR class"—Mark Lipovetsky treats the conclusion of the Strugatsky brothers' 1970s novel *Inhabited Island* as anticipating the social attitude of those members of Soviet educated, urbanized masses who came out on top in the post-Soviet transition:

> The freedom "zone" was to transform into an elite settlement, *Rubliovka* of sorts, where modernization works for the modernizers only. The irreformable scum are left on their own, free to feed on each other. It is hard to think of a more bitter and accurate satire on the transformation of the ITR discourse in the post-Soviet period.[62]

For me, it is tempting to ascribe this attitude to Listyev, and all the more so to someone like Ernst. But perhaps this urge is misplaced—not because its conclusion is wrong, but because it takes one away from the main point of ideology critique, which is to understand fully the promise and the threat of a certain way of thinking. There *was* real promise to the new *narod* as a construct. Under conditions of late socialism and perestroika, this construct created a wide range of humanist solidarities among Soviet citizens, and those solidarities may have saved Russia from a hard dictatorial turn in 1991. However, under conditions of capitalism, the new *narod* ceased to make sense, and its apparent demise contributed to the feeling of disillusionment and elitist disdain among the erstwhile "pro-democracy" camp, leading many of its former members—Lipovetsky's "modernizers"—to support and in some cases personally engineer the multiple authoritarian turns of Russia's last three decades. The invasion of Ukraine stands at the end of the line of those efforts. When the war is over and/or Putin falls, the question of popular will shall once again be front and center, because as Pomerants has stated, without such "myths" it is impossible to make history. Perhaps that history can still be made with a re-invented new *narod* construct, but one that will also incorporate a better understanding of what it means to do politics in a classed society. Or perhaps thirty years after the fall of the USSR and a hundred years after the Revolution, there is no more need to use *narod* as a referent at all. Whatever happens, reformed post-Putin mass media bosses will do well to balance their likely inevitable desire to project collective human harmony versus their need to reflect as soberly and precisely as possible on their political role, on their coalition, on that coalition's limits, and on its enemies.

Notes

1 *Est' takia bukva*, dir. Tat'iana Dmitrakova, Aleksandr Valeev (*ViD*, 2015), https://www.1tv.ru/doc/pro-shou-biznes/est-takaya-bukva, 34:40. Note how the speaker (Yulii Gusman) replaces *narodnoe* in VDNKh (the Exhibit of the Achievements of the People's Economy) with Yakubovich's name, thereby further establishing an equation between Yakubovich and the *narod* with whom he communes.

2 *Est' takia bukva*, 00:07; 35:10.

3 On "demotic nationality" in post-Soviet visual media, see Nancy Condee, *The Imperial Trace: Recent Russian Cinema* (Oxford: Oxford University Press, 2009), 39.

4 *Est' takaia bukva*, 16:15.

5 The Committee for the State of Emergency ("Gosudarstvennyi komitet po chrezvychainomu polozheniiu") comprised Politburo old-hands led by Vice President of the USSR Gennadii Yanaev, who opposed Gorbachev and attempted to seize state power in August 1991, while the Soviet president was at his vacation residence in Crimea. For a day-by-day account of the coup days, as well as the years leading up to it, see Roi Medvedev, *Sovetskii soiuz. Poslednie gody zhizni* (Moscow: ACT, 2010); see also Stephen Kotkin, *Armageddon Averted: The Soviet Collapse, 1970–2000* (Oxford: Oxford University Press, 2008); see also Vladislav Zubok, *Collapse: The Fall of the Soviet Union* (New Haven: Yale University Press, 2022).

6 *Est' takaia bukva*, 27:35.

7 See Sergei Guriev and Daniel Treisman, *Spin Dictators: The Changing Face of Tyranny in the 21st Century* (Princeton, NJ: Princeton University Press, 2022).

8 For an analysis of the "Hegelian" ambitions to render the "Spirit" of the people and their era among the founders of public opinion polling in perestroika-era Russia, see Bradley Gorski. For an account of the dynamics of late- and post-socialist state cooptation of another group of seemingly anti-establishment creative elites—Soviet rock stars, many of whom were and remain close friends of the *Vzgliad/ViD* cohort—see Rita Safariants. For a history of importation into the Russian public sphere of 1990s American "spin doctor" techniques of weaponizing public opinion, and these techniques' enabling of the "acclamatory" model of pseudo-popular legitimation of authoritarian rule in Russia today, see Maya Vinokour.

9 *Vzgliad*, October 7, 1988, Gosteleradio SSSR, https://www.youtube.com/watch?v=7HkFn5IiSag&t=2222s, 35:10–37:10.

10 On laments' social function during perestroika, see Nancy Ries, *Russian Talk: Culture and Conversation during Perestroika* (Ithaca, NY: Cornell University Press, 1997).

11 *Vzgliad*, October 2, 1987, Gosteleradio SSSR, https://www.youtube.com/watch?v=AWPcU0rn4w8&t=142s, 4:00–6:30. As Christine Evans notes, the airing of Gradsky's performance on *Vzgliad* was part of a long-time strategy of the Youth Desk on Soviet CT, where it was standard practice to toy with a carefully curated countercultural, or in other ways "anti-establishment" disposition in order to attract viewers—see Christine Evans, *Between Truth and Time: A History of Soviet Central Television* (New Haven: Yale University Press, 2016).

12 See Pavel Khazanov, "Vladimir Sappak's Humanism on Soviet TV," *EUI Max Weber Working Papers* 4 (2018), https://cadmus.eui.eu/handle/1814/56744.

13 Vladimir Sappak, *Televidenie i my: chetyre besedy* (Moscow: Iskusstvo, 1988), http://www.evartist.narod.ru/text12/85.htm.

14 Sappak, *Televidenie i my*.

15 Sappak, *Televidenie i my*, http://www.evartist.narod.ru/text12/86.htm.

16 For an in-depth interpretation of Pomerants's essay, see the first chapter in my book—Pavel Khazanov, *The Russia That We Have Lost: Pre-Soviet Past as Anti-Soviet Discourse* (Madison: Wisconsin University Press, 2023).

17 Grigorii Pomerants, "Chelovek niotkuda," http://pomeranz.ru/p/pub_man_air.htm.

18 For my part, I think the beginning of this analysis would have to start in the 1930s elite, experimental IFLI (Institute of Philosophy, Literature and History), where Soviet theoreticians of enlightenment, such as Mikhail Lifshitz, taught classes to figures like the young Pomerants, as well as some of the most important future architects of the Thaw, such as Alexander Tvardovsky. It is my sense that hearing Lifshitz's 1938 lecture on "Narodnost of Art and Class Struggle" appealed to Pomerants, then a member of a highly select cohort of Soviet humanities students, because this lecture presented a future in which people like him would be able to think of themselves as a political majority deserving to take power

in the erstwhile land of peasants and workers. As young Pomerants concluded from Lifshitz's lecture, "the people [*narod*] will someday understand art; thus it is entirely possible that one day, the philosophical lyric of Tiutchev will also become popular [*narodnoi*]." Subsequently the older Pomerants looked at the mass society of 1960s "Soviet scientists, engineers [and] teachers" presumably reasonably capable of reading Tiutchev, and cautiously surmised that perhaps this was the very collective he had been hoping for—see Grigorii S. Pomerants, *Zapiski gadkogo utenka* (Moscow: Tsentr gumanitarnykh initsiativ, 2013), 32; 224–25. For Lifshitz's lecture, see "Veter istorii. K 140-letiiu so dnia rozhdeniia Fridrikha Engel'sa," in Mikhail Lifshits, *Karl Marks. Iskusstvo I obshchestvennyi ideal* (Moscow: Khudozhestvennaia literature, 1979), available online: http://www.gutov.ru/lifshitz/texts/marks/marx-10.htm. My knowledge of the social situation among students at IFLI comes from the work of Peter Budrin—see Peter Budrin, "The Institute of Philosophy, Literature, and History (IFLI) in Moscow of the 1930s," *Oxford Research Encyclopedia of Literature* (forthcoming); Peter Budrin, "School in the Forest: The History of IFLI" (unpublished manuscript).

19 Pomerants, *Zapiski gadkogo utenka*, 224.

20 In 1970, according to Soviet official statistics, that number stood at approximately 12%—see "SSSR / naselenie SSSR na 1979 god / IV. Uroven' obrazovaniia," https://www.sovetika.ru/sssr/nas7907.htm.

21 On Pomerants, see fn18. Young Marx's hopes for a communist society, in which "each can become accomplished in any branch [of activity] he wishes," and one can "hunt in the morning, fish in the afternoon, rear cattle in the evening, [and] criticize after dinner," appear in *The German Ideology* (1845): see Karl Marx, *The German Ideology, Vol. I*, https://www.marxists.org/archive/marx/works/1845/german-ideology/ch01a.htm.

22 Evans, *Between Truth and Time*, 243.

23 Alexei Yurchak, *Everything Was Forever, Until It Was No More: The Last Soviet Generation* (Princeton, NJ: Princeton University Press, 2005), 110.

24 Alena V. Ledeneva, *Russia's Economy of Favors: Blat, Networking and Informal Exchange* (Cambridge: Cambridge University Press, 1998), 162.

25 See Kevin M. F. Platt and Benjamin Nathans, "Socialist in Form, Indeterminate in Content: The Ins and Outs of Late Soviet Culture," *Ab Imperio* 2 (2011): 301–24.

26 Platt and Nathans, "Socialist in Form," 323.

27 *Vzgliad*, October 9, 1987, https://www.youtube.com/watch?v=uxeTrsLF71s, 21:10–29:15, 37:30–44:15.

28 Vladimir Mukusev, *Razberemsia...Fragmenty interv'iu, vystuplenii, stat'I, stsenarii i rassledovaniia raznykh let* (Moscow: Flinta, 2018), 130, 74.

29 Mukusev, *Razberemsia*, 90, 102–8; see also Vladimir Sorokin, *Day of the Oprichnik*, trans. Jamey Gambrell (New York: Farrar, Straus and Giroux, 2012), 53. I take my translation of the song title from Gambrell.

30 *Vzgliad*, September 29, 1989, Gosteleradio SSSR, https://www.net-film.ru/film-81287/.

31 *Vzgliad*, October 27, 1989, Gosteleradio SSSR, https://www.youtube.com/watch?v=97DethKxNsE&t=731s.

32 For the few lines spoken by Tsoi, see *Vzgliad*, October 27, 1989, Gosteleradio SSSR, https://www.youtube.com/watch?v=kRXpv8Js3nI, 32:00.

33 In addition to her contribution to the present volume, see also Courtney Doucette, "Glasnost in the Mailroom: The Soviet Subject in Gorbachev's Perestroika, 1985–1988," *The Soviet and Post-Soviet Review* 48 (2021): 171–88.

34 *Vzgliad*, November 10, 1989, Gosteleradio SSSR, https://www.youtube.com/watch?v=XcxM-w2ZtvY. Note that the segment is mistakenly dated to 1988. The original full-length episode is no longer available on YouTube, because of copyright issues: https://www.youtube.com/watch?v=ztP3UaPMWpM.

35 For an example of this kind of understanding of what had transpired in 1991, see Kathleen Smith, *Mythmaking in the New Russia: Politics and Memory during the Yeltsin Era* (Ithaca, NY: Cornell University Press, 2002).

36 Kathleen Smith's book, cited above, was among the first Western treatments of the Yeltsin era, and rightly includes "myth" in its title.

37 *Vzgliad*, August 20–23, 1991, *ViD*, https://www.youtube.com/watch?v=_1I-qzMS8f0, 1:37:45.

38 *Vzgliad*, August 20–23, 1991, 1:50:50.

39 *Vzgliad*, August 20–23, 1991, 42:45.
40 *Vzgliad*, August 20–23, 1991, 1:09:00.
41 *Vzgliad*, November 10, 1989, 10:25.
42 *Vzgliad*, August 20–23, 1991, 1:55:30.
43 *Vzgliad*, November 10, 1989, 1:25.
44 *Vzgliad*, November 10, 1989, 12:10.
45 Mukusev, *Razberemsia*, 151.
46 Mariia Maiofis and Il'ia Kukulin, "Svoboda kak neosoznannyi pretsedent: zametki o transformatsii mediinogo polia v 1990 godu," *NLO* 1 (2007), https://magazines.gorky.media/nlo/2007/1/svoboda-kak-neosoznannyj-preczedent-zametki-o-transformaczii-medijnogo-polya-v-1990-godu.html.
47 Perhaps a similar ideological dynamic might have also been unfolding among the rock musicians examined by Safariants in the present volume.
48 Late Soviet culture often meditated on this very urge, which seemed endemic to the late-Soviet urbanized, educated masses—see, for instance, the writings of Yuri Trifonov or the films of El'dar Riazanov.
49 For Liubimov's quip, see *Vzgliad*, November 10, 1989, 11:10.
50 *Est' takaia bukva*, 32:44.
51 See *Pole chudes*, October 25, 1991, *ViD*: https://www.youtube.com/watch?v=XS_H22rAIKs&t=336s, 1:48:30.
52 For a discussion of the financial standing of Listyev and his peers in 1992–93, see my article—Pavel Khazanov, "A Petrovich Inside of Every New Russian: The Disciplinary Regime of the Capitalist 'Vanguard Group' at 1990s *Kommersant*," *Russian Review* 82 (2023): 470–85, especially 477.
53 For the commercial, see "Vladislav Listyev v reklame kruiza (1993)," YouTube, August 23, 2017, https://www.youtube.com/watch?v=p3SxVmuMjsU&t=62s.
54 *Est' takaia bukva*, 25:40–26:50.
55 "Chelovek!.. Vyvedi menia otsiuda," in Tatiana Tolstaia, *Ne Kys'*: http://loveread.ec/read_book.php?id=36252&p=122#gl_72.
56 "Kuptsy i khudozhniki," in Tatiana Tolstaya, *Ne Kys'*: http://loveread.ec/read_book.php?id=36252&p=115#gl_67.
57 *Chas pik*, March 6, 1995, *ViD*: https://www.youtube.com/watch?v=tnfvqsRVRl0&t=20s, 7:00–8:20. For a recent treatment of the term "sovok" in the Russian cultural economy of "self-hatred," see Eliot Borenstein, *Soviet Self-Hatred: The Secret Identities of Postsocialism in Contemporary Russia* (Ithaca, NY: Cornell, 2023).
58 *Chas pik*, March 6, 1995, 1:30–3:00.
59 "Pravda published Zhukov's note, written with some other academics, 'In the Interest of Truth' (which demanded the return of Stalin's name to history). I lit up, and a certain Skurlatov added fuel to the fire, with his project for educating the youth in a more severe fashion, by bringing back the ancient Russian custom of tarring the gates of lighthearted women. Both rehabilitations—of Stalin and of tar—intertwined in my consciousness." Grigorii Pomerants, *Zapiski gadkogo utenka* (Moscow: Tsentr gumanitarnykh initsiativ, 2013), 217.
60 See the case of the *Kommersant* cartoonist Andrei Bil'zho and his creation, the indelible *sovok* Petrovich, in my article—Khazanov, "A Petrovich Inside of Every New Russian."
61 On Ernst's arrival to *A Look*, see Evgenii Dodolev, *The Vzgliad* (Moscow: Alistorus, 2013), 168–203.
62 Mark Lipovetsky, "The Poetics of ITR Discourse: In the 1960s and Today," *Ab Imperio* 1 (2013): 125.

Works Cited

Borenstein, Eliot. *Soviet Self-Hatred: The Secret Identities of Postsocialism in Contemporary Russia* (Ithaca, NY: Cornell, 2023).
Condee, Nancy. *The Imperial Trace: Recent Russian Cinema* (Oxford: Oxford University Press, 2009).
Dodolev, Evgenii. *The Vzgliad* (Moscow: Alistorus, 2013).
Doucette, Courtney. "Glasnost in the Mailroom: The Soviet Subject in Gorbachev's Perestroika, 1985–1988." *The Soviet and Post-Soviet Review* 48 (2021): 171–88.

Evans, Christine E. *Between Truth and Time: A History of Soviet Central Television* (New Haven, CT: Yale University Press, 2016).

Guriev, Sergei, and Daniel Treisman. *Spin Dictators: The Changing Face of Tyranny in the 21st Century* (Princeton, NJ: Princeton University Press, 2022).

Jones, Polly. *Revolution Rekindled: The Writers and Readers of Late Soviet Biography* (Oxford: Oxford University Press, 2019).

Kotkin, Stephen. *Armageddon Averted: The Soviet Collapse, 1970–2000* (Oxford: Oxford University Press, 2008).

Khazanov, Pavel. "A Petrovich Inside of Every New Russian: The Disciplinary Regime of the Capitalist 'Vanguard Group' at 1990s *Kommersant*." *Russian Review* 82 (2023): 470–85.

Khazanov, Pavel. "Honest Jacobins: High Stalinism and the Socialist Subjectivity of Mikhail Lifshitz and Andrei Platonov." *Russian Review* 77 (2018): 576–601.

Khazanov, Pavel. *The Russia That We Have Lost: Pre-Soviet Past as Anti-Soviet Discourse* (Madison: Wisconsin University Press, 2023).

Khazanov, Pavel. "Vladimir Sappak's Humanism on Soviet TV." *EUI Max Weber Working Papers* 4 (2018). https://cadmus.eui.eu/handle/1814/56744.

Ledeneva, Alina. *Russia's Economy of Favours:* Blat, *Networking and Informal Exchange* (Cambridge: Cambridge University Press, 1998).

Lifshits, Mikhail. "Veter istorii. K 140-letiiu so dnia rozhdeniia Fridrikha Engel'sa." In *Karl Marks. Iskusstvo I obshchestvennyi ideal* (Moscow: Khudozhestvennaia literature, 1979). Available online, http://www.gutov.ru/lifshitz/texts/marks/marx-10.htm.

Lipovetsky, Mark. "The Poetics of ITR Discourse: In the 1960s and Today." *Ab Imperio* 1 (2013): 109–39.

Maiofis, Mariia, and Il'ia Kukulin. "Svoboda kak neosoznannyi pretsedent: zametki o transformatsii mediinogo polia v 1990 godu." *NLO* 1 (2007). https://magazines.gorky.media/nlo/2007/1/svoboda-kak-neosoznannyj-preczedent-zametki-o-transformaczii-medijnogo-polya-v-1990-godu.html.

Medvedev, Roi. *Sovetskii soiuz. Poslednie gody zhizni. Konets sovetskoi imperii* (Moscow: AST/Poligrafizdat, 2009).

Mukusev, Vladimir. *Razberemsia…Fragmenty interv'iu, vystuplenii, stat'i, stsenarii I rassledovaniia raznykh let* (Moscow: Flinta, 2018), 131–45.

Pelevin, Viktor. "Dzhon Faulz i tragediia russkogo liberalizma." http://pelevin.nov.ru/rass/pe-jon/1.html.

Platt, Kevin M. F., and Benjamin Nathans. "Socialist in Form, Indeterminate in Content: The Ins and Outs of Late Soviet Culture." *Ab Imperio* 2 (2011): 301–24.

Pomerants, Grigorii. "Chelovek niotkuda." http://pomeranz.ru/p/pub_man_air.htm.

Pomerants, Grigorii. *Zapiski gadkogo utenka* (Moscow: Tsentr gumanitarnykh initsiativ, 2013).

Ries, Nancy. *Russian Talk: Culture and Conversation during Perestroika* (Ithaca, NY: Cornell University Press, 1997).

Sappak, Vladimir. *Televidenie i my: chetyre besedy* (Moscow: Iskusstvo, 1988). http://www.evartist.narod.ru/text12/85.htm.

Smith, Kathleen. *Mythmaking in the New Russia: Politics and Memory during the Yeltsin Era* (Ithaca, NY: Cornell University Press, 2002).

Sorokin, Vladimir. *Day of the Oprichnik*. Translated by Jamey Gambrell (New York: Farrar, Straus and Giroux, 2012).

Tolstaia, Tatiana. Ne Kys'. https://www.youtube.com/watch?v=p3SxVmuMjsU&t=62s.

Yurchak, Alexei. *Everything Was Forever Until It Was No More: The Last Soviet Generation* (Princeton, NJ: Princeton University Press, 2005).

Zubok, Vladislav. *Collapse: The Fall of the Soviet Union* (New Haven, CT: Yale University Press, 2022).

Films, TV media:

Chas pik, March 6, 1995, *ViD*, https://www.youtube.com/watch?v=tnfvqsRVRl0&t=20s.

Est' takia bukva, dir. Tat'iana Dmitrakova, Aleksandr Valeev (*ViD*, 2015), https://www.youtube.com/watch?v=1vFB_GZCzpE.

Pole chudes, October 25, 1991, *ViD*, https://www.youtube.com/watch?v=XS_H22rAIKs&t=336s.

"Vladislav Listyev v reklame kruiza (1993)," YouTube, August 23, *2017*, https://www.youtube.com/watch?v=p3SxVmuMjsU&t=62s.

Vzgliad, October 2, 1987, Gosteleradio SSSR, https://www.youtube.com/watch?v=AWPcU0rn4w8&t=142s.

Vzgliad, October 7, 1987, Gosteleradio SSSR, https://www.youtube.com/watch?v=7HkFn5IiSag&t=2222s.
Vzgliad, September 29, 1989, Gosteleradio SSSR, https://www.net-film.ru/film-81287/.
Vzgliad, October 9, 1989, Gosteleradio SSSR, https://www.youtube.com/watch?v=UyuaTZb6lM8&t=111s.
Vzgliad, October 27, 1989, Gosteleradio SSSR, https://www.youtube.com/watch?v=97DethKxNsE&t=731s.
Vzgliad, November 10, 1989, Gosteleradio SSSR, https://www.youtube.com/watch?v=XcxM-w2ZtvY.
Vzgliad, August 20–23, 1991, ViD, https://www.youtube.com/watch?v=_1I-qzMS8f0.

CHAPTER 8

Memory and Media in Post-Soviet Russia: The 1990s to the Present

Maya Vinokour

THE ORIGINS OF PUTIN'S MEDIA CRACKDOWN AFTER FEBRUARY 24, 2022

On March 2, 2022, Ekho Moskvy, a prolific liberal radio station based in Moscow, was abruptly taken off the air for alleged violations of new speech policies around the war in Ukraine.[1] The following day, the station's Board of Directors voted to dissolve it entirely and, the day after that, formally dismissed Aleksei Venediktov, its Editor-in-Chief since 1998.[2] By March 8, Ekho's vast online archive of blog posts and broadcasts had been wiped and its YouTube channel, where it had briefly continued its existence after being taken off the air, was dead. That same day, its former radio frequency was taken over by Sputnik, a state propaganda outlet.

Even amid the chaos that followed Russia's full-scale invasion of Ukraine on February 24, the demise of Ekho came as a shock. Not only had the station been enormously popular, it was not especially oppositional, regularly hosting guests from Russia's halls of power. Venediktov himself is no revolutionary firebrand but a self-described Reagan conservative who,[3] according to journalist and editor Alexey Kovalev, had long "made a point of being on friendly terms with top regime figures."[4] Yet neither a history of compromising with the government, nor the station's affiliation with Gazprom Media, the state-owned natural gas giant that held a majority stake in Ekho, saved it in the end.

Over the course of March 2022, the Russian government blocked or deleted all remaining independent sources of information in Russia. Among the more prominent closures, the shut-down of Ekho was followed by that of TV Rain (also on March 2); the bilingual news website Meduza; and the newspaper *Novaya gazeta* (both on March 4), whose Editor-in-Chief, Dmitry Muratov, had won the 2021 Nobel Peace Prize.[5] Not content with targeting individual outlets, the Russian government also blocked Twitter, Facebook, and Instagram.[6] The blocking of Instagram was especially consequential, since in early 2022 that platform, unlike Facebook and Twitter, had a Russian user-base numbering in the tens of millions—many of whom made their living on the site.[7] Although Western social media platforms remain accessible via VPN as of this writing, and Russian courts initially clarified that individuals would not be liable simply for using them, the designation of Facebook parent company Meta as an "extremist organization" suggested precisely the opposite.[8]

The suppression of Ekho and other outlets was sudden but not surprising in the context of Putin's media policy over the last decades. Soon after coming to power in 2000, Putin began building a powerful propaganda machine that systematically dismantled, absorbed, or subverted competing sources of information. Initially focused on bringing print and television media to heel, Putin's media destruction apparatus became much more sophisticated after the mass protests of 2011–2013, which triggered a spate of Internet censorship laws.[9] Even before revelations of the Russian army's atrocities at Bucha and elsewhere in early April 2022, some Ukrainians were reporting that "the TV was winning," meaning that Russian relatives refused to believe their loved ones' eyewitness accounts of bombings.[10] One commentator noted the similarity between the Kremlin's claim that the war crimes in Bucha were either self-inflicted or staged,[11] and the rhetoric of "crisis actors" familiar to Americans from Alex Jones' campaign to deny the Sandy Hook Elementary School shooting of 2012.[12] Whatever its origins or idiosyncrasies, Putin's regime had now eliminated alternatives to state propaganda channels and instituted heavy penalties for public truth-telling, ensuring that official narratives surrounding Russia's so-called "special operation" had no real competitors.[13]

The last time Ekho had gone off the air was in August 1991 during a putsch staged by anti-Gorbachev hardliners calling themselves the "State Committee on the State of Emergency" (GKChP).[14] Led by the first and only Vice President of the Soviet Union, Gennady Yanaev, whose trembling hands betrayed his utter lack of confidence (Artifact 00012[a]), the putschists sought to undo the General Secretary's liberalizing reforms and return the Soviet Union to conservative form. As Venediktov recalled in his Telegram channel on March 9, 2022, one of the GKChP's first decrees, dated August 20, 1991, ordered the suspension of "the activities of Russian television and radio, as well as the Ekho Moskvy radio station, since these do not contribute to the process of stabilizing the situation in the country."

Venediktov's invocation of the 1990s suggests a profound continuity between that decade and the years that followed—*contra* Putin's self-positioning as the man who rescued Russia from the turmoil and humiliation of the "wild '90s [*likhie devianostye*]."[15] Even as Putin's claims of defending stability and rule of law, already suspect in 2000, became steadily less credible, some Western critics persisted in framing his regime as a fundamental departure from the Yeltsin years.[16] As I will show here, Russia's most recent authoritarian turn is not a reversion to "totalitarianism" after years of "market democracy," but the direct result of 1990s-era developments. In particular,

[a] https://postsoviet90s.com/artifacts/a-coup-d-etat-holds-a-press-conference

the contentious 1996 presidential election cycle, in which an oligarch-backed media campaign successfully discredited Yeltsin's Communist opponent, prepared the ground for Putin's dictatorial mobilization of media toward political ends.

The mediatization of post-Soviet Russian politics in 1996 marked the start of its virtualization, that is, its transformation into a simulacrum of political participation rather than a means of representing the will of the people. This lapse into political virtuality paralleled, or perhaps followed, the rise of opinion polling and triangulation as winning electoral strategies in the United States. A cherished American narrative about Yeltsin's 1996 victory holds that the beleaguered Russian president only won re-election thanks to timely intervention by consultants from Bill Clinton's 1992 campaign team. Three decades on, this narrative is impossible either to corroborate or definitively disprove. Its very existence points to the free mixing of reality and fantasy in 1990s-era history, as well as to the convergence of Western with Russian media and political technologies.

Yeltsin's 1996 re-election campaign is also notable for its weaponization of memory. Television and print outlets, including some created expressly for the purpose, presented a vote for the Communist candidate as a vote for the worst aspects of the Soviet past. One poster featured a scowling Gennady Zyuganov alongside the exhortation to "buy some food—for the last time" (Artifact 00018[b]), while a special anti-Communist newspaper, printed in color and circulated in 10 million free copies, was titled simply *God forbid!* (Artifact 00275[c]).

In another illustration of the continuity between the 1990s and the Putin era, *God Forbid!*, which had initially existed between April 20 and July 29, 1996 (just in time for the June 16 election and the July 3 runoff), was revived in February–March 2012. Although the new *God Forbid!* was not explicitly pro-Putin, it portrayed the crowds then protesting the fraudulent parliamentary elections of December 2011 as dangerous revolutionaries ready to usher in a new 1917—or 1997.

No anonymous hit job, the resurrected *God Forbid!* featured articles from well-known journalists like Maksim Shevchenko, a right-leaning commentator and frequent guest on both Ekho Moskvy and its post-March 2022 successor, a YouTube channel called *Zhivoi gvozd'* (*The Living Nail*). The inclusion of figures like Shevchenko—whose views may not have perfectly matched the official state line, but also did not dissent from it explicitly—points to the ambivalent position of journalists in post-Soviet Russia. As chroniclers of the present, on the one hand, and stewards of collective memory, on the other, journalists and other public figures were often conscripted into the creation of what would eventually become Putin's sovereign dictatorship.

---

[b] https://postsoviet90s.com/artifacts/go-buy-some-food-for-the-last-time-yeltsin-takes-on-zyuganov-in-the-1996-presidential-election

[c] https://postsoviet90s.com/artifacts/the-pro-yeltsin-propaganda-paper-god-forbid-subjects-communist-presidential-candidate-gennady-zyuganov-to-blistering-critique

FIGURE 1 Image from Artifact 00275.[d] An anti-Zyuganov cartoon published about a month before the first round of presidential elections in 1996 compares him to a Godzilla-sized dog owner training an entire city to "Beg!" for a slice of Soviet mortadella—*liubitel'skaya kolbasa*.

[d] https://postsoviet90s.com/artifacts/the-pro-yeltsin-propaganda-paper-god-forbid-subjects-communist-presidential-candidate-gennady-zyuganov-to-blistering-critique

Putin's media crackdown following the invasion of Ukraine is thus rooted in two complementary processes, both of which entered a crucial new phase in the first post-Soviet decade. The first is the consolidation of informational resources by a new class of oligarchs during the early 1990s, which enabled the media frenzy that was Yeltsin's 1996 re-election campaign. The second process is the instrumentalization of Russian cultural and historical memory—including through co-optation of grassroots variants—by the state and its supporters. Throughout the twentieth century and beyond, the perennial Russian cultural tendency to "remember" its own difficult past has generally been followed by a backlash that seeks to drive that memory back underground or reconfigure it to serve a particular political agenda.

Collective trauma cannot be repressed to the same degree as trauma afflicting individuals because of the persistence of documents, familial memory, and private conversations even where public conversation is taboo.[17] At the same time, the Russian state's manipulation of public memory has proven extremely effective in obscuring historical causes, agents, and events—for instance, when Yeltsin's 1996 campaign team invoked the specter of Stalinism to motivate an apathetic electorate to reject Zyuganov.[18] As Kevin M. F. Platt has shown on the example of Khrushchev's "Secret Speech" in 1956,[19] collective or state-sponsored memory has an inherently political, disciplinary function that helps promote Schmittean "friend"/ "enemy" distinctions—where "friends" are defined as those who remember in the "correct," officially sanctioned manner. We might also see memory culture in the latter Putin era as part of what Gavriel D. Rosenfeld classifies as the "rise of illiberal memory," noting that "the same political climate that is reinforcing the importance of studying history is generating doubts about the prophylactic power of memory"—a process exacerbated in the Russian context by the state's outright distortion and falsification of key historical episodes.[20] Since the 1990s, collective memory in Russia has become a "perpetually unreliable and even promiscuous practice," a chameleon-like entity that "can be retrofitted to any ideological end."[21]

As Putin demonstrated in the pseudo-historical lecture he gave on February 21, three days before the start of the invasion of Ukraine, controlling memory and controlling the media are mutually reinforcing processes.[22] It is no coincidence that, beyond suppressing individual outlets like Ekho or *Novaya* and banning entire platforms like Meta, Putin also prioritized liquidating Russia's most important human rights organization, Memorial, established in 1989 to document, commemorate, and ameliorate the criminal state violence of the Stalin era.[23]

THE EARLY 1990S: A "GOLDEN AGE" OF THE RUSSIAN PRESS?

The winnowing of media and memory culture that has taken place since 2000, and especially after 2012, had been prepared before Putin ever took office. For many journalists and international commentators, the early 1990s were an unprecedented time of

FIGURE 2 Image from Artifact 00276.[e] A still from *Solovki Power*, a film featuring Solovki survivor, medievalist, and prominent member of the Soviet intelligentsia Dmitry Likhachev (1906–1999).

cooperation between media and government, a kind of "golden age of the Russian press." Gorbachev's glasnost had opened the door to muckraking in the name of reform—after all, if problems could not be named and openly discussed, how could they be solved?

The last years before Soviet collapse saw the rise of a new media that sought to critique, investigate, and above all, tell the truth. A watershed moment was the 1988 release of Marina Goldovskaya's *Solovki Power* (*Vlast' Solovetskaia*), a documentary about one

---

[e] https://postsoviet90s.com/artifacts/marina-goldovskaya-s-solovki-power-excavates-painful-historical-memory/

of the oldest and most notorious Soviet gulags (Artifact 00276[f]). Distributed to 300 movie theaters simultaneously, it became the second most popular film of 1989, a true "memory vehicle for the glasnost era."[24]

Illustrating the tight links between memory and media culture in post-Soviet Russia, Goldovskaya's filmography also includes *The Bitter Taste of Freedom*, a 2011 documentary about the journalist Anna Politkovskaya, a *Novaya gazeta* correspondent known for her unflinching coverage of Russia's Chechen wars.[25] Nearly two decades after her 2006 murder, Politkovskaya remains one of the highest-profile victims of Putin's perpetual open season on independent journalists. By coincidence, an obituary for Goldovskaya, who died on March 21, 2022 at the age of eighty, became one of *Novaya*'s last articles before it was shut down.[26] A week later, the newspaper received a second written warning from Roskomnadzor for alleged violations of Russia's foreign agent law and, facing the threat of permanently losing its license to publish, announced it was suspending operations until the end of the war in Ukraine.[27] This concession failed to stem the tide of persecution and, in February 2023, *Novaya* lost its license anyway.[28]

Goldovskaya's perestroika-era work reveals her belief—shared by many of her peers in the media and creative industries at the time—that documenting the present-day ills of Soviet society was not enough to reform it, because their roots lay deep in Russia's troubled past. As the entire Soviet system lurched toward collapse, serious projects like Goldovskaya's documentaries appeared alongside tonally lighter efforts in the same vein. Youth-oriented shows like *Vzgliad* attracted enormous audiences by seamlessly blending reportage with entertainment (Artifact 00173[g]). In contrast to the stodginess and mendacity of most of Soviet television, *Vzgliad*—itself a state-sponsored effort—offered a fresh, youthful perspective on the news, alternating music videos with hard-hitting coverage of difficult topics like consumer goods shortages or urban drug use. As Pavel Khazanov demonstrates in this volume, however, the humanist aspirations of perestroika-era media experiments like *Vzgliad* became, in the final analysis, "useful tool[s] for the formation of a post-Soviet dictatorship" (p. 178), with apparently sincere and open-minded creators contributing to an environment in which their interventions could be co-opted by the state.

Indeed, the show's origins and subsequent fate are a microcosm of broader post-Soviet developments. A brainchild of Communist Party official Alexander Yakovlev, popularly known as the "godfather of perestroika" and a mentor of future Yeltsin opponent Gennady Zyuganov, the original *Vzgliad* ceased to exist after 1991. Its hosts, reporting style, and aesthetic sensibility lived on in various spinoff programs, and in 1994, *Vzgliad* returned to mainstream Russian television on the channel ORT (Russian Public Television). In the wake of the 1993 Constitutional Crisis (Artifact 00033[h]), which

---

[f] https://postsoviet90s.com/artifacts/marina-goldovskaya-s-solovki-power-excavates-painful-historical-memory/

[g] https://postsoviet90s.com/artifacts/meaning-of-pluralism-on-vzgliad

[h] https://postsoviet90s.com/artifacts/writers-demand-a-yeltsin-coup-letter-of-the-42

ended with Boris Yeltsin's bombing of the Russian parliament and the adoption of a new, executive-boosting constitution, ORT came under government control. In late 1994, a presidential decree transformed the channel into a closed joint-stock company with state agencies holding a 51 percent stake. In early 1995, popular *Vzgliad* host and new ORT director Vladislav Listyev was murdered by unknown culprits (Artifact 00130[i]). By the late 1990s, *Vzgliad* had started airing late at night rather than at prime time, and its ratings fell. It was finally canceled in 2001, and the following year, ORT became Channel One Russia (*Pervyi kanal*), today the Putin regime's main propaganda outlet.

Even nominally liberal leaders like Yeltsin found a truly independent domestic media too volatile to tolerate, but governmental overreach was not the only challenge post-Soviet outlets faced in the 1990s. Another set of problems was financial. The economic turmoil unleashed in the rigged privatization drives of the early 1990s, from "shock therapy" to "voucherization" to "loans for shares," immiserated millions of Russians while enriching a tiny minority—the future oligarchs (Artifact 00066[j], Artifact 00007[k]). For the media, newfound freedom from state control also meant "freedom" from state funding, forcing companies into desperate financial straits from which they could only emerge by compromising with state and private interests.

The case of the newspaper *Izvestia* is illustrative. Along with *Pravda*, *Izvestia* was an organ of the Soviet Supreme Soviet and therefore an official mouthpiece of the state between 1917 and 1991. Its reputation for propaganda was distilled in the ironic late-Soviet dictum "There's no truth in News [*Izvestia*], and no news in Truth [*Pravda*]." During the 1992 economic crisis, a direct consequence of forced marketization, financial difficulties caused several important papers, including *Izvestia*, to cease operations for several days. To improve their situation, Yeltsin signed a decree in February stipulating subsidies to publications with especially large readerships. When the daily was privatized in November of the same year, a dominant stake fell to Vladimir Potanin, an oligarch with close ties to the government. In 2005, *Izvestia* was sold to the Russian state energy company Gazprom—the same Gazprom that held a 66 percent stake in Ekho Moskvy. Finally, in 2011, Gazprom sold it to the National Media Group, a vast private media holding chaired by the president of Gazprombank, of which Gazprom Media is a subsidiary.[29]

The eventual return to form of a traditional propaganda megaphone like *Izvestia* is certainly poetic, but the broader contours of its co-optation were not unique to former Party papers. Many print outlets that began the decade in a spirit of proud independence—*Kommersant*, *Nezavisimaya gazeta*, *Moskovskie novosti*, *Segodnia*, to name a few examples—were eventually made to pay fealty to the state. The story of

---

[i] https://postsoviet90s.com/artifacts/list-ev-s-russian-liberals-on-chas-pik

[j] https://postsoviet90s.com/artifacts/it-s-all-chubais-fault

[k] https://postsoviet90s.com/artifacts/500-days-program-summary

Kommersant further underscores the reciprocal relationship between the manipulation of historical memory and editorial co-optation. An imitator of American financial papers like *The Wall Street Journal*, *Kommersant* signaled its allegiance to capitalism, and its break with the then-recent Soviet past, by choosing as its logo the hard sign (ъ)—a vestige of pre-1917 orthography that also appeared in the old-fashioned rendering of its name as *Коммерсантъ*. When the paper was founded in 1989, the semiotics of this move must have felt innovative, fresh, and even ironic (Artifact 00037[l]). Yet by the mid-1990s, and certainly after 2000, the state had adopted the alleged prosperity and imperial grandeur of Russia's tsarist past as prominent mnemonic references. Although the paper maintained a reputation for liberalism for another few years, its sale to billionaire and close Putin associate Alisher Usmanov in 2006 portended a sea change. In 2019, Usmanov ordered the evisceration of *Kommersant*'s politics section. By 2020, the desk had been repopulated with Putin loyalists. In the context of an accelerating imperial revival that in 2022 escalated to full-scale warfare, *Kommersant*'s symbolic play with pre-revolutionary Russian spelling no longer looked subversive. In the arena of memory, the hard sign now functioned like *Kommersant*'s editorial staff after the shakeups of 2019–2020: as a marker of its alignment with the state.

MEMORY AND MEDIA IN THE YELTSIN RE-ELECTION CAMPAIGN OF 1996

If we are looking for the fulcrum of the 1990s, the moment when politics began tilting back toward authoritarianism, there are several possibilities. For Brian McNair, the "golden age of Russian media" only lasted until the August 1991 putsch.[30] Yet there were still hopeful signs at and after that point, including the creation of *Obshchaia gazeta* during the putsch itself (Artifact 00009[m]). True, independent media outlets were severely battered by the economic turmoil attending Russia's rapid marketization. Yet I argue that their downfall came not in 1992, at the height of "shock therapy"; not in 1993, when Yeltsin reasserted the power of the executive branch by bombing Russian parliament; not in 1994, when journalists reporting on the First Chechen War courted government ire by revealing the Russian army's brutality and incompetence; and not even in 1995, which saw the assassination of *Vzgliad*'s Vladislav Listyev. Instead, the most important predecessor to Putin's contemporary crackdown came in 1996, when a small group of oligarchs, concerned about Yeltsin's re-election prospects, launched a coordinated media offensive against his Communist opponent.

As the post-Soviet economic elite amassed money and power, its representatives developed political ambitions and acquired media holdings to help pursue them.

---

[l] https://postsoviet90s.com/artifacts/petrovich-the-soviet-everyman-survives-post-soviet-russia-at-kommersant

[m] https://postsoviet90s.com/artifacts/democracy-must-know-how-to-defend-itself-obshchaia-gazeta

Business interests entering the media marketplace in the early 1990s had no interest in journalism *per se*, but saw great potential for promoting favored products, generating advertising revenue, and manipulating public opinion for political ends. Two figures deserve special mention here: Vladimir Gusinsky and Boris Berezovsky. Gusinsky, who made his money buying up metal-mining companies in the first wave of privatization, in 1993 founded the Media-MOST holding company that controlled NTV, one of Russia's most popular and influential television channels (since 2001, it has been controlled by Gazprom). Berezovsky, meanwhile, first made a fortune selling cars, then became a media magnate who took over ORT in 1994. Both oligarchs soon realized the media's potential as a tool for shaping economic and political life. Even where media holdings were not directly profitable, they could serve as conduits that funneled money and power toward those in charge. By the middle of the decade, most major media outlets were controlled by big money, a situation the oligarchs exploited to its full potential during Yeltsin's bid for re-election in 1996.

At the start of the campaign, Yeltsin was extremely unpopular, whereas Zyuganov seemed likely to win. Western and Russian elites regarded a Zyuganov victory as unacceptable from the perspective of preserving Russia's fledgling "market democracy"—and continuing the upward transfer of wealth to domestic and international players.[31] During the Davos Economic Forum that year, Gusinsky and Berezovsky aligned with several other oligarchs to form a "pact" that sought to orchestrate Yeltsin's re-election (Artifact 00034[n]).[32] Wealthy as its members were, the Davos Pact was not just about money. Gusinsky and Berezovsky alone "controlled two of the three major television channels in Russia," ensuring that the 1996 campaign was a highly mediatized affair.[33] Banding together, the oligarchs deployed their vast holdings to unleash a full-scale information war fueled by the negative campaigning known in Russia as "black PR."[34]

In yet another testament to the proximity of media history to the politics of memory, anti-Zyuganov ads continually raised the specter of the drab, meager, violent Soviet past. One cartoon spot showed a square-headed Zyuganov standing on the tip of an iceberg, which closer inspection revealed to be a nuclear submarine (Artifact 00278[o]). Behind each of the sub's portholes was a Soviet-era contradiction in terms: banners trumpeting WORLD PEACE over a landscape teeming with soldiers, tanks, and bombers; the word FREEDOM emblazoned above a cramped prison yard filled with miserable inmates; and, finally, a flag reading ABUNDANCE flying over a gigantic hungry queue. At the end of the spot, the camera zoomed out to show the vastness of the hidden underwater menace, with a final intertitle reminding viewers to "look to the root" of Zyuganov's speechifying.

---

[n] https://postsoviet90s.com/artifacts/oligarchs-collude-for-yeltsin-in-1996

[o] https://postsoviet90s.com/artifacts/iceberg-an-anti-zyuganov-television-spot

Unrelenting doomsaying was one aspect of the oligarchs' anti-Zyuganov strategy. Another tactic was to ignore him. As *Financial Times* journalist John Lloyd reported in 1997, "most of the national dailies were for Yeltsin," and while coverage by "regional papers" was more varied, "most were at least constrained because of their dependence on regional budgets for subsidies." Zyuganov was often simply omitted from the news of the day. Ahead of the first round of voting on 16 June, "out of all appearances on the three main TV channels," Yeltsin "took 53 per cent of the time devoted to all candidates, Zyuganov had 18 per cent, [General Alexander] Lebed 7 per cent, [Grigory] Yavlinsky 6 per cent, [Vladimir] Zhirinovsky 5 per cent and the other candidates 11 per cent."[35] With the benefit of twenty years of hindsight, an investigative report published on *Radio Liberty* in 2016 called the 1996 campaign "propagandistic." The report's authors also noted that "it was Boris Yeltsin who established the tradition of the leading candidate not participating in debates" with his opponents.[36] Although he had been willing to engage in 1989, already in 1991—and certainly in 1996—Yeltsin declined the opportunity.

Retrospectives of what Lloyd called "Russia's first second election" became a popular subgenre almost as soon as it was over, with attempts to explain Yeltsin's improbable success proliferating in Russia and abroad. One popular narrative, revived in the 2016 discussions around possible Russian meddling in the US presidential election, held that Yeltsin only kept his seat with help from American friends. In response to negative press coverage of Russian troll farms and other malefactors, prominent voices on the US left reminded Americans of their country's role in putting a thumb on the scale for Yeltsin twenty years earlier.[37]

According to this version of events, Yeltsin owed his second electoral victory to advice from American election consultants, who initiated his Russian staffers into the dark arts of TV advertising, photo ops, and negative campaigning.[38] It is true that, rather than focusing on Yeltsin's attributes, the oligarch-controlled media fed the public "a nonstop diet of past Soviet horrors" to discourage voting for Zyuganov.[39] It is also true that, starting in late winter 1995, the Yeltsin campaign employed three US political consultants: Joe Shumate, George Gorton, and Richard Dresner. Before this job, the trio's greatest claim to fame had been their work for California Governor Pete Wilson, an unsuccessful candidate for the Republican presidential nomination in 1995.[40] Yet their connections were rumored to be more powerful than their resumes would suggest. *Time* magazine linked them to Dick Morris, "Bill Clinton's all-purpose political aide" and the self-declared mastermind behind the US president's own 1996 re-election.[41] Whether or not Dick Morris or even Clinton himself advised them, "opinions vary greatly on the [American consultants'] influence." Their very existence "was only fully reported by *Time* magazine in July [1996], after the second round of voting" was complete.[42]

Shumate, Gorton, and Dresner themselves endorsed the idea that the Yeltsin campaign would have failed without them. Yet already in a press conference at the National

Press Club on July 9, 1996—a week after Russia's second-round election of July 3—a journalist was asking the consultants, "Did you read the *New York Times* piece this morning alleging that basically you're promoting yourselves and that in fact you had very little influence on [Yeltsin's] campaign?"[43] George Gorton responded by blaming the *Times* journalist, Alessandra Stanley, for being excessively credulous of Kremlin sources eager to diminish the Americans' role. Yeltsin insiders did, in fact, deny that the Americans significantly helped the campaign. In a 2002 interview on the NTV-based news show *Itogi*, Liudmila Pikhoya, a Yeltsin speechwriter from 1990 to 1998 and a close advisor to his second administration, stated that the American impact on Yeltsin's re-election was slim at best.[44] According to Pikhoya, none of the Americans' suggestions were "revelations" to Russian advertising and PR experts.

Fantasy mixed freely with reality not only in the 1996 campaign itself, but in its later reception, for instance in the 2003 American film *Spinning Boris*. Starring Jeff Goldblum (George Gorton), Liev Schreiber (Joe Shumate), and Anthony LaPaglia (Dick Dresner) as extremely good-looking and savvy versions of their real-life counterparts, the film depicted Yeltsin's electoral team—including the Russian president's notoriously shrewd and ruthless daughter, Tatyana Dyachenko—as a gaggle of vodka-swilling know-nothings desperate for the wisdom of their new American friends. It is clear why the various parties in this story would seek either to inflate or elide America's role in securing Yeltsin's 1996 win. Dresner and his colleagues were concerned with burnishing their reputations to boost their lucrative consulting careers. The second Clinton administration, keen to preserve America's position as the economic, political, and ideological victor in the Cold War, was not averse to being portrayed as powerful enough to influence an election half a world away.[45] It is similarly unsurprising that insiders like Pikhoya would try to claim greater credit for themselves, rather than ceding it to the Americans.

Competitive national myths aside, at least one academic study denies that TV ads—inspired by American political practices or not—made any difference at all. Just after the election, political scientist Daniel Treisman wrote that Yeltsin owed his renewed popularity to "promises of, and an outright increase in, social spending." Yeltsin, according to Treisman, "won the election in large part through state largess."[46] His public appearances and the land reform decree he had signed in March 1996 may also have played a role, as did a truce with Chechnya and the campaign's co-optation of the conservative General Alexander Lebed, who acted as a spoiler for Zyuganov. Yet while these factors "may have forestalled events that could have undermined Yeltsin's position, they did not themselves secure his victory."[47] One clue that this version of events might be correct is the absolute contempt domestic and international journalists heaped on Yeltsin's so-called "'Santa Claus' strategy." The international neoliberal establishment, from "shock therapist" Yegor Gaidar to the Editorial Board of the *New York Times*, was extremely displeased that Yeltsin was dispensing back pay, social benefits, and cars to

Russia's citizens—even though, as Treisman points out, "Yeltsin's social spending probably played a crucial role in keeping Zyuganov out of office." Far from being some outlandish Russian invention, moreover, "social welfare programs and promises have been a normal part of the politics of most Western countries" for decades.[48]

Zooming out from the question of whether American or Russian genius produced the tactic of television scare-mongering reveals the traces of a much more encompassing illusion. The international community's obsession with something called "the economy" that is disjoint from people's need to eat food and receive their wages on time—already a familiar element in international discourse around "privatizing" Russia in the early 1990s—is one of this illusion's main features. Another element is the self-congratulatory Western (and dismayed Russian) presentation of "black PR" and "opinion polling" as decisive for 1996. It is this story that has persisted in the public imagination, even in the portrayal of a satirist like Victor Pelevin (Artifact 00222[P]), whose 1999 novel *Generation P* skewered the absurdity of a fully virtual politics with the Yeltsin re-election campaign as one obvious underlying case study.

Writing in 2005, cultural and political critic Andrew Wilson pointed to the virtuality of early Putin-era politics, which in his view combined traditional "dirty tricks" with "the manipulation possibilities of modern media technology."[49] In this virtual system, "parties and politicians are only avatars, as with the graphical icons that represent users in cyberspace."[50] The journalist Peter Pomerantsev made similar claims in *Nothing Is True and Everything Is Possible*, his 2014 book on the postmodern curlicues of Putinism (the tagline calls it "a journey into the glittering, surreal heart of twenty-first-century Russia, where even dictatorship is a reality show"). Yet precisely this form of virtuality, with its dearth of "representation and accountability"[51] was already a fixture of international politics in the 1990s.

True or not, the idea that three American consultants could show up in Russia less than six months before the first round of a presidential election and, though they spoke no Russian and never met with Yeltsin, steer the unpopular incumbent to victory, suggests an improbable level of similarity between Russia and America. Despite the vast differences between the two nations and their voting publics, the techniques and slogans Dresner, Shumate, and Gorton said they deployed in Russia were nearly identical to the ones Dick Morris and others used in the Clinton campaigns of 1992 and 1996. James Carville's "It's the economy, stupid," the focus groups and photo ops, the performance of empathy with the public (Clinton's "I feel your pain")—all were apparently transposed onto the Russian context without regard for its idiosyncrasies. The perception that these efforts were the critical element that "saved" Yeltsin from defeat suggests the existence of a one-size-fits-all, magical set of strategies for manipulating the public.

[P] https://postsoviet90s.com/artifacts/an-encounter-with-america

VIRTUAL REALITY AND THE MAGIC OF OPINION POLLING

Dick Morris' own book, *Behind the Oval Office*, which he wrote after resigning in disgrace from Clinton's re-election campaign, unwittingly reveals the magical thinking behind techniques like focus grouping and triangulation.[52] Morris repeatedly denies being a "spin doctor," writing, "I don't 'spin' anything, I put new substance and ideas before the voters."[53] He is also at pains to demonstrate the scientific and rational underpinnings of opinion polling, calling it "a process that [reduces] the mysterious ways of politics to scientific testing and evaluation."[54] Elsewhere, however, Morris explains that his polling strategies are similar to those Hollywood producers use to decide how best to promote big-budget films like Steven Spielberg's shark thriller *Jaws* (1975).[55] Shaping a political narrative, for Morris, is no different from crafting a fictional one; both are stories with the potential to enrich and empower the teller.

In his 2005 study of American polling practices, political scientist George F. Bishop drew on the work of Walter Lippmann and Pierre Bourdieu to conclude that "what passes as 'public opinion' in mass media polls today represents an illusion, an artifact of measurement."[56] It is not even possible to speak of a kind of "Heisenberg uncertainty principle" whereby the very act of measuring public opinion alters it, because the entity we call "public opinion" is itself a mirage.[57] For Bishop, the media exacerbates an already virtuality-heavy situation by relying on "pseudopolls" characterized by "loaded and unfair question wording, self-selection bias in the respondents, and outright efforts to stack the results." By merely covering "pseudopolls," media outlets render their opinions "more real and credible than they might otherwise be"—further reinforcing the powerful simulacrum of reality the media exists to produce.[58]

As Bradley Gorski shows in this volume's first chapter, statistics and opinion polling in early post-Soviet Russia also sought to spin the straw of raw data into the gold of actionable metrics. During and after perestroika, data collection and analysis aimed not to model economic change or study public stances toward matters of political or social importance, but instead to "[distill] the subjective feelings of the populace into apparent social facts." As a result, "By the mid-1990s, public faith in polling was replaced by a widespread belief in the manipulability of sociologically represented truth." Barely ten years later, Russia's oldest polling agency, VTsIOM, "had become ripe for state capture," with polling set to contribute to the rise of Putinist authoritarianism (pp. 19). Ultimately, even as "polling helped bring into existence an active post-Soviet public sphere," it "also helped pave the way for its demise" (p. 42). As important as pollsters' actual techniques was the public perception of their activity, particularly after 1996. In the years that followed, Russians increasingly saw opinion polling not as a "transparent metric of popular sentiment," but as "one more tool to be manipulated" by an emerging class of "political technologists" (p. 37). Against this skeptical background, the 1996 election became a showcase of polls that "not only followed the developing narrative, but drove it" (p. 38).

According to Michael Kramer, the author of the July 1996 *Time* piece about Dresner and his colleagues' Russian sojourn, Yeltsin was so politically toxic that merely "delivering what people knew was due"—back wages and so on—would have failed to win their votes.[59] Instead of advocating for changes in policy, therefore, the American consultants worked to spin a convincing *fiction* of a Yeltsin capable of filling the Lacanian lack in Russia's wounded cultural imaginary. The members of the Davos Pact knew this void well and were all too happy to exploit it. As Natalia Rostova wrote in the *Radio Liberty* report from 2016, Russia's elites saw 1996 as an existential battle: "at issue was the formation of a new regime in which the symbolic leader" was a fig leaf "[cloaking] the rule of a narrow clan elite." The resulting structure of rule was the "epitome" of "a total merger of power and property."[60]

Like Morris, Dresner and his team insisted on the rationality of their techniques even when they were entirely fabricated. According to Kramer, Gorton told Yeltsin's aides that any campaign message had to be repeated "between eight and 12 times," numbers that were invented to serve the Russians' alleged belief that "anything that's worthwhile is scientifically based." Although there was "no data supporting how many times something needs to be repeated," Shumate told Kramer that "the Russians bought it as gospel."[61] Regardless of its veracity, this anecdote casts doubt on the potential of *any* polling method to faithfully represent the reality it purports to measure. Moreover, its smug tone shows deep contempt for both the Russian public and its elected representatives, who are equally reduced to mere objects of American political manipulation.

Despite their cynicism, Dresner and his colleagues were, in a way, entirely sincere. In *Behind the Oval Office*, Morris boasted that his methods helped create "the first fully advertised presidency in US history, which led to an extensive record of legislative accomplishment."[62] For Morris, triangulation was more than a way to get elected; it was a compass that pointed would-be leaders to the true north of political consensus.[63] The Clinton of 1996 won not because he successfully wooed different tranches of the electorate. Instead, as Morris writes, he "regained his power by finding his true voice."[64] British filmmaker Adam Curtis identifies the disturbing implications of this perspective in his 2002 documentary *Century of the Self.* In a segment on Clinton's 1992 campaign, Curtis notes in voiceover that James Carville, George Stephanopoulos, and other political strategists "did not believe that they were capitulating to the selfish desires of the middle classes," seeing promises of "tax cuts" as "the price they had to pay to regain power." They told themselves that, once in the White House, "they would still fulfill traditional Democratic policies" and "help the poor who had been neglected under [President Ronald] Reagan." Yet as soon as it began to govern, the first Clinton administration found itself stymied by the very "centrist consensus" its triangulation had helped produce. And by 1996, if we believe Morris, Clinton had "[used] polls to adjust not just his thinking" on a single issue, but his entire "frame of reference."[65] Rather than modeling some underlying reality, then, triangulation and policy-by-focus group actually created it. In poll-driven democracies, it is not the people's elected representatives who make policy, but their unaccountable, unelected political consultants. The distance between a "democracy" like the United States and the "managed democracy" Vladimir Putin began installing after his accession to Russia's presidency in 2000 may therefore be much shorter than champions of Western-style post-Soviet rule may have liked to believe.

Like Clinton, Yeltsin won re-election in 1996, but for both participants and observers, the accompanying back-room deals and media manipulation marked the end of substance and integrity in both the virtual and meatspace versions of Russian reality. As Mikhail Khodorkovsky wrote in 2005, the Yeltsin re-election campaign showed that, in post-Soviet as in Soviet and Imperial Russia, "the ends justify the means." Once lackeys of the Communist Party, many journalists now served their capitalist overlords, with formerly "independent public institutions" transforming into the "loudspeakers of sponsors." The new Russian authoritarianism, in Khodorkovsky's view, began with the compromises property made with power in 1996.[66] According to David E. Hoffman, the former Moscow bureau chief for *The Washington Post*, even Gusinsky felt that "he had made a fundamental mistake in cooperating so closely with Yeltsin in 1996." As a result, "the Kremlin got the idea that the news media—including [Gusinsky's] cherished NTV—could be treated like an obedient puppy."[67] By 2000, print and especially television media had been bought and paid for by a combination of state and private interests, preparing the way for the further consolidation—and eventually, persecution progressing into overt repression—the Putin era would bring.

Other critics dated the onset of the new Russian authoritarianism almost as far back as the collapse of the Soviet Union. A particularly prescient set of predictions belongs to Veniamin Sokolov, an astrophysicist and, as of 1995, "Russia's chief controller of the use and disposal of federal property."[68] That year, Sokolov co-authored a document titled *Program of Economic Reforms for 1995*, a macroeconomic primer for specialists. Its introduction, by contrast, offered an accessible (albeit extremely pessimistic) take on a Russian capitalism many Western and domestic observers still considered viable and exciting. As Sokolov saw it, the August 1991 putsch, though unsuccessful, signaled "the end of the democratization process" and the beginning of a slide into an "abyss" of slowly metastasizing "mafia fascism," devoid of "goals, prospects, or internal justifications for existing."[69] In an even bleaker passage, Sokolov predicted that, in the worst-case scenario, Yeltsin and his cronies would remain in power until 1999, whereupon they would "cede it, under conditions of extreme societal degradation, to the most depraved representatives of the new generation"—that is, KGB operatives and their ilk, "since no one else would [want to] remain in the government's employ."[70]

For economist and 1996 Yeltsin opponent Grigory Yavlinsky, the new authoritarianism had also started early, with the ruinous "shock therapy" of Yegor Gaidar and Anatoly

Chubais.[71] As journalist Paul Klebnikov reported in 2000 (four years before being assassinated on the streets of Moscow), Yavlinsky was "struck by how little reformers such as [former Minister for the Economy Evgeny] Yasin or Gaidar seemed to care about the Russian people." Just as "father of Socialist Realism" Maxim Gorky had viscerally hated Russia's peasants, Gaidar and his colleagues, in Yavlinsky's view, loathed its lower and middle classes.[72] Yavlinsky was horrified by their belief that "Russia was populated by *sovki* [rotten Soviets], that everything that exists in Russia should be wiped out and that only then can you build something new." For Yavlinsky, the "paradox" of the early 1990s was that the economic "reformers" tried to build capitalism "using purely Bolshevik methods," where "a Bolshevik is a man for whom the aim is important but the means are not."[73]

On March 19, 2022, Yavlinsky recapitulated this position during an appearance on *The Living Nail*, the YouTube channel Aleksei Venediktov and his colleagues established following the dismantling of Ekho.[74] The topic of conversation was the war in Ukraine, the groundwork for which, Yavlinsky asserted, "was laid in 1992 with an artificially produced inflation" of 2,600 percent. "What kind of privatization," he continued, "can possibly follow hyperinflation on that scale? Only a criminal privatization." When the interests of business and government are entirely congruent, "the result is a principled negation of the freedom of speech, of law, of parliament." Systems that produce autocrats like Putin don't form "in a [single] day," Yavlinsky concluded. The system that had coalesced into "final form" by 2000 "had a powerful trial run in 1996."

In a sense, economic reformers like Gaidar were themselves creators of an alternative public memory. By seeking to dispense instantly with fixtures of Soviet economic life like government ownership of factories, price controls, or top-down planning, they effectively denied the long-lasting impact those policies had on human behavior. The survival strategies formed over seventy years of Soviet rule—among them the cronyism, reliance on barter, and the mundane corruption of late socialism—could not be undone through rapid marketization, no matter how painful. The reformers' attempts to strong-arm Russians into global capitalism neglected the problem of historical memory, an oversight that created the perfect environment for Putin's "restorative nostalgia."[75] As the following section will show, the entire complex of measures taken in nominal service of putting the Soviet past in the rearview mirror—economically and otherwise—was already proto-authoritarian.

THE NEW RUSSIAN AUTHORITARIANISM, OR HOW CARL SCHMITT INVENTED PUTIN'S RUSSIA

Russia's 2022 invasion of Ukraine catalyzed an explosion of popular and academic discourse on totalitarianism, Eurasianism, and other dangerous and unpleasant -isms. Previously, scholars could still dismiss as hyperbolic descriptions of Putin as an all-powerful "tsar," instead trusting political technologist Gleb Pavlovsky's 2016 assessment of Russia as a stable, if corrupt, *sistema* (deep state) only nominally ruled by any one person, including Putin.[76] The war in Ukraine has displaced this paradigm, demonstrating that terms like "vertical of power," "managed democracy," and "sovereign Internet" are anything but post-ironic.

In a discussion of Russian authoritarianism, it is especially useful to recall the German legal theorist and Nazi enabler Carl Schmitt (1888–1985). As political scientist David Lewis argues, "reading Schmitt provides numerous insights" into Russia's political and social trajectory since the 2000s.[77] Indeed, Schmittean categories and concepts like sovereignty, the friend–enemy distinction, the exception, "the political," and geopolitics are longstanding fixtures of Putin's statecraft.[78] Especially salient in light of the war in Ukraine is Schmitt's belief in the inevitability of political emergency and the attendant requirement for "unexpected and sometimes unforeseeable exercises of far-reaching discretionary executive power."[79] It is precisely by invoking Schmitt that Putin's famous "pragmatism" can be reconciled with the (self-)destructiveness of the Ukraine invasion, which are only apparently in conflict. After all, Schmitt "came down on the side of facts, not norms," arguing that "for a legal order to make sense, a normal situation must exist, and he is sovereign who definitely decides whether this normal situation actually exists." Putin is certainly a sovereign in Schmitt's sense, which means he is a definer of categories; "legal order is what the sovereign makes of it."[80]

Schmitt's theory of the relationship between people and sovereign also illuminates Putin's emphasis on the legitimizing power of referenda. By law and force in Russia and by force alone in Ukraine, Putin effectively places subjects before the choice of death or what Schmitt called "acclamation," imposing "plebiscitary rule via questions posed to a passive people." In Schmitt's ideal plebiscite, the people "cannot advise, deliberate, or discuss. They cannot govern or administer." Although they help "set norms" by identifying with the sovereign, they can only "sanction [them] by consenting to a draft set of norms laid before them. Above all, they cannot pose a question, but can only answer with yes or no to a question placed before them."[81]

Finally, an appeal to Schmitt's theories clarifies the odd hybridity and hollowness of Putin's brand of fascism, perhaps more accurately called "fascism without fascism." As Jens Meierhenrich has observed, Schmitt was "astonishingly indifferent to the ideological nature of the substance that was to sustain political order," which may explain why, despite his record of antisemitism, he was never a fanatical Nazi and in fact fell out with the regime in 1936.[82] A similar hollowness attended Putin's early years in power, which were characterized by an absence of clear ideological content despite a formal allegiance to "principles" like stability, prosperity, and law and order. One example of this vacuity in action was his treatment of Anna Politkovskaya's 2006 murder. Asked about the journalist's death at the Russian-German Social Forum in October of that year, Putin emphasized that Politkovskaya had been a "radical" presence with no "serious influence on [Russia's] political mood." Her murder, he claimed, was therefore an exclusively criminal matter, its political significance limited to the embarrassment it was causing Putin abroad. Politkovskaya's death, Putin stated, did "much greater damage" to the government she had criticized that any of her publications.[83] This answer represented what was then Putin's un-ideology at its finest. Politkovskaya had certainly been a fly in Putin's ointment, and it is entirely plausible that he might have wanted her dead. But rather than denouncing her as a member of the *Lügenpresse* as Joseph Goebbels might have done, Putin cast her as an irrelevant extremist, thus leaving observers to infer her death's true significance.

Just as Veniamin Sokolov had prophesized back in 1995, "by the early 2000s, liberalism as an ideology was effectively moribund in Russia," leading to the "collapse of liberal parties at the December 2003 parliamentary elections" and the rise of *Edinaya Rossiya* as the dominant force in parliament.[84] The new Russian conservatism, which shares intellectual influences and patterns of thought with a resurgent New Right in Europe and the United States, did not appear overnight.[85] Its history begins in the late Soviet period with underground discussion groups like the Yuzhinskii circle, whose particular form of *vnenakhodimost'* (Bakhtin/ Yurchak) traveled a winding path from Yuri Mamleev's metaphysical realism all the way to Alexander Dugin's Nazi-inflected mysticism (Artifact 00194[q]).[86]

Although it may be tempting to imagine a straight line leading from Dugin's *Fourth Political Theory* (2009) to Putin's decision to invade Ukraine, the war in fact proceeds from "multiple ideological sources."[87] The diffuse nature of Russia's current ideology is the result of a longstanding triangulation in which figures like Dugin or Vladislav Surkov do not determine policy directly, but instead "fight a 'war of position' to achieve [a Gramscian] 'cultural hegemony.'" Surkov-sponsored efforts like the short-lived youth movement *Nashi* or the co-optation of the Immortal Regiment are cases in point.[88] In practice, the technique of Surkov and other "political technologists" involves "influenc[ing] public debates, shift[ing] public and elite opinion and challeng[ing] the language and discourse of liberalism"—in effect performing Dick Morris' trick of placing public and leadership into a feedback loop capable of altering entire "frame[s] of reference."[89]

As Khodorkovsky and Yavlinsky remind us, processes that culminated in the catastrophes of the present have their origins in the 1990s. The Schmitt-ification of Russian politics is no exception: in 1993, following the bombing of Parliament, Yeltsin set himself up to "rule by decree" and expanded "federal bureaucracy" to "a point where it rivaled that of the Soviet Union."[90] Several Schmittean elements attended the 1996 election: for instance, Alexander Korzhakov, Yeltsin's "longtime bodyguard and confidant," publicly called for delaying the election to avoid "civil war."[91] Meanwhile, the Davos Pact

[q] https://postsoviet90s.com/artifacts/what-is-concealed-will-be-revealed-kurekhin-s-and-dugin-s-post-ironic-political-campaign-in-saint-petersburg

sought to reduce Russia's voters to an acclamatory mass, with the oligarchs arrogating to themselves the powers of a "sovereign dictator," a term Schmitt uses to designate a ruler who parlays a temporary state of exception into an entirely new political order.[92]

The earlier period of "shock therapy" provides an even clearer instantiation of sovereign dictatorship. In 1998, political scientist Mitchell Orenstein described "shock therapy" as a "revolutionary" politico-economic doctrine that must be forced through a "'window of opportunity' created by extraordinary political events." In order that its administrators not be disturbed in the "implementation of their program," shock therapy required that they be insulated from the political consequences of their actions, "granted the power of decree when necessary to overcome opposition by entrenched interest groups." This departure from "normal democratic procedures," per Orenstein, naturally produces a "lack of accountability," which, however, is supposed to prevent entrenched interest groups from "cynically" opposing reform. Yet, as what he calls a "side effect," this lack of accountability engenders the decay of "legal institutions" and encourages governance by "executive decree," which "serves to de-legitimize state power, erode the democratic basis of state authority, undermine the fiscal capacities of the state, and thus destabilize the political system over the long term."[93]

The "revolutionary" character of Russian "shock therapy," which eliminated boundaries between executive and legislative processes and tended toward authoritarian governance by fiat, exemplifies a general feature of what Dick Morris would call a "moderate consensus" occurring at Francis Fukuyama's putative "end of history." In promoting radical steps that disrupt existing norms and practices, programs like "shock therapy" become models of sovereign dictatorship à la Schmitt. It is possible to discern, in the gulf between neoliberalism's lytic agenda and its self-positioning as a non-ideological ideology or naturalized centrist status quo,[94] a kind of haunted, magical element, a long con that presents itself as its own opposite for fun and profit. In an ideologically and culturally unstable, not to mention media-saturated, setting like post-Soviet Russia, the imposition of neoliberal economic reforms created the conditions of possibility for the meme magic of the 2010s and the further haunting of the present by the Soviet past.[95]

WEAPONIZING THE "USABLE PAST" IN THE 1990S AND BEYOND

Putin's conservative project would be unimaginable without its media component and without the specific trajectory Russian media has traveled since 1991. But it would be equally impossible without the element of memory. Since 2000, Putin's suppression of independent media has dovetailed with another longstanding cultural process: the attempt to control cultural memory and speech around the Second World War (or "Great Patriotic War") and the Stalinist terror. Both events have been contested sites of speech and memory since at least 1945, marked by alternating cycles of collective "remembering" and "forgetting." Moments like Khrushchev's "Secret Speech" of 1956, which denounced Stalin's cult of personality and ushered in a brief Thaw, and Gorbachev's glasnost, which allowed the airing of long-suppressed memory of Stalin-era crimes, seemed to herald greater openness and accountability.[96]

Instead, both moments immediately produced new waves of "forgetting."[97] The Khrushchev Thaw was followed by cultural and political "re-freezing" under Brezhnev, while glasnost dissolved first into the relative indifference of the turbulent 1990s, and then into increasingly rigid framings of the Great Patriotic War and Stalin myths starting in the 2000s. Already at the beginning of the 1996 presidential election campaign, Stalin allegedly polled better than Yeltsin.[98] Under Putin, Stalin was increasingly canonized as an "effective manager," a phrase derived from an infamous 2008 school history textbook.[99] Starting in 2011, Eksmo, one of Russia's largest publishing houses, began releasing a series of laudatory popular volumes in the same vein, including *The Great Slandered Leader: Truths and Falsehoods about Stalin* and *Beria: The Best Manager of the Twentieth Century*. For a time, resistance to the falsification of Russia's twentieth-century past prevented the seamless incorporation of these alternative facts into the national consciousness. Particularly important to these efforts was Memorial, a historical society established in 1989, during the most recent period of collective "remembering" (Artifact 00277[r]). Memorial's work aimed not only to honor the memory of victims and survivors, but also to ensure that history never repeat itself.

The reward for Memorial's painstaking, perpetually underfunded labor was a mounting campaign of repression. In 2008, police raided the organization's St. Petersburg offices; by 2015, the government had declared it a "foreign agent," a legal category introduced in 2012 to stigmatize private organizations receiving funding from abroad (in April 2022, the law was expanded to include individuals under "foreign influence," as well as their relatives).[100] In 2016, civil rights activist and historian Yury Dmitriev, head of Memorial in the northwestern region of Karelia and discoverer of a major NKVD mass execution site, was accused of disseminating child pornography, and, later, lewd acts against a minor. He remains incarcerated as of this writing despite the obviously absurd and retaliatory nature of the charges against him and international attention to his case.[101] On December 28, 2021, the day after Dmitriev's prison sentence was extended to fifteen years,[102] Russia's Supreme Court ordered the "liquidation" of Memorial, which it called a "public threat."[103] Even after it was formally dismantled, the organization's members continued to suffer persecution. In March 2023, police raided Memorial's Moscow offices and the homes of several leaders as part of a broader criminal case stemming from charges that Memorial is involved in "rehabilitating Nazism."[104] In retrospect, it is difficult not to read the destruction of Memorial as another incremental step toward Russia's invasion of Ukraine just a few months later. After all, as George Orwell put it, "who controls the past controls the future."

---

[r] https://postsoviet90s.com/artifacts/the-founding-of-the-memorial-society-in-the-late-1980s

In his televised address of February 21, 2022, Putin claimed that "modern Ukraine was entirely created" by "Lenin and his associates."[105] This assertion rested on the distorted memory culture, promoted through the state-controlled media, that his regime had cultivated since its inception. In framing himself as a kind of anti-Lenin, Putin implicitly aligned himself with the recent myth of Stalin as a harsh but fair ruler willing to make difficult choices in the name of maintaining Russia's great-power status and territorial integrity. The totalizing logic and sweep of Putin's geopolitical rhetoric is reflected in his attacks on Russian media since February 2022. The persecution of truth-tellers in Russia is certainly nothing new, but the past decades have seen many innovations in the techniques authorities use to harass, intimidate, and silence. In the 1990s and early 2000s, the stifling of dissent was still relatively decentralized. The prominent assassinations of that era involved individual journalists like Listyev, whose murder was rumored—but never proved—to have been ordered by Berezovsky,[106] or Politkovskaya, whose 2006 assassination remains unsolved to this day.[107]

Later, the technique shifted toward the elimination of specific television programs like the hit political puppet show *Kukly* (*Dolls* or *Puppets*), whose satirical depiction of Putin as a big baby in 1999 reportedly led to its demise three years later (Artifact 00168[s]).[108] Finally, the accelerating repressions of the past few years have lost any sense of anonymity. From the closing of Memorial in December 2021, to the March 2022 deletion of Ekho along with its entire archive, to the excision of Internet platforms like Twitter, Facebook, and Instagram from the Russian public sphere, the Putin regime's post-invasion media suppression has been bold and comprehensive. As Yury Dmitriev put it after his sentencing of December 27, 2021, "It all makes sense. The vertical of power works."[109]

Notes

1 https://tinyurl.com/yhd7u5rw.

2 https://tinyurl.com/2yzcvn8x and https://tinyurl.com/2fjtv6h3.

3 https://tinyurl.com/uavsaz9v.

4 https://tinyurl.com/3kvb68fa.

5 For more on the closure of each media outlet, see: https://tinyurl.com/8m83x5xz; https://tinyurl.com/mrymx9f6; and https://tinyurl.com/4v4ftz6k.

6 For more on the shutdown of each social media platform, see: https://tinyurl.com/4ayr6sm9; https://tinyurl.com/yc64p2wk; and https://tinyurl.com/yc487u4h.

7 According to Datareportal, "Data published in Meta's advertising resources indicates that Facebook had 8.60 million users in Russia in early 2022," while the corresponding figures for Twitter and Instagram were 2.95 and 64 million, respectively (https://datareportal.com/reports/digital-2022-russian-federation). By early 2023, some of these numbers had experienced drastic shifts: although Instagram still had 63.92 million Russian users, Twitter had 767.7 *thousand*. Data on Russian Facebook users in 2023, meanwhile, are inconsistent. (Data on Twitter come from https://datareportal.com/reports/digital-2023-russ

[s] https://postsoviet90s.com/artifacts/kukly-still-from-episode-2-the-old-new-year-01-07-1995-featuring-the-first-appearance-of-boris-yelstin-s-puppet-on-the-show

ian-federation, while data on Instagram are from Statista, https://www.statista.com/statistics/1024741/instagram-users-russia/). For a report on the impact of blocking access to Western social media platforms from early March 2022, see https://novayagazeta.ru/articles/2022/03/12/bolshe-nichego-nelzia.

8 https://tinyurl.com/283utdrs.

9 See Marielle Wijermars and Katja Lehtisaari, "Introduction," in *Freedom of Expression in Russia's New Mediasphere*, ed. Marielle Wijermars and Katja Lehtisaari (Routledge, 2020), 1–14. See also Markku Lonkila, Larisa Shpakovskaya, and Philip Torchinsky, "The Occupation of Runet? The Tightening State Regulation of the Russian-Language Section of the Internet" in the same volume, 17–38.

10 See, for instance, Meduza's coverage of this issue from early in the war against Ukraine: https://meduza.io/en/feature/2022/03/14/the-tv-is-winning.

11 For the invocation of "crisis actors" in Western coverage of the war in Ukraine, see https://tinyurl.com/2uf4j9y8. For more on the idea of Russian war crimes being "staged," see https://www.kp.ru/daily/27374/4567565/ and https://tinyurl.com/ys2xnte3.

12 https://tinyurl.com/z779hh5w.

13 https://tinyurl.com/bdcw4w92.

14 For more on the media dimension of the GKChP's attempted takeover, see Pavel Khazanov's account in this volume, pp. 175–202.

15 For more on the "wild" 1990s in Putin's self-conception as a leader, see "Constructing the Collective Trauma of the 1990s" (chapter 5) in Gulnaz Shafarutdinova, *Red Mirror: Putin's Leadership and Russia's Insecure Identity* (Oxford: Oxford University Press, 2020), 105–32.

16 See, for example, Michael McFaul's speculation in 2000 that Putin might be capable of "lead[ing] Russia out of its chaotic, revolutionary, and anarchic recent past and into a more stable decade of economic growth and political stability" (Carnegie Endowment for International Peace, https://carnegieendowment.org/2000/04/01/russia-s-2000-presidential-elections-implications-for-russian-democracy-and-u.s.-russian-relations-pub-421).. Raymond L. Garthoff, writing for the Brookings Institution in 2000, predicted that Putin would "pursue Russian national interests" without "[pursuing] an anti-Western policy" or "[seeking] to reestablish hegemony over former Soviet republics" ("Putin's Policies Promise Measured Change," https://www.brookings.edu/articles/putins-policies-promise-measured-change/). In 2002, a Kennan Institute report noted that, unlike Yeltsin's policies, Putin's represented "practical approaches" to Russia's "national security interests" ("National Security and Foreign Policy under Putin," https://www.wilsoncenter.org/publication/national-security-and-foreign-policy-under-putin). And as late as 2007, Timothy J. Colton of Harvard University was calling Putin an "effective leader" who might yet steer Russia toward "a more liberal course" ("The Enigmatic Mr. Putin," *Harvard Magazine*, May–June 2007, https://www.harvardmagazine.com/2007/05/the-enigmatic-mr-putin-html).

17 Thanks to Kevin M. F. Platt for his insightful comments on this topic during a guest appearance in my graduate seminar at NYU on November 20, 2023.

18 See, for example, Alessandra Stanley's account of Yeltsin's references to Stalin and Stalinism on the eve of the first round of voting in June 1996 ("The Russian Vote: Election Eve; From Yeltsin, a Reminder of Stalin and Terror," *The New York Times*).

19 Kevin M. F. Platt, "Secret Speech: Wounding, Disavowal, and Social Belonging in the USSR," *Critical Inquiry* 42, no. 3 (March 2016): 647–76.

20 Gavriel D. Rosenfeld, "The Rise of Illiberal Memory," *Memory Studies* 16, no. 4 (2023): 819–36.

21 Nancy Condee, private correspondence of April 2023.

22 https://meduza.io/en/feature/2022/02/24/fantasy-is-not-history.

23 https://www.washingtonpost.com/world/2021/12/28/russia-rights-memorial-liquidated/.

24 See Erin Alpert, "Reinventing Soviet Visual Memory: A Case Study of Marina Goldovskaya's Documentary 'Solovki Power,'" *Studies in Russian and Soviet Cinema* 7, no. 2 (2013): 207–26.

25 The 2011 film recapitulates, in title and content, Goldovskaya's 1991 documentary *A Taste of Freedom*. The earlier film had explored the changes to Russian social life occurring during perestroika, using a young Politkovskaya and her family as a case study.

26 https://novayagazeta.ru/articles/2022/03/21/skonchalas-rezhisser-dokumentalist-marina-goldovskaia-sniavshaia-film-o-zhurnalistke-novoi-anne-politkovskoi-news.

27 On April 7, 2022, a subset of the *Novaya* journalists launched a new publication from Europe, calling it *Novaya Gazeta Europe*. According to *The Moscow Times*, "the editor-in-chief of *Novaya Gazeta Europe*, Kirill Martynov, said that the paper will be independent from Russia's Novaya Gazeta, 'both

legally and in practice.' The newsroom itself will consist of Novaya Gazeta staffers who have chosen to leave Russia." See Irina Shcherbakova, "Novaya Gazeta Launches European Edition in Bid to Dodge Kremlin Censorship." *The Moscow Times*, April 7, 2022. https://www.themoscowtimes.com/2022/04/07/novaya-gazeta-launches-european-edition-in-bid-to-dodge-kremlin-censorship-a77261.

28 https://rb.gy/g46n4.

29 https://www.indexoncensorship.org/2013/12/brief-history-russian-media/.

30 Brian McNair, "Media in Post-Soviet Russia: An Overview," *European Journal of Communication* 9 (1994): 121.

31 For more on the facts and mechanisms of this upward transfer of wealth, see Nobel Prize-winning economist Joseph Stiglitz's 2003 piece for *The Guardian*, "The Ruin of Russia," April 9, 2003, https://www.theguardian.com/world/2003/apr/09/russia.artsandhumanities. For an academic discussion of Putin's "paradoxical" doubling-down on the same neoliberal policy programs enacted under Yeltsin, and the relationship of these programs to authoritarianism, see Ilya Matveev, "State, Capital, and the Transformation of the Neoliberal Policy Paradigm in Putin's Russia," *International Review of Modern Sociology* 45, no. 1 (Spring 2019): 27–48. As Matveev has written more recently elsewhere, since Putin invaded Ukraine, at least one oppositional media outlet has now explicitly connected "the (neo)liberal economic experts working with or in the state apparatus," with "Hjalmar Schacht, a skilled economist and *Reichsminister* of Economics in Nazi Germany in the 1930s." Ilya Matveev, "From the Chicago Boys to Hjalmar Schacht: The Trajectory of the (Neo)Liberal Economic Expertise in Russia," *Problems of Post-Communism* (January 2024): 1.

32 The "Davos Pact" also included Mikhail Khodorkovsky, Vladimir Potanin, Vladimir Vinogradov, Alexander Smolensky, Petr Aven, and Mikhail Fridman. David E. Hoffman, *The Oligarchs: Wealth and Power in the New Russia* (New York: Public Affairs, 2011), 328. As of 2022, Berezovsky and Vinogradov are dead, while Aven and Fridman are under international sanctions. According to *Forbes*, Alexander Smolensky "all but disappeared from view" after 2005. Meanwhile, Khodorkovsky famously spent ten years in prison under Putin and has lived in the West since his 2013 release. Like Berezovsky, Gusinsky was forced into exile soon after Putin came to power, but remains alive, in possession of his fortune, and unaffected by Western sanctions. Finally, Vladimir Potanin is Russia's richest man and as of April 2022 was not subject to Western sanctions except from Canada.

33 Hoffman, *The Oligarchs*, 328.

34 For a comprehensive discussion of "black PR," see chapter 2 in Alena Ledeneva's *How Russia Really Works: The Informal Practices That Shaped Post-Soviet Politics and Business* (Ithaca, NY: Cornell University Press, 2006), 28–57.

35 John Lloyd, "The First Second Election: Russia at the Polls," *The Political Quarterly* 68, no. 1 (1997): 19.

36 https://www.svoboda.org/a/27835237.html.

37 https://rb.gy/5j4v9.

38 For example: "If one were to look for a brief explanation of Yeltsin's electoral success, it probably lies in his campaign's exploitation of fear as an electoral tool. As election campaigns in America have proven, negative campaigning can have a decisive impact when used against parties which occupy the extreme ends of the political spectrum." Erik Depoy, "Boris Yeltsin and the 1996 Russian Presidential Election," *Presidential Studies Quarterly* 26, no. 4 (1996): 1164.

39 Michael Kramer, "Rescuing Boris," *Time*, July 15, 1996.

40 Lloyd, "The First Second Election," 18.

41 In his own book, *Behind the Oval Office: Winning the Presidency in the Nineties* (New York: Random House, 1997), Dick Morris portrayed Dick Dresner as the mind behind Yeltsin's successful re-election campaign (p. 258).

42 Lloyd, "The First Second Election," 18.

43 The piece in question may be found here: https://rb.gy/4g5oe.

44 http://www.compromat.ru/page_12520.htm.

45 According to Dick Morris, Nixon had advised George H. W. Bush that, should Russia revert back to Communism on his watch, Bush could lose his next election. Accordingly, if Morris is to be believed, "Who lost Russia?" became a fixation for Clinton and ensured his heightened interest in the Yeltsin re-election campaign. Morris, *Behind the Oval Office*, 250.

46 Daniel Treisman, "Why Yeltsin Won," *Foreign Affairs* 75, no. 5 (1996): 67.

47 Treisman, "Why Yeltsin Won," 72.

48 Treisman, 72.

49 Andrew Wilson, *Virtual Politics: Faking Democracy in the Post-Soviet World* (New Haven, CT: Yale University Press, 2005), 33.

50 Wilson, *Virtual Politics*, 39.

51 Wilson.

52 For a contemporary take on Morris' resignation, see https://rb.gy/8rh0q.

53 Morris, *Behind the Oval Office*, 40.

54 Morris, 47–8.

55 Morris, 46.

56 George F. Bishop, *The Illusion of Public Opinion: Fact and Artifact in American Public Opinion Polls* (Lanham, MD: Rowman & Littlefield, 2005), xvi.

57 Bishop, *The Illusion of Public Opinion*, 4.

58 Bishop, 143.

59 Kramer, "Rescuing Boris."

60 https://www.svoboda.org/a/27835237.html.

61 Kramer, "Rescuing Boris."

62 Morris, *Behind the Oval Office*, 145.

63 "The move to the center—triangulation—articulated a deeper and broader consensus in America than we have seen for decades" (Morris, xii).

64 Morris, xi.

65 Morris, 11.

66 https://www.svoboda.org/a/27835237.html.

67 Hoffman, *The Oligarchs*, 346.

68 "An astrophysicist by training and rector of the Krasnoyarsk State University, in 1995 [Veniamin] Sokolov was elected chief of the Chamber of Accounts, the only state body independent from the president and his government; its watchdog role is often compared to that of the U.S. General Accounting Office. As head auditor, Sokolov is now Russia's chief controller of the use and disposal of federal property—and an outspoken critic of the Yeltsin government and Western lending." Anne Williamson, "Russia's Fiscal Whistleblower," *Mother Jones*, June 16, 1998, https://www.motherjones.com/politics/1998/06/russias-fiscal-whistleblower/.

69 Veniamin Sokolov, *Programma ekonomicheskikh reform 1995 goda*, 1995, http://www.analysisclub.ru/index.php?page=econom1995&art=1.

70 Sokolov, *Programma ekonomicheskikh reform 1995 goda*.

71 For more on the differences between Yavlinsky's unrealized "500 days" program and Gaidar and Chubais' "shock therapy," see Yavlinsky's 2021 interview in the Italian magazine *Il Mulino* (original here).

72 For instance, in his 1922 essay "On the Russian Peasantry," Gorky expressed the hope that, in the new Soviet state, "the half-savage, stupid, ponderous people of the Russian villages and hamlets…will die out, and a new tribe will take their place." Maxim Gorky, "On the Russian Peasantry," *The Journal of Peasant Studies* 4, no. 1 (1976): 26.

73 Yavlinsky, qtd. in Paul Klebnikov, *Godfather of the Kremlin: Boris Berezovsky and the Looting of Russia* (New York: Harcourt, 2000), 102–3.

74 https://tinyurl.com/bddrk72d.

75 Boym. For Boym's original discussion of "restorative" vs. "reflective nostalgia," see Svetlana Boym, *The Future of Nostalgia* (New York: Basic Books, 2001), xviii–xix. The more general literature on post-Soviet nostalgia is enormous and constantly expanding. A few notable recent sources include: Alexander Etkind, *Warped Mourning: Stories of the Undead in the Land of the Unburied*. Cultural Memory in the Present (Stanford, CA: Stanford University Press, 2013); Otto Boele, Boris Noordenbos, and Ksenia Robbe, eds., *Post-Soviet Nostalgia: Confronting the Empire's Legacies*. Routledge Studies in Cultural History 76 (New York: Routledge/Taylor & Francis Group, 2020); and Kevin M. F. Platt, "Commemorating the End of History: Timelessness and Power in Contemporary Russia," in *Power and Time: Temporalities in Conflict and the Making of History*, edited by Dan Edelstein, Stefanos Geroulanos, and Natasha Wheatley (Chicago: University of Chicago Press, 2020), 400–20.

76 https://tinyurl.com/4x9crecy.

77 David Lewis, *Russia's New Authoritarianism: Putin and the Politics of Order* (Edinburgh: Edinburgh University Press, 2020), 17.

78 Stefan Auer, "Carl Schmitt in the Kremlin: The Ukraine Crisis and the Return of Geopolitics," *International Affairs* 91, no. 5 (2015): 955.

79 William E. Scheuerman, "States of Emergency," in *The Oxford Handbook of Carl Schmitt*, ed. Jens Meierhenrich and Oliver Simons (Oxford: Oxford University Press, 2013), 547–69: 547.

80 Schmitt, qtd. in Meierhenrich and Simons, *The Oxford Handbook of Carl Schmitt*, 35.

81 Schmitt, qtd. in Scheuerman, "States of Emergency," 557.

82 Meierhenrich and Simons, *The Oxford Handbook of Carl Schmitt*, 194.

83 https://tinyurl.com/mrxpx3f6.

84 Lewis, *Russia's New Authoritarianism*, 24.

85 Lewis, 29.

86 For an extensive history of the Yuzhinskii circle, see Marlene Laruelle, "The Iuzhinskii Circle: Far-Right Metaphysics in the Soviet Underground and Its Legacy Today," *The Russian Review* 74, no. 4 (2015): 563–80.

87 Laruelle, "The Iuzhinskii Circle," 2022.

88 For more on the transformation of the Immortal Regiment from a grassroots movement to a state commemoration event, see Anton Weiss-Wendt, *Putin's Russia and the Falsification of History: Reasserting Control over the Past* (New York; London: Bloomsbury Academic, 2020), 103–18.

89 Lewis, *Russia's New Authoritarianism*, 26.

90 Depoy, "Boris Yeltsin and the 1996 Russian Presidential Election," 1146.

91 Depoy, 1155.

92 For more on Schmitt's definition of "sovereign dictatorship," see Scheuerman, 554.

93 https://tinyurl.com/yp5uxb8e.

94 I draw this notion of neoliberal ideology from Mark Fisher's *Capitalist Realism*, which argues that capitalism does not "make an explicit case for [itself] in the way that propaganda does, but to conceal the fact that the operations of capital do not depend on any sort of subjectively assumed belief. It is impossible to conceive of fascism or Stalinism without propaganda—but capitalism can proceed perfectly well, in some ways better, without anyone making a case for it." Mark Fisher, *Capitalist Realism: Is There No Alternative*? (Winchester: Zero Books, 2009), 12–13.

95 For more on "meme magic," see Marc Tuters, "LARPing and Liberal Tears: Irony, Belief and Idiocy in the Deep Vernacular Web," in Maik Fielitz and Nick Thurston, eds., *Post-Digital Cultures of the Far Right: Online Actions and Offline Consequences in Europe and the US* (Bielefeld: Transcript, 2019), 37–48.

96 For more on the mnemonic functions of the Secret Speech in Soviet society after Stalin, see Platt, "Secret Speech."

97 As Kevin Platt writes, compared to the period of the Thaw, the 1980s and 1990s "brought more far-reaching, but ultimately comparable episodes of controlled exhumation of the Soviet history of collective trauma, followed by hasty reburial." Platt, "Secret Speech," 656.

98 https://tinyurl.com/3whu7dft.

99 https://tinyurl.com/bdz48eap.

100 https://tinyurl.com/yc6brk6r.

101 For more on the case against Yuri Dmitriev up to about 2020, see Weiss-Wendt, *Putin's Russia and the Falsification of History*, 225–29.

102 https://tinyurl.com/2ezuakdz.

103 https://tinyurl.com/5we72zpk.

104 For more on this episode, see https://tinyurl.com/28f96p7e.

105 http://en.kremlin.ru/events/president/news/67828.

106 https://tinyurl.com/2s3a2nwu.

107 https://www.rferl.org/a/russia-politkovskaya-murder-putin/31496138.html.

108 https://allthatsinteresting.com/vladimir-putin-satire/4.

109 https://tinyurl.com/mbxxsnd7. For more on the concept of "vertical of power," see Vladimir Gel'man and Sergei Ryzhenkov, "Local Regimes, Sub-National Governance, and the 'Power Vertical' in Contemporary Russia," *Europe-Asia Studies* 63, no. 3 (May 2011): 449–65.

Works Cited

Alpert, Erin. "Reinventing Soviet Visual Memory: A Case Study of Marina Goldovskaya's Documentary 'Solovki Power.'" *Studies in Russian and Soviet Cinema* 7, no. 2 (2013): 207–26.

Auer, Stefan. "Carl Schmitt in the Kremlin: The Ukraine Crisis and the Return of Geopolitics." *International Affairs* 91, no. 5 (2015): 953–68.

Bishop, George F. *The Illusion of Public Opinion: Fact and Artifact in American Public Opinion Polls.* Lanham, MD: Rowman & Littlefield, 2005.

Boele, Otto, Boris Noordenbos, and Ksenia Robbe, eds. *Post-Soviet Nostalgia: Confronting the Empire's Legacies.* Routledge Studies in Cultural History 76. New York: Routledge/Taylor & Francis Group, 2020.

Boycko, Maksim, Andrei Shleifer, and Robert Vishny. *Privatizing Russia.* 3. print. Cambridge, MA: MIT Press, 1997.

Boym, Svetlana. *The Future of Nostalgia.* New York: Basic Books, 2001.

Colton, Timothy. "The Enigmatic Mr. Putin." *Harvard Magazine,* June 2007. https://www.harvardmagazine.com/2007/05/the-enigmatic-mr-putin-html.

Crabtree, Lauren. "National Security and Foreign Policy under Putin." Wilson Center Insight and Analysis (blog), 2002. https://www.wilsoncenter.org/publication/national-security-and-foreign-policy-under-putin.

Depoy, Erik. "Boris Yeltsin and the 1996 Russian Presidential Election." *Presidential Studies Quarterly* 26, no. 4 (1996): 1140–64.

Etkind, Alexander. *Warped Mourning: Stories of the Undead in the Land of the Unburied.* Cultural Memory in the Present. Stanford, CA: Stanford University Press, 2013.

Fisher, Mark. *Capitalist Realism: Is There No Alternative?* Winchester: Zero Books, 2009.

Garthoff, Raymond L. "Putin's Policies Promise Measured Change." Brookings Institution (blog), April 2, 2000. https://www.brookings.edu/articles/putins-policies-promise-measured-change/.

Gel'man, Vladimir, and Sergei Ryzhenkov. "Local Regimes, Sub-National Governance, and the 'Power Vertical' in Contemporary Russia." *Europe-Asia Studies* 63, no. 3 (2011): 449–65.

Gorky, Maxim. "On the Russian Peasantry." *The Journal of Peasant Studies* 4, no. 1 (1976): 11–27.

Hoffman, David E. *The Oligarchs: Wealth and Power in the New Russia.* New York: Public Affairs, 2011.

Igo, Sarah Elizabeth. *The Averaged American: Surveys, Citizens, and Making of Mass Public.* Cambridge, MA: Harvard University Press, 2008.

Khvostunova, Olga. "A Complete Guide to Who Controls the Russian News Media." Index on Censorship, 2013. https://www.indexoncensorship.org/2013/12/brief-history-russian-media/.

Klebnikov, Paul. *Godfather of the Kremlin: Boris Berezovsky and the Looting of Russia.* New York: Harcourt, 2000.

Kramer, Michael. "Rescuing Boris." *Time Magazine,* July 15, 1996.

Laruelle, Marlene. "The Iuzhinskii Circle: Far-Right Metaphysics in the Soviet Underground and Its Legacy Today." *The Russian Review* 74, no. 4 (2015): 563–80.

Laruelle, Marlene. "The Intellectual Origins of Putin's Invasion." *UnHerd,* March 16, 2022. https://unherd.com/2022/03/the-brains-behind-the-russian-invasion/.

Ledeneva, Alena. "Chernyi Piar: Manipulative Campaigning and the Workings of Russian Democracy." In *How Russia Really Works: The Informal Practices That Shaped Post-Soviet Politics and Business,* 28–57. Ithaca, NY: Cornell University Press, 2006.

Lewis, David. *Russia's New Authoritarianism: Putin and the Politics of Order.* Edinburgh: Edinburgh University Press, 2020.

Lloyd, John. "The First Second Election: Russia at the Polls." *The Political Quarterly* 68, no. 1 (1997): 9–22.

Lonkila, Markku, Larisa Shpakovskaya, and Philip Torchinsky. "The Occupation of Runet? The Tightening State Regulation of the Russian-Language Section of the Internet." In *Freedom of Expression in Russia's New Mediasphere,* edited by Marielle Wijermars and Katja Lehtisaari, 17–38. New York: Routledge, Taylor & Francis Group, 2020.

Matveev, Ilya. "State, Capital, and the Transformation of the Neoliberal Policy Paradigm in Putin's Russia." *International Review of Modern Sociology* 458, no. 1, Special Issue on the Crisis of Neoliberalism and the Rise of Authoritarianism in the Early 21st Century (2019): 27–48.

Matveev, Ilya. "From the Chicago Boys to Hjalmar Schacht: The Trajectory of the (Neo)Liberal Economic Expertise in Russia." *Problems of Post-Communism* (January 2024), 1–10.

McFaul, Michael. "Testimony before the US Senate Committee on Foreign Relations." Washington, D.C., April 12, 2000. https://carnegieendowment.org/posts/2000/04/russias-2000-presidential-elections-implications-for-russian-democracy-and-us-russian-relations?lang=en.

McNair, Brian. "Media in Post-Soviet Russia: An Overview." *European Journal of Communication* 9 (1994): 115–35.

Meierhenrich, Jens, and Oliver Simons, eds. *The Oxford Handbook of Carl Schmitt*. Oxford: Oxford University Press, 2013.

Morris, Dick. *Behind the Oval Office: Winning the Presidency in the Nineties*. New York: Random House, 1997.

Platt, Kevin M. F. "Secret Speech: Wounding, Disavowal, and Social Belonging in the USSR." *Critical Inquiry* 42, no. 3 (2016): 647–76.

Platt, Kevin M. F. "Commemorating the End of History: Timelessness and Power in Contemporary Russia." In *Power and Time: Temporalities in Conflict and the Making of History*, edited by Dan Edelstein, Stefanos Geroulanos, and Natasha Wheatley, 400–20. Chicago: University of Chicago Press, 2020.

Rosenfeld, Gavriel D. "The Rise of Illiberal Memory." *Memory Studies* 16, no. 4 (2023): 819–36.

Sharafutdinova, Gulnaz. *The Red Mirror: Putin's Leadership and Russia's Insecure Identity*. New York: Oxford University Press, 2020.

Scheuerman, William E. "States of Emergency." In The Oxford Handbook of Carl Schmitt, edited by Jens Meierhenrich and Oliver Simons, 547–69. Oxford: Oxford University Press, 2013.

Shcherbakova, Irina. "Novaya Gazeta Launches European Edition in Bid to Dodge Kremlin Censorship." The Moscow Times, April 7, 2022. https://www.themoscowtimes.com/2022/04/07/novaya-gazeta-launches-european-edition-in-bid-to-dodge-kremlin-censorship-a77261.

Sokolov, Veniamin. *Programma ekonomicheskikh reform 1995 goda*. 1995. http://www.analysisclub.ru/index.php?page=econom1995&art=1.

Stanley, Alessandra. "The Russian Vote: Election Eve; From Yeltsin, A Reminder Of Stalin And Terror." *New York Times*, June 16, 1996, sec. 1. https://www.nytimes.com/1996/06/16/world/the-russian-vote-election-eve-from-yeltsin-a-reminder-of-stalin-and-terror.html.

Stiglitz, Joseph. "The Ruin of Russia." *The Guardian*, April 9, 2003. https://www.theguardian.com/world/2003/apr/09/russia.artsandhumanities.

Treisman, Daniel. "Why Yeltsin Won." *Foreign Affairs* 75, no. 5 (1996): 64–77.

Weiss-Wendt, Anton. *Putin's Russia and the Falsification of History: Reasserting Control over the Past*. New York; London: Bloomsbury Academic, 2020.

Wijermars, Marielle, and Katja Lehtisaari. "Introduction." In *Freedom of Expression in Russia's New Mediasphere*, edited by Marielle Wijermars and Katja Lehtisaari, 1–14. New York: Routledge, Taylor & Francis Group, 2020.

Williamson, Anne. "Russia's Fiscal Whistleblower." *Mother Jones*, June 16, 1998. https://www.motherjones.com/politics/1998/06/russias-fiscal-whistleblower/.

Wilson, Andrew. *Virtual Politics: Faking Democracy in the Post-Soviet World*. New Haven, CT: Yale University Press, 2005.

Yavlinsky, Grigory. L'economista della perestrojka (In Russian: "Ot reform 1990–x k kapitalizmu: Rossiia za 30 let"). Interview by Martina Napolitano. *Il Mulino*, December 17, 2021. https://www.rivistailmulino.it/a/intervista-a-grigorij-javlinskij. In Russian: https://www.yavlinsky.ru/article/ot-reform-1990-h-k-goskapitalizmu-rossiya-za-30-let/.

Selected Volume Bibliography

Alpert, Erin. "Reinventing Soviet Visual Memory: A Case Study of Marina Goldovskaya's Documentary 'Solovki Power.'" *Studies in Russian and Soviet Cinema* 7, no. 2 (2013): 207–26.

Andreeva, Nina. "I Cannot Forsake My Principles." *Sovetskaia Rossiia*, no. 60 (March 13, 1988).

Anemone, Tony. "About Killers, Freaks, and Real Men: The Vigilante Hero of Aleksei Balabanov's Films." In *Insiders and Outsiders in Russian Cinema*, edited by Stephen Norris and Zara Trolone, 127–41. Bloomington: Indiana University Press, 2008.

Arutunyan, Anna. *The Media in Russia*. Berkshire: Open University Press, 2009.

Astakhova, Anastasiia. "Raskryto mesto sluzhby Vacio posle aresta." *Lenta.ru*. January 16, 2024. https://lenta.ru/news/2024/01/16/raskryto-mesto-sluzhby-repera-vacio-posle-aresta/

Auer, Stefan. "Carl Schmitt in the Kremlin: The Ukraine Crisis and the Return of Geopolitics." *International Affairs* 91, no. 5 (2015): 953–68.

Avchenko, Vasily. *Teoriia i praktika politicheskikh manipuliatsyi v sovremennoi Rossii*. http://psyfactor.org/polman3.htm.

Baker, Adele Marie, ed. *Consuming Russia: Popular Culture, Sex, and Society since Gorbachev*. Durham, NC: Duke University Press, 1999.

Bakich, Olga. *Valerii Pereleshin: Life of a Silkworm*. Toronto: University of Toronto Press, 2015.

Barabanov, Boris. *ASSA: Kniga Peremen*. St. Petersburg: Amfora, 2008.

Belekhov, Leonid. "Gazeta, kotoraia tak nikomu i ne poklonilas'." *Sovsekretno.ru*. https://www.sovsekretno.ru/history/.

Benn, David Wedgewood. "The Russian Media in Post-Soviet Conditions." *Europe-Asia Studies* 48, no. 3 (1996): 471–79.

"Berberova, Nina. Mal'klo'm Braun, Simon Karlinskiy. "Peresmotr versii samoubiystva Chaykovskogo: Oproverzheniye." *Gay Slavyane* 1 (1993): 6-8" should instead be "Berberova, Nina. Mal'klo'm Braun, Simon Karlinskii. "Peresmotr versii samoubiistva Chaikovskogo: Oproverzhenie." *Gay, Slaviane!* 1 (1993): 6–8".

Berdiaev, Nikolai. "O russkom natsional'nom soznanii." *Sovershenno sekretno* 3 (December 1989): 14–15.

Beumers, Birgit. "Waiting for Change: Sergei Solov'ev and the Dreams of the Young Generation." In *Ruptures and Continuities in Soviet/Russian Cinema*, edited by Birgit Beumers and Eugenie Zvonkine, 51–68. London: Routledge, 2017.

Bishop, George F. *The Illusion of Public Opinion: Fact and Artifact in American Public Opinion Polls*. Lanham, MD: Rowman & Littlefield, 2005.

Bobrinskaia, Ekaterina. *Chuzhie? Neofitsial'noe iskusstvo: mify, strategii, kontseptsii* [*Others? Unofficial Art: Myths, Strategies, Concepts*]. Moscow: Shalva Breus, 2012.

Boele, Otto, Boris Noordenbos, and Ksenia Robbe, eds. *Post-Soviet Nostalgia: Confronting the Empire's Legacies*. Routledge Studies in Cultural History 76. New York: Routledge/Taylor & Francis Group, 2020.

Borenstein, Eliot. *Overkill: Sex and Violence in Contemporary Russian Popular Culture*. Ithaca, NY: Cornell University Press, 2007.

Borenstein, Eliot. *Plots against Russia: Conspiracy and Fantasy after Socialism*. Ithaca, NY: Cornell University Press, 2019.

Borenstein, Eliot. *Soviet Self-Hatred: The Secret Identities of Postsocialism in Contemporary Russia*. Ithaca, NY: Cornell University Press, 2023.

Boycko, Maksim, Andrei Shleifer, and Robert Vishny. *Privatizing Russia*. 3. print. Cambridge, MA: MIT Press, 1997.

Boym, Svetlana. *The Future of Nostalgia*. New York: Basic Books, 2001.

Brock, Maria, and Galina Miazhevich. "From High Camp to Post-Modern Camp: Queering Post-Soviet Pop Music." *European Journal of Cultural Studies* 25, no. 4 (2022): 993–1009.
Broido, A. "'Sviatoi' apostol Oleg." *Argumenty i Fakty* 9, no. 20 (April 17, 2003): 18–19.
Brown, Archie. *Seven Years That Changed the World*. New York: Oxford University Press, 2007.
Budraitskis, Ilya. *Dissidents among Dissidents: Ideology, Politics and the Left in Post-Soviet Russia*. New York; London: Verso, 2022.
Bykov, Dmitry. "Osnovnye tendentsii SMI v 1987 godu." *Novyi vzgliad* 34 (December 27, 1997).
Campbell, Thomas. "Homosexuality as Device: Necrorealism and Neoacademism." *In Russian Art in Translation*, edited by Nicholas Herman, Eugene Raikhel, and Elena Sorokina. Brooklyn, NY: Ante, 2007: 68–79..
Cassiday, Julie A. "Post-Soviet Pop Goes Gay: Russia's Trajectory to Eurovision Victory." *Russian Review* 73, no. 1 (2014): 1–23.
Cassiday, Julie A. "Vladislav Mamyshev-Monroe, Frog-Princess of Neoacademism." *Russian Review* 78, no. 2 (2019): 221–44.
Cassiday, Julie A., Helena Goscilo, and Jonathan Brooks Platt. "Introduction: The Allure of Retro: Neoacademism after the Fall." *Russian Review* 78, no. 2 (2019): 183–200.
Chebankova, Elena. "The State and the Public Sphere in Russia." *Demokratizatsiya* 19, no. 4 (2011): 317–41.
Clover, Charles. *Black Wind, White Snow: The Rise of Russia's New Nationalism*. New Haven, CT: Yale University Press, 2016.
Coe, Steven. "Struggles for Authority in the NEP Village: The Early Rural Correspondents Movement, 1923–1927." *Europe-Asia Studies* 48, no. 7 (November 1996): 1151–71.
Colton, Timothy. "The Enigmatic Mr. Putin." *Harvard Magazine*, June 2007. https://www.harvardmagazine.com/2007/05/the-enigmatic-mr-putin-html.
Condee, Nancy. *The Imperial Trace: Recent Russian Cinema*. Oxford: Oxford University Press, 2009.
Cunningham, Ed. "Meet Oxxymiron, the Russian Rapper Railing against Putin's Regime." *TimeOut*. March 17, 2022. Accessed January 16, 2024. https://www.timeout.com/news/meet-oxxxymiron-the-russian-rapper-railing-against-putins-regime-031722.
Davies, R. W. *Soviet History in the Gorbachev Revolution*. Bloomington: Indiana University Press, 1989.
Denisova, Anastasia. "Democracy, Protest and Public Sphere in Russia after the 2011–2012 Anti-Government Protests: Digital Media at Stake." *Media, Culture, and Society* 1, no. 19 (2016): 1–19.
Depoy, Erik. "Boris Yeltsin and the 1996 Russian Presidential Election." *Presidential Studies Quarterly* 26, no. 4 (Fall 1996): 1140–64.
Dobrenko, Evgeny. *Late Stalinism: The Aesthetics of Politics*. Translated by Jesse M. Savage. New Haven, CT: Yale University Press, 2020.
Dobson, Miriam. *Khrushchev's Cold Summer: Gulag Returnees, Crime, and the Fate of Reform after Stalin*. Ithaca, NY: Cornell University Press, 2009.
Dodolev, Evgenii. "Belyi tanets, istoriia samoi gromkoi stat'i o prostitutkakh." *Moskovskii komsomolets*, December 3, 2019. https://www.mk.ru/social/2019/12/03/belyy-tanec-istoriya-samoy-gromkoy-stati-o-prostitutkakh.html.
Dodolev, Evgenii. *Limoniana, ili neizvestnyi Limonov*. Moscow: Zebra-E, 2012.
Dodolev, Evgenii. *Vzgliad*. Moscow: Alistorus, 2013.
Doktorov, Boris. "B.A. Grushin. Chetyre desiatiletiia izucheniia rossiiskogo obshchestvennogo mneniia." *Gefter.ru*. December 2, 2015. Accessed December 15, 2022. http://gefter.ru/archive/16807.
Doucette, Courtney. "Glasnost in the Mailroom: The Soviet Subject in Gorbachev's Perestroika, 1985–1988." *The Soviet and Post-Soviet Review* 48 (2021): 171–88.
Dubin, Boris. "Chtenie i obshchestvo v Rossii." *Novyi mir* 3 (1993): 32–35.
Dubin, Boris. "Chto chitaiut rossiiane?" *Knizhnoe obozrenie* 11 (March 15, 1994): 26.
Dubin, Boris. "Ideologiia besstrukturnosti: Intelligentsiia i konets sovetskoi epokhi." *Znamia* 11 (1994): 166–79.
Dubin, Boris. "Ispytanie na sostoiatel'nost': Sotsiologicheskaia poetika russkogo romana-boevika." *Novoe literaturnoe obozrenie* 22 (1996): 252–74.
Dubin, Boris. "The Action Thriller (Boevik) in Contemporary Russia." In *Reading for Entertainment in Contemporary Russia: Post-Soviet Popular Literature in Historical Perspective*, edited by Stephen Lovell and Birgit Menzel, 101–16. Munich: Verlag Otto Sagner, 2005.
Dubin, Boris. "Uspekh po-russki." *Monitoring obshchestvennogo mneniia* 5, no. 37 (September–October 1998).

Dubin, Boris, and Lev Gudkov. *Literatura kak sotsial'nyi institut.* Moscow: Novoe literaturnoe obozrenie, 1994.

Dudinskii, Igor. "Bul'varnaia pressa i natsional'naia ideia." *Zavtra*, August 7, 2000. [Interview with Igor Dudinsky conducted by Liudmila Serova].

Dudinskii, Igor. "Desiat' dnei v ob"iat'iakh ved'my: Ira Trubina iz bezymiannoi mogily prishla v odnu iz moskovskikh kvartir." *Megapolis-ekspress* 17, no. 244 (April 26, 1995): 12.

Dugin, Aleksandr. "Gi Debor mertv. Spektakl' prodolzhaetsia." *Limonka* 14 (May 1995).

Dugin, Aleksandr. "Novye protiv starykh." *Limonka* 1 (November 1994).

Eklof, Ben. *Soviet Briefing: Gorbachev and the Reform Period.* Boulder, CO: Westview Press, 1989.

Essig, Laurie. *Queer in Russia: A Story of Sex, Self, and the Other.* Durham, NC: Duke University Press, 1999.

Est' takia bukva, dir. Tat'iana Dmitrakova and Aleksandr Valeev (*ViD*, 2015). https://www.youtube.com/watch?v=lvFB_GZCzpE.

Etkind, Alexander. "The Decay of the Russian Public Sphere." *Current History* 114, no. 774 (2015): 278–81.

Etkind, Alexander. *Warped Mourning: Stories of the Undead in the Land of the Unburied.* Cultural Memory in the Present. Stanford, CA: Stanford University Press, 2013.

Evans, Christine. *Between Truth and Time: A History of Soviet Central Television.* New Haven, CT: Yale University Press, 2016.

Fainberg, Dina. *Cold War Correspondents: Soviet and American Reporters on the Ideological Front Lines.* Baltimore, MD: Johns Hopkins University Press, 2021.

Federal'nyi zakon. "O zashchite detei ot informatsii, prichiniaiushchei vred ikh zdorov'iu i razvitiiu." Stat'ia 6.21. Propaganda netraditsionnykh seksual'nykh otnoshenii sredi nesovershennoletnikh.

Fenghi, Fabrizio. *It Will Be Fun and Terrifying: Nationalism and Protest in Post-Soviet Russia.* Madison: University of Wisconsin Press, 2020.

Firsov, Boris. *Istoriia sovetskoi sotsiologii. 1950-e–1980-e gody.* St. Petersburg: Iz-stvo Evropeiskogo universiteta, 2012.

Fisher, Mark. *Capitalist Realism: Is There No Alternative?* Winchester: Zero Books, 2009.

Foltynova, Kristyna. "The Day the Russian White House Was Shelled." *RussiaFreeEurope/ RadioLiberty.* October 4, 2019. https://rb.gy/hogvs.

Freidin, Gregory, and Victoria Bonnell. "Televorot: The Role of Television Coverage in Russia's August 1991 Coup." *Slavic Review* 52, no. 4 (1993): 810–38.

Fürst, Juliana. "In Search of Soviet Salvation: Young People Write to the Stalinist Authorities." *Contemporary European History* 15, no. 3 (August 2006): 327–45.

Fürst, Juliana. *Flowers through Concrete: Explorations in Soviet Hippieland.* Oxford: Oxford University Press, 2021.

Gabowitsch, Mischa. "Fascism as Stiob." *Kultura* 4 (December 2009).

Gallup, George, and Saul Forbes Rae. *The Pulse of Democracy: The Public-Opinion Poll and How It Works.* New York: Simon and Schuster, 1940.

Gel'man, Vladimir, and Sergei Ryzhenkov. "Local Regimes, Sub-National Governance, and the 'Power Vertical' in Contemporary Russia." *Europe-Asia Studies* 63, no. 3 (May 2011): 449–65.

Gessen, Masha. "Elena Bonner: Men'she vsego na svete menia interesuet eta problema." *Tema* 2–3 (1992): 9.

Gessen, Masha. "How Russia's Hilarious, Homoerotic 'Satisfaction' Became a Nationwide Meme of Solidarity." *The New Yorker*, January 22, 2018. https://www.newyorker.com/news/our-columnists/how-russias-hilarious-homoerotic-satisfaction-became-a-nationwide-meme-of-solidarity.

Gessen, Masha. "Masha Gessen and David Remnick on Putin." Interview with David Remnick. *The Vault*, 2014. https://newbooksnetwork.com/masha-gessen-and-david-remnick-on-putin.

Gessen, Masha. "Moscow Activists Push for Gay *Glasnost*." *The Advocate* 566 (1990): 50–51.

Gessen, Masha. *Dead Again: The Russian Intelligentsia after Communism.* London: Verso, 1997.

Gessen, Masha. *Surviving Autocracy.* New York: Riverhead Books, 2020.

Gessen, Masha. *The Future Is History: How Totalitarianism Reclaimed Russia.* New York: Riverhead Books, 2017.

Glukhov, Dmitrii. "Anatoly Gunitsky: 'Rok-klub byl gosudarstvom v gosudarstve so svoim mikroklimatom." *RokKul't*, December 10, 2021. Accessed October 22, 2024. https://rockcult.ru/interview/gunitskiy-2021/.

Golov, Aleksandr, and Orkhan Jemal. "Za chto razgoniaiut VTsIOM." *Novaia gazeta*, August 14, 2003. Accessed July 15, 2023. https://novayagazeta.ru/articles/2003/08/14/17565-za-chto-razgonyayut-vtsiom.

Gorham, Michael S. *After Newspeak: Language Culture and Politics in Russia from Gorbachev to Putin*. Ithaca, NY: Cornell University Press, 2014.

Gorky, Maxim. "On the Russian Peasantry." *The Journal of Peasant Studies* 4, no. 1 (October 1976): 11–27.

Gorshkov, Boris. "Democratizing Habermas: Peasant Public Sphere in Pre-Reform Russia." *Russian History* 31, no. 4 (Winter 2004): 373–95.

Gorski, Bradley A. "Bestseller, or the Cultural Logic of Postsocialism." *Slavic Review* 79, no. 3 (Fall 2020): 613–35.

Goscilo, Helena, ed. *Putin as Celebrity and Cultural Icon*. New York: Routledge, 2013.

Goscilo, Helena. "Style and S(t)Imulation: Popular Magazines, or the Aestheticization of Postsoviet Russia." *Russian Culture of the 1990s, Special Issue of Studies in 20th Century Literature* 24, no. 1 (2000): 15–50.

Goscilo, Helena. *Dehexing Sex: Russian Womanhood during and after Glasnost*. Ann Arbor: University of Michigan Press, 1996.

Grois, Boris, *Utopiia i obmen* [*Utopia and Exchange*]. Moscow: Znak, 1993.

Gudkov, Lev, and Boris Dubin, eds. *Obshchestvennyi razlom i rozhdenie novoi sotsiologii. Dvadtsat' let monitoringa*. Moscow: Novoe izdatel'stvo, 2008.

Gudkov, Lev. Personal interview. Zoom. August 26, 2022.

Guriev, Sergei, and Daniel Triesman. *Spin Dictators: The Changing Face of Tyranny in the 21st Century*. Princeton, NJ: Princeton University Press, 2022.

Hanukai, Maksim. "Russian Actionism as Biopolitical Performance: Shifting Grounds and Forms of Resistance." *Russian Literature* 141 (2023): 111–42.

Hegel, G. W. F. *Phenomenology of Spirit*. Translated by A. V. Miller. Oxford: Oxford University Press, 1977.

Hemment, Julie. "Satirical Strikes and Deadpanning Diplomats: Stiob as Geopolitical Performance in Russia–US Relations." *PoLAR: Political and Legal Anthropology Review* 45, no. 2 (2022): 201–23.

Hemment, Julie. *Youth Politics in Putin's Russia: Producing Patriots and Entrepreneurs*. Bloomington: Indiana University Press, 2015.

Hicks, Jeremy. "Worker Correspondents: Between Journalism and Literature." *The Russian Review* 66, no. 4 (October 2007): 568–85.

Hoffman, David E. *The Oligarchs: Wealth and Power in the New Russia*. New York: Public Affairs, 2011.

Humphrey, Caroline. *The Unmaking of Soviet Life: Everyday Economies after Socialism*. Culture and Society after Socialism. Ithaca, NY: Cornell University Press, 2002.

Hunter-Tinley, Ludovic. "Russian Rock Star Boris Grebenshikov: 'Millions Are Afraid to Think, Afraid to Speak Out.'" *Financial Times*, September 16, 2023. Accessed January 18, 2024. https://www.ft.com/content/ef51acbd-cbbc-45eb-80b6-f5794d7486be.

Huxtable, Simon. *News from Moscow: Soviet Journalism and the Limits of Postwar Reform*. Oxford: Oxford University Press, 2022.

Igo, Sarah Elizabeth. *The Averaged American: Surveys, Citizens, and Making of Mass Public*. Cambridge, MA: Harvard University Press, 2008.

Inkeles, Alex. "Critical Letters to the Soviet Press: Social Characteristics and Interrelations of Critics and the Criticized." *American Sociological Review* 18, no. 1 (1953): 12–22.

Inkeles, Alex, and Kent Geiger. "Critical Letters to the Soviet Press: Areas and Modes of Complaint." *American Sociological Review* 17, no. 6 (1952): 694–703.

Iser, Wolfgang. *The Implied Reader: Patterns of Communication in Prose Fiction from Bunyan to Beckett*. Baltimore: Johns Hopkins University Press, 1974.

Iurlov, Boris. "Dve zhizni, dve sud'by." 1/9: *literaturnoe prilozhenie k gazete* 1/10, no. 2 (1992): 2–7, 3–8.

Jackson, Matthew Jesse. *The Experimental Group: Ilya Kabakov, Moscow Conceptualism, Soviet Avant-Gardes*. Chicago: University of Chicago Press, 2010.

Jauss, Hans Robert, and Elizabeth Benzinger. "Literary History as a Challenge to Literary Theory." *New Literary History* 2, no. 1 (Autumn 1970): 7–37.

Johnson, Juliet. *A Fistful of Rubles: The Rise and Fall of the Russian Banking System*. Ithaca, NY: Cornell University Press, 2000.

Jones, Polly. *Myth, Memory, Trauma: Rethinking the Stalinist Past in the Soviet Union, 1953–70*. New Haven, CT: Yale University Press, 2013.

Jones, Polly. *Revolution Rekindled: The Writers and Readers of Late Soviet Biography*. Oxford: Oxford University Press, 2019.

Jonson, Lena. "Introduction." In *Russia—Art Resistance and the Conservative-Authoritarian Zeitgeist*, 1–25. London: Routledge, 2018.

Karlinskii, Simon. "Gomoseksualizm v russkoi istorii i kul'ture." *Tema: izdanie Assotsiatsii seksual'nykh men'shinstv* 2. Wien: Wiener Slawistischer Almanach, 1999.

Kalinsky, Yelena, ed., trans. *Collective Actions: Audience Recollections from the First Five Years, 1976–1981*. Chicago: Soberscove Press, 2012.

Kan, Aleksandr. *Kurekhin: Shkiper o kapitane*. St. Petersburg: Amfora, 2012.

Kapustsinskii, Ryshard. "Usazhivaias' za party…" *Sovershenno sekretno* 1 (June 1989), 5.

Karlinskiy, Simon. "Gomoseksualizm v russkoy istorii i kul'ture." *Tema: izdaniye Assotsiatsii seksual'nykh men'shinstv* 2 (1991): 1–3.

Karlinsky, Simon. "A Hidden Masterpiece: Valery Pereleshin's *Ariel*." *Christopher Street* 2, no. 6 (December 1977): 37–42.

Karlinsky, Simon. *A Difficult Soul: Zinaida Gippius*. Berkeley: University of California Press, 1980.

Karlinsky, Simon. *Marina Cvetaeva: Her Life and Art*. Berkeley: University of California Press, 1966.

Karlinsky, Simon. *The Sexual Labyrinth of Nikolai Gogol*. Cambridge, MA: Harvard University Press, 1976.

Kharkhordin, Oleg. *The Collective and the Individual in Russia: A Study of Practices*. Berkeley: University of California Press, 1999.

Khazanov, Pavel. "A Petrovich Inside of Every New Russian: The Disciplinary Regime of the Capitalist 'Vanguard Group' at 1990s *Kommersant*." *Russian Review* 82 (2023): 470–85.

Khazanov, Pavel. "Honest Jacobins: High Stalinism and the Socialist Subjectivity of Mikhail Lifshitz and Andrei Platonov." *Russian Review* 77, no. 4 (2018): 576–601.

Khazanov, Pavel. "Vladimir Sappak's Humanism on Soviet TV." *EUI Max Weber Working Papers* 4 (2018). https://cadmus.eui.eu/handle/1814/56744.

Khazanov, Pavel. *The Russia That We Have Lost: Pre-Soviet Past as Anti-Soviet Discourse*. Madison: Wisconsin University Press, 2023.

Khronika "Memoriala." https://www.memo.ru/ru-ru/memorial/history/.

Khvostunova, Olga. "A Complete Guide to Who Controls the Russian News Media." Index on Censorship, December 9, 2013. https://www.indexoncensorship.org/2013/12/brief-history-russian-media/.

Klebnikov, Paul. *Godfather of the Kremlin: Boris Berezovsky and the Looting of Russia*. New York: Harcourt, 2000.

Komaromi, Ann. "The Material Existence of Samizdat." *Slavic Review* 36, no. 3 (2004): 597–618.

Komaromi, Ann. *Uncensored: Samizdat Novels and the Quest for Autonomy in Soviet Dissidence*. Evanston, IL: Northwestern University Press, 2015.

Kotkin, Stephen. *Armageddon Averted: The Soviet Collapse, 1970–2000*. New York: Oxford University Press, 2008.

Kovalev, Andrei, ed. *Rossiiskii Aktsionizm 1990–2000* [*Russian Actionism 1990–2000*]. Moscow: World Art Museum (#28–29), 2007.

Kozlov, Denis. *The Readers of Novyi Mir: Coming to Terms with the Stalinist Past*. Cambridge, MA: Harvard University Press, 2013.

Kramer, Michael. "Rescuing Boris." *Time Magazine*, July 15, 1996.

Kuchkina, Ol'ga. "Kto snimaet PENKina. Telenedelia." *Komsomol'skaia pravda*, May 24, 1994.

Kukulin, Ilya. "Cultural Shifts in Russia since 2010: Messianic Cynicism and Paradigms of Artistic Resistance." *Russian Literature* 96–98 (February–May 2018): 221–54.

Kukulin, Ilya. "Longing for Fear and Darkness: 'Oppositional Grassroots Stalinism' of the 1970s–1980s and Its Influence on Legitimizing Political Elites in Today's Russia." In *Post-Soviet Nostalgia: Confronting the Empire's Legacies*, edited by Otto Boele, Boris Noordenbos, and Ksenia Robbe, 89–114. New York: Routledge, 2019.

Kulikovskaia, Galina. "Obratnogo khoda net." *Ogonëk* 23 (1987): 18–20.

Kushnir, Aleksandr. *Sergei Kurekhin: Bezumnaia mekhanika russkogo roka*. Moscow: Berstel'man Media Moscau, 2013.

Kushnir, Aleksandr. *Zolotoe podpol'e: polnaia illiustrirovannaia entsiklopediia rok-samizdata*, 1967–1994. Nizhnii Novgorod: Dekom, 1994.

Kuznetsov, Eduard. *Mordovskii marafon*. Ierusalim: Moskva-Ierusalim, 1979.

Kuznetsov, Sergei. *Oshchupyvaia slona: Zametki po istorii russkogo interneta*. Moscow: Novoe literaturnoe obozrenie, 2004.

Lankina, Tomila. "Mapping Society and the Public Sphere in Imperial Russia." In *The Estate Origins of Democracy in Russia*, 82–121. New York: Cambridge University Press, 2021.

Laruelle, Marlene. "The Intellectual Origins of Putin's Invasion." *UnHerd*, March 16, 2022. https://unherd.com/2022/03/the-brains-behind-the-russian-invasion/.

Laruelle, Marlene. "The Iuzhinskii Circle: Far-Right Metaphysics in the Soviet Underground and Its Legacy Today." *The Russian Review* 74, no. 4 (October 2015): 563–80.

Ledeneva, Alena. "Chernyi Piar: Manipulative Campaigning and the Workings of Russian Democracy." In *How Russia Really Works: The Informal Practices That Shaped Post-Soviet Politics and Business*, 28–57. Ithaca, NY: Cornell University Press, 2006.

Ledeneva, Alena. *Russia's Economy of Favours:* Blat, *Networking and Informal Exchange*. Cambridge: Cambridge University Press, 1998.

Leeds, Adam E. "Dreams in Cybernetic Fugue: Cold War Technoscience, the Intelligentsia, and the Birth of Soviet Mathematical Economics." *Historical Studies in the Natural Sciences* 46, no. 5 (2016): 633–68.

Lenoe, Matthew. "Letter-Writing and the State. Reader Correspondence with Newspapers as a Source for Early Soviet History." *Cahiers du Monde russe* 40, no. 1/2 (1999): 139–69.

Lenoe, Matthew. *Closer to the Masses: Stalinist Culture, Social Revolutions, and Soviet Newspapers*. Cambridge, MA: Harvard University Press, 2004.

Leont'ev, Oleg. "Kak stat' Agatoi Kristi v Rossii." *Knizhnoe obozrenie* 13 (April 1, 1997): 6.

Letov, Egor. "Moia oborona." *Gr-oborona.ru*. 1989. gr-oborona.ru/texts/1056898718.html.

Levada, Iurii. *Vremia peremen: Predmet i pozitsiia issledovatelia*. Moscow: Novoe literaturnoe obozrenie, 2016.

Levada, Iurii and Lev Gudkov. "Ot mnenii k ponimaniiu." *Monitoring obshchestvennogo mneniia. Sotsial'nye i politicheskie izmeneniia* 1 (January 1993): 1.

Lewis, David. *Russia's New Authoritarianism: Putin and the Politics of Order*. Edinburgh: Edinburgh University Press, 2020.

Lifshits, Mikhail. "Veter istorii. K 140-letiiu so dnia rozhdeniia Fridrikha Engel'sa." In *Karl Marks. Iskusstvo I obshchestvennyi ideal*. Moscow: Khudozhestvennaia literatura, 1979. http://www.gutov.ru/lifshitz/texts/marks/marx-10.htm.

Limonov, Eduard. "Psy voiny." *Novyi vzgliad*, no. 19, May 22, 1993.

Limonov, Eduard. *De Russische dichter houdt van grote negers*. Translated by Mieke Lindenburg. Amsterdam: Uitgeverij Bert Bakker, 1981.

Limonov, Eduard. *Eto ya—Edichka*. Roman. Moskva: Glagol, 1991.

Limonov, Eduard. *Il poeta russo preferisce i grandi negri: Romanzo*. Translated by Marina Marrazza. Milan: Frassinelli, 1985.

Limonov, Eduard. *Kniga mertvykh*. Saint Petersburg: Limbus Press, 2000.

Limonov, Eduard. *Le poète russe préfère les grands nègres*. Translated by Emmanuelle Davidov. Paris: Éditions Ramsay, 1980.

Lipovetsky, Mark. "A Trickster in Drag: Vlad Mamyshev-Monroe's Aesthetic of Camp." *Arts* 11, no. 5 (2022): 87–106.

Lipovetsky, Mark. "The Poetics of ITR Discourse: In the 1960s and Today." *Ab Imperio* 1 (2013): 109–39.

Lipovetsky, Mark. *Paralogii: Transformatsii (post)modernistskogo diskursa v russkoi kul'ture 1920–2000-kh godov*. Moscow: Novoe literaturnoe obozrenie, 2008.

Lipovetsky, Mark, Maria Engstrom, Tomas Glanc, Ilja Kukuj, and Klavdia Smola, eds. *Handbook of Soviet Underground Culture*. New York; London: Oxford University Press, 2024.

Lloyd, John. "The First Second Election: Russia at the Polls." *The Political Quarterly* 68, no. 1 (January 1997): 9–22.

Lonkila, Markku, Larisa Shpakovskaya, and Philip Torchinsky. "The Occupation of Runet? The Tightening State Regulation of the Russian-Language Section of the Internet." In *Freedom of Expression in Russia's New Mediasphere*, edited by Marielle Wijermars and Katja Lehtisaari, 17–38. New York: Routledge, Taylor & Francis Group, 2020.

Loshak, Andrei. *Broken Ties* (*Razryv Sviazi*, 2022), film.

Lovell, Stephen. *The Russian Reading Revolution: Print Culture in the Soviet and Post-Soviet Eras.* New York: St. Martin's Press, 2000.

Magun, Artemy. "Imperializatsiia (Poniatie imperii i sovremennyi mir)." *Polis: Politicheskie issledovaniia*, no. 2 (2007): 63–80.

Magun, Artemy. *Negative Revolution: Modern Political Subject and Its Fate after the Cold War.* New York: Bloomsbury Academic, 2013.

Maiofis, Mariia, and Il'ia Kukulin. "Svoboda kak neosoznannyi pretsedent: zametki o transformatsii mediinogo polia v 1990 godu." *NLO* 1 (2007). https://magazines.gorky.media/nlo/2007/1/svoboda-kak-neosoznannyj-preczedent-zametki-o-transformaczii-medijnogo-polya-v-1990-godu.html.

Mamaladze, Teimuraz. "Skazano—sdelano. Boris El'tsin v Chechne pobyval." *Izvestiia* 98, no. 24705 (May 29, 1996): 1.

Markman, Vladimir. *Na kraiu geografii.* IYerusalim: Moskva-Ierusalim, 1979.

Mason, David S., and Svetlana Sidorenko-Stephenson. "Public Opinion and the 1996 Elections in Russia: Nostalgic and Statist, Yet Pro-Market and Pro-Yeltsin." *Slavic Review* 56, no. 4 (Winter 1997): 698–717.

Matveev, Ilya. "From the Chicago Boys to Hjalmar Schacht: The Trajectory of the (Neo)Liberal Economic Expertise in Russia." *Problems of Post-Communism* (January 2024): 1–10.

Matveev, Ilya. "State, Capital, and the Transformation of the Neoliberal Policy Paradigm in Putin's Russia." *International Review of Modern Sociology* 45, no. 1, Special Issue on the Crisis of Neoliberalism and the Rise of Authoritarianism in the Early 21st Century (Spring 2019): 27–48.

Mazhaev, Aleksei. "Retsenziia na klip: Garik Sukachev i dr. – 'Ia ostaius'. Spisok razreshennykh muzykantov." *InterMedia*, July 10, 2022. https://www.intermedia.ru/news/371608.

McFaul, Michael. *Russia's 1996 Presidential Election: The End of Polarized Politics.* Stanford, CA: Hoover Institution Press, 1997.

McMichael, Polly. "'A Room-Sized Ocean': Apartments in the Practice and Mythology of Leningrad's Rock Music." In *Youth and Rock in the Soviet Bloc*, edited by William Jay Risch. Lanham: Lexington Books, 2015: 183–210.

McMichael, Polly. "'After All You're a Rock and Roll Star (At Least That's What They Say)': *Roksi* and the Creation of the Soviet Rock Musician." *The Slavonic and East European Review* 83, no. 4 (October 2005): 664–84.

McNair, Brian. "Media in Post-Soviet Russia: An Overview." *European Journal of Communication* 9 (1994): 115–35.

Medvedev, Roi. *Sovetskii soiuz. Poslednie gody zhizni. Konets sovetskoi imperii.* Moscow: AST/Poligrafizdat, 2009.

Meierhenrich, Jens, and Oliver Simons, eds. *The Oxford Handbook of Carl Schmitt.* Oxford: Oxford University Press, 2013.

Menzel, Birgit. *Bürgerkrieg um Worte: Die russische Literaturkritik der Perestrojka.* Köln: Böhlau, 2001.

Mihelj, Sabina, and Simon Huxtable. *From Media Systems to Media Cultures: Understanding Socialist Television.* Cambridge: Cambridge University Press, 2018.

Mishenin, Dima. "Tikhii Sholokhov." *Krest'ianka*, December 2008. https://web.archive.org/web/20100113143904/http://www.krestyanka.ru/archive/year2008/dec/dec_349.html.

Miss, Rosen. "The Queer Russian Photographer Who Made Global Headlines in the 90s." *Vice*, November 11, 2022. https://i-d.vice.com/en/article/n7zkyk/slava-mogutin-photography.

Mogutin, Iaroslav. "Alla Pugacheva liubit golubykh, a sama ona rozovaia." *Novyi Vzgliad* 41 (October 9, 1993).

Mogutin, Iaroslav. "Bez intelligentov, utopiia." *Novyi vzgliad* 36 (September 30, 1995). [First published in: *Limonka* 1 (November 1994).]

Mogutin, Iaroslav. "Chechenskii uzel. 13 tezisov." *Novyi vzgliad* 3 (January 28, 1992).

Mogutin, Iaroslav. "Eduard Limonov, sovetsko-frantsuzskii natsional'nyi geroi." *Novyi Vzgliad* 101 (1992).

Mogutin, Iaroslav. "Griaznye kontsy." *Novyi vzgliad* 34 (September 4, 1993).

Mogutin, Iaroslav. "Gryaznyye kontsy komoltsev." *Eshchë* 4/16 (1993).

Mogutin, Iaroslav. "Gruppovukha kak obraz mysli." *Novyi vzgliad* 129 (1994).

Mogutin, Iaroslav. "Mogutin zhiv'em." *Novyi vzgliad* 42 (October 23, 1993).

Mogutin, Iaroslav. "Sis'ki v teste." *Novyi vzgliad* 117 (1993).

Mogutin, Iaroslav. "Vospominaniia russkogo panka, ili, avtoportret bandita v molodosti." In Eduard Limonov, *U nas byla velikaia epokha*, 158–87. Moscow: Konets Veka, 1994.
Mogutin, Slava and Sonya Franeta. "Gomoseksualizm v sovetskikh tiur'makh i lageriakh." *Novoe vremia* 35 (1993), 36 (1993): 44–47, 50–54.
Moiseev, Boris. *Ptichka zhivoi zvuk*. Moskva: AST, 2007.
Monastyrskii, Andrei, ed. *Poezdki za gorod* [*Trips out of Town*]. Moscow: Ad Marginem, 1998.
Morozov, Oleg. "SPID u nas doma." *Literaturnaia gazeta* (December 14, 1988): 12.
Morris, Dick. *Behind the Oval Office: Winning the Presidency in the Nineties*. New York: Random House, 1997.
Morzhina, N. "Pis'ma, pis'ma." *Komsomol'skaia pravda* 256 (November 11, 1986): 2; 282 (December 12, 1986): 2; 10 (January 13, 1987): 2.
Morzhina, N. "Pis'ma, pis'ma." *Komsomol'skaia pravda* 29 (February 4, 1986): 2; 83 (April 8, 1986): 2; 105 (May 6, 1986): 2; 137 (June 3, 1986): 2; 165 (July 8, 1986): 2; 180 (August 6, 1986).
Mukusev, Vladimir. *Razberemsia…Fragmenty interv'iu, vystuplenii, stat'i, stsenarii i rassledovaniia raznykh let*. Moscow: Flinta, 2018, 131–45.
Mumiy Troll. "Utekai." 1997.
Muradov, Boris. "Evgeniia Debryanskaia: "Mne plevat' na obshchestvennoe mnenie"." *Argumenty i fakty* (November 19, 1997): 20.
Murtazaev, A. "1 000 000 pisem s nachala nyneshnego goda poluchila redaktsiia." *Komsomol'skaia pravda* 211 (September 16, 1986).
Nenasheva, Katrin. *Katrin Nenasheva: dokumentatsiia aktsii 2015–2020* [*Katrin Nenasheva: Documentation of Actions 2015–2020*]. Google doc shared by the artist, 2022.
Nikul'shina, Svetlana. "Artemii Troitskii o Leningradskom rok-klube: 'Muzyka ne imeet seichas takogo sakral'nogo znacheniia, kak v SSSR.'" *Sobaka*. March 11, 2021. https://www.sobaka.ru/entertainment/music/125343.
Nossik, Anton. "Russia's First Blogger Reacts to Putin's Internet Crackdown." *The New Republic*, May 15, 2014. https://newrepublic.com/article/117771/putins-internet-crackdown-russias-first-blogger-reacts.
Novodvorskaia, Valeriia. "Gore pobediteliam." *Novyi vzgliad* 24 (June 25, 1994).
Novodvorskaia, Valeriia. "Ne otdadim nashe pravo nalevo!" *Novyi vzgliad* 33 (August 28, 1993).
Novodvorskaia, Valeriia. "Rossiia no. 6." *Novyi vzgliad* 1 (January 15, 1994).
Orlova, Galina. "Kod dostupa: arkhiv nedavnego proshlogo." In *Muzei 90x: territoriia svobody*, 107–10. Moscow: Novoe literaturnoe obozrenie, 2016.
Osterberg, Ira. *Aleksei Balabanov: Brother*. Bristol: Intellect, 2022: 33–135.
Osterberg, Ira. *What Is That Song: Aleksej Balabanov's Brother and Rock as Film Music in Russian Cinema*. Helsinki: Unigrafia, 2018, 114–99.
Oswald, Ingrid, and Viktor Voronkov. "The 'Public-Private' Sphere in Soviet and Post-Soviet Society: Perception and Dynamics of 'Public' and 'Private' in Contemporary Russia." *European Societies* 6, no. 1 (March 2004): 97–117.
Oushakine, Serguei. "'Against the Cult of Things': On Soviet Productivism, Storage Economy, and Commodities with No Destination." *The Russian Review* 73, no. 2: 198–236.
Oushakine, Serguei. "The Terrifying Mimicry of Samizdat." *Public Culture* 13, no. 2 (2001): 191–214.
Paasilinna, Reino. *Glasnost and Soviet Television*. Helsinki: Finnish Broadcasting Corporation, 1995.
Pavlov, Iurii, dir. Sotvoreniie Adama, 1993; *Kinostudiia Borchaly*, 1995. VHS.
Pelevin, Victor. *Generation P*. Moscow: Vagrius, 1999. [Eng. tr.: *Homo Zapiens*. New York: Penguin Books, 2002.]
Pelevin, Viktor. "Dzhon Faulz i tragediia russkogo liberalizma." http://pelevin.nov.ru/rass/pe-jon/1.html.
Pinkhard, Terry. "Objective Spirit: The Pulse of Self-Consciousness." In *Hegel's Philosophy of Spirit: A Critical Guide*, edited by Marina F. Bykova, 147–63. Cambridge: Cambridge University Press, 2019.
Platt, Kevin M. F. "Commemorating the End of History: Timelessness and Power in Contemporary Russia." In *Power and Time: Temporalities in Conflict and the Making of History*, edited by Dan Edelstein, Stefanos Geroulanos, and Natasha Wheatley, 400–20. Chicago: University of Chicago Press, 2020.
Platt, Kevin M. F. "Secret Speech: Wounding, Disavowal, and Social Belonging in the USSR." *Critical Inquiry* 42, no. 3 (March 2016): 647–76.

Platt, Kevin M. F. and Benjamin Nathans. "Socialist in Form, Indeterminate in Content: The Ins and Outs of Late Soviet Culture." *Ab Imperio* 2 (2011): 301–24.

Podoroga, Valerii. *Mimesis. Materialy po analiticheskoi antropologii.* Moscow: Kul'turnaia revoliutsiia, 2006.

Pole chudes. ViD, October 25, 1991. https://www.youtube.com/watch?v=XS_H22rAIKs&t=336s.

Pomerants, Grigorii. *Zapiski gadkogo utenka.* Moscow: Tsentr gumanitarnykh initsiativ, 2013.

Pomerants, Grigorii. "Chelovek niotkuda." http://pomeranz.ru/p/pub_man_air.htm.

Pomerantsev, Peter. "Beyond Propaganda: How Authoritarian Regimes Are Learning to Engineer Human Souls in the Age of Facebook." *Foreign Policy*, June 23, 2015. http://foreignpolicy.com/2015/06/23/beyond-propaganda-legatum-transitions-forum-russia-china-venezuela-syria/.

Poseliagin, Nikolai. "Antropologicheskii povorot v rossiiskiikh gumanitarnykh naukakh." *Novoe literaturnoe obozrenie* 113 (January 2012).

Poznanskii, Aleksandr. *Samoubiistvo Chaikovskogo: mif i real'nost'.* Moskva: Glagol, 1993.

Pugacheva, Alla [@alla_orfey]. *Instagram.* September 18, 2022.

Putin, Vladimir. "My ikh v sortire zamochim!" September 24, 1999. REN TV/BBC/TV Tsentr.

Rezunkov, Viktor. "Rok, KGB, Komsomol." *Radio Svoboda*, April 14, 2016. https://www.svoboda.org/a/27675500.html.

Ries, Nancy. *Russian Talk: Culture and Conversation during Perestroika.* Ithaca, NY: Cornell University Press, 1997.

Roldugina, Irina. "Dissidents of Love: The Politics and Practice of Russian LGBTQ Samizdat after the Fall of the USSR." In *In Defense of the Mainstream*, 237–49. Moscow: V-A-C Press, 2021.

Rosenberg, Alyssa. "How Censorship Works in Vladimir Putin's Russia." *The Washington Post*, February 9, 2016. www.washingtonpost.com/news/act-four/wp/2016/02/09/how-censorship-works-in-vladimir-putins-russia/?utm_term=.da6c1f7ec6a1.

Rosenfeld, Gavriel D. "The Rise of Illiberal Memory." *Memory Studies* 16, no. 4 (August 2023): 819–36.

Rossiiskii gosudarstvennyi arkhiv noveishei istorii (RGANI), f. 100, op. 1, d. 285, l. 2.

Roudakova, Natalia. *Losing Pravda: Ethics and the Press in Post-Truth Russia.* Cambridge: Cambridge University Press, 2017.

Safariants, Rita. "'Thank God We're Not Alive': The Rock Star in Soviet and Post-Soviet Cinema." In *Ruptures and Continuities in Soviet/Russian Cinema*, edited by Birgit Beumers and Eugenie Zvonkine, 90–107. London: Routledge, 2017.

Safariants, Rita. "The School of Rock: Sergei Solo'vev's Workshop and Its Legacy for the Popular Music Film." *Studies in Russian and Soviet Cinema* 13, no. 2 (2019): 208–16.

Sappak, Vladimir. *Televidenie i my: chetyre besedy.* Moscow: Iskusstvo, 1988. http://www.evartist.narod.ru/text12/85.htm.

Semyonov, Iulian. "Sovershenno otkryto." *Sovershenno sekretno* 1 (June 1989), 2.

Shaburov, Alexander, ed. *B.U. Kashkin (1938–2005) Zhizn' i tvorchestvo ural'skogo pank-skomorokha* [*B.U.Kashkin (1938–2005) The Life and Work of a Ural Punk-Skomorokh*]. Ekaterinburg: Ural branch of the Government Center for Contemporary Art, 2015.

Sharafutdinova, Gulnaz. *The Red Mirror: Putin's Leadership and Russia's Insecure Identity.* New York: Oxford University Press, 2020.

Shevchenko, Olga. *Crisis and the Everyday in Postsocialist Moscow.* Bloomington: Indiana University Press, 2009.

Simon'ian, Margarita. "About Maksim Galkin." *Vecher s Vladimirom Solov'evym. Rossiia* 1 (April 26, 2022).

Sindelar, Daisy. "The Kremlin's Troll Army." *The Atlantic*, August 12, 2014. https://www.theatlantic.com/international/archive/2014/08/the-kremlins-troll-army/375932/.

Smith, Adam. "European Newspapers: Europe's Top Papers." *Campaign*, November 15, 2002. Accessed December 11, 2022. https://www.campaignlive.co.uk/article/european-newspapers-europes-top-papers/164161.

Smith, Kathleen E. *Remembering Stalin's Victims. Popular Memory and the End of the USSR.* Ithaca, NY: Cornell University Press, 1996.

Smith, Kathleen E. *Mythmaking in the New Russia: Politics and Memory during the Yeltsin Era.* Ithaca, NY: Cornell University Press, 2002.

Snegovaya, Maria. "Stifling the Public Sphere." National Endowment for Democracy, October 14, 2015. http://www.ned.org/wp-content/uploads/2015/10/Stifling-the-Public-Sphere-Media-Civil-Society-Russia-Forum-NED.pdf.

Sokolov, Veniamin. *Programma ekonomicheskikh reform 1995 goda*, 1995. http://www.analysisclub.ru/index.php?page=econom1995&art=1.

Sorokin, Vladimir. *Day of the Oprichnik*. Translated by Jamey Gambrell. New York: Farrar, Straus and Giroux, 2012.

Stanley, Alessandra. "The Russian Vote: Election Eve; From Yeltsin, A Reminder of Stalin And Terror." *New York Times*, June 16, 1996, sec. 1.

Steinholt, Yngvar Bordewich. *Rock in the Reservation: Songs from the Leningrad Rock Club* 1981–86. New York: Mass Media Music Scholars' Press, 2005.

Stel'makh, V. D., and N. K. Lobachev. *Kniga i chtenie v zerkale sotsiologii*. Moscow: Knizhnaia palata, 1990.

Stern, Mikhail. *Sex in the USSR*. New York: Times Books, 1980.

Stiglitz, Joseph. "The Ruin of Russia." *The Guardian*, April 9, 2003. https://www.theguardian.com/world/2003/apr/09/russia.artsandhumanities.

Stodolsky, Ivor A. "A 'Non-Aligned' Intelligentsia: Timur Novikov's Neo-Avantgarde and the Afterlife of Leningrad Non-Conformism." *Studies in Eastern European Thought* 63 (2011): 135–45.

Stodolsky, Ivor A. "A Multi-Lectic Anatomy of Stiob and Poshlost': Case Studies in the Oeuvre of Timur Novikov." *Laboratorium* 3, no. 1 (2011): 24–50.

Stomakhin, Igor'. "Lesbiianka Masha atakuet chinovnikov." *Megapolis ekspress* 24 (1994): 8.

Taubman, William. *Gorbachev: His Life and Times*. New York: Basic Books, 2016.

Tolstaia, Tatiana. *Ne Kys'*. https://www.youtube.com/watch?v=p3SxVmuMjsU&t=62s.

Treisman, Daniel. "Presidential Popularity in a Hybrid Regime: Russia under Yeltsin and Putin." *American Journal of Political Science* 55, no. 3 (July 2011): 590–609.

Treisman, Daniel. "Why Yeltsin Won." *Foreign Affairs* 75, no. 5 (October 1996): 64–77.

Trifonov, Gennadii. "Sovetskie gomoseksualisty: vchera, Segodnia, zavtra" *Gay, slaviane!* 1 (1993): 9–15.

Troitskii, Artemii. "Na dne. Prolog." *Novaia gazeta*, April 14, 2013. https://novayagazeta.ru/articles/2013/04/15/54350-na-dne-prolog

Troitskiy, Artemiy. *Back in the USSR: A True Story of Rock in Russia*. London: Faber & Faber, 1988.

Tsipursky, Gleb. "'As a Citizen, I Cannot Ignore These Facts.' Whistleblowing in the Khrushchev Era." *Jahrbücher für Geschichte Osteuropas* 58, no. 1 (2010): 52–69.

Tsvetkov, Aleksei. "Skinkhedy." *Limonka* 61 (March 1997).

Ukeles, Mierle Laderman. *Maintenance Art Manifesto*, 1969. Accessed June 30, 2023. https://queensmuseum.org/wp-content/uploads/2016/04/Ukeles-Manifesto-for-Maintenance-Art-1969.pdf.

Veselkin, Vladimir. "Vova Veselkin: zhizn' i tragediia rok-favna." Interv'iu Andreia Koroleva. *Nastoiashchee vremia*, December 17, 2015. https://www.currenttime.tv/a/27429551.html.

Vorob'evskii, Iurii. "Dugin i brat Markion." *Livejournal.com*, March 8, 2019. https://swinopes.livejournal.com/tag/Юрий%20Воробьевский%20Александр%20Дугин.

Wakamiya, Lisa Ryoko. *Locating Exiled Writers in Contemporary Russian Literature: Exiles at Home*. New York: Palgrave Macmillan, 2009.

Warner, Michael. "Publics and Counterpublics." *Public Culture* 14, no. 1 (2002): 49–90.

Weiss-Wendt, Anton. *Putin's Russia and the Falsification of History: Reasserting Control over the Past*. New York; London: Bloomsbury Academic, 2020.

Westemeier, Jens. *Hans Robert Jauss: Jugend, Krieg und Internierung*. Konstanz: Konstanz University Press, 2016.

White, Stephen. "Political Communications in the USSR: Letters to Party, State and Press." *Political Studies* XXXI (1983): 43–60.

Wijermars, Marielle, and Katja Lehtisaari. "Introduction." In *Freedom of Expression in Russia's New Mediasphere*, edited by Marielle Wijermars and Katja Lehtisaari, 1–14. New York: Routledge, Taylor & Francis Group, 2020.

Williamson, Anne. "Russia's Fiscal Whistleblower." *Mother Jones*, June 16, 1998. https://www.motherjones.com/politics/1998/06/russias-fiscal-whistleblower/.

Wilson, Andrew. *Virtual Politics: Faking Democracy in the Post-Soviet World*. New Haven, CT: Yale University Press, 2005.

Wolfe, Thomas C. *Governing Soviet Journalism. The Press and the Socialist Person after Stalin* (Bloomington: Indiana University Press, 2005).

Yablokova, Oksana. "Ministry Defends VTsIOM Overhaul." *Moscow Times*, September 3, 2003. Archived copy accessed July 15, 2023. https://web.archive.org/web/20110617012356/http://www.eng.yabloko.ru/Publ/2003/PAPERS/9/030903_mt.html.

Yanchuk, G. Introduction to column *Perepiska. Komsomol'skaia pravda* 164 (July 19, 1991), 2.

Yoffe, Mark. "Conceptual Carnival: National Elements in Russian Nationalist Rock Music." In *Rock 'n' Roll and Nationalism: A Multinational Perspective*, edited by Mark Yoffe and Andrea Collins, 96–119. Newcastle: Cambridge Scholars Press, 2005.

Yoffe, Mark. "The *Stiob* of Ages: Carnivalesque Traditions in Soviet Rock and Related Counterculture." *Russian Literature* 74, no. 1–2 (2013): 207–25.

Yoffe, Mark. "Why Collect Zines?: Notes on the Soviet and Russian Rock Zine Collection in the Global Resources Center of George Washington University Libraries." *Slavic and East European Information Resources* 22, no. 3–4 (2021). 276–86.

Yudin, Greg. "The War in Ukraine: Do Russians Support Putin?" *The Journal of Democracy* 33, no. 3 (July 2022): 31–37.

Yurchak, Aleksei. "A Parasite from Outer Space: How Sergei Kurekhin Proved That Lenin Was a Mushroom." *Slavic Review* 70, no. 2 (2011): 307–33.

Yurchak, Aleksei. *Everything Was Forever, Until It Was No More: The Last Soviet Generation*. Princeton, NJ: Princeton University Press, 2005.

Zamiatin, Evgenii. "Iz bloknotov 1914–1928 godov." *Sovershenno sekretno* 1, no. 8 (1990): 26–7.

Zaslavskaia, Tatiana. "K desiatiletiiu VTsIOM." *Monitoring obshchestvennogo mneniia* 1, no. 33 (1998): 9.

Zaslavskaia, Tatiana. "The Novosibirsk Report." *Survey* 28, no. 1 (March 1984): 83–109.

Zassoursky, Ivan. *Media and Power in Post-Soviet Russia*. London: M.E. Sharpe, 2004.

Zhuk, Ol'ga. *Russkie amazonki: istoriia lesbiyskoi subkul'tury v Rossii, XX ve*. Moskva: Glagol, 1998.

Zhuk, Sergei. *Rock and Roll in the Rocket City: The West, Identity, and Ideology in Soviet Dnepropetrovsk*. Baltimore: Johns Hopkins University Press, 2010.

Zubok, Vladislav. *Collapse: The Fall of the Soviet Union*. New Haven, CT: Yale University Press, 2021.

Zubok, Vladislav. *Zhivago's Children: The Last Russian Intelligentsia*. Cambridge: The Belknap Press of Harvard University, 2009.

Contributor Bios

Maya Vinokour is assistant professor in the Department of Russian and Slavic Studies at New York University and the author of *Work Flows: Stalinist Liquids in Russian Labor Culture* (Cornell University Press, 2024). Her interests include Stalinism and Nazism, late-Soviet science fiction, post-Soviet media, and the global Far Right.

Bradley A. Gorski is assistant professor of post-Soviet literature and culture in the Department of Slavic Languages at Georgetown University. He is co-editor of *Red Migrations: Transnational Mobility and Leftist Culture after 1917* (University of Toronto Press, 2024) and the author of *Cultural Capitalism: Literature and the Market after Socialism* (Cornell University Press, 2025).

Courtney Doucette is assistant professor of History at the State University of New York at Oswego. Her research focuses on the history of late Soviet reform and the evolution of popular participation in Soviet politics.

Fabrizio Fenghi is assistant professor of Slavic Studies at Brown University and the author of *It Will Be Fun and Terrifying: Nationalism and Protest in Post-Soviet Russia* (University of Wisconsin Press, 2020). His interests include contemporary Russian culture and politics, nationalism and national identity, and Soviet and post-Soviet literature and media.

Rita Safariants is assistant professor of Russian in the Department of Modern Languages and Cultures at the University of Rochester, specializing in late-Soviet, post-Soviet, and contemporary Russian film, Russian literature, media, popular music, and performance culture. She is the author of *Soviet Rock on Screen: The Life, Death, and Resurrection of a Film Genre* (forthcoming from University of Wisconsin Press).

Daniil Leiderman is an instructional associate professor at the College of Performance, Visualization & Fine Arts at Texas A&M University. His interests include the contemporary art of protest and resistance, the history of games and the emancipatory and ideological potential of the ludic, and post-Soviet media.

Thomas Keenan has served as the Slavic, East European and Eurasian Studies librarian at Princeton since 2013. His research interests include Russian literature; Russian and East European political, intellectual, and cultural history; publishing and mass communication in Eastern Europe and the Former Soviet Union; and continuities between medieval and modernist visual and verbal culture.

Pavel Khazanov is associate professor of Russian and East European Languages and Literatures at Rutgers University. His research focuses on the evolution of political ideologies in late- and post-Soviet Russian culture, between the 1950s "Thaw" and the present. He is the author of *The Russia That We Have Lost: Pre-Soviet Past as Anti-Soviet Discourse* (University of Wisconsin Press, 2023).